Data-Driven Personas

Synthesis Lectures on Human-Centered Informatics

Editor
John M. Carroll, *Penn State University*

Human-Centered Informatics (HCI) is the intersection of the cultural, the social, the cognitive, and the aesthetic with computing and information technology. It encompasses a huge range of issues, theories, technologies, designs, tools, environments, and human experiences in knowledge work, recreation and leisure activity, teaching and learning, and the potpourri of everyday life. The series publishes state-of-the-art syntheses, case studies, and tutorials in key areas. It shares the focus of leading international conferences in HCI.

Data-Driven Personas
Bernard J. Jansen, Joni Salminen, Soon-gyo Jung, and Kathleen Guan

ISBN: 978-3-031-01103-0 print
ISBN: 978-3-031-02231-9 ebook
ISBN: 978-3-031-00211-3 hardcover

DOI 10.1007/978-3-031-00211-3

A Publication in the Springer series
SYNTHESIS LECTURES ON HUMAN-CENTERED INFORMATICS
Lecture #48

Series Editor: John M. Carroll, Penn State University

Series ISSN   1946-7680   Print   1946-7699   Electronic

Data-Driven Personas

Bernard J. Jansen
Qatar Computing Research Institute, Hamad Bin Khalifa University, Doha, Qatar
Joni Salminen
Qatar Computing Research Institute, Hamad Bin Khalifa University, Doha, Qatar; Turku School of Economics at the University of Turku, Turku, Finland
Soon-gyo Jung
Qatar Computing Research Institute, Hamad Bin Khalifa University, Doha, Qatar
Kathleen Guan
University College London, London, England

SYNTHESIS LECTURES ON HUMAN-CENTERED INTERACTION #48

ABSTRACT

Data-driven personas are a significant advancement in the fields of human-centered informatics and human-computer interaction. Data-driven personas enhance user understanding by combining the empathy inherent with personas with the rationality inherent in analytics using computational methods. Via the employment of these computational methods, the data-driven persona method permits the use of large-scale user data, which is a novel advancement in persona creation. A common approach for increasing stakeholder engagement about audiences, customers, or users, persona creation remained relatively unchanged for several decades. However, the availability of digital user data, data science algorithms, and easy access to analytics platforms provide avenues and opportunities to enhance personas from often sketchy representations of user segments to precise, actionable, interactive decision-making tools—data-driven personas! Using the data-driven approach, the persona profile can serve as an interface to a fully functional analytics system that can present user representation at various levels of information granularity for more task-aligned user insights. We trace the techniques that have enabled the development of data-driven personas and then conceptually frame how one can leverage data-driven personas as tools for both empathizing with and understanding of users. Presenting a conceptual framework consisting of (a) persona benefits, (b) analytics benefits, and (c) decision-making outcomes, we illustrate applying this framework via practical use cases in areas of system design, digital marketing, and content creation to demonstrate the application of data-driven personas in practical applied situations. We then present an overview of a fully functional data-driven persona system as an example of multi-level information aggregation needed for decision making about users. We demonstrate that data-driven personas systems can provide critical, empathetic, and user understanding functionalities for anyone needing such insights.

KEYWORDS

social media analytics, user segmentation, online product, user analytics, market segmentation, interactive persona systems, persona analytics, customer analytics, audience analytics xi

Contents

Preface

In November 2015, a chance meeting between Dr. Jim Jansen and representatives of AJ+, an Al Jazeera social media channel, led to a discussion of the difficulties of using the many analytics platforms available. It was at that meeting the concept of Automatic Persona Generation (APG) emerged. That meeting led to a set of algorithmic approaches to improve user understanding by presenting analytics and numbers in a form that most people can relate to—another person!

Since that impactful meeting, the APG Project team members and collaborators have developed innovative approaches, identified and created new processes, implemented technology products, designed services, and devised delivery methods for data-driven personas—all aimed at enhanced user understanding. Many of these advances have been published in research articles, intellectual property disclosures, and online postings.

This book takes these published manuscripts, enhances them, polishes them, and integrates them into a coherent lecture that serves as a foundation for the future advancement of data-driven personas, data-driven personas systems, and data-driven personas research.

The driver for APG and the related research is inspired by Papa John's slogan—

Better Personas! Better Decisions! Better Results!

Acknowledgments

Taking a multi-year research project and research passion, with all the complexities and energies involved, and transforming all of that into a fairly concise book is difficult—really difficult!

However, challenging experiences are often rewarding, and the writing of this book is one of those situations—both challenging and rewarding! Challenges are seldom faced alone, and this book is only possible via the support of many individuals. So, here we thank the many individuals that helped make this lecture book happen. Could NOT have done it without you!

Thanks to the executive leadership team at the fabulous Qatar Computing Research Institute (QCRI), a national research institute within Hamad bin Khalifa University and a member of the Qatar Foundation. Such a great place to work! Dr. Ahmed Elmagarmid is the founding Executive Director of QCRI and is a leading computer scientist researcher, academic supporter, and business executive. Dr. Ahmed has been a consistent and enthusiastic supporter of our research. This book could not have been accomplished without the high-quality research environment he provides. We also thank Dr. Ingmar Weber, the leader of the Social Computing Group at QCRI. His steady hand at the wheel has provided the consistency needed for this book to come together. We also thank the other QCRI executives, Drs. Ashraf Aboulnaga and Mohamed F. Mokbel, for their positive support for the Team's research efforts. Good to have key leaders supporting what you do! It makes great things possible! We thank Siddharth Gulati for some fantastic last-minute copy editing! We also thank our colleagues at QCRI, both past and present, for the wonderful work environment that only great people can provide!

Much of the research presented in the book could not, would not, have happened without the support of enthusiastic collaborators from industry and non-profits in Qatar, especially Haris Alisic (Head of Audience Development and Engagement at AJ+), Dianne Robillos (CRM Analysis Manager/Consumer Research and Insights Manager at Qatar Airways), and Ali Sikandar, Manager (Digital and Social Media, Qatar Foundation). They believe in what the Team is doing and the value of research-industry collaboration! We sincerely thank them for"going out on a limb" in this collaboration. Here is to many more crazy ... and productive! ... ideas to come!

Some of the research in this book builds off of and reports research conducted with others in academia. We thank all of our collaborators, including Yisela Alvarez Trentini (independent researcher), Motahhare Eslami (Computer Science Department, University of Illinois at Urbana-Champaign, Champaign, IL), Willemien Froneman (Africa Open Institute, Stellenbosch University, Stellenbosch, South Africa), Rohan Gurunandan Rao (Indian Institute of Technology Madras, Tamil Nadu, India), Ahmed Mohamed Sayed Kamel (Department of Clinical Pharmacy,

Cairo University, Giza, Egypt), Ilkka Kaate (University of Turku, Turku, Finland), Aki Koponen (University of Turku, Turku, Finland), Ying-Hsang Liu (Department of Design, University of Southern Denmark), Lene Nielsen (IT University of Copenhagen, Copenhagen, Denmark), João M. Santos (Centre for Psychological Research and Social Intervention (CIS), ISCTE-Instituto Universitário de Lisboa, Lisbon, Portugal), Sercan Şengün (Wonsook Kim College of Fine Arts, Illinois State University, Normal, IL, USA), and Jukka Vahlo (University of Tampere, Tampere, Finland). We enjoyed working with you, and we look forward to more opportunities to work together in the future!

We also thank Chris Chapman (Principal Quantitative UX Researcher, Google). Although we have never directly worked with Chris, we have found his disdain of personas especially motivating for our research! Thanks, Chris! Keep up the pressure!

Of course, we thank the publishing team, especially the ever-professional, but loads of fun, Diane Cerra (Executive Editor at Morgan and Claypool Publishers)! Diane has been excellent throughout this process! Thanks to Jack Carroll (Distinguished Professor of Information Sciences and Technology at Pennsylvania State University and Editor, *Synthesis Lectures on Human-Centered Informatics* at Morgan & Claypool). Jack was supportive of this book from the word "go", and we thank him for his immediate and on-going support!

There are four authors of this book. Although a team, each also has individuals to acknowledge personally.

Jim Jansen dedicates his efforts on this book to Kathy Mooney, who never got the chance to pursue an education beyond 8th grade. However, she was always happy and proud to see her son do "educational" things, like writing books. Sometimes, one can trace a life-changing influence to a place. For me, that place is the Fredonia Public Library (Fredonia, Kansas, U.S.). It was a wealth of knowledge, joy, escape, and learning. Thanks also to Sara Arisara Phomdam, who spent too many weekends watching me work on this book when she could have been doing much more exciting things! Your patience is much appreciated! Thank you!

Joni Salminen extends his gratitude and thankfulness for the two women in his life: wife Parl, whose support and care makes it possible for me to focus completely on research; and to mom Helena who gave me life and all the wisdom—be it little or a lot—that I have. Also thanking Rami, Lauri, and Mekhail for always being there for me. Dedicating my part in the book to my dad Timo, who always encouraged my brother and me to do well in school. Thanks, Dad—miss you and love you.

Soon-gyo Jung dedicates this book to the endless trust of his parents, Kyung-bok Kim and Won-kyu Jung, give to him and the future with his wife, Shahanieline Flores Tapang, and his daughter, Joo-Ae Jung. Thanks to all the people who have helped me become, especially to the Team, who always encouraged and trusted me.

Kathleen Guan is indebted to the love and trust of her friends, family, and teachers, without whom this book would not have been possible. The luckiest day of my life was when I met Siddharth Singh, who has since been with me every step of the way and enabled my intellectual and emotional growth. Thanks also to Jennifer Kim and Raza Nazar, my dear friends from the Singapore days. I'm also grateful for the resources and opportunities provided to me at Georgetown, Johns Hopkins, and University College London. Finally, it goes without saying that immense gratitude is in order to Joni, Soon, and Jim for inviting me to collaborate on this manuscript in the first place and for their continued patience as I learn the ropes.

Finally, the world is a better place thanks to people who want to and actually do help and support others. It has certainly been our good fortune to be the beneficiaries of so much help from the people mentioned here. We thank them, and we thank everyone who strives to help and support others. We will pass it on.

Part 1

Setting the Stage

Introduction

This book is **not** about personas in the traditional sense of the term "personas."

It is also **not** about data.

It is also **not** about analytics.

This book is about data-driven personas, a revolutionary step forward in user-centric, customer-centric, and audience-centric focus during the planning, creation, development, and implementation of systems, campaigns, products, ergonomics, content, and so on—whatever endeavor where actionable decisions about **people** need to be made, and those decisions need to be made on actual data about real people.

Data-driven personas crystallize metrics for a specific user type into an accurate representation of a person that can be viewed and understood even by people that otherwise lack the interest or skills for user analytics.

With their integration of the **empathy** of personas and the **rationality** of analytics, data-driven personas can shift actionable focus to where it should be—**people**—in a variety of domains, including system design, marketing, advertising, content creation, hiring, education, health, retail, non-profits, customer relations, and project management.

Actionable focus on people is what data-driven personas can provide for all of these areas.

By "actionable people focus," we mean attention that is implementable.

Too often, people-centric instruments, such as personas, have been touted as emphasizing people but have lacked implementability where the rubber meets the road. Personas have, traditionally, been based on a lot of assumptions. In fact, during our decisions with many practitioners concerning their use of personas, a common phrase is something along the lines of, "*Oh, personas. That is something that we just make up.*" Personas are conventionally assumption-driven in the main, and they are mainly descriptive and not actionable for many tasks. Many people view them as "nice to have" but "not essential."

Conversely, implementable methods, such as analytics, have an inherent concentration on numbers, but they have lacked the needed relationship to people and genuine understanding. Additionally, many people do not have the skillsets or interest in acquiring the skillsets to properly understand the often-nuanced aspects of user analytics. For gaining actionable people insights, user analytics often necessitates mathematical and statistical approaches. Given the many domains that apply personas, it is neither reasonable nor realistic to expect people to become proficient in these skills, in addition to becoming and maintaining proficiency in their core jobs.

Data-driven personas leverage the intuitiveness of personas with the workability of analytics. Data-driven personas do this via a persona analytics methodology that is both people-focused and directly actionable for implementation.

The conceptual foundation is straightforward:

Better personas! Better decisions! Better results!

This benefit is what data-driven personas provide.

The objective of this book is to illustrate and communicate what data-driven personas are, how to implement data-driven personas, and what data-driven personas can do for your project, your team, or your organization in terms of actual people understanding. There are content and tools in this book that would be interesting to commercial (e.g., analytics, design, and marketing departments of companies) and academic (e.g., marketing department, business schools, HCI studies, communication schools, computer science department) purposes.

For this book, we "drank our own Kool-Aid!"

We conducted extensive market research, gathered various data from numerous sources, and benchmarked with multiple similar products, including customer reviews of personas, persona articles, and persona books. We then analyzed this data using a data-driven algorithmic approach, specifically employing factor analysis. This analysis resulted in a set of user segments from which we developed three *ad hoc* personas representing the core consumers for this book. The three data-driven personas that we used to create, develop, and refine this book about data-driven personas are as follows.

Sam: a senior designer that wants to get his company to use personas for a major design project. He is familiar with the persona concept but not so familiar with data-driven personas. His company has toyed around with personas in the past, but nothing has ever gotten off the ground. He wants to use data-driven personas for this upcoming project. He wants the data-driven persona knowledge to get buy-in from stakeholders in his company and successfully implement data-driven personas for his project.

Kristi: an academic in the human-computer interaction (HCI) program of a computer science department who will teach a course on personas, something that she has wanted to do for some time. She is familiar with personas from her HCI courses but has not personally used them in practice. Her academic department also has personas of its students and alumni, but the department hardly ever uses them except for presentations. She wants a core grounding in the latest in persona research, specifically data-driven personas, and material to show-case how data-driven personas are used in industry and academia, both for her course and to encourage her department to employ personas effectively.

Ting: a marketing researcher who wants to use personas for a large, funded research project with a commercial company concerning online advertising. She has extensive knowledge of research methods, data analytics, and marketing concepts, with several publications in these areas in top academic outlets. She is familiar and aware of personas, but not so much of data-driven personas. The company she is working with has attempted using personas in the past but with limited success. Ting has done work in segmentation using analytics, and she wants to take this avenue of research to the next level with an increased focus on the customers. She wants to employ data-driven personas to achieve these objectives.

From the Sam, Kristi, and Ting cast of data-driven personas, we then incorporated a variety of behavioral user-focus techniques, including scenarios, use cases, Jobs to be Done, and user stories, to fine-tune more granular roles that Sam, Kristi, and Ting would have.

For example, at the start of our book project, they would be buyer personas (i.e., we want them to purchase the book). Then, Sam, Kristi, and Ting would be audience personas (i.e., they would need to consume the content in the book). They would then transition to user personas (i.e., as they put the contents of the book into practice). Finally, Sam, Kristi, and Ting would be ambassador personas (i.e., we want them to be advocates for the book and the concept of data-driven personas).

This data-driven persona exercise shaped our creation, development, organization, and implementation of this book and its content.

The book is divided into six parts, which are: Part 1: Setting the Stage (this is the section that you are now reading); Part 2: Getting Ready; Part 3 Developing Data-Driven Personas; Part 4: Using Data-Driven Personas; Part 5: Evaluating Data-Driven Personas and Appropriate Persona Methods; and Part 6: Data-Driven Personas and the Road Ahead.

Part 1: Setting the Stage is the section that you are now reading, containing only the Introduction.

Part 2: Getting Ready contains two chapters. Chapter 1 provides the foundation element of personas and data-driven personas. Chapter 2 discusses getting your organization ready for personas, including techniques for stakeholder buy-in.

Part 3: Developing Data-Driven Personas contains three chapters. Chapter 3 discusses the data underlying data-driven personas. Chapter 4 discusses methods for creating data-driven personas. Chapter 5 presents a full-stack, data-driven persona system.

Part 4: Using Data-Driven Personas contains three chapters. Chapter 6 discusses the implementation challenges of data-driven personas. Chapter 7 presents the common use cases for data-driven personas. Chapter 8 aligns data-driven personas with other methods.

Part 5: Evaluating Data-Driven Personas contains two chapters. Chapter 9 is evaluating and showing value from data-driven personas. Chapter 10 compares and contrasts the three major approaches for persona creation.

Part 6: Data-Driven Personas and the Future contains the Conclusion chapter that finishes up the book with trends and the grand challenges for data-driven personas.

Along with specific topical content, each chapter includes about a half dozen or so questions for further discussion, assignment, or contemplation concerning the chapter's content. We see these as excellent for data-driven personas workshops within organizations, classroom discussions or exams, and guiding thoughts for research collaboration. So, the questions should be helpful to Sam, Kristi, and Ting!

Along with afterward, we present a glossary of persona terminology that benefit the amateur or expert alike.

The book ends with three appendices helpful for the practitioner, the teacher, or the researcher.

Appendix A: Survey Questions for Persona Perception Scale is a data collection instrument for evaluating data-driven personas.

Appendix B: User Interview Questions contains typical questions useful for customer insight and data-driven persona development.

Appendix C: Evaluation of Elements in a Variety of Persona Tools presents the elements that are common or not in a variety of persona development approaches.

With this introduction, let us begin the journey of data-driven personas!

Part 2

Getting Ready

CHAPTER   1

The Data-Driven Persona Revolution

In this chapter, we briefly introduce personas and, more specifically, data-driven personas. We compare data-driven personas with the concept of analytics. Then, we present a short history of data-driven personas. This concise history is followed by a brief discussion of user segmentation, which is the conceptual foundation of personas. We end the chapter with an overview of Automatic Persona Generation (APG), a data-driven persona system used throughout this book to illustrate key ideas.

1.1   WHAT ARE PERSONAS?

A persona is a technique for representing a segment of a user, audience, or customer population as one person (Cooper, 2004). Conceptually, personas build on the concept of user segmentation, traditionally employed in the field of advertising (Hopkins, 1923). Personas present user segments in a manner that most people can relate to—another person. This fictitious person embodies all (or most of) the users (i.e., people) in a segment.

We refer to "users" in this book, but this term also includes the audience, customers, patients, or whichever type of people the personas describe.

Many domains employ the persona approach for an enhanced understanding of the user. Some of these fields include content creation (An et al., 2018; Lee et al., 2020), marketing (Clarke, 2015; Revella, 2015), product design (Dong, Kelkar, and Braun, 2007; Guo, Shamdasani, and Randall, 2011), ergonomics (Vincent and Blandford, 2014), health (Burrows, Gooberman-Hill, and Coyle, 2015), and software development (Cooper, 2004; Pruitt and Adlin, 2006). Personas support the efforts of identifying, constructing, and assessing segments of people to optimize some performance metrics. Examples of such metrics include advertising engagement, (Salminen et al., 2021) task completion speed, ease of use, the effectiveness of effort, sales, and so on.

Personas are a part of design processes and industry workflows (Dharwada et al., ,2007; Eriksson, Artman, and Swartling, 2013; Friess, 2012; Judge, Matthews, and Whittaker, 2012; Nielsen et al., 2015; Nielsen and Hansen, 2014) for both long- and short-term projects (Judge, Matthews, and Whittaker, 2012) with a reported positive return on investment (Drego et al., 2010) and improved task performance (Salminen et al., 2020a).

The term "persona" can take on a variety of meanings. Personas can refer to the concept for representing users. A persona can also refer to the technique of data collection and analysis for user representation. More still, a persona can refer to the actual fictitious person resulting from this technique. Finally, personas can refer to the end product, which is more precisely the persona profile (i.e., a one- or two-page description of the persona) that instantiates the persona. We will try to be consistent in this book, but the meaning of the word "persona" may change somewhat depending on the context of usage.

Personas, the actual fictitious persons, are usually presented as a set of persona profiles (also called "descriptions," "narratives") that are, generally, a page or two containing personal attributes, behavioral patterns, goals, skills, name, age, and a photo, all to present the personas as real people (Nielsen et al., 2015). Although there are no set elements of persona profiles, a *de facto* standard template has emerged from accepted practice consisting of a photo, name, skills, description, goals, problems, pain points, and quotes.

It is commonly acknowledged that personas, in practice, have often been designed with little or no data to justify the persona creation.

When data has been used, personas have often been designed using user data collected via focus groups, face-to-face interviews, or online surveys (Drego et al., 2010; Nielsen et al., 2015), with this data, then being augmented with the fictitious name and photo for the end product of the persona profile. See Figure 1.1 as an example of a typical persona profile presenting one persona created from the traditional persona method of manual data collection and analysis.

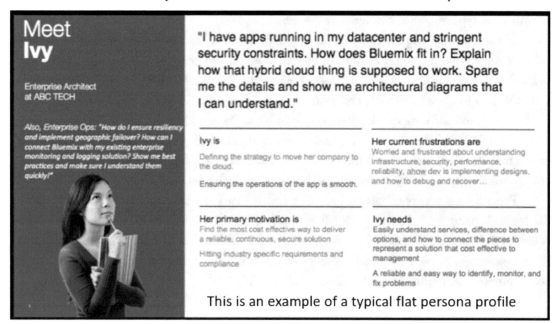

Figure 1.1: Example of a traditional flat-file persona profile (Pesot and Plantenberg, n.d.).

The foundational aim of employing personas is to provide insights concerning the demographics, behaviors, desires, goals, or needs of a targeted segment in an empathetic manner (i.e., as another person) for aiding decisions regarding a product, service, or system (Nielsen, 2013). Persona research is broad, with researchers claiming several benefits of personas that are primarily about channeling the focus on and highlighting communication concerning users to improve crafting, design, and development activities in organizations and teams (Adlin and Pruitt, 2010; Beyer and Holtzblatt, 1998; Dharwada et al., 2007; Drego et al., 2010; Eriksson et al., 2013; Friess, 2012; Miaskiewicz, Sumner, and Kozar, 2008; Pruitt and Grudin, 2003; Rönkkö, 2005).

Personas can provide "shared mental models" (Blanco, Pourroy, and Arikoglu, 2014, p. 63), facilitate team members' communication about users, and help empathize with those using the outputs created by the organization (Nielsen, 2013). In short, the employment of personas is presumed to be cognitively compelling for user understanding by placing a human face on user data.

It is suggested in prior literature that one develops personas from real data derived from actual people (Pruitt and Adlin, 2006). Using actual user data is crucial to making personas believable (Judge et al., 2012) and helping designers appropriately leverage personas. However, a recognized problem is that creating personas from real data is never an inexpensive or quick procedure, as the creation has historically involved using the ethnographic methods mentioned. As such, from our discussions with designers in many fields, personas are often "made up." Such personas are called assumption-driven personas.

Even when some data is used, as one-time data collection actions, personas created via manual methods can be quickly outdated without new rounds of data collection being conducted. Also, without real-time data, designers have no validation as to whether the currently presented personas are representative of current users (Chapman and Milham, 2006). These restrictions are especially acute in creating digital products for distribution via major online platforms (e.g., Facebook, Twitter, YouTube, etc.) or other websites, especially with changing products or products aimed at a wide and varied population. Again, in discussions with practitioners, it is often a concern that personas rapidly become stale or completely outdated.

What's more, despite the claimed benefits in the extant human-computer interaction (HCI) literature (Adlin and Pruitt, 2010; Dharwada et al., 2007; Drego et al., 2010) and the host of qualitative HCI research concerning the employment of personas (Adlin and Pruitt, 2010; Grudin and Pruitt, 2002; Jensen et al., 2017; Nielsen, 2013; Nielsen et al., 2015; Pruitt and Adlin, 2006), there is scant quantitative research empirically addressing whether or not personas are beneficial (Chapman et al., 2008; Chapman and Milham, 2006), although some such research does exist (Salminen et al., 2020).

A prevailing criticism of personas, both as concepts and as design tools, has postulated that personas are not valid methods for understanding users, that they may introduce stereotyping of users (Hill et al., 2017), and that they have limited practical value (Chapman et al., 2008; Chapman and Milham, 2006), with some even questioning whether personas can be scientifically validated at all (Chapman and Milham, 2006). In summary, traditional persona generation has been thoroughly criticized in the literature, with the main criticisms being the following.

- **Expiration:** Personas tend to expire when changes in user behavior take place. This is typical for many fast-moving online businesses, including online purchase behavior (Salminen et al., 2018), search behavior, and online content consumption.

- **High Cost:** Manual persona generation is costly in terms of time; it typically takes several months and costs tens of thousands of dollars. This timeline exceeds the waiting period for many projects. The high-cost factor, mainly in terms of time, keeps personas especially out of the reach of small to medium-size businesses and start-ups, which must react quickly to changing market conditions.

- **Lack of Scalability:** Because manual analysis relies on human labor, it scales poorly with the big user population datasets used in online analytics (An et al., 2018b). For example, classifying the sentiment of thousands of user-generated comments would be difficult for people, whereas trained algorithms can perform such classifications in a matter of seconds.

- **Non-Representative Data:** Manually created personas typically rely on data that does not represent the whole user base (Chapman and Milham, 2006). This is a side effect of using a small number of observations—for data-driven personas, the observations can originate from millions of users and content interactions.

However, despite these criticisms, personas have endured in various domains since Cooper (2004) explicitly introduced ad-hoc personas in the early 1980s (Goodwin and Cooper. 2009).

1.2   WHAT HAS CHANGED SINCE THE 1990s?

From their inception in the early 1980s (Goodwin, 2009), refinement in the early 1990s (Cooper, 2004), and following decades of use, personas were generally "flat media." As such, personas were primarily data structures—not interactive decision-making tools. A persona profile was a mechanism to organize the data concerning the imaginary person to present the information that decision-makers and others leverage to better target users.

The advent of online data, web, social media (Khan, Si, and Khan, 2019), and user analytics platforms (Baig, Shuib, and Yadegaridehkordi, 2019) allows for the possibility of data-driven personas that are created algorithmically and enable interaction between decision-makers and the underlying persona information. In this era of "personified big data" (Stevenson and Mattson, 2019, p.

4019), personas are useful for segmenting large and diverse online audiences (Salminen et al., 2018). They can bring about productivity benefits in organizations employing them (Drego et al., 2010).

These are data-driven personas. Data-driven persona development is the process of creating such data-driven personas, more formally defined as using algorithmic methods to develop accurate, representative, and up-to-date personas from numerical and textual data. In other words, they are created via a data-driven persona development process or a persona analytics methodology. Figure 1.2 shows the timeline of data-driven persona development from 1999.

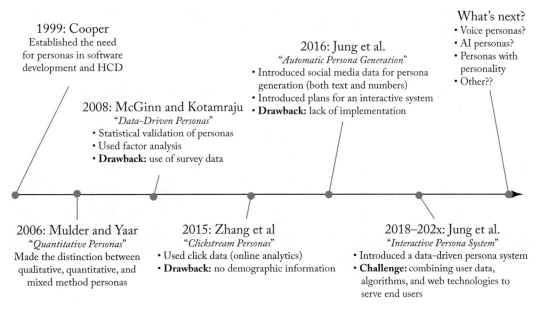

Figure 1.2: Timeline of data-driven persona development from 1999 into the future.

Besides addressing the shortcomings of assumption-driven personas, data-driven personas can increase the scientific verifiability of personas, as well as their credibility for stakeholders, as data-driven personas have the clout of using "real data" (Siegel, 2010). Ideally, data-driven personas are statistically representative, replicable, and verifiable—i.e., there is a metric that tells how well the specific method of their creation works (Chapman and Milham, 2006; Siegel, 2010). See Figure 1.3 as an example of a data-driven persona profile.

Compared to a flat-file persona profile, data-driven personas can provide an interface to an integrated full-stack persona analytics system, along the conceptual lines of task integration (Byström and Kumpulainen, 2019) that contains individual user data to the persona profile (i.e., from backend user data to frontend user conceptualization). Rather than a flat file, for these systems, the data-driven persona profile can serve as a system interface, both functioning as a data structure and equipping the persona end-users with data interactivity. Even when not serving as a system interface, data-driven personas have an inherent linkage to the underlying data from which they were created.

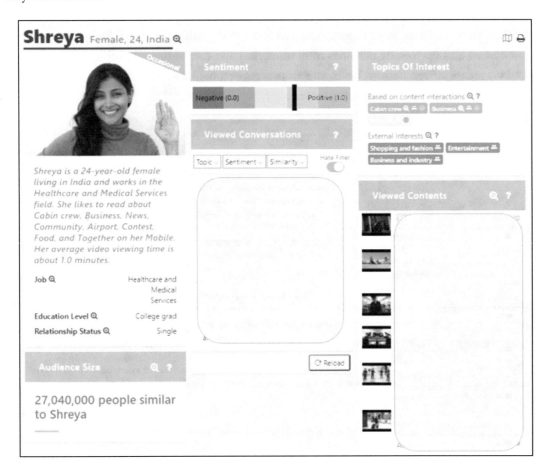

Figure 1.3: Example of a data-driven persona from the Automatic Persona Generation (APG) system. Business-sensitive content hidden.

Placing data-driven personas into the historical context of personas, the major drivers of data-driven personas are as follows.

- **Data access:** There is an abundance of data that is readily available. Abundance means users increasingly more and more leave digital traces of their behaviors and preferences, which can be employed for persona creation. Availability means that, through application programming interfaces, social media services, and online analytics platforms, there is an enabling of the automatic, large-scale harnessing of this data. Either availability or abundance is not enough per se, but both are needed to create the ideal opportunity for data-driven persona development.

- **Data science:** The rapid development of data science methods (algorithms, libraries) has made analysis easier.

- **Data expectations:** Decision-makers require more data nowadays to make informed decisions about users. This is part of the "digital transformation" taking place in many organizations worldwide (Jílková, 2020).

- **Online technologies:** Web technologies enable user interfaces and, ultimately, the interactivity between personas and end-users. We can speak about persona-user interaction in the same sense as we speak about HCI. These web technologies offer novel and exciting opportunities to make personas come to life in totally new ways, such as using automatic picture generation, voice, and simulation.

These drivers have revolutionized the possibilities of user segmentation compared to what was possible in the early days of personas. These enhanced possibilities have led to and are the drivers of the persona analytics revolution.

Researchers and practitioners are drawn to data-driven personas by the availability of such online user data (An et al., 2018a). When personas were first introduced in the 1990s, the Internet was a nascent technology, and there were few tools to collect and process large amounts of user data. The methodologies and platforms for collecting user data and automatically processing them have vastly developed since then. This development has dramatically increased the feasibility of data-driven personas in online settings where personified big data about users (Vecchio et al., 2018) can be collected through social media and online analytics platforms (e.g., Google Analytics, YouTube Analytics, or Twitter Analytics and their APIs).

Simultaneously, data science tools have evolved to new heights, including programming languages (e.g., R and Python) and libraries (e.g., scikit-learn), making a variety of statistical techniques and computational approaches accessible for persona creation. For textual data, natural language processing (NLP) provides a wide array of techniques, while numerical data can be analyzed using matrix factorization, clustering, factor analysis, principal component analysis, and so on. These developments have resulted in a "shift from using qualitative data toward using quantitative data for persona development" (Mijač, Jadrić, and Ćukušić, 2018, p. 1427).

While there have been attempts to "modernize" personas by automating their creation and tying the concept to behavioral online analytics data (Ait Hammou, Ait Lahcen, and Mouline, 2020), the question remains: Can data-driven personas offer efficiency and/or effectiveness relative to other analytics approaches and data representations for user understanding tasks?

This question can be addressed via a comparison of personas and analytics.

1.3   TRADITIONAL PERSONAS, DATA-DRIVEN PERSONAS, AND TRADITIONAL ANALYTICS

We do not discount traditionally generated personas or analytics, but our position is that the data-driven persona has certain inherent advantages relative to traditional personas and traditional analytics, as shown in Table 1.1.

Table 1.1: Attributes (including both advantages and disadvantages) of traditional personas, data-driven personas, and traditional analytics. The advantages are not highlighted, and disadvantages are highlighted in gray.

Focus	Traditional Personas	Data-driven Personas	Traditional Analytics
Representation	Gives a "face" to user data	Gives a "face" to user data	Gives no "face" to the data
Quantity of Data	Small sample size ("small data")	Large sample size ("big data")	Large sample size ("big data")
Type of Data	Qualitative data	Quantitative data but can incorporate qualitative data	Quantitative data
Creation Time	Slow to create (typically takes months)	Fast to create (typically takes days)	Fast to create graphs, charts, and reports
Current	Unresponsive to changes in user preferences	Responsive to changes in user preferences	Responsive to changes in user preferences
Cost	Expensive	Affordable	Affordable
Type of Representation	Nuanced in terms of user needs, goals, and desires	Explicit in terms of user behaviors that can be algorithmically identified	Explicit in terms of user behaviors that can be algorithmically identified

As shown in Table 1.1, data-driven personas are situated between the conceptualization of users at a high level, with personas and the granular representation of users at the analytics level. As such, using data-driven personas as the frontend interface to interactive persona analytics systems for understanding users is a natural use case. The enhancement and capabilities of data-driven personas as an interface to full-stack systems present considerable promise for data analysis practices within the field of HCI, and also offer a considerable impact on decision making in organizations that desire to understand their users. The value of data-driven personas is giving faces to data as an alternative way to present online analytics information.

Ultimately, however, the usefulness of personas comes down to specific use cases (Cooper, 2004). Personas in general, and data-driven personas specifically, are useful for tasks requiring a qualitative understanding of users, and numbers are helpful for getting a general overview of the whole user population and, in the case of machine-based decision making (i.e., marketing automation), ensuring individual-level optimization for tasks such as personalization, recommendation systems, and advertising delivery. To this end, we postulate that using individualized data is optimal for automated decision making, whereas using aggregate data such as data-driven personas works best for strategic and operational decision making, especially relating to decisions at the strategic level and those requiring human knowledge and empathy.

The claimed irrelevance of personas seems to be based on the confusion of their use in an age of online analytics data. It appears that this criticism is rooted in personas of the traditional model, while overlooking the potential of data-driven personas development. This insight further supports the purpose of conceptually separating these two types of personas, traditional and data-driven, and clearly communicating their differences to end users of online analytics data.

1.4   A SHORT HISTORY OF DATA-DRIVEN PERSONAS

The concept of a "data-driven persona" is first mentioned by Williams (2006) and popularized by McGinn and Kotamraju (2008). The purpose of being "data-driven" goes further back in the HCI literature. In fact, personas were always intended to use real data about the user. As Gaiser et al. (2006, p. 521) note, "In order to fulfill standards of a scientific method, personas can't be created arbitrarily. Personas have to be grounded in data, at best, both qualitative and quantitative data of surveys with the target audience." Similarly, Pruitt and Grudin (2003, p. 1) argue that "[personas] provide a conduit for conveying a broad range of qualitative and quantitative data, and focus attention on aspects of design and use that other method do not." Placing data-driven personas into the historical context, its major drivers are (a) the availability and abundance of user data and (b) the rapid development of data analysis algorithms that have changed since the early days of personas.

The methodological diversity for the creation of data-driven personas has been widely noted in the literature. For example, Zhu et al. (2019) cite several methods: affinity diagrams, decision trees, exploratory factor analysis (EFA), hierarchical clustering, k-means clustering, latent semantic analysis (LSA), multidimensional scaling analysis (MSA), and weighted graphs. Minichiello et al. (2017) provide a similar list of semi-automated methods: cluster analysis (including both hierarchical and k-means), factor analysis, principal component analysis (PCA), and LSA. "Semi-automatic" refers to the fact that even though the algorithm processes the data automatically, there is a need to set hyperparameters, a task often conducted by the users of the algorithms.

Data-driven persona development and research can be divided into three stages: (1) **Emergence** (2005–2008) that consists of early development and trials, (2) **Diversification** (2009–2014) that can be seen as a transition period for some transformations that would be more established in the current third stage, and (3) **Sophistication** (2015–present) that involves a revitalized interest in data-driven personas.

- **Emergence:** The first stage is marked by a focus on the basics: establishing the need for quantitative methodologies in a persona domain (McGinn and Kotamraju, 2008) and experimenting with different methods, especially those well-known in quantitative research tradition. The contextual focus is on software development, especially requirements engineering (Aoyama, 2005, 2007). There is also experimentation with using clickstreams and statistics from gaming software (Tychsen and Canossa, 2008), even though the main focus is on the use of survey data.

- **Diversification:** In the second stage, contexts expand, but the methods stale. Clustering becomes the dominant method. However, there are first experiments with NLP techniques (Bamman, O'Connor, and Smith, 2013). The field reaches a degree of self-awareness, marked by literature reviews focused on different clustering methods (Brickey, 2010). The introduction of behavioral data takes place (Masiero and Aquino, 2015), and simulation is first attempted with personas (Kanno, Ooyabu, and Furuta, 2011). From the second stage, data-driven personas have gradually been used for analyzing different demographic segments, such as Vietnamese youth (Dang-Pham, Pittayachawan, and Nkhoma, 2015) and European senior citizens (Wöckl et al., 2012). In such research, personas are merely a means to an end (i.e., understanding the data), not the focus of the research.

- **Sophistication:** In the third stage, researchers expand the notion of behavior, not only for behavioral data (An et al., 2018a) but also for using behavioral theories for interpreting quantitative personas (Jansen, Van Mechelen, and Slegers, 2017). Deep learning is applied to make personas interactive (Li et al., 2016) using sophisticated neural networks (Chu, Vijayaraghavan, and Roy, 2018), and new data sources, most notably web and social media data, emerge. Research starts to pay attention to the longitudinal aspect of personas evolving over time (Holmgard et al., 2014). Health context is introduced (Holden et al., 2017; Vosbergen et al., 2015), along with other new domains. The goal of fully automated persona generation emerges (An et al., 2018b) with an associated system development that enables persona users to interact with the personas (An et al., 2018a). In the third stage, clustering remains popular but is no longer dominant; rather, researchers apply multiple quantitative methods simultaneously.

As online analytics data has become more prevalent and accessible, researchers have proposed novel methods for data-driven persona generation that uses digital, rather than analog, data for persona creation (Zhang, Brown, and Shankar, 2016). Researchers have applied different types of data, such as follows.

- **Quantitative Analysis of Survey Data:** Several prior attempts at data-driven persona creation rely on survey-based data collection (Chapman, Krontiris, and Web, 2015; Dupree et al., 2016; Vahlo and Koponen, 2018). This survey data is most typically analyzed via cluster or factor analysis. However, survey-based data collection can be costly and fallible compared to using behavioral data due to many possible respondents and researcher biases associated with survey data collection in general (Podsakoff et al., 2003).

- **Simulation:** In the context of video games, researchers have created procedural personas that capture the sequential game-playing choices. The applied techniques include, e.g., evolutionary algorithms and neural networks (Holmgard et al., 2018). The procedural personas are given names based on their behaviors while playing the game (e.g., "Monster Killers"). Rather than being rounded personas (Nielsen, 2004) with a name and demographic information, these personas can be seen as virtual agents that simulate various game-playing behaviors (Vahlo et al., 2017).

- **System Log Data:** In addition to survey data, personas can be created from system logs and organizational records describing the users (Brickey, Walczak, and Burgess, 2012). For example, Molenaar (2017) analyzed 400,000 clickstreams from a period of 3 months, grouping them into common workflows and classifying users into these workflows. Using a similar approach, Zhang et al. (2016) applied hierarchical clustering to generate five data-driven personas from clickstream data.

- **Textual Data:** Methods such as LSA have been applied to create personas by differentiating users based on their use of language (Miaskiewicz, Grant, and Kozar, 2009). The weakness of this approach is the dependency on the text corpus, which is not always available in online analytics datasets. In addition, user-generated content such as social media posts can be considered a weaker form of data than behavioral data (e.g., analyzing users' writings of what they bought instead of observing actual sales records).

- **User Preference Data:** In the discrete choice methodology for data-driven persona creation (Chapman et al., 2015), users explicitly state their preferences. A conjoint analysis algorithm is then used to match respondents to their best-fit persona. The method was developed in response to the criticism of personas as lacking quantitative information (Chapman et al., 2008); through forced assignment, this method helps determine the representativeness of a persona within the overall user base. The method also makes it possible to compare the algorithmic persona assignments to randomly generated persona assignments. However, the major limitation is that stated preference data can be expensive to collect and can also be more unreliable than observed behavioral data. This is also the limitation of creating personas with principal component analysis (PCA) (Sinha, 2003) that uses preference data from a limited number of users.

1.5   RELATING DATA-DRIVEN PERSONAS TO SEGMENTATION

A data-driven persona is a representation of an actual segment of users presented as an imaginary person. As such, user segmentation is the conceptual foundation of the data collection and analysis for data-driven personas. Identifying user segments in many situations is difficult for a variety of reasons, from lack of data to privacy concerns to isolating what data to use (Leyva López et al., 2020). Notably, user segmentation and granularity are discussed by Claycamp and Massy (1968), who found aggregation beneficial for marketing practice. The optimal segmentation of user groups has also been pursued in computer science without a definitive solution as of yet (Jiang and Tuzhilin, 2009). We note that some view that personas, conceptually, differ from segments (Brangier and Bornet, 2011).

Our view is that personas, profiles, segments, etc., are human-designed constructs, so the boundaries are somewhat porous. Therefore, there is little applied value in attempting to definitively define each. These user representations all serve the purpose of better user understanding.

Concerning these user segmentation attempts, there have been various efforts from various domains and fields, so we mention only a few here to provide a flavor of the research area. Increasingly, user segmentation processes leverage social media data for both behavioral and demographic grouping (Jansen, Sobel, and Cook, 2011) of users. Website data has been used to segment users into various revenue segments (Ortiz-Cordova and Jansen, 2012), which is an example of behavioral segmentation. Search query data has been used to classify the gender of searchers and to then relate this demographic attribute to revenue generation (Jansen, Moore, and Carman, 2013). Tuna and colleagues (2016) examine the identification of segments from social media, specifically from user attributes such as gender and age, among others.

Dursun and Caber (2016) employ RFM (recency, frequency, monetary) analysis on data from a major hotel chain's user relationship management system, with results showing eight user segments and categorizing the majority of the users as "Lost Users," who stay for shorter periods and spend less relative to other segments. RFM analysis is a marketing technique used to quantitatively determine which users are the best ones by examining how recently a user has purchased a product (recency), how often the user purchases (frequency), and how much the user spends (monetary).

Zhang et al. (2016) analyzed user-level clickstreams to identify ten common workflows using hierarchical clustering. They then present five user facets based on the probability of platform use that they then gave a name (thus creating "personas"). Antoniou (2017) uses segmentation from online platforms in cultural heritage applications by extracting user personality and cognitive style profiles.

Concerning the specific use of social media data, Kamboj, Kumar, and Rahman (2017) find that social use, hedonic use, and cognitive use positively influence the financial and market performance of firms. Across the spectrum of research, we see the increasing reliance on online data for user segmentation (Shpak et al., 2020).

Major online social media platforms present unique challenges for user segmentation efforts attempting to rely on online user data. User segmentation relies on identifying key attributes from which one can separate users into segments (Cooil, Aksoy, and Keiningham 2008).

Targeting users via behavioral segmentation involves dividing the user base based on their collective behavior. A behavior can be a single attribute (e.g., viewing online content) or a set of behaviors (e.g., viewing online content, length of video watched, etc.), but it is typically focused on how the segment responds to, uses, or engages with a product.

Targeting users via demographic segmentation includes segmenting the users based on one or more differentiating characteristics, often including, but not limited to, gender, age, race, location, education, income, or career. However, much prior work in user segmentation has focused on using individual website data, such as that available from the analytics platforms. However, there is an increasing effort to employ user segmentation using social media data from the major online platforms. This data presents unique challenges, as it is typically aggregated to preserve the privacy of individuals, so methods must be employed to deal with the issues this aggregation causes in inferring user attributes.

Data-driven personas are based on automatically creating user segments using real user data, often aggregated by online platforms, meaning it is grouped by user attributes (e.g., Male, 25–34, South Korea) (Jung et al., 2017). This grouping is more common due to privacy concerns that prompt online platforms to provide only aggregated user data rather than session- or user-level data. Data-driven persona efforts have investigated using aggregated social media data for isolating user segments based on both the behaviors and on the demographics of those users and then linking the two user segments groupings for a complete representation of the user base. However, one can also apply similar techniques to individual user data. So, data-driven persona development is possible using either individual or aggregated user data.

1.6   DATA-DRIVEN PERSONAS FROM APG

Throughout this book, we will be employing data-driven personas from APG as the practical example implementation of the points presented. APG is both a methodology and a system for automatically creating data-driven personas from online analytics data (Jung et al., 2017).

APG generated data-driven personas are: (1) representative, as APG processes the entire online analytics dataset; (2) behaviorally descriptive, inferring latent patterns from users' engagement with products (e.g., digital content, e-commerce products, flight destinations, etc.); (3) rapidly generated due to fast processing time of the applied algorithms and web technologies; and (4) continuously up-to-date due to periodical retrieval of current data and the associated regeneration of the personas (Jansen, Salminen, and Jung, 2020).

See Figure 1.4 for an illustration of the APG interface as a data-driven persona, highlighting the unique aspects of data-driven personas of loyalty, sentiment, and interests. Note the persona cast listed on the left-hand side, along with the navigational and predictive features.

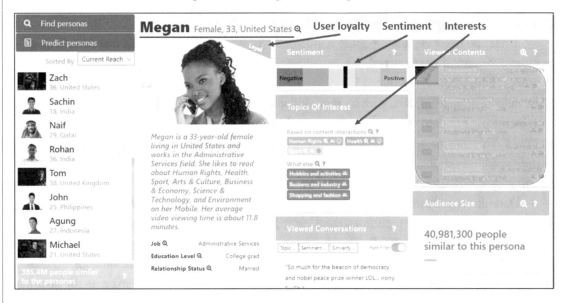

Figure 1.4: Example of a data-driven persona from the Automatic Persona Generation (APG) system. The persona cast is the listing of data-driven personas (screen left) and a displayed data-driven persona profile. The data-driven persona profiles contain the usual persona profile attributes, along with direct access provided to the underlying user data. There are also unique aspects, such as loyalty, sentiment, and interests.

APG leverages a novel approach for isolating user segments using online user data for products that are distributed via online social media platforms and analytics platforms. APG uses non-negative matrix factorization to first identify behavioral user segments and then to identify demographic user segments. APG employs a methodology for linking the two segments to present integrated and holistic user segments, i.e., personas. Behavioral segments are generated from user interactions with online content. Demographic segments are generated using the gender, age, and location of these users. In a variety of research studies (Jansen et al., 2020; Jung et al., 2017; Salminen et al., 2020), it has been shown that APG can accurately identify both behavioral and demographical user segments using actual online user data from which we can generate personas representing real groups of people.

As such, APG represents the state of the art in data-driven persona creation, and these data-driven personas are illustrative of the concepts, methods, and techniques discussed further in this book.

1.7   CHAPTER TAKE-AWAYS

- Data-driven personas are an approach for empathically understanding users based on user analytics.

- Personas are traditionally developed using manual data collection and primarily qualitative analysis methods.

- Data-driven personas employ automatic data collection and algorithmic analysis methods to create and update personas rapidly.

- Data-driven personas are foundationally based on user segmentation.

- Data-driven personas can serve as interfaces to fully functional persona analytics systems, a system integration that combines the advantages and offsets the shortcomings of both persona and analytics techniques.

- APG is a state-of-the-art data-driven persona system used as a conceptual demonstration for the examples in this book.

1.8   DISCUSSION AND ASSESSMENT QUESTIONS

1. List the benefits of personas in general and the benefits of data-driven personas. Compare and contrast the two lists. Describe design situations in which the benefits of each would be most beneficial.

2. List the possible criticisms of personas in general and the criticisms of data-driven personas. Compare and contrast the two lists. Describe design situations in which the criticisms of each would be most valid.

3. Explain the major changes in user segmentation since the concept of personas was first introduced. Elaborate on how these changes relate to persona development.

4. What are the three main evolutionary stages in data-driven persona development over time? Define each stage. Provide examples of contexts and methods for each stage.

5. What is meant by "flat-file" and "full-stack" when referring to data-driven personas? List the implications of each of these concepts in terms of enhanced user understanding.

6. Tease apart the term "persona." What meanings can the term have? List these meanings and then compare and contrast each for theoretical or practical similarities and differences.

7. List situations when individual user data is better than aggregated user data for user-related decision making. List situations when aggregated data is better. For each, which data type do personas represent?

8. Compare and contrast personas, analytics, and data-driven personas in terms of advantages and disadvantages. What is inherent in each that results in these advantages and disadvantages?

9. Using a common user-facing technology that you are familiar with, create a persona profile that you imagine would represent the typical user of this technology, including demographics, behaviors, and goals. Now identify possible data sources and analysis methods that you could use to create a data-driven persona for the typical user of this technology.

1.9   REFERENCES

Adlin, T. and Pruitt, J. (2010). *The Essential Persona Lifecycle: Your Guide to Building and Using Personas*. 1st ed. San Francisco, CA: Morgan Kaufmann Publishers Inc. DOI: https://doi.org/10.1016/B978-0-12-381418-0.00001-2. 5

Ait Hammou, B., Lahcen, A. A., and Mouline, S. (2020). Towards a real-time processing framework based on improved distributed recurrent neural network variants with fasttext for social big data analytics. *Information Processing and Management* 57(1), 102122. DOI: 10.1016/j.ipm.2019.102122. DOI: 10.1016/j.ipm.2019.102122. 9

An, J., Kwak, H., Jung, S., Salminen, J., and Jansen, B. J. (2018a). Customer segmentation using online platforms: Isolating behavioral and demographic segments for persona creation via aggregated user data. *Social Network Analysis and Mining* 8(1), 54. DOI: 10.1007/s13278-018-0531-0. DOI: 10.1007/s13278-018-0531-0. 3, 6, 9, 12

An, J., Kwak, H., Salminen, J., Jung, S., and Jansen, B. J. (2018b). Imaginary people representing real numbers: Generating personas from online social media data. *ACM Transactions on the Web (TWEB)* 12(4), 27. DOI: 10.1145/3265986. 12

Antoniou, A. (2017). Social network profiling for cultural heritage: Combining data from direct and indirect approaches. *Social Network Analysis and Mining* 7(1), 39. DOI: 10.1007/s13278-017-0458-x. 15

Aoyama, M. (2005). Persona-and-scenario based requirements engineering for software embedded in digital consumer products. In *Proceedings of the 13th IEEE International Conference on Requirements Engineering (RE'05)*. Pp. 85–94. Washington, DC. DOI: 10.1109/RE.2005.50. 12

Aoyama, M. (2007). Persona-scenario-goal methodology for user-centered requirements engineering. In *Proceedings of the 15th IEEE International Requirements Engineering Conference (RE 2007)*. pp. 185–94. Delhi, India. DOI: 10.1109/RE.2007.50. 12

Baig, M. I., Shuib, L., and Yadegaridehkordi, E. (2019). Big data adoption: State of the art and research challenges. *Information Processing and Management*, 56(6), 102095. DOI: 10.1016/j.ipm.2019.102095. 6

Bamman, D., O'Connor, B., and Smith, N. A. (2013). Learning latent personas of film characters. In *Proceedings of the 51st Annual Meeting of the Association for Computational Linguistics*. p. 10. Sofia, Bulgaria. 12

Beyer, H. and Holtzblatt, K. (1998). *Contextual Design: Defining Customer-Centered Systems*. Morgan Kaufmann Publishers Inc. DOI: 10.1145/286498.286629. 5

Blanco, E., Pourroy, F., and Arikoglu, S. (2014). Role of personas and scenarios in creating shared understanding of functional requirements: An empiricalstudy. In *Design Computing and Cognition'12*. pp. 61–78. Springer. DOI: 10.1007/978-94-017-9112-0_4. 5

Brangier, E. and Bornet, C. (2011). Persona: A method to produce representations focused on consumers' needs. In *Human Factors and ergonomics in Consumer Product Design*. pp. 37–61. Taylor and Francis. DOI: 10.1201/b10950-5. 14

Brickey, J., Walczak, S., and Burgess, T. (2012). Comparing semi-automated clustering methods for persona development. *IEEE Transactions on Software Engineering*. 38(3), 537–46. DOI: 10.1109/TSE.2011.60. 13

Brickey, J. (2010). *System for Persona Ensemble Clustering: A Cluster Ensemble Approach to Persona Development*. University of Colorado at Denver. 12

Burrows, A., Gooberman-Hill, R., and Coyle, D. (2015). Empirically derived user attributes for the Ddesign of home healthcare technologies. *Personal and Ubiquitous Computing*, 19(8), 1233–45. DOI: 10.1007/s00779-015-0889-1. 3

Byström, K. and Kumpulainen, S. (2019). Vertical and horizontal relationships amongst task-based information needs. *Information Processing and Management* 102065. DOI: 10.1016/j. ipm.2019.102065. 7

Chapman, C., Krontiris, K., and Webb, J. (2015). Profile CBC: Using conjoint analysis for consumer profiles. In *Sawtooth Software Conference Proceedings*. Google Research. 13

Chapman, C. N., Love, E., Milham, R. P., ElRif, P., and Alford, J. L. (2008). Quantitative evaluation of personas as information. In *Proceedings of the Human Factors and Ergonomics Society Annual Meeting*. Vol. 52, pp. 1107–11. DOI: 10.1177/154193120805201602. 5, 14

Chapman, C. N. and Milham, R. P. (2006). The personas' new clothes: Methodological and practical arguments against a popular method. In *Proceedings of the Human Factors and Ergonomics Society Annual Meeting*. Vol. 50, pp. 634–36. DOI: 10.1177/154193120605000503. 5, 6, 7

Chu, E., Vijayaraghavan, P., and Roy, D. (2018). Learning personas from dialogue with attentive memory networks. In *Proceedings of the 2018 Conference on Empirical Methods in Natural Language Processing*. Brussels, Belgium: Association for Computational Linguistics. pp. 2638–46. DOI: 10.18653/v1/D18-1284. 12

Clarke, M. F. (2015). The work of mad men that makes the methods of math men work: Practically occasioned segment design. In *Proceedings of the 33rd Annual ACM Conference on Human Factors in Computing Systems*. Seoul, Republic of Korea: ACM. pp. 3275–84. DOI: 10.1145/2702123.2702493. 3

Claycamp, H. J. and Massy, W. F. (1968). A theory of market segmentation. *Journal of Marketing Research*, 5(4), 388–94. DOI: 10.2307/3150263. 14

Cooil, B., Aksoy, L., and Keiningham, T. L. (2008). Approaches to customer segmentation. *Journal of Relationship Marketing*, 6(3–4), 9–39. DOI: 10.1300/J366v06n03_02. 15

Cooper, A. (2004). *The Inmates Are Running the Asylum: Why High Tech Products Drive Us Crazy and How to Restore the Sanity*, 2nd edition. Pearson Higher Education. 3, 6, 11

Dang-Pham, D., Pittayachawan, S., and Nkhoma, M. (2015). Demystifying online personas of Vietnamese young adults on Facebook: A Q-Methodology approach. *Australasian Journal of Information Systems*, 19(1). DOI: 10.3127/ajis.v19i0.1204. 12

Dharwada, P., Greenstein, J. S., Gramopadhye, A. K., and Davis, S. J. (2007). A case study on use of personas in design and development of an audit management system. In *Human Factors and Ergonomics Society Annual Meeting Proceedings*. Vol. 51, pp. 469–73. DOI: 10.1177/154193120705100509. 3, 5

Dong, J., Kelkar, K., and Braun, K. (2007). Getting the most out of personas for product usability enhancements. *Usability and Internationalization, HCI and Culture*, 4559, 291–96. DOI: 10.1007/978-3-540-73287-7_36. 3

Drego, V. L., Dorsey, M., Burns, M., and Catino, S. (2010). *The ROI of Personas. Report*. Forrester Research. 3, 4, 5, 7

Dupree, J. L., Devries, R., Berry, D. M., and Lank, E. (2016). Privacy personas: Clustering users via attitudes and behaviors toward security practices. In *Proceedings of the 2016 CHI Conference on Human Factors in Computing Systems, CHI '16*. pp. 5228–39. New York, NY: ACM. DOI: 10.1145/2858036.2858214. 13

Dursun, A. and Caber, M. (2016). Using data mining techniques for profiling profitable hotel customers: An application of RFM analysis. *Tourism Management Perspectives*, 18, 153–60. DOI: 10.1016/j.tmp.2016.03.001. 14

Eriksson, E., Artman, H., and Swartling, A. (2013). The secret life of a persona: When the personal becomes private. In *Proceedings of the SIGCHI Conference on Human Factors in Computing Systems*. ACM. pp. 2677–86. DOI: 10.1145/2470654.2481370. 3, 5

Friess, E. (2012). Personas and decision making in the design process: An ethnographic case study. In *Proceedings of the SIGCHI Conference on Human Factors in Computing Systems*, CHI '12. New York, NY: ACM. pp. 1209–18. DOI: 10.1145/2207676.2208572. 3, 5

Gaiser, B., Panke, S., and Arnold, P. (2006). Community design-The personas approach. In *E-Learn: World Conference on E-Learning in Corporate, Government, Healthcare, and Higher Education. Association for the Advancement of Computing in Education (AACE)*. pp. 520–25. 11

Goodwin, K.. (2009). *Designing for the Digital Age: How to Create Human-Centered Products and Services*, 1st edition. Indianapolis, IN: Wiley. 6

Goodwin, K. and Cooper, A. (2009). *Designing for the Digital Age: How to Create Human-Centered Products and Services*. Indianapolis, IN: Wiley. 6

Grudin, J. and Pruitt, J. (2002). Personas, participatory design and product development: An infrastructure for engagement. In *Proceedings of Participation and Design Conference (PDC2002)*. Vol. 2, pp. 144–61. Sweden. 5

Guo, F. Y., Shamdasani, S., and Randall, B. (2011). Creating effective personas for product design: Insights from a case study. In *Internationalization, Design and Global Development, Lecture*

Notes in Computer Science, edited by P. L. P. Rau. Berlin, Heidelberg: Springer. pp. 37–46. DOI: 10.1007/978-3-642-21660-2_5. 3

Hill, C. G., Haag, M., Oleson, A., Mendez, C., Marsden, N., Sarma, A., and Burnett, M. (2017). Gender-inclusiveness personas vs. stereotyping: Can we have it both ways? In *Proceedings of the 2017 CHI Conference*. Denver, CO: ACM Press. pp. 6658–71. DOI: 10.1145/3025453.3025609. 5

Holden, R. J., Kulanthaivel, A., Purkayastha, S., Goggins, K. M., and Kripalani, S. (2017). Know thy EHealth user: Development of biopsychosocial personas from a study of older adults with heart failure. *International Journal of Medical Informatics*. 108, 158–67. DOI: 10.1016/j.ijmedinf.2017.10.006. 12

Holmgard, C., Green, M. C., Liapis, A., and Togelius, J. (2018). Automated playtesting with procedural personas with evolved heuristics. *IEEE Transactions on Games PP*(99), 1–1. DOI: 10.1109/TG.2018.2808198. 13

Holmgard, C., Liapis, A., Togelius, J., and Yannakakis, G. N. (2014). Evolving personas for player decision modeling. In *Computational Intelligence and Games (CIG), 2014 IEEE Conference on*. IEEE. pp. 1–8. DOI: 10.1109/CIG.2014.6932911. 12

Hopkins, C. C. (1923). *Scientific Advertising*. Laurus-Lexecon Kft. 3

Jansen, A., Van Mechelen, M., and Slegers, K. (2017). Personas and behavioral theories: A case study using self-determination theory to construct overweight personas. In *Proceedings of the 2017 CHI Conference on Human Factors in Computing Systems, CHI '17*. Denver, CO: ACM. pp. 2127–36. DOI: 10.1145/3025453.3026003. 12

Jansen, B. J., Moore, K., and Carman, S. (2013). Evaluating the performance of demographic targeting using gender in sponsored search. *Information Processing and Management,* 49(1), 286–302. DOI: 10.1016/j.ipm.2012.06.001. 14

Jansen, B. J., Salminen, J. O., and Jung, S. (2020). Data-driven personas for enhanced user understanding: Combining empathy with rationality for better insights to analytics. *Data and Information Management*, 4(1), 1–17. DOI: 10.2478/dim-2020-0005. 16, 17

Jansen, B. J., Sobel, K., and Cook, G. (2011). Classifying ecommerce information sharing behaviour by youths on social networking sites: *Journal of Information Science*. DOI: 10.1177/0165551510396975. 14Jensen, I., Hautopp, H., Nielsen, L., and Madsen, S. (2017). Developing international personas: A new intercultural communication practice in globalized societies. *Journal of Intercultural Communication*, (43). 5, 14

Jiang, T. and Tuzhilin, A. (2009). Improving personalization solutions through optimal segmentation of customer bases. *IEEE Transactions on Knowledge and Data Engineering*, 21(3), 305–20. DOI: 10.1109/TKDE.2008.163. 14

Jílková, P. (2020). Customer behaviour and B2C client segmentation in data-driven society. *International Advances in Economic Research*, 26(3,) 325–26. DOI: 10.1007/s11294-020-09799-9. 9

Judge, T., Matthews, T., and Whittaker, S. (2012) Comparing collaboration and individual personas for the design and evaluation of collaboration software. in *Proceedings of the SIGCHI Conference on Human Factors in Computing Systems*, CHI '12. New York, NY: ACM. pp. 1997–2000. DOI: 10.1145/2207676.2208344. 3, 5

Jung, S., An, J., Kwak, H., Ahmad, M., Nielsen, L., and Jansen, B. J. (2017). Persona generation from aggregated social media data. In *Proceedings of the 2017 CHI Conference Extended Abstracts on Human Factors in Computing Systems, CHI EA '17*. Denver, CO: ACM. pp. 1748–55. DOI: 10.1145/3027063.3053120. 15, 16, 17

Kamboj, S., Kumar, V., and Rahman, Z. (2017). Social media usage and firm performance: The mediating role of social capital. *Social Network Analysis and Mining* 7(1), 51. DOI: 10.1007/s13278-017-0468-8. 15

Kanno, T., Ooyabu, T., and Furuta, K. (2011). Integrating human modeling and simulation with the persona method. In *Universal Access in Human-Computer Interaction. Users Diversity, Lecture Notes in Computer Science*, edited by C. Stephanidis. Springer Berlin Heidelberg. pp. 51–60. DOI: 10.1007/978-3-642-21663-3_6. 12

Khan, F., Si, X., and Khan, K. U. (2019). Social media affordances and information sharing: An evidence from Chinese public organizations. *Data and Information Management*, 3(3), 135–54. DOI: 10.2478/dim-2019-0012. 6

Lee, M., Kwahk, J., Han, S. H., Jeong, D., Park, K., Oh, S., and Chae, G. (2020). Developing personas and use cases with user survey data: A study on the millennials' media usage. *Journal of Retailing and Consumer Services*, 54, 102051. DOI: 10.1016/j.jretconser.2020.102051. 3

Leyva López, J. J., Figueroa Pérez, J. J., Contreras, E. O. P., and Sánchez, P. S. (2020). A marketing decision support system for product design based on an outranking approach. In *Customer Oriented Product Design: Intelligent and Fuzzy Techniques, Studies in Systems, Decision and Control*, edited by C. Kahraman and S. Cebi. Cham: Springer International Publishing. pp. 303–25. DOI: 10.1007/978-3-030-42188-5_16. 14

Li, J., Galley, M., Brockett, C., Spithourakis, G., Gao, J., and Dolan, B. (2016). A persona-based neural conversation model In *Proceedings of the 54th Annual Meeting of the Association for*

Computational Linguistics (Volume 1: Long Papers). Berlin, Germany: Association for Computational Linguistics. pp. 994–1003. DOI: 10.18653/v1/P16-1094. 12

Masiero, A. A. and Aquino, P. T. (2015). Creating personas to reuse on diversified projects. In *Human-Computer Interaction: Design and Evaluation*. Vol. 9169, *Lecture Notes in Computer Science*, edited by M. Kurosu. Cham: Springer International Publishing, pp. 238–47. DOI: 10.1007/978-3-319-20901-2_22. 12

McGinn, J. J. and Kotamraju, N. (2008). Data-driven persona development. In *Proceedings of the SIGCHI Conference on Human Factors in Computing Systems*. Florence, Italy: ACM. pp. 1521–24. DOI: 10.1145/1357054.1357292. 11, 12

Miaskiewicz, T., Grant, S. J., and Kozar, K. A. (2009). A preliminary examination of using personas to enhance user-centered design. Article 697. http://aisel.aisnet.org/amcis2009/697 in *AMCIS 2009 Proceedings*. 13

Miaskiewicz, T., Sumner, T., and Kozar, K. A. (2008). A latent semantic analysis methodology for the identification and creation of personas. In *Proceedings of the SIGCHI Conference on Human Factors in Computing Systems*. ACM. pp. 1501–10. DOI: 10.1145/1357054.1357290. 5

Mijač, T., Jadrić, M., and Ćukušić, M. (2018). The potential and issues in data-driven development of web personas. In *2018 41st International Convention on Information and Communication Technology, Electronics and Microelectronics (MIPRO)*. pp. 1237–42. DOI: 10.23919/MIPRO.2018.8400224. 9

Minichiello, A., Hood, J. R., and Harkness, D. S. (2017). *Work In Progress: Methodological Considerations for Constructing Nontraditional Student Personas with Scenarios from Online Forum Usage Data in Calculus. Working Paper*. Paper ID #17980. American Society for Engineering Education. DOI: 10.18260/1-2--29171. 11

Molenaar, L. (2017). Data-driven personas: Generating consumer insights with the use of clustering analysis from big data. *Undefined*. Retrieved June 28, 2020 (https://repository.tudelft.nl/islandora/object/uuid%3A12d7f261-20b4-4656-93d7-fed2b437aefb). 13

Nielsen, L. (2004). Engaging Personas and Narrative Scenarios. Ph.D. Thesis, Samfundslitteratur, Copenhagen, Denmark. 13

Nielsen, L. (2013). *Personas - User Focused Design*. 1st ed. London, UK: Springer-Verlag. DOI: 10.1007/978-1-4471-4084-9. 5

Nielsen, L. and Hansen, K.S. (2014). Personas is applicable: a study on the use of personas in Denmark. In *Proceedings of the SIGCHI Conference on Human Factors in Computing Systems (CHI '14)*. Association for Computing Machinery, New York, NY, 1665–1674. DOI: 10.1145/2556288.2557080. 3

Nielsen, L., Hansen, K. S., Stage, J., and Billestrup, J. (2015). A template for design personas: Analysis of 47 persona descriptions from Danish industries and organizations. *International Journal of Sociotechnology and Knowledge Development*, 7(1), 45–61. DOI: 10.4018/ijskd.2015010104. 3, 4, 5

Ortiz-Cordova, A. and Jansen, B. J. (2012). Classifying web search queries in order to identify high revenue generating customers. *Journal of the American Society for Information Sciences and Technology*, 63(7), 1426–41. DOI: 10.1002/asi.22640. 14

Pesot, J. and Plantenberg, S. (n.d.) Define personas - IBM garage practices. *Define Personas.* Retrieved October 20, 2020 (https://www.ibm.com/garage/method/practices/think/practice_personas/). 4

Podsakoff, P. M., MacKenzie, S. B., Lee, J-Y., and Podsakoff, N. P. (2003). Common method biases in behavioral research: A critical review of the literature and recommended remedies. *Journal of Applied Psychology*, 88(5), 879–903. DOI: 10.1037/0021-9010.88.5.879. 13

Pruitt, J. and Adlin, T. (2006). *The Persona Lifecycle: Keeping People in Mind Throughout Product Design.* 1st edition. Boston: Morgan Kaufmann. DOI: 10.1145/1167867.1164070. 3, 5

Pruitt, J. and Grudin, J. (2003). Personas: Practice and theory. In *Proceedings of the 2003 Conference on Designing for User Experiences, DUX '03.* San Francisco, CA: ACM. pp. 1–15. DOI: 10.1145/997078.997089. 5, 11

Revella, A. (2015). *Buyer Personas: How to Gain Insight into Your Customer's Expectations, Align Your Marketing Strategies, and Win More Business.* Wiley. 3

Rönkkö, K. (2005). An empirical study demonstrating how different design constraints, project organization and contexts limited the utility of personas. In *Proceedings of the Proceedings of the 38th Annual Hawaii International Conference on System Sciences - Volume 08, HICSS '05.* Washington, DC: IEEE Computer Society. 5

Salminen, J., Jansen, B. J., Haewoon Kwak, J. I., and Jung, S. (2018). Are personas done? Evaluating their usefulness in the age of digital analytics. *Persona Studies*, 4(2), 47–65. DOI: 10.21153/psj2018vol4no2art737. 6, 7

Salminen, J., Jung, S., Chowdhury, S. A., Sengün, S., and Jansen, B. J. (2020). Personas and analytics: A comparative user study of efficiency and effectiveness for a user identification task. In *Proceedings of the ACM Conference of Human Factors in Computing Systems (CHI'20).* Honolulu, HI: ACM. DOI: 10.1145/3313831.3376770. 17

Salminen, J., Kaate, I., Sayed Kamel, A., Jung, S.G., and Jansen, B. J. (2021) How does personification impact ad performance and empathy? An experiment with online advertising, *International Journal of Human–Computer Interaction*, 37, 2, 141–155, DOI: 10.1080/10447318.2020.1809246. 3

Salminen, J., Jung, S-G., Chowdhury, S., Sengün, S., and Jansen, B. J. (2020a). Personas and analytics: A comparative user study of efficiency and effectiveness for a user identification task. *Proceedings of the 2020 CHI Conference on Human Factors in Computing Systems. Association for Computing Machinery*, New York, NY, 1–13. DOI: 10.1145/3313831.3376770. 3

Shpak, N., Kuzmin, O., Dvulit, Z., Onysenko, T., and Sroka, W. (2020). Digitalization of the marketing activities of enterprises: Case study. *Information*, 11(2), 109. DOI: 10.3390/info11020109. 15

Siegel, D. A. (2010). The mystique of numbers: Belief in quantitative approaches to segmentation and persona development. In *CHI '10 Extended Abstracts on Human Factors in Computing Systems, CHI EA '10*. New York, NY: ACM. pp. 4721–32. DOI: 10.1145/1753846.1754221. 7

Sinha, R. (2003). Persona development for information-rich domains. In *CHI '03 Extended Abstracts on Human Factors in Computing Systems*. ACM. pp. 830–31. DOI: 10.1145/765891.766017. 14

Stevenson, P. D. and Mattson, C. A. (2019). The personification of big data. *Proceedings of the Design Society: International Conference on Engineering Design*, 1(1), 4019–28. DOI: 10.1017/dsi.2019.409. 6

Tuna, T., Akbas, E., Aksoy, A., Canbaz, M. A., Karabiyik, U., Gonen, B., and Aygun, R. (2016). User characterization for online social networks. *Social Network Analysis and Mining*, 6(1), 104. DOI: 10.1007/s13278-016-0412-3. 14

Tychsen, A. and Canossa, A. (2008). Defining personas in games using metrics. In *Proceedings of the 2008 Conference on Future Play: Research, Play, Share, Future Play '08*. Toronto, Ontario, Canada: ACM. pp. 73–80. DOI: 10.1145/1496984.1496997. 12

Vahlo, J. and Koponen, A. (2018). Player personas and game choice. In *Encyclopedia of Computer Graphics and Games*, edited by N. Lee. Cham: Springer International Publishing. pp. 1–6. DOI: 10.1007/978-3-319-08234-9_149-1. 13

Vahlo, J., Kaakinen, J. K., Holm, S. K., and Koponen, A. (2017). Digital game dynamics preferences and player types. *Journal of Computer-Mediated Communication*. 22, 2, 88–103. DOI: 10.1111/jcc4.12181. 13

Vecchio, P. del, Mele, G., Ndou, V., and Secundo, G. (2018). Creating value from social big data: Implications for smart tourism destinations. *Information Processing and Management*, 54(5), 847–60. DOI: 10.1016/j.ipm.2017.10.006. 9

Vincent, C. J. and Blandford, A. (2014). The challenges of delivering validated personas for medical equipment design. *Applied Ergonomics*, 45(4), 1097–1105. DOI: 10.1016/j. apergo.2014.01.010. 3

Vosbergen, S., Mulder-Wiggers, J. M. R., Lacroix, J. P., Kemps, H. M. C., Kraaijenhagen, R. A., Jaspers, M. W. M., and Peek,N. . (2015). Using personas to tailor educational messages to the preferences of coronary heart disease patients. *Journal of Biomedical Informatics*, 53, 100–112. DOI: 10.1016/j.jbi.2014.09.004. 12

Williams, K. L. (2006). Personas in the Design Process: A Tool for Understanding Others. Ph.D. Thesis, Georgia Institute of Technology. 11

Wöckl, B., Yildizoglu, U., Buber, I., Diaz, B. A., Kruijff, E., and Tscheligi, M. (2012) Basic senior personas: A representative design tool covering the spectrum of European older adults. In *Proceedings of the 14th International ACM SIGACCESS Conference on Computers and Accessibility, ASSETS '12*. New York, NY: ACM. pp. 25–32. DOI: 10.1145/2384916.2384922. 12

Zhang, X., Brown, H-F., and Shankar, A. (2016). Data-driven personas: Constructing archetypal users with clickstreams and user telemetry. In *Proceedings of the 2016 CHI Conference on Human Factors in Computing Systems, CHI '16*. San Jose, CA: ACM. pp. 5350–59. DOI: 10.1145/2858036.2858523. 13, 15

Zhu, H., Wang, H., and Carroll, J. M. (2019). Creating persona skeletons from imbalanced datasets: A case Sstudy using U.S. older adults' health data. In *Proceedings of the 2019 on Designing Interactive Systems Conference - DIS '19*. San Diego, CA: ACM Press. pp. 61–70. DOI: 10.1145/3322276.3322285. 11

CHAPTER 2

Getting Your Organization Data-Driven Persona Ready

This chapter discusses the challenging process of getting data-driven personas integrated within an organization. More precisely, it requires effort to bring the stakeholders within an organization to understand, develop, and productively employ data-driven personas for enhanced user understanding. We outline and discuss details of a three-step data-driven-personas process consisting of **educate**, **invest**, and **employ**. We end the chapter with an example of the Automatic Persona Generation (APG), a data-driven-persona system, to illustrate the fundamental idea of motivating your organization to employ data-driven personas productively. Some of the insights in this chapter are useful for *any* persona project, although throughout the chapter we maintain a particular focus on data-driven personas.

2.1   WHY IS THE ONBOARDING OF DATA-DRIVEN PERSONAS NEEDED?

Introduced for the software-design field, personas gained popularity in the late 1990s (Cooper, 1999), eventually leading to data-driven personas. Data-driven personas can be a powerful tool for user understanding in design, sales, advertising, and marketing (Guan et al., 2021). However, their actual use within organizations is more challenging than one might believe—an organization needs to be ready for personas.

In some organizations, the value of personas, in general, is often lost among stakeholders across departments who either do not regularly utilize this type of primary user-standing technique or question its worthiness (Matthews et al., 2012). Even when data-driven personas are created within organizations, they often are not actively deployed in many managerial or design settings (Friess, 2012). As such, they are developed, placed in a "desk drawer," and never actually employed, except maybe just for show. There are many possible reasons, such as not including stakeholders in the creation process, data-driven personas being viewed as unrealistic or not being based on relevant user insights (i.e., bad persona-creation methodologies). This has been a common issue with assumption-based personas (i.e., personas not based on real data). Furthermore, non-adoption and inactive use are consequences of the lack of readiness in a broader organizational scheme of culture, capabilities, and clear articulation of goals and metrics for the persona project

Thus, an organization must be primed and ready for data-driven personas to use them effectively. A foundational way to start is to assess the organizational maturity for data-driven personas.

Evaluating the need for data-driven personas is only the beginning of a long journey toward adopting personas. The steps of a persona project are: (1) persona readiness assessment, (2) persona readiness improvement, (3) persona creation, (4) persona deployment, and (5) persona performance monitoring. Table 2.1 provides useful indicators for this purpose for need evaluation.

Table 2.1: Maturity readiness of an organization for effective persona employment		
Maturity	**Maturity Indicator**	**Action Item**
Higher	We have defined the industry or industries we are part of.	Need to do before personas
	We have defined target markets (countries) we want to do business in.	
	We have defined target clients in these countries that we want to do business with.	Personas can help with this
	We have defined buyer types within these target clients to reach and learn about.	
	We have actually reached people representing these buyer types and interviewed them.	
	We have formed buyer personas based on these interviews (and/or other data).	Data-driven persona ready
	We have actually tested these buyer personas using advertising/sales outreach.	
	We are frequently updating these buyer personas based on how well they work and/or to reflect the changes in our buyer types in the market.	

Maturity	Maturity Indicator	Action Item
	Industries we are part of are defined.	Do that first
	Target market to do business in are defined	
	Target clients in these markets to do business with are defined.	Personas can help
	Buyer types within these target clients to reach and learn about are defined.	
	People representing these buyer types are actually reached and interviewed.	
	Buyer personas are formed based on these interviews (and/or other data).	Data-driven persona ready
	Buyer personas are tested using advertising/sales outreach.	
	Buyer personas are frequently updated based on how well they work and/or to reflect the changes in our buyer types in the market.	

2.2   THE ORGANIZATION'S DATA-DRIVEN PERSONA READINESS

The issue of data-driven persona readiness within an organization brings additional questions relative to just personas in general. Specifically, the focus of persona development is often on the needs of the end-users of analytics systems. Organizations that are struggling with adopting human-based data representations and large and diverse datasets can provide great benefit from this approach. Data-driven persona readiness is a much larger issue as it involves aspects like top management support, basic knowledge of personas in the organization, data sophistication, and technology maturity.

To be successful, data-driven persona projects need top management support, financial resources, a concrete plan to make use of personas, and so on. The measurement of these factors is addressed by the Persona Readiness Scale (PRS) (see Table 2.2). Scale dimension justifications are provided in the following subsections.

Table 2.2: Persona Readiness Scale. "We" is "our organization." "User" can be replaced by "customer." Items marked with [D] are considered optional for qualitative personas, whereas items marked with [T] are considered optional for quantitative personas. Mixed-method personas may utilize all statements.

Construct	Statements
Need Readiness	Our organization needs personas.
	We consider personas important.
	Personas would be useful for us.
	We need personas now.
Culture Readiness	User understanding is crucial for us.
	Empathy is required for understanding users.
Knowledge Readiness	Most of the people in our organization know what a persona is.
	Most of the people in our organization have used personas in their work.
	We know how to use personas.
Resource Readiness	We have a person in our organization who is strongly advocating for personas.
	We have a dedicated budget for persona creation and implementation.
	Training is available for team members not familiar with personas.
Data and Systems Readiness	We actively collect user data. [D]
	We have extensive user data, including behavioral and demographic information.
	Our user data is frequently updated. [D]
	Our user data is rich and includes user interviews or written feedback. [T]
Capability Readiness	We have data science expertise. [D]
	We have advanced know-how on user segmentation.
Goal Readiness	We have a plan for implementing personas after their creation.
	We have quantitative goals for persona use.
	We have clearly defined use cases for personas.
	We have defined quantitative metrics to measure the results of persona use.

The implementation of the PRS can be done using the standard Likert Scale, with options ranging from Strongly Disagree (1) to Strongly Agree (5). Given this, the maximum number of "points" an organization can achieve using the scale is 22 constructs × 5 ratings = 110. The minimum score, in turn, is 22 × 1 = 22. This leaves a range of 110 − 22 = 88 points in between. When dividing the points evenly across three classes, the interpretation is as follows.

- Low Persona Readiness: 22–51 points

- Average Persona Readiness: 52–81 points

- High Persona Readiness: 82–110 points

Knowing the current state of the persona readiness of a given organization can help locate areas of improvement. Addressing these areas before even starting the persona creation can improve the chances of success with data-driven personas.

As data-driven persona creation is costly, time-consuming, and resource-intensive, any activities that improve the prospect of success should be undertaken when pursuing persona projects. In particular, (a) design consultants or service providers offering persona services to organizations and (b) organizations themselves can use the PRS along with the suggested scoring system to gauge their persona readiness before launching costly projects. The scale can help identify specific areas of improvement in the current persona knowledge and attitudes in the organization, in the adequacy of financial and other resources, in the capabilities for carrying out a data-driven persona project from start to finish, and in the implementation plan with concrete goals and success metrics. The following subsections provide academic support for the scale dimensions.

2.2.1   NEED READINESS

"Need readiness" implies that the organization has an awareness of the benefits of personas, which is not always the case. Negative connotations may be associated with personas (Howard, 2015; Matthews et al., 2012; Rönkkö et al., 2004; Salminen et al., 2018a), and management support may be lacking. These benefits are also accepted as feasible or lucrative for the organization. In other words, there is a recognized "need" for personas. This perceived need for technology can vary depending on the organizational level. Senior management may perceive personas as important for strategic decisions, middle management for tactical decisions, and operational staff (e.g., software developers, designers, and user support) for operational (daily) decisions. Therefore, the organization must have the tactical, operational, and strategic awareness and need for data-driven personas, including an appreciation of their value and importance. This management buy-in is critical (Seidelin et al., 2014) and just as important as the buy-in at the design and implementation level.

2.2.2   CULTURE READINESS

"Culture readiness" expresses the commitment to understanding users in general and valuing empathy (Nielsen, 2019; Nielsen and Storgaard Hansen, 2014) as part of the user-centric decision-making process can be referred to as UX Maturity (Sauro et al., 2017). The importance of empathy arises from the persona literature, where the consensus is that empathy, on the one hand, is enhanced by data-driven personas and, on the other hand, results in more user-centric (and therefore better) design and product development choices. Therefore, the organization needs to have the motivation to understand users, a commitment to understanding users, a focus on user-centric thinking, and the employment of empathetic thinking about users.

2.2.3   KNOWLEDGE READINESS

"Knowledge readiness" involves a basic understanding of the concept of data-driven personas among the team members and experience in applying personas for real use cases. The lack of experience can be detrimental for persona application simply because questions, doubts, and lack of reference examples hinder a decision maker's ability to make use of personas in a meaningful way (Matthews et al., 2012). Lack of clarity on what personas are is a prime proponent in making them appear abstract, impersonal, and untrustworthy to decision-makers. To avoid this, the organization needs to have a foundational understanding of personas, including personas, and knowledge of the applications of these personas in real use cases for the organization. These use cases need to be defined before starting the persona creation to avoid the situation where personas are created, and then the organization does not know what to do with them.

2.2.4   RESOURCE READINESS

"Resource readiness" relates to the availability of crucial resources for the data-driven persona project, which includes persona creation, evaluation, and implementation. This may be conducted by in-house personnel or an external consultancy. Lifecycle thinking of personas (Pruitt and Adlin, 2006) is important, as organizations might not properly follow through with persona application after their creation. Moreover, the organization should appoint a point of contact with the responsibility to ensure the success of the persona project, including their creation, application, and updating for the organization's needs. This person is sometimes characterized as a "persona champion." Also, training is provided for the team members not familiar with personas to educate these users on the concept and opportunities of data-driven personas. Overall, the organization needs to have resource availability, including finances and people. Again, it is key that the organization have a "data-driven persona advocate" appointed with the responsibility for updating the data-driven personas, championing their use, and ensuring personas are a priority in the organization to better understand users in their daily jobs. So, for this, there needs to be executive support for the use of personas if hiring is needed.

2.2.5   DATA AND SYSTEMS READINESS

"Data and systems readiness" refers to activities supporting the creation of high-quality data-driven personas. This is characterized by the continuous collection of user data that corresponds with the big user data characteristics of volume, variability, veracity, and velocity (Jung et al., 2020; Stevenson and Mattson, 2019). The data must satisfy the requirements of creating truthful and diverse persona sets that contain complete information to be helpful for team members' decision-making tasks (the "rounded persona" principle [Nielsen et al., 2015]). The exact data requirements depend on the applied persona creation approach. For personas especially, the organization needs to have sufficient data to create the personas. The data and systems readiness needs to be either internal to the organization, outsourced to those with the expertise, or employed through reliance on SaaS data-driven persona systems (Jung et al., 2018).

2.2.6   CAPABILITY READINESS

While the question of readiness is applicable to all kinds of personas (Jansen et al., 2021), the organization's decision to pursue algorithmically generated data-driven personas sets additional requirements for data science and technology competencies (Salminen et al., 2020). This is not often well understood. Based on our encounters with practitioners, many stakeholders assume that since their organization has a social media account, they can automatically generate personas. This is an incorrect assumption as the requirements involve the quantity, quality, and structure of the data. Hence, "capability readiness" involves technical competence to operate systems and data required for data-driven persona generation. This includes knowledge of algorithms, data structures, databases, external data sources such as APIs, as well as a sound understanding of user segmentation principles and how these relate to statistical techniques, such as dimensionality reduction, which is often used for persona generation.

Therefore, the organization needs to have, or have access to, data science competencies, including data collection from internal databases and online sources, algorithmic know-how to process that data, and system development know-how to build interactive persona systems the integrate the information generated from the raw data. Data-driven SaaS personas (Jung et al., 2018) can supplement or augment this capability. The exact capabilities depend on the persona creation approach (qualitative, quantitative, or mixed) applied.

2.2.7 GOAL READINESS

"Goal readiness" refers to the tracking of performance outcomes. If data-driven personas are left unattended after their creation, the effort put into the project can easily become wasted. Personas also need to support the achievement of the team's goals to make the team receptive to personas. For these reasons, performance metrics (e.g., marketing outcomes, user satisfaction) are required to gauge the success of the persona project. The metrics should be aligned with an implementation plan (i.e., a list of campaigns/projects/activities/ programs where personas are to be applied, along with a description of who and by whom) and tangible numerical goals (e.g., deploying personas will improve the surveyed user satisfaction by 15% within 6 months of the introduction of the finalized personas). The organization must have defined goals and metrics to support persona implementation and follow-through. For this, we suggest creating a plan for *Persona Performance Monitoring* (PPM)—a formal document explaining how the personas will be used after their creation and how the results will be measured. An example of such a plan is shown in Figure 2.1.

Project Statement: The data-driven personas are created for the overall purpose of

_____ .

The responsible: _____

Specific use cases for the data-driven personas:

_____
_____
_____

Teams/team members involved in data-driven persona creation:

_____
_____

Teams/team members involved in data-driven persona use:

_____
_____

Goals for the persona project:

_____

Metrics for measuring the goals:

_____

Figure 2.1: Template for data-driven persona project plan.

2.3   ARE DATA-DRIVEN PERSONAS RIGHT FOR YOUR ORGANIZATION, EVEN IF THE ORGANIZATION IS READY FOR THEM?

In addition, organizations are encouraged to consider the following questions before initiating data-driven personas projects, specifically:

- **User-facing Products:** Does your organization offer products/services in online environments? (e.g., e-commerce, social media)

- **Diverse User Population:** Does your organization have a large and diverse user/customer base? (e.g., international audience, patient population)

- **User Population Data:** Has your organization collected digital information on your users/customers? (e.g., customer relationship management (CRM) system, Weblog files, electronic health records, etc.)

- **Measurable User Characteristics:** Are the user attributes your organization is interested in easily quantifiable? (e.g., engagement with online content)

If the answers to these questions are mostly positive, data-driven personas techniques can be beneficial for the organization's enhanced user insights, as these are the environments where data-driven personas provide the most benefits. In other words, the data structure, offering, and customer base all indicate compatibility with data-driven personas. If the answers to these questions are primarily negative, traditional persona techniques might make more sense for the organization. For example, startups with limited pre-existing customer data could pursue a handful or more customer interviews (so-called "customer development;" Batko, 2013) to get a general understanding of the prospective users' needs for their product. Therefore, the feasibility of data-driven personas is associated with the volume and variability of the customer data—with small datasets, one can easily perform manual analyses without the use of sophisticated algorithms.

The guiding questions and the statements in Tables 2.1 and 2.2 are essential for mapping the data-driven personas readiness of an organization and avoiding conflated expectations about the applicability of data-driven personas. In some cases, especially when a deep understanding of the users' goals and motivations is needed, qualitative persona creation may be more applicable than pure-form data-driven personas. Naturally, mixed methods can also be applied to enhance quantitative personas with qualitative insights, which is an approach discussed in detail in a later chapter.

2.4   THREE-STEP PROCESS FOR DEPLOYING DATA-DRIVEN PERSONAS IN THE ORGANIZATION

Once you have determined that the organization is ready for data-driven personas (or at least personas), here is a three-step data-driven persona onboarding process dubbed **Educate—Invest—Employ** (EIE). The steps are as follows.

- **Step 1: Educate—Introduce, define, and clarify data-driven personas.** Ensure stakeholders understand the costs and benefits of data-driven personas and how to best use data-driven personas. Lay the foundation in data, technology, capabilities, and management support.

- **Step 2: Invest—Get key stakeholders involved with data-driven persona creation from the outset.** Get stakeholders invested in creating data-driven personas to ensure trust and further use of the personas in the future. This requires organization expertise in data, technology, and understanding. If these readiness features do not exist internally, then the organization needs external expertise.

- **Step 3: Employ—Set up the processes and culture where data-driven personas are used in the organizational workflow.** Assist stakeholders in ensuring that data-driven personas' benefits are tangible and incorporated into the organization's workflow and the measured key performance indicators (KPIs). It is essential to have a persona champion and managerial support.

We will now discuss each of these steps in more detail and provide supporting content for their implementation.

2.4.1   STEP 1: EDUCATE: INTRODUCE, DEFINE, AND CLARIFY PERSONAS

The stakeholders' education concerning what data-driven personas are and what differentiates data-driven personas from analytics tools, such as user segmentation, is the first step for incorporation into the organization. There must be an advocate for the meaningful use of data-driven personas within the organization, followed soon, hopefully, by a team of advocates for data-driven personas' meaningful employment. Educational efforts are instrumental in getting organizational buy-in for data-driven personas.

For the education, start with the basics by showing what data-driven personas are, explaining the value of data-driven personas to stakeholders, demonstrating how they contribute to a user-centered organization, and validating how they could be used. Like nearly any technology project, the employment of personas, especially data-driven personas, benefits from a champion or evangelist.

This education step may mean having discussions multiple times with various stakeholders to clarify what data-driven personas are. Many stakeholders may not have been exposed to personas at all, not to mention data-driven personas. Get the conversation started by asking them what their perception of personas are and then show them an example of a cast of data-driven personas.

This might also require educating, especially the analytics personal, about the difference between data-driven personas and segmenting—segmentation does not equal data-driven personas. Table 2.3 shows the differences among traditional personas, data-driven personas, and segmentations.

Table 2.3: Compare and contrast of personas, data-driven personas, and segments; • means has			
Features	Traditional Persona	Data-driven Personas	Segments
Humanizing Attributes (e.g., photo, name)	•	•	
Demographic Attributes (e.g., nationality, age)	•	•	•
Goals, Pain Points, etc. (e.g., get promoted, wants reasonable price)	•	•	
Specific Behaviors (e.g., purchases online, wants images)		•	•
Personalizing Capability (e.g., uses a mobile phone, watches videos)			•

Since personas were introduced, HCI researchers and practitioners have highlighted both their positive and negative aspects. Stated benefits aside (Goodwin and Cooper, 2009), there are still concerns about personas' value. During the evangelizing process, one will most likely encounter statements about the possible negatives, of personas in general. So, one must be knowledgeable of these, and one must also be knowledgeable of the perceived benefits of data-driven personas in particular.

We present these positive and negative aspects of data-driven personas and then explore the underlying assumptions of both, as the data-driven personas implementation in practical situations is tied explicitly to these foundational assumptions about personas in general. Then, we illustrate the advantages of data-driven personas.

Table 2.4: Benefits (3Cs) and drawbacks (3Es) of personas, as reported in prior HCI literature

Positives about personas (3Cs)		Negatives about personas (3Es)	
Communication	Personas aid in facilitating organizational communication by providing a common reference point for user focusing.	Envision	Personas have no credibility, are inaccurate, and are unverifiable; the personas' profile information is not pertinent for decision-makers, and persona information is inconsistent.
Consideration	Personas are enhancing the immersion in designing "for a person" versus nameless user segments. Personas generate user empathy.	Execution	Persona creation takes a considerable amount of effort, time, and money; personas may be biased by the motives and misbeliefs of their creators, and they are often built using non-representative data.
Concentration	Personas challenge the existing assumptions and assist in focusing on the user when conflicting design needs arise.	Evaluation	Personas, once created, are practically useless, or they are used only for organizational politics. There is limited empirical backing that personas provide actual benefits when employed.

Positives about Personas

The reported positive aspects of personas can be summarized into the groupings of *Communication*, *Consideration*, and *Concentration* (labeled as the "3Cs"), as presented in Table 2.4 and discussed below.

Communication: Personas reportedly offer collaboration benefits derived from the personas' ability to encapsulate user information into the intuitive representation of a real person, which can be readily communicated (Watanabe et al., 2017) to the various stakeholders within organizations (Matthews et al., 2012) in a manner that is more immersive than analytics data (Hill et al., 2017). At their best, personas are *shared mental models* that decision-makers can rely upon when creating plans and designs (Nielsen, 2019) concerning an explicit user (Cooper, 1999). Personas enable communication of user preferences that may deviate from inherent viewpoints (Miaskiewicz et al., 2009).

Consideration: Personas purportedly have psychological benefits rooted in the natural emotional identification with people represented by personas (Miaskiewicz et al., 2009), helping decision-makers understand and predict user behavior under different contexts (Pruitt and Grudin, 2003). This mental modeling depends on the innate ability of *empathy* and *immersion* (Krashen, 1984) in humans as social beings. Personas are also alleged to challenge the conventional preconceptions about the users within organizations (Miaskiewicz and Kozar, 2011) by conveying factual information concerning users (Pruitt and Adlin, 2006) and rectifying incorrect preconceptions (Matthews et al., 2012).

Concentration: Personas can allegedly facilitate concentration on the most significant user segments (Miaskiewicz et al., 2009) by isolating an archetype user to develop products and services. This concentration helps decision-makers define appropriate features (Cooper, 1999; Le-Rouge et al., 2013) while also curbing the egocentric bias that may occur during a design process (Miaskiewicz et al., 2009).

Negatives about Personas

There are substantial negative aspects of personas detailed in the HCI literature. We tag these negatives as *Envision*, *Execution*, and *Evaluation* (labeled as the 3Es) as summarized in Table 2.4 and discussed below.

Envision: Chapman and Milham (2006) contend that personas have no direct association with real user data and that they represent few actual users (Chapman and Milham, 2006) and are not scientifically valid (Cabrero et al., 2016) because a persona is not falsifiable in any meaningful way (Popper, 2002). Vincent and Blandford (2014) claim that persona creation adapts not to user data but to what their creators want to accomplish politically within the organization. Thus, personas quite often are not representative of actual user segments (Chapman and Milham, 2006) but reflect private or organizational dynamics and preferences of stakeholders. Also, no definitive information must be included in a persona profile (Bødker et al., 2012; Chapman and Milham, 2006), causing confusion and a lack of trust among end users of personas.

Execution: Hill et al. (2017) highlight that it takes considerable effort, money, and time to create high-quality personas. Accordingly, as Rönkkö (2005) reports, the volume of effort leads many stakeholders to question the return on investment (ROI) of a persona development process. One of the most noted concerns is that multiple or periodic data collection rounds may be needed to keep the personas updated (Mulder and Yaar, 2006) or at least verify that the personas have not staled. This criticism, widely present in the persona literature, is based on the assumption that there are times of instability and change in user populations (Chapman and Milham, 2006), resulting in changes to personas created (Drutsa et al., 2017).

Furthermore, the high effort and cost of persona creation tend to exclude personas from the reach of small and medium businesses, including startups (Salminen et al., 2018). Finally, personas are also reported to be inconsistent; they are often created via merging information from numerous unrelated sources into a piecemeal (Bødker et al., 2012) profile without confirming that the informational components are proportionate (Matthews et al., 2012).

Evaluation: The prior literature on persona evaluation has commonly either presented a criticism of personas as a methodology or employed soft metrics for the personas' successes, such as anecdotal responses from personas' end users stating that personas appeared "correct" and "good." Similarly, Rönkkö reports how organizational factors often led to limited persona usage (Rönkkö, 2005). Ma and LeRouge (2007) claim that profiles are often preferred to personas. Also, numbers-oriented end users may consider personas as little more than "nice narratives" while resisting their adoption for practical use in day-to-day decision-making (Massanari, 2010). The findings of Matthews et al. (2012) indicate that personas can be seen as abstract and misleading, and they are not a replacement for the actual user data. There has been a limited quantitative empirical evaluation of personas' use compared to another user-centric technique (Salminen et al., 2020b).

Benefits of Data-Driven Personas

While manual and data-driven methods are often used in conjunction, the lack of resources incentivizes researchers and practitioners to choose one or the other (Thoma and Williams, 2009). When facing this choice and due to the benefits of the creation process above, data-driven personas provide some distinct advantages, listed as follows.

Enhanced objectivity. Manually created personas are associated with a high degree of subjectivity that may hinder the validity of the developed personas (An et al., 2018). In contrast, data-driven personas are seen as a "way to overcome subjectivity [of manually created personas] both in interpretation and segmentation of available data" (Jansen et al., 2017, p. 2128) (n.p.). Besides, data-driven persona approaches tend to be replicable and use large sample sizes to increase the representativeness of the personas of the user population (Chapman and Milham, 2006; Siegel, 2010). This statistical robustness can boost both the validity and credibility of the developed personas.

Decreased cost. Manual personas development typically requires several months to complete from start to finish, including the financial cost of tens of thousands of dollars when conducted by consultancies (Drego et al., 2010). The high-cost factor, mainly in terms of time, makes high-quality personas inaccessible for organizations with limited financial resources (e.g., startup companies and non-profit organizations). Data-driven personas can mitigate this cost by relying on automation in persona development's critical processes, including data collection and analysis, thus offering ways to "democratize" persona development for organizations of all kinds. Although the development of a data-driven persona system in-house may be expensive in terms of both time and money, Software-as-a-Service (Saas) puts data-driven personas within most organizations' reach.

Updatability. Shifts in user demographics and behaviors are typical in many fast-moving industries, such as e-commerce (Salminen, Jung, and Jansen, 2019b), Web search engines (Jenkinson, 1994), and social media platforms (Li et al., 2016). When the underlying user data changes, personas become redundant unless they are updated according to the new data. For manual personas, updating personas tends to require excessive amounts of costly and non-scalable manual labor, resulting in the personas often not being updated at all. In contrast, data-driven personas are based on automated processes for periodic data collection. Its re-analysis uses standard algorithms to capture user behavior change over time (Jansen et al., 2019; Jung et al., 2019).

Scalability and "data readiness." Manual analysis of data is costly and requires specific expertise, making many manual persona development efforts incompatible with large datasets that are becoming increasingly common with the rise of social media and Web analytics (Guo and Razikin, 2015). The more distinct user segments in the baseline data, the more difficult it is to discover them using manual personas. In turn, large datasets are typically not a concern for data-driven persona methods, as data science and machine learning algorithms have been developed to process large amounts of data.

Data-driven methods make persona creation easy, efficient, and affordable—so all types of organizations can get access to personas, including those with limited financial resources such as non-profits and startups.

Education Take-Away

The main takeaway concerning the education step, also known as "evangelizing," is communicating that data-driven personas are an invaluable tool for stakeholders aiming to build consensus and alignment for their user's goals and behaviors. With this common understanding and knowledge with the organization, user-focused conversations can shift from a product-based to a solution-based empathic understanding of users. This empathic solution-based communication allows leading stakeholders to create synergies among organizational departments around users.

2.4.2   STEP 2: INVEST: GET KEY STAKEHOLDERS INVOLVED WITH DATA-DRIVEN PERSONA CREATION FROM THE OUTSET

The process of creating data-driven personas needs to be highly collaborative to get buy-in from organizational stakeholders. Colleagues with little to no say in the research data collection, data analysis, or other aspects of data-driven personas development process are likely to question the findings and insights or even reject the use of personas all together. Therefore, all stakeholder need to be involved, the best, or at least aware of the details of how the personas are created.

The effective employment of data-driven persona requires everyone, from design engineers to marketing representatives to managers to customer service employees, to actively participate in the process of designing personas. As a result of this participatory engagement, stakeholders can better shape the type of data-driven personas insights, trust the developed data-driven personas, and then actually apply the data-driven personas for user understanding tasks. Bring personas using stakeholders onboard the journey of creating data-driven personas! Get the key stakeholders involved from the onset of the process.

The stakeholders who will be using the data-driven personas need to participate in their creation as much as possible. This participation helps internalize important user segment information during the creation process and helps avoid rejection of the data-driven personas for being "artificial." The Investment step might vary somewhat organization and among different stakeholders, but investing stakeholders would most likely include activities such as follows.

- Before data-driven personas creation, form "persona hypotheses" by interviewing stakeholders like salespeople, marketers, and executives.

- Capture their tacit knowledge into the data-driven personas hypotheses (e.g., "our typical user is a young woman from Helsinki that loves outdoor experiences").

- Analyze quantitative data from users. Which of the hypotheses hold?

- Get stakeholders involved in the data collection (even with data-driven personas, there will usually be some) and the selection of online data to create data-driven personas.

- Invite stakeholders to any workshops when creating the data-driven personas, even to things like names and pictures.

- Let stakeholders comment on work-in-progress data-driven personas versions (Norman, 2004).

- Invite stakeholders to observe the user research that the data-driven personas are to be based on. This can be somewhat challenging with data-driven personas, requiring activities such as review social media account, service call logs, survey results, CRM data, and web analytics data.

The point of this investment is to make the "buyer of the persona" part of the data-driven personas creation process. This lowers their possible resistance when coming back with findings based on real data to confirm, refute, or add to their understanding of the user segments. When stakeholders participate in the creation of data-driven personas, they are more likely to accept and adopt data-driven personas in their professional decision-making.

Based on empirical findings (Salminen et al., 2020b), the experience of the stakeholders is an important antecedent to realizing the full value of personas. While previous research alludes to this same point (Howard, 2015; Long, 2009), our research has empirically quantified the impact of the data-driven personas experience on user perceptions. Basically, from a design point of view, all "desirable" perceptions (apart from clarity) of personas increase by experience. This finding has important implications for persona design and adoption.

These findings (Salminen et al., 2020b) suggest that experience represents a peripheral route to obtaining the widely cited empathy benefits of personas, possibly because more experienced persona users can perceive personas as real people. In a sense, the data-driven personas need to be likable to the stakeholders. Likability, while not a design goal per se (i.e., unlikable personas can be important for understanding user groups that are different from the designers' worldview and attitudes), can affect other perceptions (Salminen et al., 2019b). Thus, the finding that experience increases likability is interesting and corroborates that people with less experience in personas are more likely to consider personas as "inanimate" profiles rather than real people they could empathize with.

Our prior experience (and research (Salminen et al., 2020b)) of deploying data-driven personas in the field suggest that experience with personas is a factor that supports the reception of personas by itself. Consequently, the focus on persona developers (e.g., user experience professionals and consultancies) should be on applying techniques that increase stakeholders' exposure and experience with personas. For this, several possibilities exist, including training courses, presentations, workshops, experimenting with personas via controlled experiments such as marketing campaigns, and so on.

Therefore, exposing stakeholders to data-driven personas to try out personas for real or simulated scenarios can enhance the experience and make personas more valuable. From our experiences in the field (some of which are reported in (Salminen et al., 2019; Salminen et al., 2018b), decision-makers often face a "mental obstacle" of getting started with personas, which involve uncertainty and resistance. Thus, accumulating more experience seems like a hygiene factor for persona adoption. Experience enhances the understanding of the persona technique (What are personas? How are they used? What information should I pay attention to?) and improves the use of personas by managers, designers, and software developers for user-centric decision-making.

During Step 2, here are some additional investment aspects to consider that specifically pertain to data-driven personas.

- **Avoid the "mystique of numbers."** One should not blindly believe the outputs of statistical methods. Additional steps, such as ensuring data quality and triangulating the results with other methods, such as qualitative interviews, are necessary. Therefore, practitioners with limited knowledge about quantitative methods should ask as many "stupid" questions as possible to avoid the "mystique of numbers" (Siegel, 2010), including asking clarification about how the data-driven personas were created, what judgment calls the creative process involved, and how the results were evaluated. Being critical pays off.

- **Consider the human bias.** Surveys are the most popular data format for data-driven personas. However, even when analyzed quantitatively, survey data may include several validity issues, such as social desirability bias (Fisher, 1993), especially relative to behavioral data. In a similar vein, setting the number of data-driven personas, applying hyperparameters for algorithms, and other steps that involve human judgment are subject to human bias. Therefore, "quantitative" does not automatically mean objective or truthful, which is critical to acknowledge. Data-driven persona creation involves human decisions, and these decisions should be reported and scrutinized.

- **Consider the algorithmic bias.** The research community is increasingly aware of algorithmic biases, meaning that data and algorithms may introduce undesired generalizations into the personas (Hajian et al., 2016; Salminen, Jung, and Jansen, 2019a). The blind application of data and algorithms might lead to adverse outcomes, such as ignoring minority groups (Luo et al., 2019). Statistical methods tend to favor majority groups and obscure the outliers and deviations within the user groups. Sometimes, these are interesting, like the most loyal users that comprise only a small portion of the whole but have a decisive impact. To counter this, data-driven persona applications can, e.g., split the dataset into "majority" and "minority" and generate data-driven personas separately for each.

- **Target real use cases and measures.** Several authors of data-driven persona articles suggest ways of going beyond mere persona creation to testing the usefulness of the data-driven personas in meeting stakeholder goals (Goodman-Deane et al., 2018; Miaskiewicz and Luxmoore, 2017; Rahimi and Cleland-Huang, 2014; Tanenbaum et al., 2018; Watanabe et al., 2017). These efforts can take the form of longitudinal studies on how the data-driven personas are adapted and used by stakeholders and to what effect. For example, in healthcare, such initiatives would involve designing tailored medical interventions to subpopulations represented by the personas and evaluating how health outcomes develop over time (Tanenbaum et al., 2018; Vosbergen et al., 2015). Some studies show promise using longitudinal data and standardized algorithms to compare persona casts over time (Jung et al., 2019) and organizational units

(Zaugg and Ziegenfuss, 2018). Evaluation of data-driven personas can also be inspired by qualitative persona evaluation studies (Friess, 2012; Matthews et al., 2012).

2.4.3   STEP 3: EMPLOY: SET UP THE PROCESSES AND CULTURE IN WHICH PERSONAS ARE USED IN THE ORGANIZATIONAL WORKFLOW

Step 3, the hardest of the three steps, is the employment of the data-driven personas once created and gotten buy-in for from stakeholders. However, the organization now needs to use the personas for empathic user understanding and the importance of putting the users at the heart of organizational business decisions. However, this employment does not happen immediately. It takes effort to ensure that the data-driven personas developed by the organization are going to get used. Personas are valuable if they are used in the right way to reap organizational benefits. Data-driven personas do not tell which feature is a priority unless they are actually employed in the design and development process. As illustrated in Step 2, the efforts for the employment of data-driven personas never ends.

However, there are some recommended techniques for integrating data-driven personas into the organization's expectations and culture.

- **Integrate data-driven personas into people's workflow.** When employing data-driven personas into organizations, one should seek opportunities where enhanced user understanding and data-driven personas can be of value. These opportunities are often organization specific. Investigating, prior to their creation, where data-driven personas can be integrated is a necessary exercise.

- **Use data-driven personas for strategic guidance.** Identify the points in the organization's workflows when data-driven personas can be effective for focusing on the users. Some examples of when data-driven personas can be instrumental for successful user understanding are:

  - **Design workshops:** A design workshop is an opportunity for a team to untangle a problem together by going through a series of exercises designed to reach a specific outcome. Design workshops are about getting stuff done, and they are often used as milestones to start projects or make decisions. Bringing data-driven personas "into the room" results in system designers, developers, engineers, C-level executives, and so on, creating a more empathetic and personalized experience for users.

  - **Ideation workshops:** An ideation workshop is a dedicated session for developing new ideas, with the primary goal of sparking innovation. Have each workshop attendee represent a data-driven persona in a role-playing scenario. This way, stakeholders can get in touch with their personas and start empathizing with them as real people. This role-playing results in a considerable amount of valuable user understanding brainstorming ideas that otherwise might not be achieved without personas.

- **Making business decisions:** Business decision-making is the process of making choices by identifying a needed decision, collecting relevant information, developing courses of action, assessing these alternatives, and then determining the optimal business solution. Again, data-driven personas are tailor-made for these situations (i.e., think about "What would Sara want? When will she need this? Is this going to help her?" etc.).

- **Making design decisions:** Design decisions take into account human considerations, from ergonomics to cognitive capabilities. A good design solution has to be useable and useful. Data-driven personas are tailor-made for these situations (i.e., think about "How is Tracey going to use this? When will she use it? Is this going to help her?" etc.).

- **Roadmap planning sessions:** A roadmap is a strategic plan that defines a goal or desired outcome and includes the major steps or milestones needed to reach those goals or outcomes. Using data-driven personas, one can prioritize roadmap features around the needs of the different personas.

- **Keep data-driven personas alive:** Data-driven personas need to be living entities in order to be effectively employed. With data-driven personas, you cannot carry out research once and think you are done learning about your users. For maximum effectiveness, one must continually conduct new research and understand more users, updating the cast of data-driven personas throughout. Our research shows that for large organizations, there can be rapid persona changes month-to-month (Jansen et al., 2019), and large personas casts change year-to-year (Jung et al., 2019). Expect the data-driven personas to change and plan accordingly.

- **Make data-driven personas visible:** Quite simply, do not place your data-driven personas in a shared organizational Intranet server, on your organizational Intranet, or print them off so folks can place them in desk drawers. Data-driven personas can change rapidly. Incorporate your personas into corporate presentations. Develop the culture of discussion personas in electronic communication. Put personas up in communal areas that people frequently pass by and see every day. Given that data-driven personas can change rapidly, we encourage using digital screens and interactive systems to present personas and keep them fresh, as demonstrated in Figure 22.

Figure 2.2: Four data-driven personas displayed on a digital screen; great for wall mounting in common organizational areas.

Here are some possible contexts for your organization to incorporate data-driven personas into the workflow, with specific methods for possible integration.

- **Brand Discovery:** Use data-driven personas to uncover how your core users feel about your product or service and how they rationalize the purchasing decision.

- **Channel and Offering Alignment:** Use data-driven personas to align product offering and marketing activity, identifying new channels, needs, and opportunities.

- **Communication:** Data-driven personas are great for communication among team members and across departments. Personas are great for meetings! Data-driven personas keep folks focused on the big picture with regard to users.

- **Data-Driven Persona Discovery:** Use data-driven personas to document users involved in the system engagement process in a way that allows decision-makers to empathize with them consistently.

- **Experimentation and Optimization:** Use data-driven personas to utilize well-thought usability experiments to produce statistically significant user-focused insights.

- **Journey Mapping:** Use data-driven personas to plot the stages and paths of the persona lifecycle, documenting unique states of mind, needs, and concerns of users at each stage.

- **Marketing:** Use data-driven personas to understand where your core users spend their time online or interacting with your system, their interests, and their pain points.

- **Reporting and Feedback:** Use data-driven personas to report and review user data and insights to drive strategic decisions and provide consistent user information to the organization as a whole.

- **Sales:** Use data-driven personas for targeted offerings to help your organization increase user engagement with products or systems, with all stakeholders holding a common view of the user.

Here are some possible roles in which your organization can incorporate data-driven personas into the daily routine. We discuss various methods of incorporation specifically in Chapter 8.

- **Content creators** can use data-driven personas to deliver content that will be the most relevant and useful to their users, with all content creators in the organization having a consistent view of "who is the user(s)."

- **Executives** can use data-driven personas to keep users in mind while making strategic decisions. In fact, a data-driven persona can become a "silent member in the boardroom," which is one reason some organizations post images of personas (see Figure 2.2).

- **Product managers** can use data-driven personas as information to design features that meet core users' needs or desires, and marketing can use data-driven personas to craft organizationally consistent messages that resonate with these users.

- **Researchers** can use data-driven personas to conduct user experiments to produce statistically significant business insights that are focused on actual organizational users.

- **System designers** can use data-driven personas for the identification, planning, scoping, and implementation of system features and/or capabilities.

User understanding is part of the path toward achieving organizational objectives. Data-driven personas constitute an instrument for enhanced user understanding. Therefore, data-driven personas only have value when put into action.

2.5   EDUCATE–INVEST–EMPLOY IS A CYCLICAL PROCESS

EIE is a never-ending cycle. New stakeholders arrive in the organization, needing to be onboarded with the personas. New data-driven personas need to be developed. New products are developed, targeting new users.

Organizations need one or more data-driven persona advocates to keep the EIE process in motion. During this cyclical process, one should internalize the readiness criteria and address them during the EIE process for your organization.

With advancements in data collection, machine learning, and artificial intelligence from the data-driven persona side and continual personnel, strategy, technology, and product changes from the organization side, EIE is an ongoing process throughout the data-driven persona project's lifecycle.

2.6   ILLUSTRATION USING APG

APG creates data-driven personas by leveraging behavioral and demographic user segments from social media and other analytics data for many different applications and services with minimal manual efforts. APG is a SaaS system. APG can create data-driven personas from millions of data points in a matter of hours. APG is flexible and resilient for application in a wide range of contexts. User-centric data needs to be transformed into easy-to-understand representations for decision-making and customer insights.

APG uses this analytics data to identify customer behaviors, generate customer segments, and then enriche these customer segments with gender, age, and nationality-appropriate names and pictures. Customer loyalty rating, customer interests, product interactions, brand sentiment, and segment sizes are represented by the personas, and all of this is done in a privacy-preserving process using only aggregated data.

As one example of how APG can add value through user understanding for organizations, APG uses algorithmic approaches to calculate the sentiment of the data-driven personas. Additionally, APG shows you the underlying data for this sentiment analysis for validity with the persona stakeholders (see Figure 2.3).

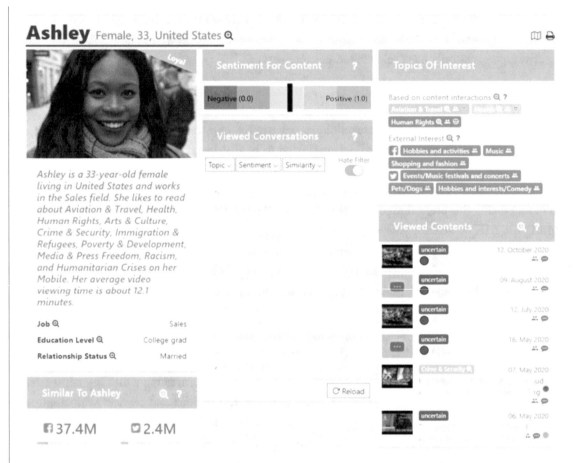

Figure 2.3: APG shows the sentiments of the user segment represented by the data-driven persona. This sentiment analysis provides insights into possible pain points, as even loyal users (like those represented by this persona) can have frustrations with a system, service, or product. APG also shows the sentiments of the user segment represented by the data-driven persona, including the underlying sentiment analysis scores.

This is a value-enhancing feature of data-driven personas relative to flat persona profiles or complex analytics systems.

2.7   CHAPTER TAKE-AWAYS

- Personas need to be well-made, data-driven, empathetic, realistic, complete, relevant, consistent, and insightful to work within the organization. If stakeholders do not view the personas as valid, the personas will not be used.

- Key stakeholders in the organization need to be on board with data-driven persona creation and their acceptance via education. Resistance or apathy can reduce the meaningful employ of data-driven personas.

- Persona readiness can be measured using the Persona Readiness Scale, a questionnaire for decision-makers of a given organization.

- Need readiness indicates the organization's perceived need for personas.

- Culture readiness indicates the organization's positive attitude toward customer understanding.

- Knowledge readiness indicates the organization's understanding of personas and how to use them.

- Resource readiness indicates financial and human resources to implement high-quality persona projects.

- Data and systems readiness indicates the required systems and data variables for persona creation.

- Capability readiness indicates data science competencies for development and maintenance of data-driven personas and supporting systems.

- Goal readiness indicates clearly defined plans and metrics for monitoring performance outcomes from the data-driven persona project.

- The data-driven persona onboarding process in an organization consists of three major phases: (1) Education, (2) Investment, and (3) Employment.

2.8 DISCUSSION AND ASSESSMENT QUESTIONS

1. List and define the three steps of successfully deploying data-driven personas in an organization.

2. Explain the eight dimensions of the Persona Readiness Scale.

3. Explain the challenges of each step in a data-driven persona deployment process. Identify possible techniques for mitigation of the challenges.

4. Describe three advantages of personas in general. Compare and contrast with the benefits of data-driven personas.

5. Describe three criticisms of personas in general. Compare and contrast with the criticisms of data-driven personas.

6. List and define the six readiness criteria to assess whether or not the organization can implement data-driven personas effectively.

7. Formulate a plan for introducing data-driven personas into an organization's culture for an organization of your choosing, with specifics defined for each of the three steps discussed above.

2.9   REFERENCES

An, J., Kwak, H., Jung, S., Salminen, J., and Jansen, B. J. (2018). Customer segmentation using online platforms: Isolating behavioral and demographic segments for persona creation via aggregated user data. *Social Network Analysis and Mining*, 8(1), 54. DOI: 10.1007/s13278-018-0531-0. 42

Batko, M. (2013). *The Four Steps to the Epiphany* (2nd ed.). K&S Ranch. https://medium.com/mbreads/the-four-steps-to-the-epiphany-7aee0c8e0f8e. 37

Bødker, S., Christiansen, E., Nyvang, T., and Zander, P.-O. (2012). Personas, people and participation: Challenges from the trenches of local government. *Proceedings of the 12th Participatory Design Conference on Research Papers: Volume 1 - PDC '12*, 91. DOI: 10.1145/2347635.2347649. 41, 42

Cabrero, D. G., Winschiers-Theophilus, H., and Abdelnour-Nocera, J. (2016). A critique of personas as representations of "the Other" in cross-cultural technology design. *Proceedings of the First African Conference on Human Computer Interaction*. pp. 149–154. DOI: 10.1145/2998581.2998595. 41

Chapman, C. N. and Milham, R. P. (2006). The personas' new clothes: Methodological and practical arguments against a popular method. *Proceedings of the Human Factors and Ergonomics Society Annual Meeting*, 50, 634–636. DOI: 10.1177/154193120605000503. 41, 42

Cooper, A. (1999). *The Inmates Are Running the Asylum: Why High Tech Products Drive Us Crazy and How to Restore the Sanity.* 1st edition. Sams-Pearson Education. 29, 40, 41

Drego, V. L., Dorsey, M., Burns, M., and Catino, S. (2010). *The ROI of Personas* [Report]. Forrester Research. https://www.forrester.com/report/The+ROI+Of+Personas/-/E-RES55359. 42

Drutsa, A., Gusev, G., and Serdyukov, P. (2017). Periodicity in user engagement with a search engine and its application to online controlled experiments. *ACM Transactions on the Web*, 11(2), 1–35. DOI: 10.1145/2856822. 42

Fisher, R. J. (1993). Social desirability bias and the validity of indirect questioning. *Journal of Consumer Research*, 20(2), 303–315. DOI: 10.1086/209351. 46

Friess, E. (2012). Personas and decision making in the design process: An ethnographic case study. *Proceedings of the SIGCHI Conference on Human Factors in Computing Systems*, pp. 1209–1218. DOI: 10.1145/2207676.2208572. 29, 47

Goodman-Deane, J., Waller, S., Demin, D., González-de-Heredia, A., Bradley, M., and Clarkson, J. P. (2018). Evaluating inclusivity using quantitative personas. In *Proceedings of Design Research Society Conference 2018. Design Research Society Conference 2018*, Limerick, Ireland. DOI: 10.21606/drs.2018.400. 46

Goodwin, K. and Cooper, A. (2009). *Designing for the Digital Age: How to Create Human-Centered Products and Services*. Wiley. 39

Guo, H. and Razikin, K. B. (2015). Anthropological user research: A data-driven approach to personas development. *Proceedings of the Annual Meeting of the Australian Special Interest Group for Computer Human Interaction*, pp. 417–421. DOI: 10.1145/2838739.2838816. 43

Guan, K.W., Salminen, J., Nielsen, L., Jung, S.G., and Jansen, B. J. (2021) Information design for personas in four professional domains of user experience design, healthcare, market research, and social media strategy. *54th Annual Hawaii International Conference on System Sciences (HICSS 2021)*, Koloa, HI. 5–8. 29

Hajian, S., Bonchi, F., and Castillo, C. (2016). Algorithmic bias: From discrimination discovery to fairness-aware data mining. *Proceedings of the 22nd ACM SIGKDD International Conference on Knowledge Discovery and Data Mining*. pp. 2125–2126. DOI: 10.1145/2939672.2945386. 46

Hill, C. G., Haag, M., Oleson, A., Mendez, C., Marsden, N., Sarma, A., and Burnett, M. (2017). Gender-inclusiveness personas vs. stereotyping: Can we have it both ways? *Proceedings of the 2017 CHI Conference*. pp. 6658–6671. DOI: 10.1145/3025453.3025609. 40, 41

Howard, T. W. (2015). Are personas really usable? *Communication Design Quarterly Review*, 3(2), 20–26. DOI: 10.1145/2752853.2752856. 33, 45

Jansen, A., Van Mechelen, M., and Slegers, K. (2017). Personas and behavioral theories: A case study using self-determination theory to construct overweight personas. *Proceedings of the 2017 CHI Conference on Human Factors in Computing Systems*. pp. 2127–2136. DOI: 10.1145/3025453.3026003. 42

Jansen, B. J., Jung, S., and Salminen, J. (2019). Capturing the change in topical interests of personas over time. *Proceedings of the Association for Information Science and Technology*, 56(1), pp. 127–136. DOI: 10.1002/pra2.11. 43, 48

Jansen, B. J., Jung, S., Salminen, J., Guan, K., and Nielsen, L. (2021). Strengths and weaknesses of persona creation methods: Outlining guidelines for novice and experienced users and opportunities for digital innovations. *Proceedings of the Hawaii International Conference on System Sciences (HICSS)*. 35

Jenkinson, A. (1994). Beyond segmentation. *Journal of Targeting, Measurement and Analysis for Marketing*, 3(1), 60–72. 43

Jung, S., Salminen, J., and Jansen, B. J. (2019). Personas changing over time: Analyzing variations of data-driven personas during a two-year period. *Extended Abstracts of the 2019 CHI Conference on Human Factors in Computing Systems - CHI EA '19*. pp. 1–6. DOI: 10.1145/3290607.3312955. 43, 48

Jung, S.-G., Salminen, J., An, J., Kwak, H., and Jansen, B. J. (2018). Automatically conceptualizing social media analytics data via personas. *Proceedings of the International AAAI Conference on Web and Social Media (ICWSM 2018)*. p. 2. 35

Jung, S.-G., Salminen, J., and Jansen, B. J. (2020). Giving faces to data: Creating data-driven personas from personified big data. *Proceedings of the 25th International Conference on Intelligent User Interfaces Companion*. pp. 132–133. DOI: 10.1145/3379336.3381465. 35

Krashen, S. D. (1984). Immersion: Why it works and what it has taught us. *Language and Society*, 12(1), 61–64. 41

LeRouge, C., Ma, J., Sneha, S., and Tolle, K. (2013). User profiles and personas in the design and development of consumer health technologies. *International Journal of Medical Informatics*, 82(11), e251–e268. DOI: 10.1016/j.ijmedinf.2011.03.006. 41

Li, J., Galley, M., Brockett, C., Spithourakis, G., Gao, J., and Dolan, B. (2016). A persona-based neural conversation model. *Proceedings of the 54th Annual Meeting of the Association for Computational Linguistics (Volume 1: Long Papers)*. pp. 994–1003. DOI: 10.18653/v1/P16-1094. 43

Long, F. (2009). Real or imaginary: The effectiveness of using personas in product design. *Proceedings of the Irish Ergonomics Society Annual Conference*. p. 14. 45

Luo, Y., Liu, P., and Choe, E. K. (2019). Co-designing food trackers with dietitians: Identifying design opportunities for food tracker customization. *Proceedings of the 2019 CHI Conference on Human Factors in Computing Systems - CHI '19*, 1–13. DOI: 10.1145/3290605.3300822. 46

Ma, J. and LeRouge, C. (2007). Introducing user profiles and personas into information systems development. *AMCIS 2007 Proceedings*. p. 237. https://aisel.aisnet.org/amcis2007/237. 42

Massanari, A. L. (2010). Designing for imaginary friends: Information architecture, personas, and the politics of user-centered design. *New Media and Society*, 12(4), 401–416. DOI: 10.1177/1461444809346722. 42

Matthews, T., Judge, T., and Whittaker, S. (2012). How do designers and user experience professionals actually perceive and use personas? *Proceedings of the 2012 ACM Annual Conference on Human Factors in Computing Systems - CHI '12*. pp. 1219. DOI: 10.1145/2207676.2208573. 29, 33, 34, 40, 41, 42, 47

Miaskiewicz, T., Grant, S. J., and Kozar, K. A. (2009). A preliminary examination of using personas to enhance user-centered design. *AMCIS 2009 Proceedings,* Article 697, http://aisel.aisnet.org/amcis2009/697. http://aisel.aisnet.org/amcis2009/697. 41

Miaskiewicz, T. and Kozar, K. A. (2011). Personas and user-centered design: How can personas benefit product design processes? *Design Studies*, 32(5), 417–430. DOI: 10.1016/j.destud.2011.03.003. 41

Miaskiewicz, T. and Luxmoore, C. (2017). The use of data-driven personas to facilitate organizational adoption–A case study. *The Design Journal*, 20(3), 357–374. DOI: 10.1080/14606925.2017.1301160. 46

Mulder, S. and Yaar, Z. (2006). *The User is Always Right: A Practical Guide to Creating and Using Personas for the Web*. New Rider. 41

Nielsen, L. (2019). *Personas—User Focused Design*, 2nd ed. 2019 edition. Springer. DOI: 10.1007/978-1-4471-7427-1. 34, 40

Nielsen, L., Hansen, K. S., Stage, J., and Billestrup, J. (2015). A template for design personas: Analysis of 47 persona descriptions from Danish industries and organizations. *International Journal of Sociotechnology and Knowledge Development*, 7(1), 45–61. DOI: 10.4018/ijskd.2015010104. 35

Nielsen, L. and Storgaard Hansen, K. (2014). Personas is applicable: A study on the use of personas in Denmark. *Proceedings of the SIGCHI Conference on Human Factors in Computing Systems*. pp. 1665–1674. DOI: 10.1145/2556288.2557080. 34

Norman, D. (2004). *Ad-Hoc Personas and Empathetic Focus* [Personal website]. http://www.jnd.org/dn.mss/personas_empath.html. 44

Popper, K. (2002). *The Logic of Scientific Discovery*, 2nd edition. Routledge. 41

Pruitt, J. and Adlin, T. (2006). *The Persona Lifecycle: Keeping People in Mind Throughout Product Design*. 1st edition. Morgan Kaufmann. 34, 41

Pruitt, J. and Grudin, J. (2003). Personas: Practice and theory. *Proceedings of the 2003 Conference on Designing for User Experiences*. pp. 1–15. DOI: 10.1145/997078.997089. 41

Rahimi, M. and Cleland-Huang, J. (2014). Personas in the middle: Automated Ssupport for creating personas as focal points in feature gathering forums. *Proceedings of the 29th ACM/IEEE International Conference on Automated Software Engineering*. pp. 479–484. DOI: 10.1145/2642937.2642958. 46

Rönkkö, K. (2005). An empirical study demonstrating how different design constraints, project organization and contexts limited the utility of personas. *Proceedings of the Proceedings of the 38th Annual Hawaii International Conference on System Sciences*, Volume 08. DOI: 10.1109/HICSS.2005.85. 41, 42

Rönkkö, K., Hellman, M., Kilander, B., and Dittrich, Y. (2004). Personas is not applicable: Local remedies interpreted in a wider context. *Proceedings of the Eighth Conference on Participatory Design: Artful Integration: Interweaving Media, Materials and Practices*, Volume 1. pp. 112–120. DOI: 10.1145/1011870.1011884. 33

Salminen, J., Guan, K., Jung, S., Chowdhury, S. A., and Jansen, B. J. (2020). A literature review of quantitative persona creation. *CHI '20: Proceedings of the 2020 CHI Conference on Human Factors in Computing Systems*. pp. 1–14. DOI: 10.1145/3313831.3376502. 35

Salminen, J., Jansen, B. J., An, J., Kwak, H., and Jung, S. (2018a). Are personas done? Evaluating their usefulness in the age of digital analytics. *Persona Studies*, 4(2), 47–65. DOI: 10.21153/psj2018vol4no2art737. 33, 42

Salminen, J., Jung, S., An, J., Kwak, H., Nielsen, L., and Jansen, B. J. (2019a). Confusion and information triggered by photos in persona profiles. *International Journal of Human-Computer Studies*, 129, 1–14. DOI: 10.1016/j.ijhcs.2019.03.005. 45

Salminen, J., Jung, S., Chowdhury, S. A., Sengün, S., and Jansen, B. J. (2020a). Personas and analytics: A comparative user study of efficiency and effectiveness for a user identification task. *Proceedings of the ACM Conference of Human Factors in Computing Systems (CHI'20)*. DOI: 10.1145/3313831.3376770. 35

Salminen, J., Jung, S., and Jansen, B. J. (2019). Detecting demographic bias in automatically generated personas. *Extended Abstracts of the 2019 CHI Conference on Human Factors in Computing Systems*, LBW0122:1-LBW0122:6. DOI: 10.1145/3290607.3313034. 45, 46

Salminen, J., Jung, S., and Jansen, B. J. (2019b). The future of data-driven personas: A marriage of online analytics numbers and human attributes. *ICEIS 2019 - Proceedings of the*

21st International Conference on Enterprise Information Systems. pp. 596–603. DOI: 10.5220/0007744706080615. 45

Salminen, J., Jung, S., Santos, J. M., Chowdhury, S., and Jansen, B. J. (2020b). The effect of experience on persona perceptions. *Extended Abstracts of the 2020 CHI Conference on Human Factors in Computing Systems Extended Abstracts*. pp. 1–9. DOI: /10.1145/3334480.3382786. 42, 44, 45

Salminen, J., Jung, S., Santos, J. M., and Jansen, B. J. (2019b). Does a smile matter if the person is not real?: The effect of a smile and stock photos on persona perceptions. *International Journal of Human–Computer Interaction*, 0(0), 1–23. DOI: 10.1080/10447318.2019.1664068. 45

Salminen, J., Nielsen, L., Jung, S., An, J., Kwak, H., and Jansen, B. J. (2018b). "Is more better?": Impact of multiple photos on perception of persona profiles. *Proceedings of ACM CHI Conference on Human Factors in Computing Systems (CHI2018)*. DOI: 10.1145/3173574.3173891. 45

Sauro, J., Johnson, K., and Meenan, C. (2017). From snake-oil to science: Measuring UX maturity. *Proceedings of the 2017 CHI Conference Extended Abstracts on Human Factors in Computing System*s. pp. 1084–1091. DOI: 10.1145/3027063.3053350. 34

Seidelin, C., Jonsson, A., Høgild, M., Rømer, J., and Diekmann, P. (2014). Implementing personas for international markets: A question of UX maturity. *Proceedings at SIDER*. p. 14. 33

Siegel, D. A. (2010). The mystique of numbers: Belief in quantitative approaches to segmentation and persona development. *CHI '10 Extended Abstracts on Human Factors in Computing Systems*. pp. 4721–4732. DOI: 10.1145/1753846.1754221. 42, 46

Stevenson, P. D. and Mattson, C. A. (2019). The personification of big data. *Proceedings of the Design Society: International Conference on Engineering Design*, 1(1), 4019–4028. DOI: 10.1017/dsi.2019.409. 35

Tanenbaum, M. L., Adams, R. N., Iturralde, E., Hanes, S. J., Barley, R. C., Naranjo, D., and Hood, K. K. (2018). From wary wearers to d-embracers: personas of readiness to use diabetes devices. *Journal of Diabetes Science and Technology*, 12(6), 1101–1107. DOI: 10.1177/1932296818793756. 46

Thoma, V. and Williams, B. (2009). Developing and validating personas in e-commerce: A heuristic approach. In T. Gross, J. Gulliksen, P. Kotzé, L. Oestreicher, P. Palanque, R. O. Prates, and M. Winckler (Eds.), *Human-Computer Interaction – INTERACT 2009*. pp. 524–527. Springer Berlin Heidelberg. DOI: 10.1007/978-3-642-03658-3_56. 42

Vincent, C. J. and Blandford, A. (2014). The challenges of delivering validated personas for medical equipment design. *Applied Ergonomics*, 45(4), 1097–1105. DOI: 10.1016/j.apergo.2014.01.010. 41

Vosbergen, S., Mulder-Wiggers, J. M. R., Lacroix, J. P., Kemps, H. M. C., Kraaijenhagen, R. A., Jaspers, M. W. M., and Peek, N. (2015). Using personas to tailor educational messages to the preferences of coronary heart disease patients. *Journal of Biomedical Informatics*, 53, 100–112. DOI: 10.1016/j.jbi.2014.09.004. 46

Watanabe, Y., Washizaki, H., Honda, K., Noyori, Y., Fukazawa, Y., Morizuki, A., Shibata, H., Ogawa, K., Ishigaki, M., Shiizaki, S., Yamaguchi, T., and Yagi, T. (2017). ID3P: Iterative data-driven development of persona based on quantitative evaluation and revision. *Proceedings of the 10th International Workshop on Cooperative and Human Aspects of Software Engineering*. pp. 49–55. DOI: 10.1109/CHASE.2017.9. 40, 46

Zaugg, H. and Ziegenfuss, D. H. (2018). Comparison of personas between two academic libraries. *Performance Measurement and Metrics*, 19(3), 142–152. DOI: 10.1108/PMM-04-2018-0013. 47

Part 3

Developing Data-Driven Personas

CHAPTER 3

Getting Meaningful Data

In this chapter, we discuss the aspects of getting data that is useful for creating data-driven personas. We start by introducing the concept of persona information needs, which refers to stakeholders' requests for information. We then proceed to persona information display and design, which refers to how the selected information is displayed to end-users of data-driven personas. After this, we present the primary data collection strategies for data-driven personas, including surveys, text quantification, and automated data collection. Finally, we discuss five central data challenges: (1) availability; (2) specifications; (3) unknown measurement error; (4) bias; and (5) ethical concerns. We conclude by presenting takeaways and educational questions.

3.1 DATA-DRIVEN PERSONA USERS' INFORMATION NEEDS

When it comes to the application areas, personas have been applied in so many areas, including digital services (Miaskiewicz and Kozar, 2011), learning (Dantin, 2005), and health care (LeRouge et al., 2013), which are among the most common areas, and target groups are both children (Antle, 2006), adults, and users with special needs (Loitsch et al., 2016) using both mobile devices (Sedlmayr et al., 2019) and web services (Jung et al., 2018). In each of these areas, and others, data-driven personas can be a powerful tool for user understanding. Data-driven personas help increase user understanding by identifying user pain points, potential objections, information needs, behaviors, interests, and so on.

Data-driven-persona systems can be seen as repositories that record snapshots of user data over time. Hence, they can be deployed for recording a persona change and communicating the change to stakeholders. For example, users can be alerted when a new persona enters their user population or when a preexisting persona becomes inactive. Such intelligent functions are made possible by longitudinal user data.

Moreover, the system can show each persona's status in terms of loyalty: New, Loyal, Occasional, Inactive. A crucial commercial use case is the reactivation of disengaged users or customers; data-driven personas can facilitate these reactivation campaigns by pinpointing the customer segments that are falling behind. Moreover, new personas can be welcomed by tailored outreach campaigns. For these actions, the personas must be operationalizable—i.e., connected to an underlying data source (e.g., CRM system) in which each individual can be traced to a specific persona (the full-stack principle).

Persona users' information needs drive the personas' information design, meaning that the information presented in the data-driven persona profiles needs to correspond with what the stakeholders perceive as valuable (useful, actionable) information. The steps before the actual persona creation include:

- define the information needs,

- collect data,

- preprocess the data, and

- analyze the data.

However, the actual design of data-driven personas and the generation of meaningful data within organizations can be somewhat challenging for various reasons. For example, Anvari et al., (2015) discuss the use of personality traits in personas: it is unclear how well such traits that require subject-matter expertise and human analysis could be automatically added to data-driven personas. Also, the specifics of what data to collect for persona creation seems to be an open question. Information needs refer to the type of information that stakeholders want to get out of the personas. This information can include, for example, the following.

- **Audience size** (how many people the persona represents)

- **Demographics** (e.g., age, gender, country)

- **Pain points** (e.g., sources of stress and concerns, typically illustrated as quotes)

- **Psychological traits** (e.g., the Big Five—extroversion, agreeableness, openness, conscientiousness, and neuroticism (Salminen et al., 2020a))

- **Sentiment** (the attitude of persona toward various issues)

- **Sociographics** (e.g., job, marital status, education)—sometimes, this information is seen as a subcategory of demographics

- **Topics of interest** (e.g., what news topics the persona likes)

To investigate what information persona creators tend to be interested in, we collected a large sample of persona interview questions from popular persona blog posts. After removing duplicate questions, we identified 276 unique persona interview questions[1], classified into ten themes (see Table 3.1). It is evident that this many questions cannot be asked, and this many pieces of information cannot be provided in a concise persona profile. Instead, persona information design needs to be approached from contextual premises. *What is the information the persona users want to know*

---

[1] https://persona.qcri.org/blog/the-most-comprehensive-list-of-persona-interview-questions-on-the-web/

about their users/customers? The information that the stakeholder organization specifies as important is the starting point for persona data collection.

Table 3.1: Themes of persona information

No.	Theme	Definition
1	Demographics	This theme contains the most basic questions that organizations should be asking about their target users. The demographic theme divides users based on many variables, such as age, gender, family size, income, occupation, race, religion, and education.
2	Life Situation	This theme includes questions designed to find out more about the user's general day-to-day life. As well as offering insights into their core personality, these questions reveal a lot about what products and services users are likely to be interested in and what would be useful to them.
3	Working Life	This theme contains questions about the users' working life, such as their current job, position, career goals, obstacles, and pain points in their job. Questions about users' working life reveal many interesting details about the users in professional aspects. That said, the role one assumes at work may not be an accurate reflection of the person we are at home or with friends.
4	Decision Making	This theme contains questions about the user's process of making decisions. These questions usually consist of goals to be achieved, problem awareness, evaluation, decision-making tactics, and post-decision sentiments. How users make decisions can determine the right product or feature for the user.
5	Information Sources	This theme is important because organizations need to understand how the user consumes information. Do they go online, prefer to learn in-person, or pick up newspapers and magazines? If they are online learners, do they visit social networks? Do they use search engines such as Google, Baidu, or Yandex? Which sources do they trust the most—friends, family, coworkers, or industry experts?
6	Consumer Habits	This theme contains the habits and preferences of users when buying products and services.
7	Marketing Team	This theme contains questions regarding the work of marketing team members.
8	Sales Team	This theme contains questions regarding the work of sales team members.

No.	Theme	Definition
9	Pain Points	This theme contains the users' problems and how organizations can see and find solutions to these user pain points.
10	School Life	This theme contains questions about the lives of users during their school days. What subjects did they take, what extracurricular activities did they participate in, what kind of school they did they attend? The attitude we have in our younger years is a strong hint as to the type of person we will grow into.

The questions and themes we found seem to correspond well with the persona information proposed in popular textbooks and research articles (Cooper, 2004; Nielsen, 2019; Nielsen et al., 2015; Pruitt and Adlin, 2006). Nevertheless, the specific information needs of stakeholders may vary greatly from these questions and themes. Consider, for example, the case of a human resources agency trying to understand why employees are applying to fill various positions. This agency would like to know information such as (a) what kind of job types the applicants are interested in, (b) how many work hours can they put in, (c) whether they have any disabilities or limitations affecting the jobs they can accept, and (d) what skills they possess. In many cases, such industry-specific information is needed.

Therefore, the information needs of those using the personas are decisive for the data collection. Generic question lists can provide inspiration for drilling down to information needs. Still, ultimately the information needs are case-specific and should be clarified in close collaboration and dialogue between the persona creators and the stakeholders.

3.2   PERSONA INFORMATION DESIGN

Overall, persona information design has been recognized as one of the prominent research subfields of persona creation (Salminen et al., 2019a; Salminen et al., 2019). Persona information design refers to design choices regarding the presentation of persona information to stakeholders. These choices relate to the template (layout) being used, modes of information (text, numbers, graphs, tables, bullet points), colors, font size, portrait picture style (or no picture, or several pictures), organization of the information elements (which ones are presented "top," which ones "below-the-fold"?), as well as providing supporting information such as explanations of how a certain piece of information was inferred and definitions of each information element.

An information element refers to a "block" of information. For example, "Pain Points" is an information element—it is a visually independent and distinct part of the persona profile that usually includes a title and the actual information (e.g., listing the pain points of the persona as bullet points). In the following sections, we discuss the information design for conventional and data-driven personas.

3.2.1   CONVENTIONAL PERSONA DESIGN

The conventional way of presenting a persona is with a portrait picture, age, gender, and country while including a text description with information about the persona. However, there is no single template for persona information (Nielsen et al., 2015). Instead, templates vary by professional domains and use cases. The lack of such a generic template is a consequence of the persona being applied in different decision-making situations that require varying baseline information.

Example of de facto standard layout of persona profile

Figure 3.1: Even though there is no industry-wide standard for what data is needed or what information is contained within the persona profile, a *de facto* standard has developed with the persona's profile being one or two pages, with some demographic information, some behavioral attributes, usually a photo, a name, or a "user type" (e.g., "Alice—The Engaged Marketer"), and some qualitative aspects such as goals or pain points. Image credit: Xtensio (https://xtensio.com/user-persona/)l.

Personas typically contain demographic information and user goals and motivations (Nielsen et al., 2015). The principle of rounded personas (Nielsen, 2019) calls for the persona to contain all the necessary information for stakeholders using the personas. Thus, it is essential to identify and discuss the boundaries of the information design of personas. For this, Nielsen et al. (2015) analyzed 12 templates from articles published between 2006 and 2013. The study shows that the attitude toward the product and the context of use is often intertwined; thus, the information can be divided into three broad information types.

1. **Demographics:** includes basic information such as gender, age, and ethnicity.

2. **Context:** includes information related to the specific area to design for, such as technology use, a-day-in-the-life, product goals, and behavioral information.

3. **Personality:** includes information about personality traits and attitudes.

Apart from this, some researchers suggest adding business information, such as user segment size, brand relationships (Jones and Marsden, 2006; Mulder and Yaar, 2006; Pruitt and Adlin, 2006), and different behaviors according to, for example, disabilities (Pichler, 2012).

The information design of personas has been studied empirically, using experimental designs, and conceptually, by crafting research agendas that entail open questions for what is considered as an "optimal" persona template. For example, Hill et al. (2017) experimented with two persona designs: one that includes multiple pictures (consisting of both males and females) for a given persona and another one that has only one picture. Using a controlled laboratory study with eye-tracking measurement, they found that the use of multiple pictures may represent an appropriate technique to expand the persona users' understanding of the persona as a gender-free (or multi-gender) user segment rather than evoking gender stereotypes (Hill et al., 2017).

Similarly, Salminen et al. (2018) experimented with persona profiles: one with lifestyle photos and a single portrait picture. Contrary to Hill et al., (2017), their findings indicated that the use of multiple images could distract and confuse the persona users, possibly because these are more used to the conventional template of the persona, including only one photo (Salminen et al., 2018). Nonetheless, neither Hill et al. (2017) nor Salminen et al., (2018) found that multiple photos would decrease the user engagement with the persona.

In another experimental study, Salminen et al. (2020a) presented 38 professionals with 2 alternate layouts: one that used a numbers-oriented information presentation style and another one that used a text-oriented style. They found that analysts' numbers-oriented template was perceived as significantly more useful but remarkably less complete by both marketers and analysts (Salminen et al., 2020b). The visual engagement with the persona profiles was found not to vary significantly between the templates (Salminen et al., 2020b).

Interestingly, some of the empirical findings concerning persona design are conflicting (such as those by Hill et al., (2017) and Salminen et al. (2018) regarding the use of multiple photos). We surmise that this is due to variations in the implementation of persona templates—both small and large variations can affect user experiences in crucial ways. In other words, the persona templates tested by different studies look and feel different and thus are perceived as and engaged with in different ways.

The only way, it appears, is to produce consistent research insights that are generalizable across at least some of the nuanced implementations of personas and include more design variations in these user studies. Consequently, this would require the use of large-scale data collection, potentially prompting for more scalable data collection such as persona crowd experiments (Salminen et al., 2019b).

3.2.2 DATA-DRIVEN PERSONA DESIGN

Data-driven persona design inherits its fundamental design principles from conventional personas. Simultaneously, interactive systems enable new ways of information presentation, such as scrollable information that extends what can be fitted into the persona profile, as well as clickable information that means that details can be made available beyond the visible information.

Research has shown that data-driven personas can take many forms and shapes. For example, Aoyama (2005) used conjoint analysis to create data-driven personas for software embedded in digital consumer products. Holden et al. (2017) developed "biopsychosocial" data-driven personas of elderly patients with heart failure using quantitative survey data. Data-driven personas have also been applied in fashion (Dhakad et al., 2017), e-commerce (Al-Qirim, 2006), news (Salminen et al., 2018), and many other domains. Thus, the diversity in persona information design appears to originate on the one hand from the:

- specificity of the methods applied—with the intuition that the outputs of different methods enable different information to be used for data-driven personas development—and, on the other hand, from

- varying information needs of persona users, which inarguably affect the goals of the persona development endeavor.

As those for design personas, data-driven persona templates are diverse and fragmented. To investigate data-driven persona templates, we conducted a literature review of 31 data-driven persona research articles. Data from each article's persona profile layout(s) was recorded using a standardized data extraction form (Zhu et al., 2014) with subcategories built on the previous work of Nielsen et al. (2015). Table 3.2 displays our findings.

Table 3.2: Information used in data-driven personas profiles		
Subcategory	**Description of Information Content**	**Examples (verbatim whenever possible)**
Name	Full name, first name, or epithet	Eric Transon (Tempelman-Kluit and Pearce, 2014) (p. 632), "Lazy Experts" (Dupree et al., 2016)
Age	Age (or age range) ascribed to the persona	Age 23, "senior student" (Aoyama, 2005) (p. 6)

Subcategory	Description of Information Content	Examples (verbatim whenever possible)
Gender	Gender ascribed to the persona	Male/female
Personality and psychographics	Character traits and disposition of the persona	"Very satisfied with life, usually gets the social support she needs" (Zhu et al., 2019) (p. 66)
Lifestyle	Living situation, leisure, work-life balance	"Lives in central California, frequently walks and gardens" (Zhu et al., 2019) (p. 66)
Experience	The persona's experience with the product	"Never interacted with a robot before (…)" (dos Santos et al., 2014) (p. 8)
Daily work context	The persona's role and duties in the workplace	"Daily use of e-mail, browsing the web" (Aoyama, 2005) (p. 6)
Product-related behaviors	How the persona interacts with technology and/or tools in the workplace	"How the persona interacts with technology and AIBO was cute and she was enjoying it" (dos Santos et al., 2014) (p. 8) Note: AIBO is a robotic dog.
Product goals	What the persona hopes to achieve	"Wants reliable access to all journal articles he needs" (Tempelman-Kluit and Pearce, 2014) (p. 632)
Scenarios	Specific events involving the persona in relation to the product	"I mainly use the library website to find citations or to check whether I can get articles I've found in Google Scholar for free" (Tempelman-Kluit and Pearce, 2014) (p. 632)
A day in the life	The daily context for the persona in relation to the product	"She goes out at least once in every two weeks with fellow hikers… frequently jogs in the field of Shenzhen University" (Tu et al., 2010b) (p. 599)
Market size	The sample size of the analyzed population that matches a particular persona	Percentage of time spent in a knowledge worker action section (Ford et al., 2017)

Subcategory	Description of Information Content	Examples (verbatim whenever possible)
Color coding to indicate the segment	Color tagging for details of the persona	Yellow highlight
Use of facial picture	Photograph of a real person included	N/A
Use of cartoon picture	Cartoon image to represent the persona	Cartoon image depicting a girl
Reference to sources	Source of data or explanation of metrics	Link to research references (Miaskiewicz and Luxmoore, 2017)
Disabilities	Handicaps of the persona (particularly for papers written in healthcare contexts)	Heart health metrics (Holden et al., 2017)
International considerations	Cultural heritage, ethnicity, and/or citizenship	Non-aboriginal (Brooks and Greer, 2014)
Explanations	Tooltip definitions	Link to research references (Miaskiewicz and Luxmoore, 2017)

Analyzing the 31 templates for data-driven personas, we found that such personas vary greatly by their information richness, as the most informative layout has four times as many information categories as the least informative layout (Salminen et al., 2020a). We also found that graphical complexity and information richness do not necessarily correlate. Furthermore, the chosen persona development method may carry over to the information presented, with quantitative data typically presented as scores, metrics, or tables and qualitative data as text-rich narratives. Like Nielsen et al. (2015) for design personas, we did not locate one "general template" for data-driven personas. Defining this template is difficult due to the variety of the outputs of different methods and different persona users' information needs.

The persona profile layouts varied in "richness," which we define as *containing multifaceted, well-rounded information regarding the persona*. We quantitatively calculated personas' richness by tallying the total pieces of information (i.e., subcategories present) within each persona profile layout. The most complex persona profile layout contained data for 14 subcategories (Miaskiewicz and Luxmoore, 2017), while the least complex contained only 4 (Dang-Pham et al., 2015; Dhakad et al., 2017). The mean number of subcategories was 8.83, while the standard deviation was 2.57.

Based on the descriptive statistics, the persona profile layouts were divided into three levels of richness styles: "simple" (four to seven subcategories), "moderate" (eight–ten subcategories), and "high" (11–14 subcategories) (see Table 3.3 for examples). We selected the number of subcategories for the levels after examining the entire dataset and identifying the natural breakpoints in the subcategories. Half of the persona profile layouts (50%) fell under the "moderate" category, with the remainder falling relatively evenly between either "simple" (26.6%) or "high" (23.3%) richness.

The graphical complexity and information richness of the personas do not necessarily correlate. For example, one persona layout (Dang-Pham et al., 2015), while an interesting graphical way of presenting personas, was questionable in its informativeness for end-users; such extreme cases of abstraction were categorized under "simple" style, despite their graphical complexity (see Table 3.3). Persona layouts falling under the most "simple" information style, as exemplified by the layout from Dupree et al., (2016) in Table 3.3, contained sparse information limited to bullet points detailing common behaviors. The persona is not identified with characteristics to make it human, such as a name or demographic and psychographic information; instead, it may only be labeled with a general epithet, such as "Lazy Experts," close to what Floyd et al. (2008) term as user archetypes.

Most "simple" persona profile layouts could be regarded as "skeleton personas" (Zhu et al., 2019) that can be further enriched with details once time, costs, or limited data are removed as barriers. Persona layouts falling under the "moderate" information style—the most common category—reflect what such an upgrade in resources can result. As exemplified by Kanno et al. (2011), personas in this category are enriched with human-like elements, such as a full name, age, gender, and details on leisurely activities and temperament. In many cases, a photo of a real person is enclosed. The persona layout also contains a short narrative (or, in some cases, detailed bullet points) about the persona's daily life scenarios and design-related goals.

Finally, persona profile layouts falling under the "high" information category are enriched with the most details (see "C" in Table 3.3). They extend beyond "moderate" information layouts by including quotes, graphical representations, and categorization of the persona's information. In short, persona layouts in this category contain more comprehensive information on demographic and psychographic details and categorize details in direct relation to the authors' objectives. For example, Tempelman-Kluit and Pearce (2014) organize specific details under library usage and frustrations directly with the authors' topics of inquiry. Graphical symbols illustrate what relevant devices or subscriptions the persona has (the authors' point of interest). This contrasts with the personas in the "moderate" category (see "B" in Table 3.3) that usually contain only a short narrative with details that are not necessarily arranged into meaningful categories. As such, persona layouts in the "high" category go beyond mere personification and become mediums of analysis, as users can view these layouts to discern relevant information from various categories quickly.

Table 3.3: Persona layouts with varying richness

A: Simple (4–7 subcategories included) (Dupree et al., 2016)

Lazy Experts
- Helpers, assist others with security concerns.
- Trust and maintains home network
- Chooses convenience over security
- Chooses being social over privacy
- Rationalize lower level of concern (e.g. OS).
- Mostly unique passwords
- Write down passwords securely
- Shares passwords only rarely with trusted people
- Treats most of the web like its public domain

- Monitoring or being watched would be okay.
- "I don't matter" (Honest man)

Marginally Concerned
- Learning sources include TV shows (like CSI) and Word of Mouth/Friends.
- Doesn't grasp more basic technical terms (Cookies)
- Basic trust of all wireless networks
- Trust what website says about security. (We won an award for security, or we promise not to sell your information!)
- In favor of using Fallback Authentication questions
- Only identified software protection is anti-virus scanner
- Small changes from triggers, e.g. change password from 123456 to <birthday> if prompted by password policy.
- A small set of passwords, one heavily favored.
- Knows threats exist but doesn't worry about them. "I'm not very secure."

- Advanced software manipulation knowledge
- Advanced security knowledge, independent learning
- Hate Fallback authentication

- Make changes based on previous attacks

Amateurs
- Understands basic technical terms (ie. cookies)
- Make changes based on weak or inaccurate advice
- Stuck in their set up. Fallback authentication question has caused them not to log in.
- Identified software protection as anti-virus scanner and something extra (ie. Firewall or malware scanner)
- Trust but does not maintain their usual wireless network (i.e. uses the schools network, their landlord's network)
- Likes to limit the information that is given out
- Occasional distrust of software (ie. Norton, Windows)
- Somewhat inaccurate view of others as uneducated, unsecure
- Odd cases of sharing passwords
- Typically 1 stronger password or mid-level of layered password schemes, usually categories

- Does understand security certificate.
- Passwords often written down insecurely
- "I don't know"; "I haven't bothered to look it up"

- "I take extra care to protect my bank"
- Generalization of Concerns (hackers or id thieves)
- "You can't find me" (Obscurity)

- Determining trust based on popularity, size of website

Fundamentalists
- Non or reluctant helpers
- Views general public as uneducated and unsecure
- Little trust of network (WPA/2 is questionable)
- Looks for security claims on websites (https, padlock)
- Multi-layer passwords, important passwords unique
- May extend protection beyond computer
- Sometimes refuses to sign up or participate online
- Monitoring or watching is not okay
- Maintains global concerns (censorship or tracking)

- Chooses security over convenience

Technicians
- Learning sources include news and blogs
- Made changes based on sound advice
- Limited trust of privacy settings onlin e.g. Facebook
- Passive user of social networking
- Chooses privacy over being social
- Few layers of passwords, usually just low and high.
- Passwords all similarly themed, but unique and personal
- One off cases of writing down passwords
- Physical security concerns
- Will put things off or forget about them occasionally
- Trusts look and feel of website, "I know it when I see it"
- "I used to worry about those things"
- "I monitor very closely"

B: Medium (8–10 subcategories included) (Kanno et al., 2011)

Name Kaori Ayase (Female)
Address Toka:-mura village Ibaraki Pref
Age 80
Family husbanc(live with) two sons (not live with)
Hobby Cooking
Personality Cheerful and extrovert

Profile
Kaori Ayase is 80 years old and lives with her husbanc They are happily married Her personality is very cheerful and extrovert She and her husband run a farm and she usually works on the farm during the day She loves the farm and crops as her children She is in good health but she has a pain in her back and knee after her many years of farming She believes that public announcements about disasters are always nothing to be alarmed about

C: High (11–14 sub-categories included) (Tempelman-Kluit and Pearce, 2014)

Eric Transon

I mainly use the library website to find citations or to check whether I can get articles I've found in Google Scholar for free.

How Eric uses the library:
- Checks BobCat for citations found in bibliographies of papers assigned to him
- Books study room on LL2 for class projects
- Follows NYULibraries on Facebook and Twitter

Eric's library frustrations:
- Wants reliable access to all journal articles he needs
- All educational resources should be in one place
- Wants universal alerts for forthcoming articles and new research across sources
- Wants to easily locate call numbers on rare occasions when he gets books from Bobst

Profession:	Full-time Senior Instructional Designer, Sesame Street Workshop; Master of Arts, in Digital Media Design for Learning program at Steinhart, part-time student
Location:	Lives in New York, NY
Age:	32
Home life:	Studio in East Village; single
Hobbies:	Lighting Design

Motivation: Mainly Intrinsic
Information need: Mechanical
Portion of sample: 42%
Internet experience: Advanced, knows programming languages
Computer & devices: iPhone 5S, MacBook Pro, iPad

part-time student

uses laptop to research for articles

follows library social media

Data-driven personas often contain a chart-like presentation of the details, with "scores" directly representing the survey's quantitative data. On the other hand, the mixed-method approach (Tu et al., 2010b) results in more narrative-like, contextual descriptions. Information such as work-related issues, daily life context, and product-related issues may be more difficult to infer from data than information with a more direct numerical constituency (e.g., "customer lifetime value"). Moreover, personality and psychographic information may be easier to infuse into a narrative format than to a quantitative structure. However, there is an example of presenting quantitatively inferred personality traits (Salminen et al., 2020d) as narrative information (see Figure 3.2).

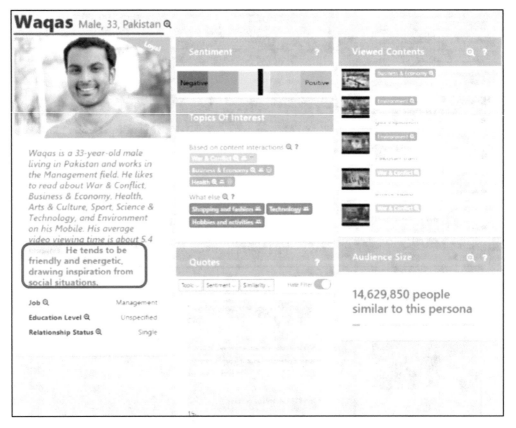

Figure 3.2: An example of incorporating a textual description of personality in data-driven personas. The bolded text, "He tends to be friendly and energetic, drawing inspiration from social situations," corresponds to the general description of high extroversion (Agarwal, 2014), reflected in the personas' comments based on automatic personality detection. The generic personality trait descriptions can be automatically inserted based on the personality scores obtained.

Overall, we surmise that the type of information collected for persona profile development (i.e., quantitative vs. qualitative) may carry over to the actual design of the data-driven persona or another type of persona, with numerical details such as graphs, scores, metrics, and tables being more familiar with purely quantitative personas and text-focused, narrative-like descriptions that are more prevalent in mixed-method personas. However, most layouts (especially in the "high" information richness category) combine both information styles, with some numerical cues and textual information. The degree of text versus numbers in data-driven personas is an open research question. Previous research shows that persona developers' choices can affect users' persona perceptions (Salminen et al., 2020c).

The consequence is that the field is embedded in the diversity of proposed design templates for data-driven personas. This diversity reflects the increasing relevance of data-driven personas for researchers and practitioners in user-centric industries.

3.2.3   OPEN QUESTIONS ON THE DESIGN OF DATA-DRIVEN PERSONAS

HCI scholars have proposed many types of persona profiles and layouts for data-driven personas (An et al., 2018a; Aoyama, 2005; Dhakad et al., 2017; Holden et al., 2017), with varying complexity and informational content. The overarching goal of these is to increase quantitatively reliable information in personas for stakeholders. Nonetheless, the multitude of layouts and templates for data-driven personas has resulted in two challenges.

1. First, there is a lack of a general template for data-driven personas, meaning that researchers and practitioners are uncertain of what information to include when using quantitative methods and data for the creation of data-driven personas.

2. Second, it is not well-known what the boundaries are of data-driven personas that are relative to manually created personas. Qualitative personas are based on social constructivism and human meaning-making (Denzin and Lincoln, 1998) and the understanding that human persona creators infer from other humans (the users) when creating the persona. It has been postulated that persona creation is an immersive practice that enhances understanding about the users.

Data-driven personas might be limited in their ability to capture human nuances and understand meanings of social importance, as the persona creation takes place via probabilistic calculations that humans have little or no interaction. Previous research on data-driven personas fails to deliver a critical analysis such as this, focusing primarily on evaluating data-driven personas using technical accuracy metrics (Brickey et al., 2012). Figure 3.3 illustrates this concern with an example of a statistically valid but potentially non-useful persona.

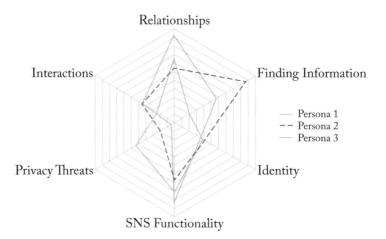

Figure 3.3: Data-driven persona based on quantitatively identified patterns of user behavior (Dang-Pham et al., 2015).

Understanding data-driven personas (versus personas of other types or analytics) is important because in-depth information about user motivations and pain points may not be readily available when relying solely on quantitative methods. This is because data-driven persona creation methods rely on probabilistic learning rather than on a true understanding of human nature. Thus, they have limited ability to detect human pain points, needs and wants, and goals of individuals (Salminen et al., 2019b). Algorithms cannot capture tacit information or understand why a person acts the way he or she does. This limitation might form a fundamental obstacle for the value and usefulness of data-driven personas, as personas traditionally rely on their ability to convey human-centric information. For HCI, it is a principle of primary importance that personas appear as realistic profiles of otherwise cold and unempathetic "target groups" (as descriptions that cannot evoke empathy), thus enhancing stakeholders' focus on end-user needs (Cooper, 1999).

When comparing data-driven personas or other analytics solutions, the "disappearing numbers" paradigm refers to the overall goal of favoring personified information, which is qualitative, labeled, and descriptive, rather than using "cold" statistical information such as tables, charts, and metrics. Hence, numbers can be replaced with textual descriptors, such as "many," "few," and so on (Salminen et al., 2020c). This paradigm is inspired by the concept of "disappearing computer" (Streitz and Nixon, 2005) that refers to ubiquitous and invisible computing all around us. However, it is an open question as to what extent stakeholders actually require numbers in data-driven personas. According to our experience, stakeholders do appreciate numerical information in personas and ask for it if it is missing. For example, if launching a target marketing campaign, a reasonable question that requires a number is the number of potential users in the targeted segment.

Finally, a novel but interesting aspect of persona information design is automation. Automated persona design refers to the use of algorithms for generating persona information. Information such as interest topics can be generated using text classification or topic modeling (An et al., 2018b). Similar techniques could be used for inferring users' pain points, motivations, needs, and wants. Sociographics can be inferred by matching the persona's demographic information with population-level data sources using, e.g., Facebook Marketing API (Jung et al., 2018).

Text descriptions could be generated automatically using advanced text generation networks such as GPT-3 (Floridi and Chiriatti, 2020), although we are not aware of anyone carrying this out successfully at the time of writing. Persona quotes could also be generated automatically, which is an exciting research direction.

As an example of using deep learning technologies as part of the persona creation process, there have been attempts to automatically generate facial pictures in persona profiles (see Figure 3.3). A user study shows that generative adversarial networks (GANs) can produce realistic enough pictures for persona profiles (Salminen et al., 2020b). However, the automatic allocation of age, gender, and country to the artificially generated persona pictures is still an open issue (Salminen et al., 2020b).

Given the novel area of image creation, there is the potential for unintended consequences and concerns about the responsible use of data. Finally, demographically appropriate persona names can be inferred from social network usernames, as our research demonstrates (Jung et al., 2021).

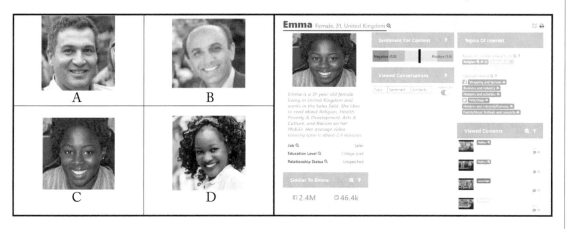

Figure 3.4: An example of artificially generated persona pictures Generator: StyleGAN (Karras et al., 2018). A, B, C, and D show pairs of demographically corresponding real and artificial facial pictures. A and C are artificial pictures. In the example, C is incorporated into a demographically corresponding persona profile.

3.3   DATA COLLECTION STRATEGIES

Three general strategies of data collection for data-driven personas can be identified.

- **Survey:** collecting data from the end-users with the help of standardized or tailored questionnaires.

- **Quantification of text material:** coding or otherwise quantifying interviews or user-generated content, such as social media comments or posts.

- **Automatic collection of numerical data:** collecting numerical analytics data from social media and online analytics platforms using APIs, most typically regarding engagement (e.g., views, clicks, visits, conversions).

In addition to these three, there is a fourth strategy, which is their combination.

- **Mixed:** a strategy combining several data sources for creating the personas.

Depending on the stakeholders' information needs, some persona profile information (e.g., motivation, needs, and wants) may be difficult to obtain using purely quantitative methods. The required information also affects the data collection strategy; qualitative insights are often required to portray the needed information realistically. Persona experts often advocate a mixed approach whenever possible (Pruitt and Grudin, 2003). However, in practice, data collection strategy is often constrained by the time, budget, and skills available.

According to our literature review, the most often applied data collection strategy (Salminen et al., 2020e) is survey data. In our study of 60 data-driven persona articles published from 2005–2019, we found that, in total, 50% (N = 30) of the papers reported the use of **surveys**, making it the most common source for data collection. The second most popular data source is the **web and social media data** (N = 18; 30% of total). This category includes social media platforms (e.g., YouTube [An et al., 2018b]) and discussion forums (Huh et al., 2016), as well as user click logs (Thoma and Williams, 2009) and telemetry (Zhang et al., 2016). Two articles also notably used **device-collected data**, including GPS signals (Guo and Ma, 2018) and physical comfort levels (dos Santos et al., 2014). Even though this use of device-collected data was marginal, it reveals how "personal big data" can provide interesting information about users, e.g., their health and wellness.

For example, behavioral data describing actual user interactions with devices is increasingly common (Minichiello et al., 2018). Nine articles (15%) used more than one data source. The most common data-source combination was surveys and interviews (N = 7, 77.8% of the multiple data sources). The authors regarded this as enhancing both the breadth (through quantitative data) and depth (through qualitative data) of the generated personas. We grouped the data-driven-persona research articles into three periods and discovered that the dataset sizes tend to increase over time (see Table 3.4).

Table 3.4: Survey sample sizes of data-driven personas. Percentages in parentheses indicate an increase from the previous era

	Quantification (2005–2008)	Diversification (2009–2014)	Digitalization (2015–present)
Mean	343	2,034 (493%)	**12,339 (506.6%)**
Max	1,300	12,496 (861.2%)	**170,704 (1266.1%)**
Median	31	100 (222.6%)	**199 (99%)**
SD	638	4,003 (527.4%)	**36,371.1 (808.6%)**

Even though surveys have been a consistently popular data format, the focus is shifting from survey to web data post-2015. Web and social media data sources are seeing a rise since 2015, and 2018 marks the first year that web data exceeded survey data. This trend continued throughout 2019. Also noteworthy is the increase in the data being collected from system logs and interfaces, enabling the creation of personas representing various user behaviors (Mijač et al., 2018; Wang et al., 2018; Zhang et al., 2016).

While behavioral data from product interaction is considered an essential advantage of data-driven personas (An et al., 2018a; dos Santos et al., 2014), the most popular data source for data-driven personas is survey data. Survey data has at least three issues unique to the survey data collection approach. First, Tu et al. (2010b) highlight the potential problems with objectivity when authors select which questions to ask (and, therefore, which answers to consider) from surveys. Second, Ford et al. (2017) also highlight the subjectivity of survey participants' self-reported answers. Some participants may exaggerate in their answers depending on the context, such as rating their productivity levels. Third, survey data collection requires recruiting a robust sample of participants and thus carries a high cost. These limitations hinder the representativeness and validity of personas.

Due to these shortcomings, API-based data collection, both text and numbers, is gaining momentum. A case example of API-based data collection is APG. APG links to and accesses the specific online social media platforms (e.g., Facebook Insights, Google Analytics, YouTube Analytics) via the API of each analytics platform, given the account holder's permission. These platforms' typical user data include the demographic variables of gender, age, and country of the person, provided at an aggregated group level. Via the APIs, APG collects users' detailed interactions with each of the online content pieces on the corresponding platform. This data is available to only owners of a particular social media channel (e.g., YouTube channel) and not available to the general public.

3.4   DATA CHALLENGES

Data collection for persona development involves several challenges, the main ones being identified in the ASUBE model.

- **A**vailability

- **S**pecifications

- **U**nknown measurement errors

- **B**ias

- **E**thical concerns

Availability: First, the dominant online platforms can be possessive of their data. Not all data variables—the same that the platform collects—are shared via APIs. Important behavioral or demographic information can be left out. The user information can be aggregated to make it impossible to use for a seamless data-driven persona generation. There are API restrictions on usage, such as thresholds for data collection. The variables can abruptly change or be removed while new ones are added without quality documentation. These are real experiences we have encountered dealing with API-based data collection over several years. Stakeholders are often oblivious to these challenges and expect data to appear automatically.

One of the most striking concerns of data-driven persona application is the restrictions on data availability, which crucially hinders the development of "fully rounded" persona profiles. For example, information on pain points and motivations is rarely available for data-driven personas, prompting the necessity of either additional (manual) data collection to perfect the personas or the creation of new algorithmic techniques for inferring this information reliably from textual data associated with a given persona. Moreover, online platforms periodically change their rules about what data they share and how stakeholders can use this data. The fact that rules change means resources are required to maintain persona systems relying on these data sources.

Specifications: Each data-driven persona algorithm has its inherent limitations as well as specific requirements for the data type and structure it can process, making not all data work with all algorithms. Particular methods may require explicit data or a data structure that is not always available. Figure 3.5 shows an example.

In some cases, stakeholders may be oblivious to these limitations, resulting in the "fallacy of perfection" concerning data-driven personas' applicability. We advise persona creators to understand automation and algorithms' limits in providing accurate and comprehensive user representations rather than expecting full automation and objectivity from data-driven personas. The field is advancing, but a lot more progress needs to be made before the craft of data-driven personas is perfected.

◉Instances ◯Groups

Simple Example

Country	Gender	Age	Movie
QA	female	19	Titanic
US	male	52	Arrival
KR	female	36	The Terminator
QA	female	24	Titanic

Example with combinable content (Movie Title + Subtitle)

Country	Gender	Age	Movie	Subtitle
QA	f	18–24	Titanic	ar
US	m	45–54	Arrival	en
KR	f	35–44	The Terminator	ko
QA	f	18–24	Titanic	en

Choose File   No file chosen

Figure 3.5: Data structure from APG. The data has to conform to this structure; otherwise, personas cannot be used by the algorithm applied in APG.

Unknown error: On a related note, a larger quantity of data does not automatically mean better quality. The personas inherit any biases and errors in the data. For example, when generating personas from online analytics data, the measurement error is unknown. There is no information about the baseline population, the estimation methods used, or any missing data. A data-driven persona represents the best efforts made with available data; however, data sources should not be blindly trusted. To increase trust in quantitative personas, creators can (a) apply triangulation by independent samples to corroborate personas and (b) increase persona transparency (Salminen et al., 2019c; Salminen et al., 2020), including clear statements of where the data originates, how it was collected, and the analysis steps that resulted in the visible personas.

Bias/Skewness: The data can be biased or skewed, meaning that it represents one user group well but another user group poorly. There is a trade-off between accuracy and biased source data. On the one hand, the generated personas inherit the source data's biases and yield personas that do not represent all users fairly. On the other hand, this very property exposes the source data's biases, which can be useful to stakeholders (e.g., to spot underserved user segments). If the algorithm is objective, but the data is biased, the "biased personas" reveal flaws in the real world that can then (ideally) be addressed. For example, one can focus on a subset of data consisting of vulnerable classes or minority segments and generate personas that precisely portray these user types. For persona designers, it is highly important to analyze and describe the bias in the source data, be transparent in the pros and cons of their preferred algorithmic techniques, and work together with stakeholders to understand their biases and how the data-driven personas could be used to co-create fair decision-making outcomes in real use cases.

Ethical concerns: Due to privacy, legal issues, and difficulty of collection, user data from the major online social media platforms is not individualized. It is aggregated along typically coarse attributes such as gender, which complicates generating customer segments. Therefore, one must develop techniques to decompose this aggregated data for customer segment generation while still respecting data privacy. Our method of APG is flexible in terms of the number of possible customer segments generated. Typically, user segmentation and persona creation focus on a small number of segments or personas.

From this premise, ethical data collection for data-driven personas encompasses:

a.   mining aggregated large-scale privacy-preserving online customer data,

b.   avoiding the use of personally identifiable information such as usernames, and

c.   aiming to objectively cover different demographic and socioeconomic groups in the wild.

Perhaps one of the most perplexing data challenges for drafting data-driven persona profiles is the "problem of every choice," referring to the situation that every single choice of persona profile information—whether an algorithm or human makes the choice—excludes users from the segment with non-corresponding attributes from the same underlying data representation. For example, working from two genders, if the persona is "Male," it cannot be "Female" simultaneously. The underlying data could indicate that 30% of the group's data-driven persona is based on women. Thus, there is an opportunity cost of ignoring 30% of the audience. Every choice is an inherent part of the persona concept—as long as the persona is one person with one gender, other genders are not represented.

That being said, there are ways to add diversifying information to the data-driven persona profile that mitigates users' chance of overlooking the persona's underlying diversity. First, the concept of information hierarchy enables ways of representing the data-driven persona group's diversity, even in such cases (see Figure 3.6). For stakeholders, it is important to make clear that the data-driven persona is one fictive person, typically the most typical one, that describes many users, some of which deviate from the generated persona in terms of some traits while still sharing a fundamental trait of similarity (the trait the persona generation is based on).

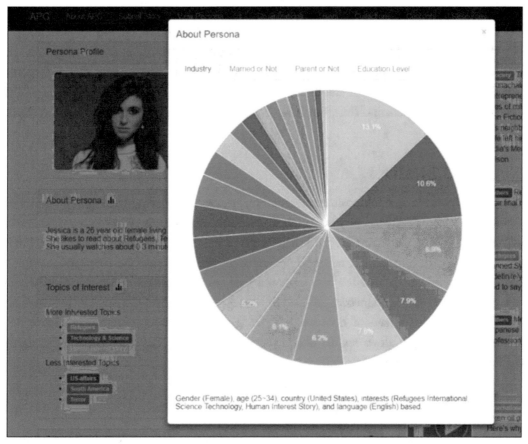

Figure 3.6: Information callout in APG showing the probabilities of the data-driven persona having a career in a given set of industries. Example of introducing diversity to data-driven personas. The persona has one chosen industry (Sales), but the data from Facebook Marketing API show that several other industries are associated with the profile matching the persona's characteristics. Therefore, even though the persona profile shows one predominant industry, the layered data approach shows the data's full distribution.

Second, estimates, proportions, or error margins can be provided. For example, "Persona is Single" can be expressed as "There is a 65% probability that the persona is Single." Similarly, "Persona is Male" can be expressed as "Out of the individuals categorized under this persona, 70% are men," or, alternatively, by saying, "<u>Most</u> people represented by this persona are male."

Third, for some variables, ranges can be indicated. For example, if we say a persona is a 26-year-old male, that will exclude 27-year-old-males. Instead, we can rely on ranges: 26 and 27 are both within the range of 25–34. When a range or confidence interval is available, communicating it to the end-user increases the persona's informativeness. It can also increase trust, as the user is now aware of how confident the algorithm is in the provided information.

Whether or not adding such information "breaks the spell" of the persona being a real person is not known. It is possible that, in some cases, the inclusion of more numerical information would decrease the perceptions of credibility and empathy if the users become more aware of the artificial nature of the persona. Thus, involving diversity is likely a balancing act between realism and informativeness.

3.5   CONCLUSION

A data-driven persona is a composite representation of users, portraying both demographics and behaviors. A persona also has a picture, name, and various other pieces of information. This additional information tends to concern the things users do in the real world as well as their hidden attitudes. The varied information needs of stakeholders require data-driven persona creators to collect various kinds of data. Often, the most practical way to conduct this data collection is to obtain quantitative behavioral metrics grouped by demographics and texts written by the users. Demographically grouped behavioral data enables a straightforward application of many data science algorithms. Moreover, it allows textual data to be analyzed using NLP, thus providing a starting point for data-driven personas.

3.6   CHAPTER TAKE-AWAYS

- The space of potential information to select for personas is excessive. To narrow down this data space, persona creators need to define the persona stakeholders' information needs.

- The basic data elements of a persona profile include a user's picture, age, and name. These can be automatically inferred from a suitable dataset for data-driven personas.

- Further information can include pain points, motivations, needs, and wants. These are often difficult to infer using automation, but there are data-driven ways, mainly relying on natural language processing (NLP) and text classification.

- Data-driven personas' information design involves collecting and combining numerical and textual information to meet stakeholders' information needs in a user-friendly manner.

- There are data-driven approaches for inferring persona profile attribute information from social media and other online datasets. For example, persona pictures and names can be manually curated or automatically generated using data-driven approaches.

- The main strategies of data collection involve surveys (the most popular method), text quantification (e.g., using NLP), and automatic data collection (e.g., using APIs).

- Data collection and use for personas require awareness of bias regarding (a) data source, (b) the algorithmic process of data collection, and (c) human bias (i.e., manual choices made for data sources and sampling criteria).

3.7   DISCUSSION AND ASSESSMENT QUESTIONS

1. List and define the ten themes of persona profile information.

2. List and describe the steps of the ASUBE model for persona data collection.

3. Explain in what situations one would apply mixed-data collection for personas. When would one not?

4. Label and define Nielsen's three broad persona profile information types. Provide a context for possible use for each and explain why.

5. Explain how the persona profile picture, as data, affects the stakeholder's perceptions of the persona?

6. Describe the manner in which persona information design can be defined.

7. Define persona information needs? Provide some examples.

8. List and describe the three richness styles of data-driven personas.

3.8   REFERENCES

Agarwal, B. (2014). Personality detection from text: A review. *International Journal of Computer System*, 1(1). 74

Al-Qirim, N. (2006). Personas of e-commerce adoption in small businesses in New Zealand. *Journal of Electronic Commerce in Organizations (JECO)*, 4(3), 18–45. DOI: 10.4018/jeco.2006070102. 69

An, J., Kwak, H., Jung, S., Salminen, J., and Jansen, B. J. (2018a). Customer segmentation using online platforms: Isolating behavioral and demographic segments for persona creation via aggregated user data. *Social Network Analysis and Mining*, 8(1), 54. DOI: 10.1007/s13278-018-0531-0. 75, 79

An, J., Kwak, H., Salminen, J., Jung, S., and Jansen, B. J. (2018b). Imaginary people representing real numbers: Generating personas from online social media data. *ACM Transactions on the Web (TWEB)*, 12(4), 27. DOI: 10.1145/3265986. 77, 78

Antle, A. N. (2006). Child-personas: Fact or fiction? *Proceedings of the 6th Conference on Designing Interactive Systems*. pp. 22–30. DOI: 10.1145/1142405.1142411. 63

Anvari, F., Richards, D., Hitchens, M., and Babar, M. A. (2015). Effectiveness of persona with personality traits on conceptual design. *2015 IEEE/ACM 37th IEEE International Conference on Software Engineering*, 2, 263–272. DOI: 10.1109/ICSE.2015.155. 64

Aoyama, M. (2005). Persona-and-scenario based requirements engineering for software embedded in digital consumer products. *Proceedings of the 13th IEEE International Conference on Requirements Engineering (RE'05)*. pp. 85–94. DOI: 10.1109/RE.2005.50. 69, 70, 75

Brickey, J., Walczak, S., and Burgess, T. (2012). Comparing semi-automated clustering methods for persona development. *IEEE Transactions on Software Engineering*, 38(3), 537–546. DOI: 10.1109/TSE.2011.60. 75

Brooks, C. and Greer, J. (2014). Explaining predictive models to learning specialists using personas. *Proceedins of the Fourth International Conference on Learning Analytics And Knowledge – LAK '14*. pp. 26–30. DOI: 10.1145/2567574.2567612. 71

Cooper, A. (1999). *The Inmates Are Running the Asylum: Why High Tech Products Drive Us Crazy and How to Restore the Sanity*, 1st edition. Sams—Pearson Education. 76

Cooper, A. (2004). *The Inmates Are Running the Asylum: Why High Tech Products Drive Us Crazy and How to Restore the Sanity*, 2nd edition. Pearson Higher Education. 66

Dang-Pham, D., Pittayachawan, S., and Nkhoma, M. (2015). Demystifying online personas of Vietnamese young adults on Facebook: A Q-methodology approach. *Australasian Journal of Information Systems*, 19(1). DOI: 10.3127/ajis.v19i0.1204. 71, 72, 76

Dantin, U. (2005). Application of personas in user interface design for educational software. *Proceedings of the 7th Australasian Conference on Computing Education*, 42, 239–247. 63

Denzin, N. K. and Lincoln, Y. S. (1998). Introduction: Entering the field of qualitative research. In Strategies of Qualitative Inquiry. Thousand Oaks, CA: Sage, pp. 1–34. http://ls-tlss.ucl.ac.uk/course-materials/PUBLGC32_50089. 75

Dhakad, L., Das, M., Bhattacharyya, C., Datta, S., Kale, M., and Mehta, V. (2017). SOPER: Discovering the influence of fashion and the many faces of user from session logs using stick breaking process. *Proceedings of the 2017 ACM on Conference on Information and Knowledge Management - CIKM '17.* pp. 1–341609–1618. DOI: 10.1145/3132847.3133007. 69, 71, 75

dos Santos, T. F., de Castro, D. G., Masiero, A. A., and Junior, P. T. A. (2014). Behavioral persona for human-robot interaction: A study based on pet robot. *International Conference on Human-Computer Interaction.* pp. 687–696. DOI: 10.1007/978-3-319-07230-2_65. 70, 79

Dupree, J. L., Devries, R., Berry, D. M., and Lank, E. (2016). Privacy personas: Clustering users via attitudes and behaviors toward security practices. *Proceedings of the 2016 CHI Conference on Human Factors in Computing Systems.* pp. 5228–5239. DOI: 10.1145/2858036.2858214. 69, 72, 73

Floridi, L. and Chiriatti, M. (2020). GPT-3: Its nature, scope, limits, and consequences. *Minds and Machines*, 1–14. DOI: 10.1007/s11023-020-09548-1. 77

Floyd, I. R., Jones, M. C., and Twidale, M. B. (2008). Resolving incommensurable debates: A preliminary identification of persona kinds, attributes, and characteristics. *Artifact*, 2(1), 12–26. DOI: 10.1080/17493460802276836. 72

Ford, D., Zimmermann, T., Bird, C., and Nagappan, N. (2017). Characterizing software engineering work with personas based on knowledge worker actions. *Proceedings of the 11th ACM/IEEE International Symposium on Empirical Software Engineering and Measurement.* pp. 394–403. DOI: 10.1109/ESEM.2017.54. 70, 79

Guo, A. and Ma, J. (2018). Archetype-based modeling of persona for comprehensive personality computing from personal big data. *Sensors*, 18(3), 684. DOI: 10.3390/s18030684. 78

Hill, C. G., Haag, M., Oleson, A., Mendez, C., Marsden, N., Sarma, A., and Burnett, M. (2017). Gender-inclusiveness personas vs. stereotyping: Can we have it both ways? *Proceedings of the 2017 CHI Conference.* pp. 6658–6671. DOI: 10.1145/3025453.3025609. 68

Holden, R. J., Kulanthaivel, A., Purkayastha, S., Goggins, K. M., and Kripalani, S. (2017). Know thy eHealth user: Development of biopsychosocial personas from a study of older adults with heart failure. *International Journal of Medical Informatics*, 108, 158–167. DOI: 10.1016/j.ijmedinf.2017.10.006. 69, 71, 75

Huh, J., Kwon, B. C., Kim, S.-H., Lee, S., Choo, J., Kim, J., Choi, M.-J., and Yi, J. S. (2016). Personas in online health communities. *Journal of Biomedical Informatics*, 63, 212–225. DOI: 10.1016/j.jbi.2016.08.019. 78

Jones, M. and Marsden, G. (2006). *Mobile Interaction Design.* Wiley. DOI: 10.1145/1085777.1085872. 68

Jung, S. G., Salminen, J. O., and Jansen, B. J. (2021). All about the name: Assigning demographically appropriate names to data-driven entities. *Proceedings of the Hawaii International Conference on System Sciences (HICSS2021).* 77

Jung, S.-G., Salminen, J., An, J., Kwak, H., and Jansen, B. J. (2018). Automatically conceptualizing social media analytics data via personas. *Proceedings of the International AAAI Conference on Web and Social Media (ICWSM 2018).* p. 2. 63, 77

Kanno, T., Ooyabu, T., and Furuta, K. (2011). Integrating human modeling and simulation with the persona method. In C. Stephanidis (Ed.), *Universal Access in Human-Computer Interaction. Users Diversity.* Springer Berlin Heidelberg. pp. 51–60. DOI: 10.1007/978-3-642-21663-3_6. 72, 73

Karras, T., Laine, S., and Aila, T. (2018). A style-based generator architecture for generative adversarial networks. *ArXiv Preprint ArXiv:1812.04948.* DOI: 10.1109/CVPR.2019.00453. 77

LeRouge, C., Ma, J., Sneha, S., and Tolle, K. (2013). User profiles and personas in the design and development of consumer health technologies. *International Journal of Medical Informatics,* 82(11), e251-268. DOI: 10.1016/j.ijmedinf.2011.03.006. 63

Loitsch, C., Weber, G., and Voegler, J. (2016). Teaching accessibility with personas. In K. Miesenberger, C. Bühler, and P. Penaz (Eds.), *Computers Helping People with Special Needs,* 9758, Springer International Publishing. pp. 453–460. DOI: 10.1007/978-3-319-41264-1_62. 63

Miaskiewicz, T. and Kozar, K. A. (2011). Personas and user-centered design: How can personas benefit product design processes? *Design Studies,* 32(5), 417–430. DOI: 10.1016/j.destud.2011.03.003. 63

Miaskiewicz, T. and Luxmoore, C. (2017). The use of data-driven personas to facilitate organizational adoption–A case study. *The Design Journal,* 20(3), 357–374. DOI: 10.1080/14606925.2017.1301160. 71

Mijač, T., Jadrić, M., and Ćukušić, M. (2018). The potential and issues in data-driven development of web personas. *2018 41st International Convention on Information and Communication Technology, Electronics and Microelectronics (MIPRO).* pp. 1237–1242. DOI: 10.23919/MIPRO.2018.8400224. 79

Minichiello, A., Hood, J. R., and Harkness, D. S. (2018). Bringing user experience design to bear on STEM education: A narrative literature review. *Journal for STEM Education Research,* 1(1–2), 7–33. DOI: 10.1007/s41979-018-0005-3. 78

Mulder, S. and Yaar, Z. (2006). *The User is Always Right: A Practical Guide to Creating and Using Personas for the Web*. New Riders. 68

Nielsen, L. (2019). *Personas—User Focused Design*, 2nd ed. 2019 edition. Springer. DOI: 10.1007/978-1-4471-7427-1. 66, 67

Nielsen, L., Hansen, K. S., Stage, J., and Billestrup, J. (2015). A template for design personas: Analysis of 47 persona descriptions from Danish industries and organizations. *International Journal of Sociotechnology and Knowledge Development*, 7(1), 45–61. DOI: 10.4018/ijskd.2015010104. 66, 67, 68, 71

Pichler, R. (2012). A template for writing great personas, Volume 2017. http://www.romanpichler.com/blog/persona-template-for-agile-product-management/. 68

Pruitt, J. and Adlin, T. (2006). *The Persona Lifecycle: Keeping People in Mind Throughout Product Design*, 1st edition. Morgan Kaufmann. DOI:10.1145/1167867.1164070. 66, 68

Pruitt, J. and Grudin, J. (2003). Personas: Practice and theory. *Proceedings of the 2003 Conference on Designing for User Experiences*. pp. 1–15. DOI: 10.1145/997078.997089. 66

Salminen, J., Guan, K., Nielsen, L., Jung, S., Chowdhury, S. A., and Jansen, B. J. (2020a). A template for data-driven personas: Analyzing 31 quantitatively oriented persona profiles. In *Proceedings of the 22nd International Conference on Human-Computer Interaction (HCII'20)*. DOI: 10.1007/978-3-030-50020-7_8. 64, 68, 71

Salminen, J., Jansen, B. J., An, J., Kwak, H., and Jung, S. (2019a). Automatic persona generation for online content creators: Conceptual rationale and a research agenda. In L. Nielsen (Ed.), *Personas—User Focused Design* (2nd ed.). Springer London. pp. 135–160. DOI: 10.1007/978-1-4471-7427-1_8. 66

Salminen, J., Jung, S., and Jansen, B. J. (2020). Explaining data-driven personas. *Proceedings of the Workshop on Explainable Smart Systems for Algorithmic Transparency in Emerging Technologies Co-Located with 25th International Conference on Intelligent User Interfaces (IUI 2020)*. pp. 7. DOI: urn:nbn:de:0074-2582-4. 81

Salminen, J., Jung, S., and Jansen, B. J. (2019). The future of data-driven personas: A marriage of online analytics numbers and human attributes. *ICEIS 2019 - Proceedings of the 21st International Conference on Enterprise Information Systems*. pp. 596–603. https://pennstate.pure.elsevier.com/en/publications/the-future-of-data-driven-personas-a-marriage-of-online-analytics. DOI: 10.5220/0007744706080615. 66

Salminen, J., Jung, S., Kamel, A. M. S., Santos, J. M., and Jansen, B. J. (2020b). Using artificially generated pictures in customer-facing systems: An evaluation study with data-driven personas. *Behaviour and Information Technology*, 0(0), 1–17. DOI: 10.1080/0144929X.2020.1838610. 68, 77

Salminen, J., Jung, S., Santos, J. M., and Jansen, B. J. (2019b). Does a smile matter if the person Is not real?: The effect of a smile and stock photos on persona perceptions. *International Journal of Human–Computer Interaction*, 0(0), 1–23. DOI: 10.1080/10447318.2019.1664068. 69, 76

Salminen, J., Liu, Y.-H., Sengun, S., Santos, J. M., Jung, S., and Jansen, B. J. (2020c). The effect of numerical and textual information on visual engagement and perceptions of AI-driven persona interfaces. *IUI '20: Proceedings of the 25th International Conference on Intelligent User Interfaces*. pp. 357–368. DOI: 10.1145/3377325.3377492. 75, 76

Salminen, J., Nielsen, L., Jung, S., An, J., Kwak, H., and Jansen, B. J. (2018). "Is more better?": Impact of multiple photos on perception of persona profiles. *Proceedings of ACM CHI Conference on Human Factors in Computing Systems (CHI2018)*. DOI: 10.1145/3173574.3173891. 68, 69

Salminen, J., Rao, R. G., Jung, S., Chowdhury, S. A., and Jansen, B. J. (2020d). Enriching social media personas with personality traits: A deep learning approach using the big five framework. In *Proceedings of the 22nd International Conference on Human–Computer Inter-action (HCII'20)*. DOI: 10.1007/978-3-030-50334-5_7. 74

Salminen, J., Guan, K., Jung, S.G., Chowdhury, S., and Jansen, B. J. (2020e) A literature review of quantitative persona creation. *ACM CHI Conference on Human Factors in Computing Systems (CHI'20)*, Honolulu, HI, pp. 25–30. DOI: 10.1145/3313831.3376502. 78

Salminen, J., Santos, J. M., Jung, S., Eslami, M., and Jansen, B. J. (2019c). Persona transparency: Analyzing the impact of explanations on perceptions of data-driven personas. *International Journal of Human–Computer Interaction*, 0(0), 1–13. DOI: 10.1080/10447318.2019.1688946. 81

Sedlmayr, B., Schöffler, J., Prokosch, H.-U., and Sedlmayr, M. (2019). User-centered design of a mobile medication management. *Informatics for Health and Social Care*, 44(2), 152–163. DOI: 10.1080/17538157.2018.1437042. 63

Streitz, N. and Nixon, P. (2005). The disappearing computer. *Communications-ACM*, 48(3), 32–35. DOI: 10.1145/1047671.1047700. 76

Tempelman-Kluit, N. and Pearce, A. (2014). Invoking the user from data to design. *College and Research Libraries*, 75(5), 616–640. DOI: 10.5860/crl.75.5.616. 69, 70, 72, 73

Thoma, V. and Williams, B. (2009). Developing and validating personas in e-commerce: A heuristic approach. In T. Gross, J. Gulliksen, P. Kotzé, L. Oestreicher, P. Palanque, R. O. Prates, and

M. Winckler (Eds.), *Human-Computer Interaction – INTERACT 2009*, Springer Berlin Heidelberg. pp. 524–527. DOI: 10.1007/978-3-642-03658-3_56. 78

Tu, N., Dong, X., Rau, P. P., and Zhang, T. (2010a). Using cluster analysis in Persona development. *2010 8th International Conference on Supply Chain Management and Information*. pp. 1–5.

Tu, N., He, Q., Zhang, T., Zhang, H., Li, Y., Xu, H., and Xiang, Y. (2010b). Combine qualitative and quantitative methods to create persona. *2010 3rd International Conference on Information Management, Innovation Management and Industrial Engineering*, 3, 597–603. DOI: 10.1109/ICIII.2010.463. 70, 74, 79

Wang, L., Li, L., Cai, H., Xu, L., Xu, B., and Jiang, L. (2018). Analysis of regional group health persona based on image recognition. *2018 Sixth International Conference on Enterprise Systems (ES)*. pp. 166–171. DOI: 10.1109/ES.2018.00033. 79

Zhang, X., Brown, H.-F., and Shankar, A. (2016). Data-driven personas: Constructing archetypal users with clickstreams and user telemetry. *Proceedings of the 2016 CHI Conference on Human Factors in Computing Systems*. pp. 5350–5359. DOI: 10.1145/2858036.2858523. 78

Zhu, E., Hadadgar, A., Masiello, I., and Zary, N. (2014). Augmented reality in healthcare education: An integrative review. *PeerJ*, 2, e469. DOI: 10.7717/peerj.469. 69

Zhu, H., Wang, H., and Carroll, J. M. (2019). Creating persona skeletons from imbalanced datasets: A case study using U.S. older adults' health data. *Proceedings of the 2019 on Designing Interactive Systems Conference - DIS '19*. pp. 61–70. DOI: 10.1145/3322276.3322285. 70, 72

CHAPTER 4

Creating Data-Driven Personas

In this chapter, we review the literature on data-driven persona development. We discuss popular data-driven persona development algorithms to show the diversity of algorithmic approaches. We then summarize the primary challenges of data-driven persona development, pointing to the road ahead with general data-driven persona creation methods. We then demonstrate data-driven persona development with a detailed description of the Automatic Persona Generation (APG) system's six stages. This is a data-driven persona development methodology employing non-negative matrix factorization to develop rich, holistic personas. We end the chapter by discussing other computer science domains' contributions to this concept traditionally linked with HCI.

4.1   MULTIPLE METHODOLOGIES FOR CREATION

The increasing abundance of digital data (Khan et al., 2019), social media (Spiliotopoulos et al., 2020), and user analytics (Deng et al., 2020) have paved the way for algorithmically created personas that facilitate interaction between the users represented by personas and the stakeholders. In this age of "personified big data" (Stevenson and Mattson, 2019, p. 4019), data-driven personas are useful for splitting up and categorizing large, diverse digital communities (Salminen et al., 2018a). Data-driven persona development uses algorithms to create accurate, representative, and up-to-date personas from quantitative data.

Employing algorithmic methods and online data to generate data-driven personas emerged in the early 2000s. The usefulness of algorithms for creating personas was highlighted by Aoyama (2005, 2007). In 2008, McGinn and Kotamraju coined the phrase data-driven persona development (McGinn and Kotamraju, 2008). Since then, data-driven persona development has become increasingly applied in HCI in various contexts, including video game design (Smith and Nayar, 2016; Tychsen and Canossa, 2008), health informatics (Holden et al., 2017; Zhu et al., 2019), cybersecurity (Dupree et al., 2016; Kim et al., 2019), marketing (An et al., 2018a), and many others.

Over the years, researchers have also utilized a diverse variety of algorithms for data-driven persona development. In their review of data-driven persona development, Zhu et al. (2019) observed the use of exploratory factor analysis (EFA), decision trees, weighted graphs, k-means clustering, hierarchical clustering, latent semantic analysis (LSA), and multi-dimensional scaling analysis (MSA). Minichiello et al. (2018) highlighted a similar list of methods: factor analysis, principal component analysis (PCA), cluster analysis (CA), and LSA.

A systematic review of quantitative persona creation (Salminen et al., 2020) identified five general algorithmic approaches (see Table 4.1), including CA, PCA, LSA, latent Dirichlet allocation (LDA), and non-negative matrix factorization (NMF).

Table 4.1: Five common methods for data-driven persona development based on the results of a systematic review (Salminen et al., 2020)

Method	Description
Cluster analysis	Groups a dataset using a predetermined number of clusters. Popular approaches are partitioning based approaches such as k-means and agglomerative such as hierarchical clustering.
Latent Dirichlet allocation	A generative statistical model that models each item of a collection (typically text) as a finite mixture over an underlying set of patterns.
Latent semantic analysis	Data analysis algorithm that uses singular value decomposition to detect hidden semantic relationships between words.
Non-negative matrix factorization	Matrix factorization method in which matrices are constrained as non-negative and decomposed to extract sparse and meaningful features.
Principal component analysis	Linear dimension-reduction algorithm used to extract information by removing non-essential elements with a relatively small variation.

Due to the divergence of the methods, there is no unified metric for measuring the quality of quantitative personas, apart from preliminary attempts to create a standardized questionnaire for measuring user perceptions of the personas (Salminen et al., 2018b). In the absence of standards, researchers struggle to benchmark the quality of personas. The lack of standardization of data-driven persona methods makes the comparison of different methods difficult. For example, clustering is typically evaluated with a different metric than matrix factorization. Having a unified way to compare different methods would enable benchmarking of results and clear demarcation of scientific progress in data-driven persona methods.

4.2   MULTIPLE METHODOLOGIES FOR VALIDATION

A common feature of the aforementioned methods is the process of simplifying data of a large-user population into smaller user segments, which are, in turn, enriched into the final persona profile form. This data simplification process commonly involves a step called dimensionality reduction. Data with several variables are projected into smaller representations that have limited yet distinct components and still retain essential information about the subpopulations (Huang et al., 2019). Once the selected algorithm pinpoints the most "essential" dimensions, these smaller representations can be enriched by combining heuristic rules and relevant datasets to generate richer persona profiles. As such, data-driven persona development is characterized by its compression of large datasets of audiences into a small number of distinct personas. This enables stakeholders to engage with a simplified representation of their user population without compromising numerical rigor (Brickey et al., 2012; Chapman et al., 2008).

Validation methods to confirm that the analytical procedure employed is suitable also differed across algorithms and individual studies. For example, Tanenbaum et al. (2018) used k-means CA to create diabetes patients' personas to determine how suitable various medical interventions were for different patient subpopulations. They validated the results by calculating the Euclidean distance between the different variables and then conducting Chi-squared tests. Meanwhile, Holden et al. (2017) used hierarchical CA to evaluate geriatric patients' psychosocial variables with heart failure. The authors validated their results using the Kruskal-Wallis test and Welch's ANOVA to determine statistical significance. Additionally, Mesgari, Okoli, and Guinea (2015) used hierarchical CA to develop university users' personas of institutional knowledge systems. They conducted validation by using Pearson correlation to consider the relations between variables.

Some have attempted combined algorithmic approaches. For example, k-means CA was used in combination with PCA by Wang et al. (2018) to develop regional groups' health personas. They validated their results by calculating the Euclidean distances of different demographic and medical variables. Similarly, Brickey et al. (2012) combined PCA with both LSA and k-means CA to develop personas for users of a military institutional knowledge platform. Indeed, combining methods is quite common, with a recent literature review observing that most existing data-driven persona development studies using PCA complement it with at least one other algorithm (Salminen et al., 2020).

Similarly, Miaskiewicz et al. (2008) combined LSA with hierarchical CA to create university library users' personas. They validated their results through cosine similarity tests. Meanwhile, Dupree et al. (2016) used LSA to explore cyber privacy attitudes among university students. They qualitatively validated their results by recruiting additional students to provide feedback on the accuracy of the personas.

As for LDA, studies have utilized the method to create personas for e-commerce portal shoppers (Dhakad et al., 2017) and video game characters (Smith and Nayar, 2016). LDA was combined with NMF to create personas for YouTube channel subscribers (An et al., 2018b; An et al., 2017). In the two studies, the authors used LDA to build initial topic models to construct matrices for NMF, which was then used to validate the generated data-driven personas.

NMF has been used to develop data-driven personas in several studies (An et al., 2017; An et al., 2018a, 2018b; Kwak et al., 2017; Salminen et al., 2019). For example, some studies have obtained content consumption patterns and used NMF to associate these patterns with user demographics (An et al., 2018a, 2018b). For validation, the Kendall rank correlation coefficient was used to compare the generated demographic groups' rankings versus correct rankings based on real content interactions.

Many data-driven persona development research projects have also conducted qualitative validation through subject expert and user consultations (Dupree et al., 2016; Salminen et al., 2018c; Tu et al., 2010; Vosbergen et al., 2015; Zhang et al., 2016; Zhu et al., 2019). For example, researchers have asked potential users to rate how realistically they perceived the resulting personas (Dupree et al., 2016; Tu et al., 2010).

Moreover, some researchers have developed and introduced unique data-driven persona development algorithms for their datasets, such as the Hanako method by Aoyama (2005, 2007), the Dirichlet persona model by Bamman et al. (2013), the neural speaker model by Li et al. (2016), and the ego-splitting algorithm by Epasto et al. (2017), among several others. Some studies have also developed their clustering methods based on specific variables determined for their end goals (Aoyama, 2007; Bamman et al., 2013; Tu et al., 2010).

4.3   DESIGN PRINCIPLES FOR DATA-DRIVEN PERSONAS

We have proposed several "simple guiding principles" for the development of data-driven persona systems (Salminen et al., 2019). They are as follows.

- **Authenticity:** data comes first—we do not knowingly manipulate the persona representations to deviate from the data, even if this means showing stakeholders information that they consider unpleasant (e.g., toxic comments).

- **Consistency:** the independent elements of the persona match one another to create a coherent profile of the underlying user segment; all parts of the persona system are reliable.

- **Relevance:** the shown persona information and the provided features are of immediate use and relevance to the end-users of the persona system.

- **Non-stereotyping:** the systems communicate to the stakeholders the multi-dimensional nature of the segment that the persona represents (e.g., even though the representative gender is "Male," there can be female segments that correspond with the persona's behavioral pattern). For example, we can provide a deeper layer of information of the persona to end-users, thereby clarifying that the persona is based on a group of people (a distribution) rather than on one predominant demographic trait.

When designing data-driven personas, creators can benefit from the following process.

Determine what information should be included.

➤ Devise ways to computationally infer that information.

➤ Develop models, experiment with them, and evaluate results.

➤ Implement the most suitable models.

➤ Communicate model performance to end-users.

When defining the information elements included in the persona profile, which is the artifact consisting of the persona presentation, it seems that implicit or explicit user feedback is required to provide appropriate information. Moreover, after defining the desired information content (what information to include), comes a question of its retrieval (how to get that information). Data-driven personas consist of essential information elements, such as image, name, and topics of interest. Additionally, social media enables us to infer a wide range of other attributes, such as political affiliation, personality traits, socioeconomic status, and relationship status. The applied methodologies are broad, including graph analysis, matrix factorization, NLP, and so on. These approaches involve their specific design choices, such as feature selection and extraction requiring subject matter knowledge.

4.4   CHALLENGES OF DATA-DRIVEN PERSONA DEVELOPMENT

As mentioned in previous chapters, data-driven personas' primary strength is that they address qualitative personas' limitations. By using quantitative data, the algorithmic processes enhance credibility and the scientific verifiability of personas (Siegel, 2010). The ideal data-driven persona is verifiable, replicable, and statistically representative (Chapman and Milham, 2006; Siegel, 2010).

Nonetheless, data-driven persona development is not without its challenges. There are at least four central concerns (Salminen et al., 2020), which are:

1. availability of data,

2. quality of data,

3. weaknesses associated with specific methods, and

4. bias (both human and machine).

All of these pose potential barriers to creating verifiable, replicable, and statistically representative data-driven personas. As the data-specific concerns were addressed in Chapter 3, the following section will focus on data-driven persona development's method-specific weaknesses and how to counter issues with bias.

4.4.1   METHOD-SPECIFIC WEAKNESSES OF DATA-DRIVEN PERSONA DEVELOPMENT

As formerly noted by researchers, each data-driven persona development method has its own strengths and weaknesses (Brickey et al., 2012; Kwak et al., 2017). For example, one major disadvantage of cluster algorithms is that it requires "specialists to use expert judgment during clustering" to define hyperparameters (Minichiello et al., 2018, p. 19). Further, k-means CA requires a single group to fit into one persona when, in reality, distinct behavioral segments often exist simultaneously within a demographic group. This is because individuals belonging to the same demographic group are not all homogenous and often behave differently depending on situations and contexts (Kwak et al., 2017).

On the other hand, non-negative matrix factorization (NMF) requires manual parameter settings that are usually set using rules of thumb (An et al., 2018a). Further, latent semantic analysis's (LSA's) disadvantage is that it greatly depends on the availability of linguistic corpora that is typically unavailable on digital analytics platforms. This means that LSA cannot incorporate behavioral data, such as user engagement metrics. Therefore, its data quality is severely limited (Salminen et al., 2019).

As different algorithms involve strengths and weaknesses, the choice of a persona generation algorithm can be context-dependent and subject to human judgment. If we have a large sample, we may not care about small-sample properties. If we are working with noisy data, we might prioritize algorithms that are not easily influenced by extreme values. Thus, it is important to understand that there is no algorithm that is "the" algorithm for data-driven persona development. In modern data-driven persona creation, multiple algorithms are involved at different steps toward the finalized persona profiles, and even within each step, several alternative approaches exist.

4.4.2   HUMAN AND MACHINE BIAS

It is important to understand that quantity of data does not automatically equal a greater quality of the personas. Any biases, human or machine-made, in the data will be transferred onto the final personas. When using algorithmic methods, persona creators still face the challenge of how to instill in-depth interpretations of the data into holistic personas, especially the rich narratives that are traditionally part of the persona profile. This is an issue with all methods of persona creation. This interpretative step highlights the major challenge of going from data to the narrative. As expressed by Wöckl et al. (2012, p. 3), "a main challenge when creating personas from quantitative data is the translation of numerical output into text."

For example, say one is using data from an online analytics data platform to create data-driven personas. The measurement errors are unknown, as these platforms neither provide error margins (confidence intervals) nor transparently clarify the processes they use to infer user characteristics (Jansen et al., 2020). This means that one cannot blindly trust the data from social media and online analytics platforms. However, even when one uses in-house data sources with known reliability, there are still risks. For example, imbalanced user datasets can result in stereotyping in the data-driven persona development process, which can be very harmful to decision-making (Turner and Turner, 2011).

Algorithmic bias originates from the interaction between the algorithm and the data, and it can result in "unfair" personas—i.e., those that do not represent the data correctly. For example, if 20% of the users in the baseline data are from the Philippines, but only 10% (1 out of 10 personas) in the persona set are Filipino, then we can argue that Filipinos are underrepresented.

There is a lack of work on debiasing persona generation and moving toward the creation of unbiased personas. "Unbiased personas" refer to personas in whose creation the algorithm has not biased the persona characteristics (e.g., demographic traits) from what they should be based on data (cf., the principle of demographic parity (Hardt et al., 2016)). Note that "fair personas" might be defined slightly differently so that fair personas represent the predominant user groups in the data and marginalized groups that are underrepresented in the data. Often, marginalized groups are at risk of being excluded from the generated set of personas or are underrepresented in the persona set relative to the baseline data (e.g., the Filipino example). Some of the techniques that could be explored for "fair personas" include:

a. outlier detection algorithms, with the rationale that marginalized groups are "outliers," i.e., they are not detected or covered by algorithms that focus on representing central tendencies of the data;

b. data pre-processing techniques (e.g., stratification, sub-sampling, and transforming data distributions), with the rationale that fixing the imbalanced data also "corrects" the output personas (Bera et al., 2019; Chierichetti et al., 2017); and

c. modifying the objective function of persona creation algorithm to make them fairer. The literature currently does not include examples of accomplishing this for personas, but there are examples of "fair clustering" for other purposes (Backurs et al., 2019; Chierichetti et al., 2017).

To some extent, supplemental manual methods can alleviate these challenges. In the literature, researchers often use qualitative methods to resolve issues with depth and representativeness in their personas (Dupree et al., 2016; Salminen et al., 2018c; Tu et al., 2010; Vosbergen et al., 2015;

Zhang et al., 2016; Zhu et al., 2019), using fairness metrics such as demographic parity. Qualitative methods can enhance the strength of data-driven persona development in the following ways.

- **Evaluation:** evaluating if stakeholders adopt the personas for decision-making and whether the personas are effective. Ask your team: "*Are the personas realistic and useful for the decision-makers?*"

- **Hyperparameters:** setting the values for hyperparameters (i.e., manually adjustable parameters) for algorithms. This means selecting the "right" number of personas for creation.

- **Write-up:** constructing narrative descriptions alongside personas shown to personas' end-users (Wöckl et al., 2012).

As such, even data-driven persona development, characterized by its leveraging of algorithms, involves some degree of human creativity and judgment calls. Data-driven personas do not automatically project onto the digital "paper." Some manual efforts are necessary for refining the user data into holistic and meaningful personas that best serve decision-makers' needs. A standard approach uses algorithms to explore user characteristics and subsequently enhance these behavioral traits with qualitative insights to create richer personas.

Therefore, data-driven persona development does not only deal with the choice of an algorithm. Instead, the development contains many interconnected linkages: *creation* (dimensionality reduction, *supporting* algorithms), *presentation* (interaction techniques, multimedia), and *adoption* (acceptance, readiness). Data-driven persona development needs to consider both technical and organizational factors.

4.4.3   SETTING THE NUMBER OF PERSONAS

Algorithmic persona creation is essentially a task of clustering or dimensionality reduction. In clustering, variables are grouped together based on their differences or similarities. There are many different clustering algorithms, usually divided into partitive (e.g., K-Means) and hierarchical (e.g., agglomerative, divisive) clustering. Similarly, there are many ways to compute distances between data points to determine the clusters, such as Ward's, cosine, Manhattan, or Euclidean distance. Based on applying these algorithms and techniques, data points are grouped into clusters, representing variability in the dataset.

Dimensionality reduction, in turn, is a more general term for reducing the complexity of a dataset by determining components that explain the variability. These components are sometimes referred to as clusters or patterns. When applying algorithms for data-driven persona creation, the components are the "strawman" (skeleton) personas—they are not directly interpretable. For this reason, additional enrichment steps are required to create usable persona profiles.

For data-driven personas, dimensionality reduction involves the tangible issue of losing some of the data, which is an issue not only for personas but also for market segmentation in general. Regarding this issue, a major question is how many components (personas) one should obtain to best describe the data. Depending on the specific algorithm, the techniques for determining this number vary. For example, in PCA, one can look at the proportion of variance explained by the different number of components or the cumulative variance explained.

Different algorithms may converge at different numbers of components. Ultimately, persona creators can use two alternative strategies to set the number of personas: (1) predetermination (e.g., "We want five personas") or (2) data-driven (i.e., using quantitative analysis for finding the "data-optimal" number of personas). This can be achieved, for example, by modifying the hyper-parameters of the algorithmic model. Such analysis can be based on metrics like the proportion of variance, or it can be based on exploratory data analysis (EDA), an inductive process through which the analyst manually investigates the data and suggests the number of personas. EDA can help persona creators choose the number of personas.

The general limitation of dimensionality reduction algorithms is that the number of components cannot be larger than the number of variables, although there are techniques for increasing data dimensionality by kernel conversions. Nonetheless, in theory, with thousands of columns, the number of personas can be very high if necessary. Ultimately, the choice is influenced by the manageability tradeoff; *even though more personas would represent the data better, there is a limit in how many personas stakeholders can actively process and use.* Interactive features, such as search options and filters, can help stakeholders narrow down the number of personas efficiently. Developing and testing such features is an ongoing area of research.

4.4.4   DESIGN TRADEOFFS

In general, there is a diversity tradeoff in data-driven persona development (Salminen et al., 2020). The tradeoff is that if your personas are optimized for diversity, then consistency decreases. Conversely, if your personas are optimized for consistency or fairness, your personas will be less diverse.

As such, diversity, fairness, and consistency are conflicting design goals in data-driven persona development. In addition, as the number of personas decreases, fringe or marginalized groups may become excluded from representation. As discussed in the previous section, some researchers have combined several algorithms to offset issues associated with specific methods and/or bias (Brickey et al., 2012).

Moreover, persona information design is not a trivial task. Chapman and Milham (2006) observed the problem of representativeness, meaning the more attributes one adds, the more possible personas with different attribute combinations there are. This exponentially increases the required data to describe all the possible segments in the data accurately. Thus, Chapman and Milham

(2006) argue that persona information selection is, by definition, *arbitrary*, as persona developers do not even attempt to cover all possible personas in the ideal world.

Researchers also argue that it is not possible to distinguish between relevant and irrelevant attributes of a persona, as *any* information can matter for a given use case. In the worst case, the chosen information takes away the stakeholders' attention from the task at hand instead of serving their needs (Long, 2009; Matthews et al., 2012).

Although there is some truth to this idea of "infinite possibility, and therefore no absolute value," persona systems can, in theory, solve this issue. This is because the stakeholders can be given tools to select the information according to their own needs, without the need for the persona creator to do this selection *a priori*. What is still needed *a priori* from the system is a pool of available information elements that the stakeholders can then select, with the system parsing them together into a coherent whole. While, as far as we know, such systems do not exist currently, their creation is possible and provides a critical avenue for future research on data-driven persona development.

Finally, there is a philosophical question of what we want the personas to represent. Should the data-driven personas capture *average* behaviors in the dataset? Should they capture the *range* of behaviors, including deviant behaviors? Should the personas be maximally different? Should they be temporally consistent or indicate "spiking" behaviors, such as trends?

These questions, although they are critical for data-driven persona development, are often not explored in detail. However, according to our experience, persona creators should ponder and reflect upon these questions before deciding their persona creation approach.

4.5   THE AUTOMATIC PERSONA GENERATION APPROACH

This section provides a general explanation of one methodological approach: the APG methodology that we believe to be one of the best methods for resolving common data-driven persona development challenges. In later chapters, we will demonstrate how the APG methodology can be applied to real user data from a major social media platform.

Figure 4.1 gives an overview of the data-driven persona creation process used by APG. The configuration involves the data assets, including client organizations, user accounts, API access tokens, and periodic data collection parameters. "Configuration" also includes resources used in the persona enrichment state, including demographically tagged pictures, names, and ethnicity information. The "Collection" part involves the scripts for data collection from social media and online analytics platforms that are currently connected to the system. In-house data sources can also be deployed. The "Persona Generation" stage involves building the persona profiles (explained later in this chapter). "Interaction" encompasses the parts of the system that end-users can interact with, including information pages, persona profiles, and features such as comparison. There is also an API for passing the persona information to third-party systems.

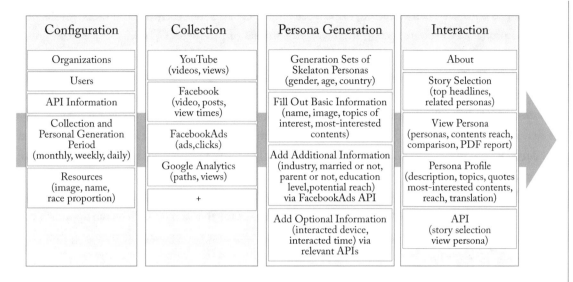

Figure 4.1: An outline of the APG persona system—from data collection to interaction with end-users.

The APG methodology consists of the six steps shown in Figure 4.2.

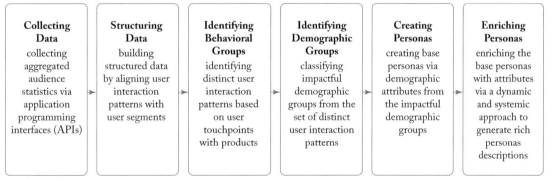

Figure 4.2: The Automatic Personas Generation (APG) approach. The APG approach is a six-step process to convert web analytics data into holistic persona profiles.

The first step uses NMF to identify the number of significant behavioral patterns and prevalent demographic groups. This allows us to decompose attributes to persona skeletons. The second phase adds complementary personal attributes, such as user interests, demographics, photos, names, and other personal details, to build the holistic persona descriptions.

4.5.1 STEPS 1 AND 2: STRUCTURING THE DATA

Chapter 3 provides an in-depth investigation of how to collect meaningful and reliable data for data-driven persona development.

Once data has been collected, APG first builds a matrix representing the users' interaction with the product. A user group (G_i) interacts with the set of products ($C_1, C_2,..., C_n$). A user group is defined as a set of interaction points with a set of products. We denote by $\mathbf{V}$ the g × c matrix of g user groups ($G_1, G_2,..., G_g$) and c the online products for all of C_i. The elements in interaction matrix $\mathbf{V}$, V_{ij}, are any statistics that represent the interaction of users G_i with product C_j. For example, in the case of YouTube Analytics, V_{ij} is a view count for a specific video, C_j, from user group G_i. This is defined by gender, age, and nationality (i.e., Female, 35–44, Denmark). Depending on the data available or your needs, V_{ij} can also be classified as total minutes watched a particular video, C_j, from a user group G_i. For example, columns could be videos, and rows can be minutes viewed.

Note that a user group, G_i, can be an individual user if the data is available at that level of granularity, and privacy concerns are accounted for. This means that the APG research approach can be generalized to both user-level as well as aggregated data usage. As such, this matrix approach is broadly applicable across both data of varying granularity and data of any content type.

In addition, the APG approach can be used for any domain where the matrix $\mathbf{V}$ can be defined. For example, suppose an app store provides statistics concerning app downloads by different demographic user groups. In that case, $\mathbf{V}_{ij}$ can be defined as the number of downloads from a particular user group for a specific app. In this scenario, our approach can be used to identify app store personas. The assumption is that there are demographics variables for each group.

4.5.2 STEPS 3 AND 4: IDENTIFYING BEHAVIORAL AND DEMOGRAPHIC GROUPS

Once we have the matrix $\mathbf{V}$, the next step is to identify underlying latent factors that will form the basis of the data-driven personas. Matrix decomposition is illustrated in Figure 4.3.

$$\mathbf{V} = \mathbf{W} \quad \underset{(p \times c)}{\mathbf{H}} + \varepsilon \qquad (1)$$

$$(g \times c) \qquad (g \times p) \qquad\qquad (g \times c)$$

Figure 4.3: Overview of matrix decomposition for identifying latent interaction patterns and prevalent demographic segments. This process forms the basis for the resulting personas.

From Figure 4.3, one can see that $\mathbf{V}$ is our matrix of $\mathbf{V}$, the g × c matrix of g user groups (G_1, $G_2,..., G_g$) and c products ($C_1, C_2,..., C_c$). Once it is decomposed, $\mathbf{W}$ is a g × p matrix, $\mathbf{H}$ is a p × c matrix, and ε is an error term. Here, p is the number of latent factors (behavioral patterns) identified, which are used to highlight unique sets of user interactions with products. The column in $\mathbf{W}$

forms the basis for the personas or user segment, and the column in **H** is an encoding that consists of coefficients that represent a linear combination of the bases. The resulting matrix decomposition equation is:

$$V = WH + \varepsilon \text{ or } V_{ij} = \sum_{k=1}^{p} W_{ik} H_{kj} + \varepsilon_{ij}$$

The basis and the encoding depend on what decomposition technique is employed. APG employs NMF (Lee and Seung, 1999). NMF (Lee and Seung, 1999) does not allow negative coefficients **W** and **H**. This non-zero constraint makes it straightforward to interpret the matrix decomposition. This is why APG ultimately leverages NMF to identify common patterns from the aggregated data. As such, a data-driven persona is a de-aggregated profile based on aggregated data.

4.5.3   STEP 5: CREATING THE DATA-DRIVEN PERSONAS

As mentioned, each row in **W** represents a different user group, which consists of common patterns. The coefficient, W_{ij}, is a relative proportion of a consumption pattern, P_j, in a user group, G_i (i.e., impactful user demographic group). This means that a row in **W** represents how different behavioral patterns can characterize each user group. A column in **W** shows how a distinct behavioral pattern is associated with different user groups. Thus, for each column, the user group with the largest coefficient can be considered the most prevalent user group for that corresponding pattern.

To determine the user groups' demographics, the most efficient way is to use the demographic breakdown from the building process of **V** (Step 1). Using the example from Step 2, if **V** has a row mapping into a group defined as [age group, gender, country], it is redundant to identify a persona's representative demographics. Indeed, many social media analytics platforms already provide user statistics in a format that can be leveraged for persona profiles.

This can be accomplished in two steps: (1) find the representative user group for the persona, as outlined above, and then (2) identify the representative demographics of this group. Once one has identified the column in **W** with the largest coefficient, one can then choose the corresponding demographic grouping from the dataset.

Now that we have identified the behavioral patterns and representative demographics of the user groups, this information can form the basis of the personas. The next step is enriching these persona skeletons.

4.5.4   STEP 6: ENRICHING THE PERSONAS

Behavioral patterns and representative demographics form the basis of the persona skeletons, but more information is required to ensure the personas reflect real people. This information includes name, photo, hobbies, topics of interest, and more (Nielsen and Storgaard Hansen, 2014).

The APG method automates this enrichment process. To generate a name, we utilize a pre-built lexicon of popular names by gender and year from each of the countries represented in the dataset (Jung et al., 2021). Then, APG can dynamically assign a gender to the age (based on year born) and country of the identified demographic groups. For example, for a 30-year-old male from Canada, APG can assign one of the popular male baby names in Canada from 30 years ago. This process relies on a custom-built algorithm (Jung et al., 2021) that use metadata for images and names based on nationality.

To assign a photo to each persona in the APG system, we have obtained copyright permissions for real photographs of stock photo models ahead of time (Salminen et al., 2021). We ensure that these photos reflect the ages, genders, and nationalities of the dataset, and tag the images with the corresponding metadata. This allows us to quickly retrieve photos from our pre-existing database for the personas (Figure 4.4).

NMF can be seen as the "core" algorithm of APG, as the personas are directly dependent on this algorithm, and it outperformed other algorithms that we evaluated. In addition, there are various "supporting" algorithms that participate in the enrichment process that results in the final data-driven persona profiles. Each supporting algorithm is dedicated to a specific subsection of persona information. Some examples of the supporting algorithms that contribute to the enrichment of the personas include the following.

- **eXtreme Gradient Boosting (XGBoost)** (Chen and Guestrin, 2016): This is a commonly applied algorithm in data science. It is a boosted tree-based method that performs very well for classification tasks. XGBoost enables the creation of supervised machine learning models. These can be used to categorize the persona's topics of interest from content text descriptions and associated labels. Alternatives: Random Forest, LightGBM.

- **Bidirectional Encoder Representations from Transformers (BERT)** (Devlin et al., 2019): This is a method for feature extraction in order to preserve the meaning of the text in context. BERT can be used for data-driven personas for topic classification and even sentiment scoring for persona's quotes. Alternatives: TF-IDF, Word2Vec.

- **Latent Dirichlet Allocation (LDA)** (Blei et al., 2003): LDA is a topic modeling algorithm. It can be used to infer personas' topics of interest. The difference between XGBoost and LDA for this purpose is that LDA is an unsupervised method that aims to discover topics from word distributions, whereas XGBoost (and similar algorithms) require labeled training data. Experiments with APG have shown that supervised methods tend to output more useful results, as LDA outputs are more difficult to interpret and may not be stable.

Ameerah Female, 25, Qata

Ameerah is a 25-year-old female living in Qatar and works in the Administrative Services field. She likes to read about Heritage, Design, Technology, Environment, Youth, Health, Research, Culture, and Community on her Mobile. Her average video viewing time is about 1.6 minutes.

Job Q	Administrative Services
Education Level Q	College 1 c
Relationship Status Q	Unspecified

Figure 4.4: Enriching of the persona descriptions with appropriate names and photos for the user segment.

An additional consideration of using multiple algorithms for persona generation is evaluation. As several algorithms can independently contribute to the whole of the data-driven persona, then each separate algorithm's evaluation scores can be tallied up to form a composite score. Suppose that Algorithm A's score would be 0.8 (on a range of 0 to 1), Algorithm B would have 0.2, and Algorithm C would have 0.5. The average "quality score" of the persona is then (0.8 + 0.2 + 0.5) / 3 = 0.5. Since this is in the midrange of 0–1, we could argue that the persona is of "mediocre quality" (in other words, there is room for improvement).

Figure 4.5 illustrates how these algorithms contribute to enriching the persona profile. Conceptually, algorithms are used for creating models that process persona data (and external data, such as names). These models output predicted scores and classes to become part of the data-driven persona construction.

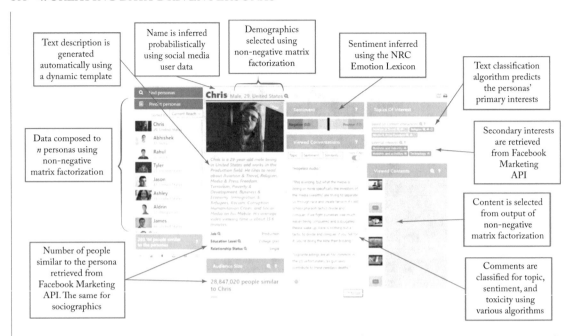

Figure 4.5: Algorithms under the hood of a data-driven persona (from Automatic Persona Generation).

In addition, we can also employ qualitative approaches to contextualize further the behaviors of the automatically generated personas. For example, Salminen et al. (2018c) manually coded and analyzed public Instagram profiles that represented "real" social media users in the Middle East to complement their data-driven persona development of YouTube users in the Middle East. The authors also recruited five social media users from the Middle East to discuss their usage of various social media services via semistructured interviews. Interviews were coded using action-implicative discourse analysis to contextualize social media use (Tracy, 1995). By integrating the APG personas with the qualitative findings, one can create rich personas and corresponding social media usage characteristics.

As such, the APG system and methodology is a practical demonstration of data-driven persona development from "soup to nuts."

4.6   CROSS-DOMAIN CONTRIBUTIONS TO DATA-DRIVEN PERSONA DEVELOPMENT

Traditionally, personas have been associated with HCI, and more recently, marketing and advertising.

Data-driven personas do not weaken this association to the HCI field since user studies, UI/ UX design, and understanding of how stakeholders perceive and use personas for user-centric decision-making is still needed (perhaps more than ever). Nevertheless, conceptually, data-driven persona development is related to different sub-fields of computer science (Table 4.2). As such, these linkages by data-driven personas expand the research horizons of data-driven persona development and introduce new technical challenges of various magnitudes to a wide range of disciplines.

Table 4.2: Relationships between information in data-driven personas and computer science fields and techniques

Persona Element	Description	Goal/Benefit	Field of Computer Science
Image	Generating descriptive and demographically correct pictures of personas.	Generating variations from baseline images to fill in all the gaps in the image database while considering the underlying demographic variety (age, ethnicity, gender). Eliminates the need for manually downloading stock photos.	Artificial image generation, computer vision, generative adversarial networks
Description	Describing the persona in a fluent way based on data.	Using natural language to summarize online numerical data makes the end-users more receptive to persona descriptions.	Text generation, topic modeling, natural language processing
Topics of interest	Creating topic classifications of online content and discovering probable interests by bridging social media platforms.	Creating a taxonomy by either supervised or unsupervised methods, the taxonomy needs to be scalable and cover multiple domains, eliminating the need for creating an organization- or industry-specific taxonomy each time a new one is added.	Topic modeling, text classification, natural language modeling, conjoint analysis
Comments	Finding representative, relevant, and non-toxic comments describing the persona.	Need to match a persona (consistency criteria), increase empathy and customer insight received by end-user; the goal is to prevent distraction from useful information.	Sentiment analysis, natural language processing, predictive modeling

Persona Element	Description	Goal/Benefit	Field of Computer Science
Story selection	Predicting and choosing content for personas or content creators.	A feature that enables to formulate headlines correctly before publishing the stories; the goal is to enable users to test content before publishing it.	Predictive modeling, recommendation systems
Temporal analysis	Observing change in personas over time.	Identifying trends in the underlying customer base, so that appropriate actions can be taken by end-users when there are shifts in customer behavior.	Tensor factorization, time-series, data stream analysis, anomaly detection, concept drift
Information architecture	Choosing the correct information elements and layout for a given user or industry.	Showing the right information to the decision-maker in the right format, so that the system satisfices information needs of the organization and individual users in it, thereby making possible better decisions.	User studies, human-computer interaction, ethnography, crowd experiments, adaptive systems, information science
Evaluation	Validating accuracy, consistency, and usefulness of personas for individuals and organizations.	Ensuring that personas are reliable and valid so that they can be trusted in real decision-making situations.	Eye tracking, user studies, surveys, factor analysis, structural equation modeling case study

The "giving faces to data" slogan of APG aims to capture the diversity and complexity of research and development problems about data-driven personas. Moreover, organizational issues, such as acceptance/adoption and active use of personas, typically studied in management information systems (MIS) or information system sciences (ISS), are also highly relevant research topics to ensure value creation with personas. In addition, natural language processing (NLP) offers quintessential tools for the creation of (social media) personas. This is because psychographic variables, such as interests, lifestyles, and values, help create a more holistic and realistic portrayal of a persona. At the same time, inferring these attributes from quantitative data can be challenging.

The most promising source of data for such in-depth insights is *text*: the user-generated social media comments of users that correspond with a specific persona. By using advanced NLP techniques for text classification, it is possible to learn from the users' needs and wants beyond what pure numerical data would enable.

In conclusion, at their core, data-driven personas represent a field of inter-disciplinary effort, with potential contributions from multiple inquiry fields. The data-driven persona project can be defined as a junction of interesting computer science problems to tackle. This means that state-of-the-art methods are needed for solving problems of data-driven personas, but the developed solutions can have value beyond the context of personas.

4.7   CHAPTER TAKE-AWAYS

- Data-driven persona development is the process of using algorithms to create rich personas from quantitative and textual data.

- Data-driven personas are useful for segmenting and categorizing large, diverse user populations of which there is digital information available.

- Several algorithms have been used in data-driven persona development. Sometimes these methods are combined to strengthen results.

- Data-driven persona development is characterized by dimensionality reduction. This is when multi-dimensional data are projected into fewer dimensions that contain essential information about user segments.

- Data-driven persona development challenges include method-specific weaknesses, human or machine bias, and various design tradeoffs. The challenges can be addressed by using complementary manual methods and by developing new system features.

- The ideal data-driven persona is verifiable, replicable, and statistically representative.

- The APG methodology consists of six steps: (1) data collection, (2) data structuring (using NMF), (3) identifying behavioral groups, (4) identifying demographic groups, (5) creating skeletal personas, and (6) enriching the skeletal personas.

- Decision-makers may have different information needs depending on their use case, so the requested persona information may vary. A static persona profile cannot keep up with changing information needs. As such, there is a need for fluid and flexible interfaces and backend systems that process information "just in case" a decision-maker requests it for their task.

- Data-driven personas rely on innovations from various sub-fields of computer science, and the data-driven persona can be seen as a nexus of technology research and development.

4.8   DISCUSSION AND ASSESSMENT QUESTIONS

1.   List four popular algorithms used in data-driven persona development, with their strengths and weaknesses.

2.   List two quantitative methods for data-driven persona development validation and two qualitative methods for data-driven persona development validation. Compare and contrast the advantages and disadvantages of each.

3.   Define dimensionality reduction and give an example for data-driven persona development. Explain how the example achieves or demonstrates dimensionality reduction.

4.   Define and discuss one method-related weakness of data-driven persona development. How can this weakness be addressed for data-driven persona development?

5.   Identify a manual method for alleviating bias in data-driven persona development. Discuss why this method can be effective at alleviating bias in data-driven persona development.

6.   List the six steps in the APG methodology. Define each step of the APG methodology. Identify an analytics platform from which you could potentially collect data and apply the APG methodology. Explain how you will do this following the six steps in the APG methodology.

4.9   REFERENCES

An, J., Kwak, H., and Jansen, B. J. (2017). Personas for content creators via decomposed aggregate audience statistics. *2017 IEEE/ACM International Conference on Advances in Social Networks Analysis and Mining (ASONAM)*. pp. 632–635. DOI: 10.1145/3110025.3110072. 95

An, J., Kwak, H., Jung, S., Salminen, J., and Jansen, B. J. (2018a). Customer segmentation using online platforms: Isolating behavioral and demographic segments for persona creation via aggregated user data. *Social Network Analysis and Mining*, 8(1), 54. DOI: 10.1007/s13278-018-0531-0. 93, 95, 98

An, J., Kwak, H., Salminen, J., Jung, S., and Jansen, B. J. (2018b). Imaginary people representing real numbers: Generating personas from online social media data. *ACM Transactions on the Web (TWEB)*, 12(4), 27. DOI: 10.1145/3265986. 95

Aoyama, M. (2005). Persona-and-scenario based requirements engineering for software embedded in digital consumer products. *Proceedings of the 13th IEEE International Conference on Requirements Engineering (RE'05)*. pp. 85–94. DOI: 10.1109/RE.2005.50. 93, 96

Aoyama, M. (2007). Persona-scenario-goal methodology for user-centered requirements engineering. *Proceedings of the 15th IEEE International Requirements Engineering Conference (RE 2007)*. pp. 185–194. DOI: 10.1109/RE.2007.50. 93, 96

Backurs, A., Indyk, P., Onak, K., Schieber, B., Vakilian, A., and Wagner, T. (2019). Scalable fair clustering. *ArXiv Preprint ArXiv:1902.03519.* 99

Bamman, D., O'Connor, B., and Smith, N. A. (2013). Learning latent personas of film characters. *Proceedings of the 51st Annual Meeting of the Association for Computational Linguistics.* pp. 10. 96

Bera, S., Chakrabarty, D., Flores, N., and Negahbani, M. (2019). Fair algorithms for clustering. *Advances in Neural Information Processing Systems.* pp. 4954–4965. 99

Blei, D. M., Ng, A. Y., and Jordan, M. I. (2003). Latent dirichlet allocation. *Journal of Machine Learning Research*, 3, 993–1022. 106

Brickey, J., Walczak, S., and Burgess, T. (2012). Comparing semi-automated clustering methods for persona development. *IEEE Transactions on Software Engineering*, 38(3), 537–546. DOI: 10.1109/TSE.2011.60. 95, 98, 101

Chapman, C. N., Love, E., Milham, R. P., ElRif, P., and Alford, J. L. (2008). Quantitative evaluation of personas as information. *Proceedings of the Human Factors and Ergonomics Society Annual Meeting.* Volume 52. pp. 1107–1111. DOI: 10.1177/154193120805201602. 95

Chapman, C. N. and Milham, R. P. (2006). The personas' new clothes: Methodological and practical arguments against a popular method. *Proceedings of the Human Factors and Ergonomics Society Annual Meeting.* Volume 50. pp. 634–636. DOI: 10.1177/154193120605000503. 97, 102, 103

Chen, T. and Guestrin, C. (2016). Xgboost: A scalable tree boosting system. *Proceedings of the 22nd Acm Sigkdd International Conference on Knowledge Discovery and Data Mining.* pp. 785–794. http://dl.acm.org/citation.cfm?id=2939785. 106

Chierichetti, F., Kumar, R., Lattanzi, S., and Vassilvitskii, S. (2017). Fair clustering through fairlets. *Advances in Neural Information Processing Systems*, 5029–5037. 99

Deng, S., Jiang, Y., Li, H., and Liu, Y. (2020). Who contributes what? Scrutinizing the activity data of 4.2 million Zhihu users via immersion scores. *Information Processing and Management*, 57(5), 102274. DOI: 10.1016/j.ipm.2020.102274. 93

Devlin, J., Chang, M.-W., Lee, K., and Toutanova, K. (2019). BERT: Pre-training of deep bidirectional transformers for language understanding. ArXiv:1810.04805 [Cs]. http://arxiv.org/abs/1810.04805. 106

Dhakad, L., Das, M., Bhattacharyya, C., Datta, S., Kale, M., and Mehta, V. (2017). SOPER: Discovering the influence of fashion and the many faces of user from session logs using stick breaking process. *Proceedings of the 2017 ACM on Conference on Information and Knowledge Management - CIKM '17*. pp. 1609–1618. DOI: 10.1145/3132847.3133007. 95

Dupree, J. L., Devries, R., Berry, D. M., and Lank, E. (2016). Privacy personas: Clustering users via attitudes and behaviors toward security practices. *Proceedings of the 2016 CHI Conference on Human Factors in Computing Systems*. pp. 5228–5239. DOI: 10.1145/2858036.2858214. 93, 95, 96, 99

Epasto, A., Lattanzi, S., and Paes Leme, R. (2017). Ego-splitting framework: From non-overlapping to overlapping clusters. *Proceedings of the 23rd ACM SIGKDD International Conference on Knowledge Discovery and Data Mining*. pp. 145–154. DOI: 10.1145/3097983.3098054. 96

Hardt, M., Price, E., and Srebro, N. (2016). Equality of opportunity in supervised learning. *Advances in Neural Information Processing Systems*. pp. 3315–3323. 99

Holden, R. J., Kulanthaivel, A., Purkayastha, S., Goggins, K. M., and Kripalani, S. (2017). Know thy eHealth user: Development of biopsychosocial personas from a study of older adults with heart failure. *International Journal of Medical Informatics*, 108, 158–167. DOI: 10.1016/j.ijmedinf.2017.10.006. 93, 95

Huang, X., Wu, L., and Ye, Y. (2019). A review on dimensionality reduction techniques. *International Journal of Pattern Recognition and Artificial Intelligence*, 33(10), 1950017. DOI: 10.1142/S0218001419500174. 94

Jansen, B. J., Salminen, J., and Jung, S. (2020). Data quality in website traffic metrics: A comparison of 86 websites using two popular analytics services. *ACM Transactions on the Web (TWEB)*, 25. 99

Jung, S. G., Salminen, J. O., and Jansen, B. J. (2021). All about the name: Assigning demographically appropriate names to data-driven entities. *Proceedings of the Hawaii International Conference on System Sciences (HICSS2021)*. 106

Khan, F., Si, X., and Khan, K. U. (2019). Social media affordances and information sharing: An evidence from Chinese public organizations. *Data and Information Management*, 3(3), 135–154. DOI: 10.2478/dim-2019-0012. 93

Kim, E., Yoon, J., Kwon, J., Liaw, T., and Agogino, A. M. (2019). From innocent Irene to parental Patrick: Framing user characteristics and personas to design for cybersecurity. *Proceedings of the Design Society: International Conference on Engineering Design*, 1(1), 1773–1782. DOI:10.1017/dsi.2019.183. 93

Kwak, H., An, J., and Jansen, B. J. (2017). Automatic generation of personas using YouTube social media data. *Proceedings of the Hawaii International Conference on System Sciences (HICSS-50)*. pp. 833–842. 95, 98

Lee, D. D. and Seung, S. H. (1999). Learning the parts of objects by non-negative matrix factorization. *Nature*, 401(6755), 788–791. DOI: 10.1038/44565. 105

Li, J., Galley, M., Brockett, C., Spithourakis, G., Gao, J., and Dolan, B. (2016). A persona-based neural conversation model. *Proceedings of the 54th Annual Meeting of the Association for Computational Linguistics (Volume 1: Long Papers)*. pp. 994–1003. DOI: 10.18653/v1/P16-1094. 96

Long, F. (2009). Real or imaginary: The effectiveness of using personas in product design. In *Proceedings of the Irish Ergonomics Society Annual Conference*, Volume 14, pp. 1-10. 102

Matthews, T., Judge, T., and Whittaker, S. (2012). How do designers and user experience professionals actually perceive and use personas? In *Proceedings of the SIGCHI Conference on Human Factors in Computing Systems (CHI '12)*. Association for Computing Machinery, New York, NY, pp. 1219–1228. DOI: 10.1145/2207676.2208573. 102

McGinn, J. J. and Kotamraju, N. (2008). Data-driven persona development. *Proceedings of the SIGCHI Conference on Human Factors in Computing Systems*. pp. 1521–1524. DOI: 10.1145/1357054.1357292. 93

Mesgari, M., Okoli, C., and de Guinea, A. O. (2015, June 26). Affordance-based user personas: A mixed-method approach to persona development. *AMCIS 2015 Proceedings*. https://aisel.aisnet.org/amcis2015/HCI/GeneralPresentations/1. 95

Miaskiewicz, T., Sumner, T., and Kozar, K. A. (2008). A latent semantic analysis methodology for the identification and creation of personas. *Proceedings of the SIGCHI Conference on Human Factors in Computing Systems*. pp. 1501–1510. http://dl.acm.org/citation.cfm?id=1357290. DOI: 10.1145/1357054.1357290. 95

Minichiello, A., Hood, J. R., and Harkness, D. S. (2018). Bringing user experience design to bear on STEM education: A narrative literature review. *Journal for STEM Education Research*, 1(1–2), 7–33. DOI: 10.1007/s41979-018-0005-3. 93, 98

Nielsen, L. and Storgaard Hansen, K. (2014). Personas is applicable: A study on the use of personas in Denmark. *Proceedings of the SIGCHI Conference on Human Factors in Computing Systems*. pp. 1665–1674. DOI: 10.1145/2556288.2557080. 105

Salminen, J., Guan, K., Jung, S., Chowdhury, S. A., and Jansen, B. J. (2020). A literature review of quantitative persona creation. *CHI '20: Proceedings of the 2020 CHI Conference on Human Factors in Computing Systems*. pp. 1–14. DOI: 10.1145/3313831.3376502. 94, 95, 97, 101

Salminen, J., Jansen, B. J., An, J., Kwak, H., and Jung, S. (2018a). Are personas done? Evaluating their usefulness in the age of digital analytics. *Persona Studies*, 4(2), 47–65. DOI: 10.21153/psj2018vol4no2art737. 93

Salminen, J., Jansen, B. J., An, J., Kwak, H., and Jung, S. (2019). Automatic persona generation for online content creators: Conceptual rationale and a research agenda. In L. Nielsen (Ed.), *Personas—User Focused Design*, 2nd ed. pp. 135–160. Springer London. DOI: 10.1007/978-1-4471-7427-1_8. 95

Salminen, J., Jung, S., and Jansen, B. J. (2019). The future of data-driven personas: A marriage of online analytics numbers and human attributes. *ICEIS 2019 - Proceedings of the 21st International Conference on Enterprise Information Systems*. pp. 596–603. https://pennstate.pure.elsevier.com/en/publications/the-future-of-data-driven-personas-a-marriage-of-online-analytics. DOI: 10.5220/0007744706080615. 96, 98

Salminen, J., Jung, S.G., Santos, J., Kamel, A. M., and Jansen, B. J. (2021) Picturing it!: The effect of image styles on user perceptions of personas. *ACM CHI Conference on Human Factors in Computing Systems (CHI2021)*, Yokohama, Japan. 106

Salminen, J., Kwak, H., Santos, J. M., Jung, S., An, J., and Jansen, B. J. (2018b). Persona perception scale: Developing and validating an instrument for human-like representations of data. *Extended Abstracts of the 2018 CHI Conference on Human Factors in Computing Systems - CHI '18*. pp. 1–6. DOI: 10.1145/3170427.3188461. 94

Salminen, J., Şengün, S., Kwak, H., Jansen, B. J., An, J., Jung, S., Vieweg, S., and Harrell, D. F. (2018c). From 2,772 segments to five personas: Summarizing a diverse online audience by generating culturally adapted personas. *First Monday*. DOI: 10.5210/fm.v23i6.8415. 96, 99, 108

Siegel, D. A. (2010). The mystique of numbers: Belief in quantitative approaches to segmentation and persona development. *CHI '10 Extended Abstracts on Human Factors in Computing Systems*. pp. 4721–4732. DOI: 10.1145/1753846.1754221. 97

Smith, B. A. and Nayar, S. K. (2016). Mining controller inputs to understand gameplay. *Proceedings of the 29th Annual Symposium on User Interface Software and Technology*. pp. 157–168. DOI: 10.1145/2984511.2984543. 93, 95

Spiliotopoulos, D., Margaris, D., and Vassilakis, C. (2020). Data-assisted persona construction using social media data. *Big Data and Cognitive Computing*, 4(3), 21. DOI: 10.3390/bdcc4030021. 93

Stevenson, P. D. and Mattson, C. A. (2019). The personification of big data. *Proceedings of the Design Society: International Conference on Engineering Design*, 1(1), 4019–4028. DOI: 10.1017/dsi.2019.409. 93

Tanenbaum, M. L., Adams, R. N., Iturralde, E., Hanes, S. J., Barley, R. C., Naranjo, D., and Hood, K. K. (2018). From wary wearers to d-embracers: personas of readiness to use diabetes devices. *Journal of Diabetes Science and Technology*, 12(6), 1101–1107. DOI: 10.1177/1932296818793756. 95

Tracy, K. (1995). Action-implicative discourse analysis. *Journal of Language and Social Psychology*, 14(1–2), 195–215. DOI: 10.1177/0261927X95141011. 108

Tu, N., Dong, X., Rau, P. P., and Zhang, T. (2010). Using cluster analysis in persona development. *2010 8th International Conference on Supply Chain Management and Information*. pp. 1–5. 96, 99

Turner, P. and Turner, S. (2011). Is stereotyping inevitable when designing with personas? *Design Studies*, 32(1), 30–44. DOI: 10.1016/j.destud.2010.06.002. 99

Tychsen, A. and Canossa, A. (2008). Defining personas in games using metrics. *Proceedings of the 2008 Conference on Future Play: Research, Play, Share*. pp. 73–80. DOI: 10.1145/1496984.1496997. 93

Vosbergen, S., Mulder-Wiggers, J. M. R., Lacroix, J. P., Kemps, H. M. C., Kraaijenhagen, R. A., Jaspers, M. W. M., and Peek, N. (2015). Using personas to tailor educational messages to the preferences of coronary heart disease patients. *Journal of Biomedical Informatics*, 53, 100–112. DOI: 10.1016/j.jbi.2014.09.004. 96, 99

Wang, L., Li, L., Cai, H., Xu, L., Xu, B., and Jiang, L. (2018). Analysis of regional group health persona based on image recognition. *2018 Sixth International Conference on Enterprise Systems (ES)*. pp. 166–171. DOI: 10.1109/ES.2018.00033. 95

Wöckl, B., Yildizoglu, U., Buber, I., Aparicio Diaz, B., Kruijff, E., and Tscheligi, M. (2012). Basic senior personas: A representative design tool covering the spectrum of european older adults. *Proceedings of the 14th International ACM SIGACCESS Conference on Computers and Accessibility*. pp. 25–32. DOI: 10.1145/2384916.2384922. 98, 100

Zhang, X., Brown, H.-F., and Shankar, A. (2016). Data-driven personas: Constructing archetypal users with clickstreams and user telemetry. *Proceedings of the 2016 CHI Conference on Human Factors in Computing Systems*. pp. 5350–5359. DOI: 10.1145/2858036.2858523. 96, 100

Zhu, H., Wang, H., and Carroll, J. M. (2019). Creating persona skeletons from imbalanced data-sets: A case study using u.s. older adults' health data. *Proceedings of the 2019 on Designing Interactive Systems Conference – DIS '19*. pp. 61–70. DOI: 10.1145/3322276.3322285. 93, 96, 100

CHAPTER   5

Data-Driven Personas as Interfaces for Persona Analytics System

With increasing access to analytics data, personas are more commonly generated from online user analytics data, using algorithmic approaches and, less often, from assumptions. This integration of data and algorithms offers new opportunities to shift personas from flat files to interactive persona systems. We illustrate this transition with Automatic Persona Generation (APG), a persona system. In pushing advancements of both persona and analytics conceptualization, development, and use, APG presents a multi-layered, full-stack integration. APG affords three levels of user data presentation, which are (a) <u>the conceptual data-driven personas</u>, (b) <u>the analytical user metrics</u>, and (c) <u>the foundational user data</u>. Moving to a persona-as-interface approach offers the benefits of both personas and analytics, and their integration addresses many of the shortcomings of each. The result of a persona analytics system is a better user-understanding instrument than either personas or analytics alone.

5.1   INTRODUCTION

A persona is a descriptive user model presented as an imaginary figure representing a segment of real people (Cooper, 2004; Pruitt and Grudin, 2003). This segment can be customers, audiences, or users of a product, content, or a service or system, respectively. For brevity, we use the term "user" in this chapter but also imply a customer or audience. We use the word "product" but also include content or a service or system feature. When data is used, which based on our research was surprisingly not often, personas are typically created using data from surveys or focus groups (Nielsen, 2019b; Pruitt and Grudin, 2003). In such approaches, the user data is usually collected and analyzed manually to create the personas (Pruitt and Adlin, 2006), although many assumptions about users are often included in the final persona profile.

From their inception in the early 1990s (Cooper, 1999, 2004), persona profiles have generally been "flat" (i.e., paper or electronic documents such as PDFs) (Gao and Gao, 2019), encompassed within a one or two-page summary (Nielsen and Storgaard Hansen, 2014). These flat persona profiles (see Figure 5.1 as an example) generally contain a collection of attributes about the persona, such as name, age, demographic attributes, a picture, a quote, and so on. As such, from their initial creation through several decades of their use, persona profiles were mainly data structures, i.e., static frameworks or representation of user attributes (Nielsen, 2019a; Pichler, 2012), with which the stakeholders only had a limited interaction. A persona was a descriptive tool.

A persona profile was a means to organize the data about the imaginary person to present information that stakeholders of the personas could then use for their design goals of, ideally, better understanding a segment of users.

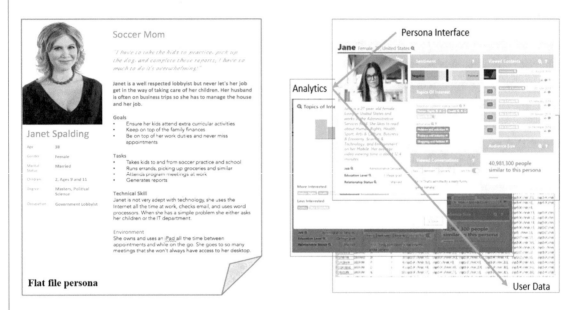

Figure 5.1: Left: example of a flat persona Profile.[2] Right: example of an interface persona profile that is interactive and provides access to system features and underlying analytics and user data.[3]

The explosion of online user analytics (Stamatelatos et al., 2020), social media analytics (Ma et al., 2020), system analytics (Ait Hammou et al., 2020), and customer databases make it possible to create data-driven personas using computational algorithms (An et al., 2018) that represent the underlying data (Stevenson and Mattson, 2019).

Instead of flat documents, these data-driven personas can become part of a cohesive (Aboelmaged and Mouakket, 2020) full-stack persona analytics system containing data about the users in a hierarchy of layered information—from backend user data to probabilistic analytics to frontend data-driven persona conceptualization.

As the persona profile is interactively connected to the underlying user segment and also the individual user data, the persona is changed from a flat data structure document to an interactive system interface for an analytics and data system—a persona analytics system. The data-driven

---

[2]   Image credit: https://launchschool.com/books/agile_planning/read/concept_to_personas.
[3]   See https://persona.qcri.org/.

persona becomes predictive and actionable, rather than just descriptive. In addition, the information structures in the persona profile can be altered with ease, for example, substituting numerical information for textual or vice versa (Salminen et al., 2020b).

For such an integrated system, the persona profile:

- functions as a **user interface** (UI) (see Figure 5.2) for conceptually understanding the user,

- provides a **data structure** for empathic user understanding of the analytics data, and

- has **interactive** functions to support the process of learning about the persona, segment, or user.

In this chapter, we demonstrate these principles through the APG system (Jung et al., 2017), showing the capabilities and functions at three levels of granularity:

- conceptualization (i.e., the data-driven personas),

- analytics (i.e., percentages, probabilities, and weights), and

- data (i.e., the foundational user data).

Data-driven, algorithmically derived persona systems such as APG transform the persona creation process, how persona profiles can be used (Johanssen, 2018) as an interface, and the notion of personas as design tools. As such, personas as interfaces to persona analytics systems provide both theoretical and practical implications (Bonnardel and Pichot, 2020).

We note that we are not presenting APG as *the* definitive persona analytics system. Instead, we offer APG as an instantiation of the persona analytics system for the ongoing research in the data-driven personas to further develop.

5.2   FLAT PERSONAS LEADING TO INTERACTIVE DATA-DRIVEN PERSONAS

Since their inception, personas have typically been presented through non-interactive, flat media, either actual paper or PDF-like electronic documents, serving mainly as a data format (e.g., framework, representation, structure) to present assorted information for decision-makers. These flat files provide little means for stakeholders to interact with the persona profiles beyond cognitively processing the information presented (Szczuka and Krämer, 2019) and communicating that information to others. Partly because of this, personas have come under substantial critique (Chapman and Milham, 2006) for:

- being of little practical value in the actual design process,

- lacking actual employment between the personas and among the various stakeholders, and

- providing little actionable information that the stakeholders can directly operationalize.

The concern about the value of personas is even more pressing because a range of online analytics tools, services, and platforms have emerged (Cooper, 2004; Jung et al., 2018; Springer and Whittaker, 2019) since personas were first proposed—e.g., Facebook Insights, Google Analytics, IBM Analytics, YouTube Analytics—as well as integrating services (e.g., SocialBaker, SocialFlow, Tableau) that organizations can use to understand their users and user segments.

These analytics services provide platform stakeholders access to both individuals (Ricotta and Costabile, 2007) and aggregated big data (Oliveira et al., 2018; Vecchio et al., 2018) about users, raising questions about the value of using traditional personas for user insights, with a plethora of analytics information, services, and systems. However, the concern with these analytics systems is three-fold.

- Their efficient use requires a level of *analytical sophistication* that not all end-users (e.g., journalists, nurses, politicians, etc.) might have or want to have.

- The "raw and cold" numbers and tables afforded by the analytics systems are not ideal for creating a *sense of empathy* toward the users that the numbers and metrics in these analytics systems represent.

- There is often little *intelligent processing* and/or *humanizing* conducted for the data in these analytics platforms beyond aggregate reporting.

Numbers also lack explanations of who the users are as people and why they behave as they do. In contrast, personas typically include such information, wrapped up in goals, pain points, and interests. So, analytics systems may encourage increased personalization without really aiding user understanding or empathizing with the users' underlying goals, focuses, or pain points. Instead, analytics may lead to personalizing on the incorrect, minor, or flawed data points, based only on prior user interactions recorded in the analytics data.

One obvious solution is combining data-driven personas and analytics, where each approach's strengths help counterbalance the deficiencies of the other. Conceptually, data-driven personas are easy for people to understand and generate empathy for the user and can be generated in numbers to represent large user populations (Pruitt and Grudin, 2003), but personas are perceived as not granular and not actionable (Chapman and Milham, 2006). Analytics data can be granular and actionable (Misuraca et al., 2020), but it can also be cumbersome for employment and confusing for end-users to comprehend (Webb, 2018). The combination of data-driven personas and analytics into a persona analytics system leverages the strengths and offsets the weaknesses (Salminen et al., 2020a).

Data-driven personas that are automatically generated from analytics data have all the power of personas. When serving as the interface to analytics systems, data-driven personas provide all of the strengths of user analytics, too, as illustrated in Figure 5.2.

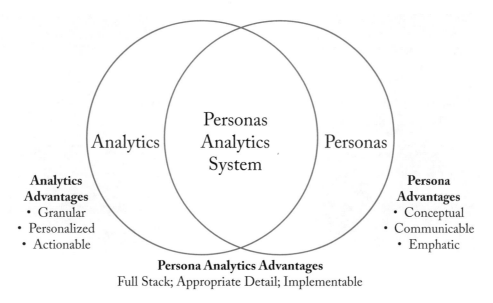

Figure 5.2: Comparison of the advantages of persona analytics with analytics and personas.

Combining data-driven personas with analytics makes the user data less challenging to use with the additional benefit of presenting an empathetic understanding of users via the representation of another person in the persona. Other advantages of this persona-as-interface approach is that, relative to traditionally crafted personas that are manually created and typically include 3–7 personas per set (Hong et al., 2018), one can create hundreds of such data-driven personas (Spilio-topoulos et al., 2020) to reflect the different behavioral and demographic nuances in the underlying user population (Salminen et al., 2018a) and segments. Although theoretically achievable, and with some prior work in the area (Zhang et al., 2016), there are limited working and deployed persona analytics systems.

Therefore, the question arises: *Can we actually create persona analytics systems that enable stake-holders to interact with both the data-driven personas and the quantitative data that the personas are based, while still retaining the empathetic user experience of persona profiles?* There has been some prior work concerning making personas interactive (Bonnardel and Pichot, 2020; Chu et al., 2018; Li et al., 2016), but the focus here is also integrating personas with underlying user data.

Toward addressing this question, we present the APG implementation of a full-stack da-ta-driven persona analytics system, highlighting the multiple levels—a full stack—of data access afforded by a "persona as an interface" (PAAI) implementation to an integrated persona analytics system.

We believe that such a full-stack system offers the empathy of personas and the idea of the rationality of analytics (Jansen et al., 2020).

5.3   APG SYSTEM OVERVIEW

APG generates a set of persona profiles (see the left-hand side listing of personas in Figure 5.3) representing the user population segments. Each user segment has a complete data-driven persona profile (see the displayed persona profile in Figure 5.3).

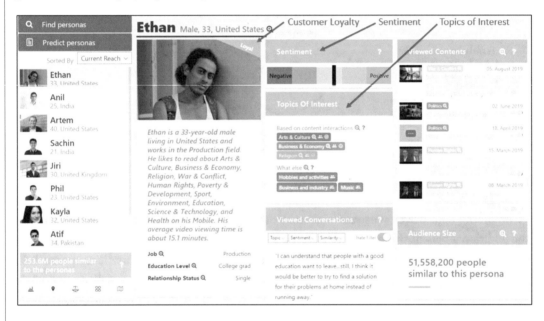

Figure 5.3: APG is interactive from the start, allowing the end-user to select the number of personas, from 5–15. An APG persona contains the standard persona profile attributes, plus direct access to the underlying data used for creation.

Data-driven personas, relying on regular data collection intervals, can enrich the traditional persona profile with additional elements such as (a) user loyalty, (b) sentiment analysis (Tahara et al., 2019), and (c) topics of interest, which are features requested by the stakeholders. Also, the data-driven persona profile is interactive, functioning as the interface to the additional level of data, as discussed in the next subsections.

5.4   APG: INTERACTION WITH DATA-DRIVEN PERSONAS

The APG system employs the foundational user data, which the system algorithms act upon, transforming this data into information about users. This algorithmic processing's outcomes are actionable metrics and measures about the user population (e.g., percentages, probabilities, weights) of the type that one would typically see in industry-standard analytics packages.

Employing these actionable metrics is the next level of abstraction taken by the APG system to leverage this analytics data, along with corresponding meta-tagged information, such as photos and names, to create sets of data-driven personas profiles at the conceptual level. The result is a data-driven persona analytics system capable of presenting user insights at different granularity levels, with levels both integrated and appropriate to the task (see Figure 5.4).

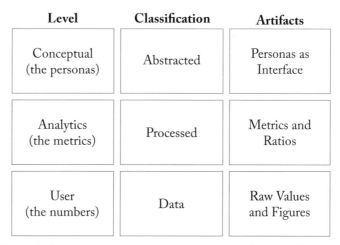

Level	Classification	Artifacts
Conceptual (the personas)	Abstracted	Personas as Interface
Analytics (the metrics)	Processed	Metrics and Ratios
User (the numbers)	Data	Raw Values and Figures

Figure 5.4: APG full-stack data integration, from user level to analytics level to conceptual level.

We now discuss these three levels illustrated in Figure 5.4.

5.4.1   CONCEPTUAL LEVEL: DATA-DRIVEN PERSONAS

The highest level of abstraction is the set of data-driven personas that APG generates from the data using the method described above, with a default of ten personas. However, the APG system can generate as many personas as needed within the boundaries of data. The general limitation of dimensionality reduction algorithms such as non-negative matrix factorization (NMF) is that the number of components cannot be larger than the number of columns. With thousands of columns, the number of personas can be very high if needed. The persona profile has nearly all the typical attributes that one finds in the traditional flat-file persona profiles.

However, as in APG, data-driven persona system interfaces allow for dramatically increased interactivity in leveraging personas within organizations. Interactivity is provided such that the stakeholders can alter this number to generate more or fewer data-driven personas, with the system currently set for between 5 and 15 personas. The system can search for a set of personas (see Figure 5.5) or leverage analytics for the prediction of persona interests (see Figure 5.6).

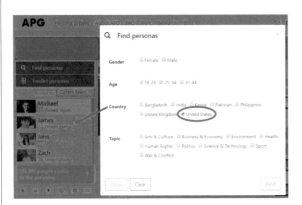
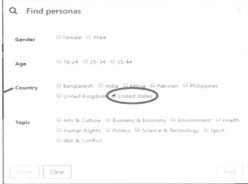

Figure 5.5: Left: Searching a set of personas to locate just those from the U.S. (See callout to the right). Right: Callout of display of the percentage of the overall population of the persona.

Figure 5.6: Left: Entering a topic ("What is happening in China with the riots?"), which the system automatically classifies topically, showing which personas would be most interested and least interested (Red Down Arrows) in the topic. (See callout to the right). Right: Callout of entering a topic ("What is happening in China with the riots?"), which the system automatically classifies topically, showing which personas would be most interested.

5.4.2   ANALYTICS LEVEL: PERCENTAGES, PROBABILITIES, AND WEIGHTS

APG data-driven persona profiles act as interfaces to the underlying information and data used to create the persona profiles. The specific information may vary somewhat by the data source. Still, the analytics level will reflect the particular metrics and measures generated from the foundational user data and used to create the personas. The personas profile in the APG system provides affordance to the various analytics information via clickable icons on the persona interface. We highlight three examples.

As shown in Figure 5.7 for audience size (i.e., number of people in the user segment), APG displays the percentage of the entire user population that a particular persona is representing (calculated from Facebook Marketing API data). This analytics insight is valuable for decision-makers to determine the importance of designing or developing for a particular persona and helps address the issue of the persona's validity in representing actual users (Chapman et al., 2008).

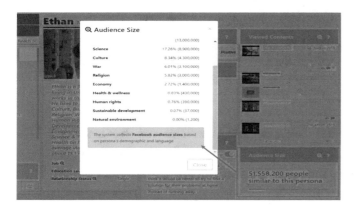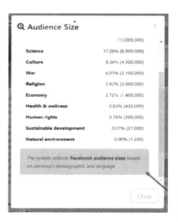

Figure 5.7: Left: Display of the percentage of the overall population represented by the persona (see callout to the right). Right: Callout of display of the percentage of the overall population of the persona.

APG gathers general demographic information from the online platforms, which typically includes gender, age grouping, and nationality. Using these attributes and results derived from NMF (Lee and Seung, 1999), APG then leverages the appropriate analytics platform application program interface (API) to determine the probability of other demographic characteristics. The persona profiles provide access to these probabilities (see Figure 5.8 for the probability of relationship status).

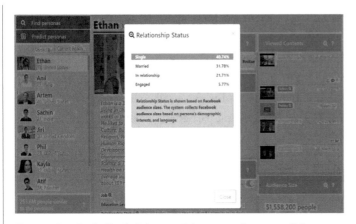 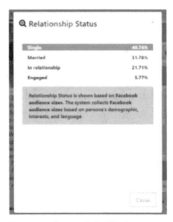

Figure 5.8: Left: Probabilities of the marital status of the persona (see callout to the right). Right: Probabilities of Marital Status of the Persona.

As mentioned above, APG identifies unique behavioral patterns and then associates these unique patterns via latent factors to one or more demographic groups, assigning a weight to each of these demographic groups based on the strength of its association with the unique pattern. These weights provide insights to the stakeholder about the data-driven personas concerning both (a) the strength of the behavior and (b) the association of this behavioral pattern with other groups. Therefore, APG provides access to these demographic group weights (Figure 5.9), addressing concerns of what actual customers the personas represent (Chapman et al., 2008).

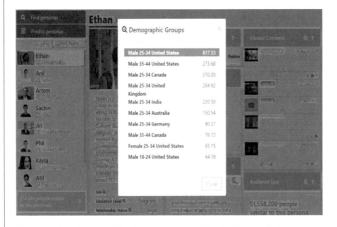

Figure 5.9: Left: Weights generated by NMF of the various demographic segments associated with a unique behavior pattern (see callout to the right). Right: Weights generated by NMF of the various demographic segments associated with a unique behavior pattern.

5.4.3 USER LEVEL: INDIVIDUAL DATA

By leveraging the demographic meta-data output from the NMF, the decision-maker can access the specific customer level (i.e., individual or aggregate), as shown in Figure 5.10. It is the numerical user data (in various forms) that are the foundation of the personas and analytics presented in prior figures.

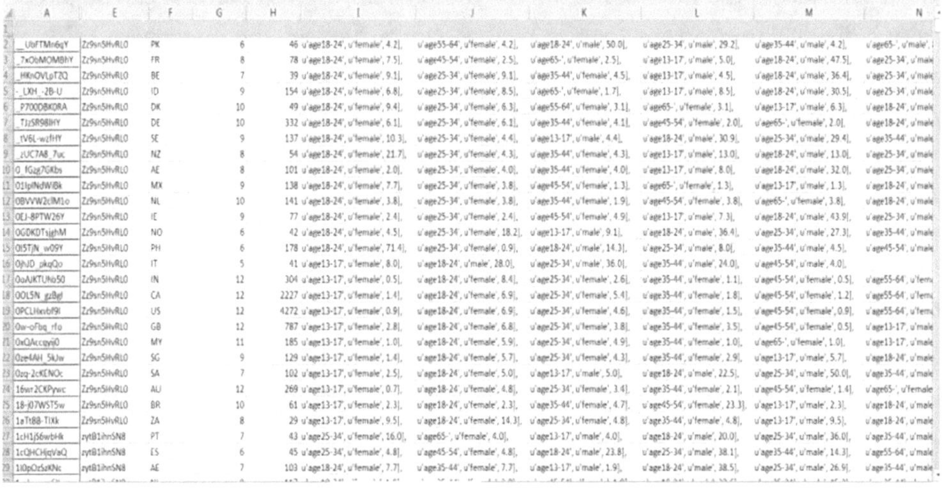

	A	E	F	G	H	I	J	K	L	M	N
1											
2	_UbFTMn6qY	Zz9sn5HvRL0	PK	6	46	u'age18-24', u'female', 4.2],	u'age55-64', u'female', 4.2],	u'age18-24', u'male', 50.0],	u'age25-34', u'male', 29.2],	u'age35-44', u'male', 4.2],	u'age65-', u'male',
3	_7xObMOMBhY	Zz9sn5HvRL0	FR	8	78	u'age18-24', u'female', 7.5],	u'age45-54', u'female', 2.5],	u'age65-', u'female', 2.5],	u'age13-17', u'male', 5.0],	u'age18-24', u'male', 47.5],	u'age25-34', u'male
4	_HKnOVLpT2Q	Zz9sn5HvRL0	BE	7	39	u'age18-24', u'female', 9.1],	u'age25-34', u'female', 9.1],	u'age35-44', u'female', 4.5],	u'age13-17', u'male', 4.5],	u'age18-24', u'male', 36.4],	u'age25-34', u'male
5	-_LXH_-2B-U	Zz9sn5HvRL0	ID	9	154	u'age18-24', u'female', 6.8],	u'age25-34', u'female', 8.5],	u'age65-', u'female', 1.7],	u'age13-17', u'male', 8.5],	u'age18-24', u'male', 30.5],	u'age25-34', u'male
6	_P700DBKDRA	Zz9sn5HvRL0	DK	10	49	u'age18-24', u'female', 9.4],	u'age25-34', u'female', 6.3],	u'age55-64', u'female', 3.1],	u'age65-', u'female', 3.1],	u'age13-17', u'male', 6.3],	u'age18-24', u'male
7	_TJzSR98IHY	Zz9sn5HvRL0	DE	10	332	u'age18-24', u'female', 6.1],	u'age25-34', u'female', 6.1],	u'age35-44', u'female', 4.1],	u'age45-54', u'female', 2.0],	u'age65-', u'female', 2.0],	u'age18-24', u'male
8	_tV6L-wzfHY	Zz9sn5HvRL0	SE	9	137	u'age18-24', u'female', 10.3],	u'age25-34', u'female', 4.4],	u'age13-17', u'male', 4.4],	u'age18-24', u'male', 30.9],	u'age25-34', u'male', 29.4],	u'age35-44', u'male
9	_zUC7A8_7uc	Zz9sn5HvRL0	NZ	8	54	u'age18-24', u'female', 21.7],	u'age25-34', u'female', 4.3],	u'age35-44', u'female', 4.3],	u'age13-17', u'male', 13.0],	u'age18-24', u'male', 13.0],	u'age25-34', u'male
10	0_fGzg7GKbs	Zz9sn5HvRL0	AE	8	101	u'age18-24', u'female', 2.0],	u'age25-34', u'female', 4.0],	u'age35-44', u'female', 4.0],	u'age13-17', u'male', 8.0],	u'age18-24', u'male', 32.0],	u'age25-34', u'male
11	01IplNdWiBk	Zz9sn5HvRL0	MX	9	138	u'age18-24', u'female', 7.7],	u'age25-34', u'female', 3.8],	u'age45-54', u'female', 1.3],	u'age65-', u'female', 1.3],	u'age13-17', u'male', 1.3],	u'age18-24', u'male
12	0BVVW2clM1o	Zz9sn5HvRL0	NL	10	141	u'age18-24', u'female', 3.8],	u'age25-34', u'female', 3.8],	u'age35-44', u'female', 1.9],	u'age45-54', u'female', 3.8],	u'age65-', u'female', 3.8],	u'age18-24', u'male
13	0EJ-8PTW26Y	Zz9sn5HvRL0	IE	9	77	u'age18-24', u'female', 2.4],	u'age25-34', u'female', 2.4],	u'age45-54', u'female', 4.9],	u'age13-17', u'male', 7.3],	u'age18-24', u'male', 43.9],	u'age25-34', u'male
14	0GDKDTsjghM	Zz9sn5HvRL0	NO	6	42	u'age18-24', u'female', 4.5],	u'age25-34', u'female', 18.2],	u'age13-17', u'male', 9.1],	u'age18-24', u'male', 36.4],	u'age25-34', u'male', 27.3],	u'age35-44', u'male
15	0I5TjN_w09Y	Zz9sn5HvRL0	PH	6	178	u'age18-24', u'female', 71.4],	u'age25-34', u'female', 0.9],	u'age18-24', u'male', 14.3],	u'age25-34', u'male', 8.0],	u'age35-44', u'male', 4.5],	u'age45-54', u'male
16	0jhJD_pkqQo	Zz9sn5HvRL0	IT	5	41	u'age13-17', u'female', 8.0],	u'age18-24', u'male', 28.0],	u'age25-34', u'male', 36.0],	u'age35-44', u'male', 24.0],	u'age45-54', u'male', 4.0],	
17	0oAJKTUhb50	Zz9sn5HvRL0	IN	12	304	u'age13-17', u'female', 0.5],	u'age18-24', u'female', 8.4],	u'age25-34', u'female', 2.6],	u'age35-44', u'female', 1.1],	u'age45-54', u'female', 0.5],	u'age55-64', u'fem
18	0OL5N_gzBgl	Zz9sn5HvRL0	CA	12	2227	u'age13-17', u'female', 1.4],	u'age18-24', u'female', 6.9],	u'age25-34', u'female', 5.4],	u'age35-44', u'female', 1.8],	u'age45-54', u'female', 1.2],	u'age55-64', u'fem
19	0PCLHxvbf9I	Zz9sn5HvRL0	US	12	4272	u'age13-17', u'female', 0.9],	u'age18-24', u'female', 6.9],	u'age25-34', u'female', 4.6],	u'age35-44', u'female', 1.5],	u'age45-54', u'female', 0.9],	u'age55-64', u'fem
20	0w-oFbq_rfo	Zz9sn5HvRL0	GB	12	787	u'age13-17', u'female', 2.8],	u'age18-24', u'female', 6.8],	u'age25-34', u'female', 3.8],	u'age35-44', u'female', 3.5],	u'age45-54', u'female', 0.5],	u'age13-17', u'male
21	0xQAccqyij0	Zz9sn5HvRL0	MY	11	185	u'age13-17', u'female', 1.0],	u'age18-24', u'female', 5.9],	u'age25-34', u'female', 4.9],	u'age35-44', u'female', 1.0],	u'age65-', u'female', 1.0],	u'age13-17', u'male
22	0ze4AH_5kUw	Zz9sn5HvRL0	SG	9	129	u'age13-17', u'female', 1.4],	u'age18-24', u'female', 5.7],	u'age25-34', u'female', 4.3],	u'age35-44', u'female', 2.9],	u'age13-17', u'male', 5.7],	u'age18-24', u'male
23	0zq-2cKENOc	Zz9sn5HvRL0	SA	7	102	u'age13-17', u'female', 2.5],	u'age18-24', u'female', 5.0],	u'age13-17', u'male', 5.0],	u'age18-24', u'male', 22.5],	u'age25-34', u'male', 50.0],	u'age35-44', u'male
24	16wr2CKPywc	Zz9sn5HvRL0	AU	12	269	u'age13-17', u'female', 0.7],	u'age18-24', u'female', 4.8],	u'age25-34', u'female', 3.4],	u'age35-44', u'female', 2.1],	u'age45-54', u'female', 1.4],	u'age65-', u'female
25	18-j07WST5w	Zz9sn5HvRL0	BR	10	61	u'age13-17', u'female', 2.3],	u'age18-24', u'female', 2.3],	u'age35-44', u'female', 4.7],	u'age45-54', u'female', 23.3],	u'age13-17', u'male', 2.3],	u'age18-24', u'male
26	1aTt8B-TIXk	Zz9sn5HvRL0	ZA	8	29	u'age13-17', u'female', 9.5],	u'age18-24', u'female', 14.3],	u'age25-34', u'female', 4.8],	u'age35-44', u'female', 4.8],	u'age13-17', u'male', 9.5],	u'age18-24', u'male
27	1cH1jS6wbHk	zytB1ihnSN8	PT	7	43	u'age25-34', u'female', 16.0],	u'age65-', u'female', 4.0],	u'age13-17', u'male', 4.0],	u'age18-24', u'male', 20.0],	u'age25-34', u'male', 36.0],	u'age35-44', u'male
28	1cQHCHjqVaQ	zytB1ihnSN8	ES	6	45	u'age25-34', u'female', 4.8],	u'age45-54', u'female', 4.8],	u'age18-24', u'male', 23.8],	u'age25-34', u'male', 38.1],	u'age35-44', u'male', 14.3],	u'age55-64', u'male
29	1l0pOzSzKNc	zytB1ihnSN8	AE	7	103	u'age18-24', u'female', 7.7],	u'age35-44', u'female', 7.7],	u'age13-17', u'male', 1.9],	u'age18-24', u'male', 38.5],	u'age25-34', u'male', 26.9],	u'age35-44', u'male

Figure 5.10: Foundational user-level data from which the personas are generated.

The conceptual shift of personas from flat data structures to data-driven personas as interfaces for understanding users opens new possibilities for interaction among stakeholders, data-driven personas, and analytics. By using data-driven personas as the interfaces for analytics data, decision-makers can imbue analytics systems with the benefits of both empathic psychological bonds of personas between stakeholders and user data, creating data-driven persona analytics systems.

5.5 THE ROAD AHEAD FOR THEORY AND PRACTICE

Data-driven personas from online analytics data can be used to "give faces to data" as the frontend interface to interactive systems for understanding users (Jansen et al., 2020). To this end, there are ample research opportunities, including increasing levels of data granularity and user studies concerning the deployment of such systems and persona interactivity (Eiband et al., 2018). Optimal persona UIs and features are other central targets for future research.

The features and functionalities presented here are based on discussions with real users in several user studies (Salminen et al., 2019; Salminen et al., 2018b). However, the actual interaction between the users and these experimental interaction features needs to be empirically addressed, calling for future work in HCI domains, computing science, information science, and other related fields focused on user understanding.

The approach of combining data-driven personas and analytics into an integrated persona analytics system has several theoretical implications. First, it addresses the conceptual criticism that personas are not actionable (Chapman and Milham, 2006) at the individual user level. With data-driven personas as the interface to an analytics system, a given persona can be directly associated with individual users in the foundational user data. Second, the integration helps offset the issue with a reliance on numbers solely for personalization without conceptually understanding user goals, pain points, and underlying needs (Nielsen, 2019b). Third, the combination of data-driven personas and analytics makes possible the generation of tens to hundreds to thousands of data-driven personas for a given user population (Jansen et al., 2019), increasing the personas' coverage of the underlying user data.

The practical implications for managers and practitioners of combining data-driven personas and analytics into an integrated persona analytics system are derived from the direct linkage from conceptualization with personas to implementation with actual user data. First, data-driven personas are now actionable, as the personas accurately reflect the data (Sim et al., 2019). As an illustrative scenario, executives can make <u>strategic</u> decisions about users or customers based on a set of data-driven personas, given that ease of communication is one of the hallmarks of personas. Mid-level managers (Cai et al., 2020), using the system's analytics aspect, can isolate the specific user segment represented by a given data-driven persona and communicate <u>tactical</u> goals relating to that segment. Finally, designers, information managers, or marketers can identify the individual users represented by the given data-driven persona and contained within the market segment and then carry out <u>operative</u> tasks based on this information. This full-stack implementation aspect has not been available with personas or analytics previously.

Overall, the capabilities and conceptual enhancement of data-driven personas as an interface to full-stack persona analytics systems (Springer and Whittaker, 2019) present much promise for employing data-driven personas for leveraging user information and impacting decision-making in organizations.

5.6   CHAPTER TAKE-AWAYS

- Traditionally, personas as flat files were primarily a data structure.

- Data-driven personas can function as interfaces to persona analytics systems and underlying user data.

- These persona analytics systems become full-stack implementations, going from conceptual personas to operational analytics and linked user data.

- These persona analytics systems address some of the shortcomings of personas and analytics through the integration.

5.7   DISCUSSION AND ASSESSMENT QUESTIONS

1. List the advantages of personas, and list the advantages of analytics. Compare and contrast the two.

2. Select a current analytics tool/service/platform. Identify areas where the incorporation of data-driven personas could improve its functionality.

3. Compare and contrast assumption-driven personas and data-driven personas in their ability to relate to and simplify the presentation of both user data and users.

4. Rank the pros and cons of a persona analytics system relative to some other system that you are familiar with to understand users. Explain your ranking of the pros and cons.

5. List, describe, and explain the implementation of the three levels of a persona analytics system.

6. Describe the impact of interactive data-driven personas on managerial work.

5.8   REFERENCES

Aboelmaged, M. and Mouakket, S. (2020). Influencing models and determinants in big data analytics research: A bibliometric analysis. *Information Processing and Management*, 57(4), 102234. DOI: 10.1016/j.ipm.2020.102234. 120

Ait Hammou, B., Ait Lahcen, A., and Mouline, S. (2020). Towards a real-time processing framework based on improved distributed recurrent neural network variants with fastText for social big data analytics. *Information Processing and Management*, 57(1), 102122. DOI: 10.1016/j.ipm.2019.102122. 120

An, J., Kwak, H., Jung, S., Salminen, J., and Jansen, B. J. (2018). Customer segmentation using online platforms: Isolating behavioral and demographic segments for persona creation via aggregated user data. *Social Network Analysis and Mining*, 8(1), 54. DOI: 10.1007/s13278-018-0531-0. 120

Bonnardel, N. and Pichot, N. (2020). Enhancing collaborative creativity with virtual dynamic personas. *Applied Ergonomics*, 82, 102949. DOI: 10.1016/j.apergo.2019.102949. 121, 123

Cai, M., Wang, Y., and Gong, Z. (2020). An extension of social network group decision-making based on TrustRank and personas. *International Journal of Computational Intelligence Systems*, 13(1), 332–340. DOI: 10.2991/ijcis.d.200310.001. 130

Chapman, C. N., Love, E., Milham, R. P., ElRif, P., and Alford, J. L. (2008). Quantitative evaluation of personas as information. *Proceedings of the Human Factors and Ergonomics Society Annual Meeting*. Volume 52, pp. 1107–1111. DOI: 10.1177/154193120805201602. 127, 128

Chapman, C. N., and Milham, R. P. (2006). The personas' new clothes: Methodological and practical arguments against a popular method. *Proceedings of the Human Factors and Ergonomics Society Annual Meeting*. Volume 50, pp. 634–636. DOI: 10.1177/154193120605000503. 121, 122, 130

Chu, E., Vijayaraghavan, P., and Roy, D. (2018). Learning personas from dialogue with attentive memory networks. *Proceedings of the 2018 Conference on Empirical Methods in Natural Language Processing*. pp. 2638–2646. https://www.aclweb.org/anthology/D18-1284. DOI: 10.18653/v1/D18-1284. 123

Cooper, A. (1999). *The Inmates Are Running the Asylum: Why High Tech Products Drive Us Crazy and How to Restore the Sanity*, 1st edition. Sams - Pearson Education. 119

Cooper, A. (2004). *The Inmates Are Running the Asylum: Why High Tech Products Drive Us Crazy and How to Restore the Sanity*, 2nd edition. Pearson Higher Education. 119, 122

Eiband, M., Schneider, H., Bilandzic, M., Fazekas-Con, J., Haug, M., and Hussmann, H. (2018). Bringing transparency design into practice. *23rd International Conference on Intelligent User Interfaces*. pp. 211–223. DOI: 10.1145/3172944.3172961. 129

Gao, G. and Gao, G. (2019). A survey of user profiles methods. *Data Analysis and Knowledge Discovery*, 3(3), 25–35. DOI: 10.11925/infotech.2096-3467.2018.0784. 119

Hong, B. B., Bohemia, E., Neubauer, R., and Santamaria, L. (2018). Designing for users: The global studio. *DS 93: Proceedings of the 20th International Conference on Engineering and Product Design Education (E&PDE 2018)*, Dyson School of Engineering, Imperial College, London. September 6–7, 2018, pp. 738–743. 123

Jansen, B. J., Jung, S., and Salminen, J. (2019). Creating manageable persona sets from large user populations. *Extended Abstracts of the 2019 CHI Conference on Human Factors in Computing Systems*. pp. 1–6. DOI: 10.1145/3290607.3313006. 130

Jansen, B. J., Salminen, J., and Jung, S. (2020). Data-driven personas for enhanced user understanding: Combining empathy with rationality for better insights to analytics. *Data and Information Management*, 4(1). https://content.sciendo.com/view/journals/dim/4/1/article-p1.xml. DOI: 10.2478/dim-2020-0005. 124, 129

Johanssen, J. O. (2018). Continuous user understanding for the evolution of interactive systems. *Proceedings of the ACM SIGCHI Symposium on Engineering Interactive Computing Systems.* pp. 1–6. DOI: 10.1145/3220134.3220149. 121

Jung, S., An, J., Kwak, H., Ahmad, M., Nielsen, L., and Jansen, B. J. (2017). Persona generation from aggregated social media data. *Proceedings of the 2017 CHI Conference Extended Abstracts on Human Factors in Computing Systems.* pp. 1748–1755. 121

Jung, S., Salminen, J., An, J., Kwak, H., and Jansen, B. J. (2018). Automatically conceptualizing social media analytics data via personas. *Proceedings of the International AAAI Conference on Web and Social Media (ICWSM 2018). International AAAI Conference on Web and Social Media (ICWSM 2018),* San Francisco, California. 122

Lee, D. D. and Seung, S. H. (1999). Learning the parts of objects by non-negative matrix factorization. *Nature*, 401(6755), 788–791. DOI: 10.1038/44565. 127

Li, J., Galley, M., Brockett, C., Spithourakis, G., Gao, J., and Dolan, B. (2016). A persona-based neural conversation model. *Proceedings of the 54th Annual Meeting of the Association for Computational Linguistics (Volume 1: Long Papers).* pp. 994–1003. DOI: 10.18653/v1/ P16-1094. 123

Ma, Y., Mao, J., Ba, Z., and Li, G. (2020). Location recommendation by combining geographical, categorical, and social preferences with location popularity. *Information Processing and Management*, 57(4), 102251. DOI: 10.1016/j.ipm.2020.102251. 120

Misuraca, M., Scepi, G., and Spano, M. (2020). A network-based concept extraction for managing customer requests in a social media care context. *International Journal of Information Management*, 51, 101956. DOI: 10.1016/j.ijinfomgt.2019.05.012. 122

Nielsen, L. (2019a). Persona writing. In L. Nielsen (Ed.), *Personas—User Focused Design.* Springer. pp. 55–81 DOI: 10.1007/978-1-4471-7427-1_4. 120

Nielsen, L. (2019b). *Personas—User Focused Design,* 2nd edition 2019 edition. Springer. DOI: 10.1007/978-1-4471-7427-1. 119, 130

Nielsen, L. and Storgaard Hansen, K. (2014). Personas is applicable: A study on the use of personas in Denmark. *Proceedings of the SIGCHI Conference on Human Factors in Computing Systems.* pp. 55–811665–1674. DOI: 10.1145/2556288.2557080. 119

Oliveira, M. L., Rivero, L., de Oliveira Neto, J. N., Santos, R., and Viana, D. (2018). Developing an application for dealing with depression through the analysis of information and requirements found in groups from a social network. *Proceedings of the XIV Brazilian Symposium on Information Systems.* pp. 1–10. DOI: 10.1145/3229345.3229354. 122

Pichler, R. (2012). A template for writing great personas (Vol. 2017). http://www.romanpichler.com/blog/persona-template-for-agile-product-management/. 120

Pruitt, J. and Adlin, T. (2006). *The Persona Lifecycle: Keeping People in Mind Throughout Product Design*, 1st edition. Morgan Kaufmann. DOI: 10.1145/1167867.1164070. 119

Pruitt, J.,and Grudin, J. (2003). Personas: Practice and theory. *Proceedings of the 2003 Conference on Designing for User Experiences*. pp. 1–15. DOI: 10.1145/997078.997089. 119, 122

Ricotta, F. and Costabile, M. (2007). Customizing customization: A conceptual framework for interactive personalization. *Journal of Interactive Marketing*, 21(2), 6–25. DOI: 10.1002/dir.20076. 122

Salminen, J., Jansen, B. J., An, J., Kwak, H., and Jung, S. (2018a). Are personas done? Evaluating their usefulness in the age of digital analytics. *Persona Studies*, 4(2), 47–65. DOI: 10.21153/psj2018vol4no2art737. 123

Salminen, J., Jung, S., An, J., Kwak, H., Nielsen, L., and Jansen, B. J. (2019). Confusion and information triggered by photos in persona profiles. *International Journal of Human-Computer Studies*, 129, 1–14. DOI: 10.1016/j.ijhcs.2019.03.005. 129

Salminen, J., Jung, S., Chowdhury, S. A., Sengün, S., and Jansen, B. J. (2020a). Personas and analytics: A comparative user study of efficiency and effectiveness for a user identification task. *Proceedings of the ACM Conference of Human Factors in Computing Systems (CHI'20)*. DOI: 10.1145/3313831.3376770. 123

Salminen, J., Liu, Y.-H., Sengun, S., Santos, J. M., Jung, S., and Jansen, B. J. (2020b). The effect of numerical and textual information on visual engagement and perceptions of AI-driven persona interfaces. *IUI '20: Proceedings of the 25th International Conference on Intelligent User Interfaces*. pp. 357–368. DOI: 10.1145/3377325.3377492. 121

Salminen, J., Nielsen, L.,Jung, S., An, J., Kwak, H., and Jansen, B. J. (2018b). "Is more better?": Impact of multiple photos on perception of persona profiles. *Proceedings of ACM CHI Conference on Human Factors in Computing Systems (CHI2018)*. DOI: 10.1145/3173574.3173891. 129

Sim, G., Shrivastava, A., Horton, M., Agarwal, S., Haasini, P. S., Kondeti, C. S., and McKnight, L. (2019). Child-generated personas to aid design across cultures. In D. Lamas, F. Loizides, L. Nacke, H. Petrie, M. Winckler, and P. Zaphiris (Eds.), *Human-Computer Interaction – INTERACT 2019* (pp. 112–131). Springer International Publishing. DOI: 10.1007/978-3-030-29387-1_7. 130

Spiliotopoulos, D., Margaris, D., and Vassilakis, C. (2020). Data-assisted persona construction using social media data. *Big Data and Cognitive Computing*, 4(3), 21. DOI: 10.3390/bdcc4030021. 123

Springer, A. and Whittaker, S. (2019). Progressive disclosure: Empirically motivated approaches to designing effective transparency. *Proceedings of the 24th International Conference on Intelligent User Interfaces*. pp. 107–120. DOI: 10.1145/3301275.3302322. 122, 130

Stamatelatos, G., Gyftopoulos, S., Drosatos, G., and Efraimidis, P. S. (2020). Revealing the political affinity of online entities through their Twitter followers. *Information Processing and Management*, 57(2), 102172. DOI: 10.1016/j.ipm.2019.102172. 120

Stevenson, P. D. and Mattson, C. A. (2019). The personification of big data. *Proceedings of the Design Society: International Conference on Engineering Design*, 1(1), 4019–4028. DOI: 10.1017/dsi.2019.409. 120

Szczuka, J. M. and Krämer, N. C. (2019). There's more to humanity than meets the eye: Differences in gaze behavior toward women and gynoid robots. *Frontiers in Psychology*, 10. DOI: 10.3389/fpsyg.2019.00693. 121

Tahara, S., Ikeda, K., and Hoashi, K. (2019). Empathic dialogue system based on emotions extracted from tweets. *Proceedings of the 24th International Conference on Intelligent User Interfaces*. pp. 52–56. DOI: 10.1145/3301275.3302281. 124

Vecchio, P. D., Mele, G., Ndou, V., and Secundo, G. (2018). Creating value from social big data: implications for smart tourism destinations. *Information Processing and Management*, 54(5), 847–860. DOI: 10.1016/j.ipm.2017.10.006. 122

Webb, R. (2018). *12 Challenges of Data Analytics and How to Fix Them*. https://www.clearrisk.com/risk-management-blog/challenges-of-data-analytics. 123

Zhang, X., Brown, H.-F., and Shankar, A. (2016). Data-driven personas: Constructing archetypal users with clickstreams and user telemetry. *Proceedings of the 2016 CHI Conference on Human Factors in Computing Systems*. pp. 350–5359. DOI: 10.1145/2858036.2858523. 123

Part 4

Using Data-Driven Personas

CHAPTER 6

Challenges of Applying Data-Driven Persona Development

This chapter reviews issues and challenges of data-driven-persona development. We introduce an analytical framework for ethical dimensions to assess if data-driven personas are fair and representative of minority groups while also countering the perpetuation of stereotypes. The complicated intersections of people and technology form the basis of this ethical inquiry of data-driven persona development. By exploring how the individual steps in data-driven persona development correspond with algorithms, we present a model for considering data-driven persona ethics. This is based on procedural justice—that fairness can best be assured when considering every step of an algorithmic process. We also introduce four values of algorithmic transparency. The result is a set of guiding questions that consider the entire life cycle of data-driven persona development from collecting datasets to the interface between personas and end-users. We conclude with three key principles of ethical decision-making in data-driven persona development.

6.1 COMMON CHALLENGES OF APPLYING DATA-DRIVEN PERSONA DEVELOPMENT

With the increased availability of online user data, be it in-house or online, alongside more advanced algorithmic techniques (An et al., 2018a, 2018b), data-driven persona development opportunities are growing (Vecchio et al., 2018). As noted in earlier chapters, this user data can be obtained through social media platforms (e.g., Facebook, YouTube), digital analytics services (e.g., Adobe Analytics, Google Analytics), or CRM data. Much of the earlier chapters have focused on the benefits of this approach.

Data-driven persona development has some weaknesses, however, particularly pertaining to the following.

- **Complexity:** User data obtained through this method may require complex algorithms for interpretation (Dhakad et al., 2017; Holmgard et al., 2014).

- **Disconnection:** Segmentation may not represent the goals and priorities of the end-users (Goodman-Deane et al., 2018; Hirskyj-Douglas et al., 2017).

- **Outliers:** The statistical weight of the majority of users may hide insightful outliers (Tychsen and Canossa, 2008; Zhang et al., 2016).

- **Targeting:** Personas may only depict some existing users and not all desired users (Bamman et al., 2013; Brickey et al., 2012; Holden et al., 2017).

Interestingly, data-driven persona development often-cited concerns that may closely resemble the reported advantages of data-driven persona development or even parallel the concerns with qualitative research (see Table 6.1). This indicates that the idealized rewards of data-driven persona development are not always accomplished in reality. For example, many research articles begin with the premise: "data-driven persona development is ideal because it does require manual steps and is objective," but conversely conclude by suggesting that "data-driven persona development might be improved if enhanced manual steps and subjectivity" (Salminen et al., 2020). Moreover, the manual processes are part of the data-driven persona development methods aimed at establishing the hyperparameters for the algorithms and determining the persona description by, for example, selecting a photo and writing a detailed description for the persona profiles.

Table 6.1: SWOT analysis of each of the major persona creation approaches. Note that the concerns of data-driven persona developments correspond with qualitative persona creation but manifest in different ways.

	Qualitative	Data-Driven	Mixed-Methods
Strengths	Detailed and nuanced insights	Detailed and testable observations of behaviors	More subtle explanations of observed behaviors
Weakness	Limited data and testable hypotheses	Circumscribe insights into goals, desires, and pain points	Difficult to integrate disparate data
Opportunities	Enhanced methods of data collection	Availability of online analytics data	Algorithmic approaches for understanding qualitative data
Threats	Rapidly changing user population requiring further rounds of data collection	Constant change to APIs, services, and platforms	Diverge user segments resulting in conflicting insights

Evidently, as shown in Table 6.1, the data-driven persona development concerns correspond with those of the qualitative methods, but they are expressed in different ways for each approach. In particular, manual steps in the data-driven persona development must address the superficiality of the data-driven persona development outputs. But manual choices, from initial data to final personas, elicit several possible opportunities for bias in decision-making. For example, the decision of what photo to use for a persona is not random at all, and the photo could have a significant impact on end-user stereotyping of the persona along with variables, such as gender, age, and ethnicity (Hill et al., 2017; Salminen et al., 2018a).

In addition, some cite that manual persona development data collection is costly (An et al., 2018a). Yet survey data collection, the most common data source for data-driven persona development, necessitates the recruitment of a rich sample of participants and therefore requires a high cost.

There is, therefore, a dilemma in the automation of persona creation: *how do we make data-driven personas more rich, convincing, and informative?*

This endeavor requires increasing versatility in data-driven persona development approaches, with more and more algorithmic techniques needing to distinguish the specific nuances of online audiences. For example, one algorithm might need to identify demographic characteristics and another algorithm to identify behavioral characteristics. Because each novel method adds to the personas' accumulated measurement error, computationally intensive data-driven persona development methods are highly susceptible to a cascading failure of user representation.

Suppose even one category of information in the persona is incorrectly projected. In that case, this error will also be misrepresented in the other information in the persona, as the information sources are interconnected in the database.

The following section will briefly summarize common issues that have arisen in discussions of data-driven persona development challenges. Specifically, these involve:

    a.   lack of standardized measures,

    b.   method-specific weaknesses,

    c.   data quality,

    d.   data availability,

    e.   consistency,

    f.   human and machine biases, and

    g.   lack of concern for outliers.

6.1.1   LACK OF STANDARDIZED EVALUATION MEASURES

There are no centralized standards for assessing data-driven personas' quality due to the diversity of quantitative approaches. Validation metrics can verify the methods; however, the lack of a unified metric transferable across the various techniques is a severe disadvantage. By necessity, authors become obliged to generalize findings because of the limited number of final personas produced.

While authors can certainly create more personas for documenting subtler and esoteric characteristics, this could result in personas being too detailed to be useful. Based on their objectives, researchers must, therefore, consider the opportunity cost of including and/or excluding fringe personas.

Method-Specific Weaknesses

Every data-driven persona development approach has its advantages and disadvantages. As mentioned in an earlier chapter, one of the main problems of k-means clustering is that it requires a single demographic group to fit neatly into a unique persona (Kwak et al., 2017). In reality, however, several behavioral segments can be identified in one demographic group, as individuals in the same demographic can, and often do, act differently depending on the context. Also, data-driven personas do not immediately project themselves into a final form. Instead, several manual steps are required to translate the quantitative findings into persona profiles.

Wöckl et al. (2012, p. 3) have noted: "a main challenge when creating personas from quantitative data is the translation of numerical output into text." This underscores the complicated relationship between automation and manual input when it comes to data-driven personas. Therefore, rather than expecting full automation and objectivity from data-driven persona development, decision-makers are urged to know the limits of automation and algorithms in delivering accurate and reliable user representations.

Data Quality

Numerical data is often identified as the most significant benefit of data-driven persona development compared to qualitative personas. Even so, many papers identify obstacles to data-driven methods. Mijač et al. (2018) highlight time and/or cost factors as a barrier to the volume of data that can be compiled and subsequently evaluated, particularly due to the high cost of recruiting survey participants.

Tu et al. (2010) discuss significant concerns with objectivity when survey designers choose which questions are asked (and, thus, which responses to evaluate) from surveys. Ford et al. (2017) also outline survey responses' subjectivity and note that some participants may overstate their experiences depending on the context, such as evaluating their productivity levels.

Data Availability

Another major concern of data-driven persona development is the limitation on data availability that crucially reduces the effectiveness of fully rounded persona profiles (Nielsen, 2019). Data concerns are attributed not only to the quality of the original data but also to the lack of rich user insights. This illustrates the major breadth-depth trade-off of using data-driven versus qualitative data. As a result, data-driven personas may appear superficial and incapable of providing a rich narrative understanding that designers often seek.

Moreover, data is not always accessible in the form that research teams need, as analytics platforms place restrictions on what user data can be accessed (e.g., not reporting engagement metrics by demographics) and the quantity (e.g., enforcing thresholds or sampling for data exports). As described by Wöckl et al. (2012, p. 4), "*Due to numerical constraints, the number of variables used for creating clusters is limited, and additional associated variables are needed to allow a more detailed precision.*"

Furthermore, restricted datasets lead to issues with the applicability and/or adoption of findings to other settings, since the datasets reflect only one context (e.g., one academic institution; Kim and Wiggins, 2016) or users of one website (e.g., YouTub; An et al., 2018a). This limits researchers from extending the generalizability of their personas to other contexts. A further challenge involves combining data from different sources, as file formats and features may vary greatly between digital platforms (Mijač et al., 2018). Hence, there is a lack of "cross-platform" personas in the literature. Online platforms also regularly change their practices on what data they share and how this information can be used, requiring continuing resource expenditure to maintain persona processes reliant on these datasets.

Data Consistency

A practical issue when adapting machine learning models to persona creation is that these models tend to expire. New data, data science algorithms, and feature extraction techniques tend to improve predictive performance over time. However, when applying updated models to the persona system, previous characteristics of personas can change (e.g., names, pictures, topics of interest). This can cause inconsistency for users who want to visit older personas. The following quote describes the issue from an end-user's perspective: "I've faced [this problem], as there are certain personas I like (or dislike), then at some point can't find them."

This problem can significantly disrupt the user experience. Consider the case of "Where did Jessica go?" There is a persona named "Jessica" that appears one month and disappears the next. In the January generation of personas, the user sees five personas, one of which is "Jessica." In February, there are again five personas, but this time none of them are Jessica. Now, where did Jessica disappear to? (see Table 6.2).

Table 6.2: After only a few months, the personas generated from the same source channel have drastically changed when using a data-driven methodology

(a) Old Personas					(b) New Personas from the Same Data Source				
	Name	Gender	Age	Country		Name	Gender	Age	Country
	Jessica	Female	25	U.S.		Andrew	Male	30	U.S.
	Salih	Male	26	Pakistan		Vihaan	Male	33	Philippines
	Elon	Male	25	U.S.		Camila	Female	22	U.S.
	Ning	Male	25	Philippines		Tyler	Male	22	U.S.
	Joseph	Male	25	UK		Vivaan	Male	25	India

There are a few potential explanations here. First, the concept drift issue: The user attributes have drastically changed, causing Jessica to disappear. But that is not the only potential explanation. It may also be that the persona generation algorithm is overly sensitive for data drifts, with a small tolerance for change in the baseline data. In such cases, at different periods, one would receive very different personas, causing inconsistencies for users familiarizing themselves with and expecting a particular persona to appear over time.

One solution is to "lock" the older persona generations so that they remain always available. However, at times this may be difficult, for example, when it would result in the co-existence of several topic taxonomies (old and new) for the same data. In such cases, manual reconciliation is needed.

Human and Machine Biases

It is essential to note that the data quantity does not automatically result in a higher quality of people. Instead, the personas inherit any biases and errors in the results. Online data platforms rarely disclose their methods of interpreting user attributes. This makes the measurement error unknown when creating personas from digital analytics data. Similarly, algorithms, especially when combined with skewed user data, can contribute to intensified prejudices, causing the applicability of personas to be inaccurate or even detrimental to decision-making in the wild.

For example, stereotyping is the classic problem of qualitative persona creation (Marsden and Haag, 2016a). In the earlier days of data-driven personas, it was believed that algorithms would solve this problem by being "objective," but it was soon realized that this is not the case. Algorithms generalize, too. They tend to rely on means and other central tendencies when processing data. So, although the human bias is removed in data-driven persona creation, it is replaced by algorithmic bias (Kirkpatrick, 2016; Salminen et al., 2019b; Salminen et al., 2019b).

Therefore, using algorithms for de-stereotyping (or de-biasing) the personas is a crucial concern for data-driven personas. Solving the concern is impaired by the intractable way data-driven algorithms pick persona features. In other words, an algorithm's choices are not always entirely understood. Some algorithms also involve random initialization that can make the personas inconsistent when repeating their generation from the same user data. However, there are broadly available means to manage the randomness of algorithms, such as recording the random seed for replicating a given persona generation.

Lack of Consideration for Outliers

Most data-driven persona development research focuses on majority users (i.e., the user segment that is the largest). Moreover, since most researchers are limited in resources and are also generating personas for particular applications, identifying outlier personas is often not a major concern. Therefore, outliers are usually intentionally removed from the data (Jansen et al., 2016).

Statistical algorithms in data science tend to emphasize means and averages, which means anomalies are considered less relevant (or so difficult to deal with it is easier to ignore them). This is at odds with the current push toward the inclusiveness of personas by the HCI research community (Goodman-Deane et al., 2018; Hill et al., 2017) by examining outliers, deviating behaviors, and underrepresented minorities (Hill et al., 2017; Marsden and Haag, 2016). These so-called fringe personas are not just a statistical consideration of outliers but an ethical issue of justice for understanding these user segments.

The design of personas to represent fringe communities requires special attention to data collection methods and collaborative efforts with minority stakeholders to generate the necessary information.

Addressing the Challenges

Overall, data-driven persona development methods represent the best attempts to use the tools and approaches that are obtainable at a given time. To increase trust in data-driven persona development, authors can (a) apply triangulation using independent samples to validate personas and (b) increase algorithmic transparency by including detailed steps on where the data originates, how it was extracted, and what analysis steps resulted in the final persona profiles. Unfortunately, few studies deploying data-driven persona development follow this best practice of reporting the results.

6.2   ETHICS IN DATA-DRIVEN PERSONA DEVELOPMENT APPLICATION

As the topic of ethics has emerged in the field of computing systems, the ethics of data-driven persona development have also come under more scrutiny. Per the escalating demands for normative analysis of algorithms (Eslami et al., 2018), an ethical review of data-driven persona development is necessary. While data-driven persona development resolves certain concerns with qualitative persona creation (Jung et al., 2019; Salminen et al., 2018, 2019a), current methods can still present new sources of prejudice, a lack of transparency (Salminen et al., 2019b), and other ethical challenges.

In an overarching view, data-driven persona development may be thought of as an attempt to disaggregate aggregated data, which is how analytic platforms typically present such user data. Therefore, the most salient normative issues concern the (a) ethics of categorization, bias, and discrimination, as well as (b) the question of algorithmic transparency. Above all, data-driven persona development can be interpreted as an attempt to extrapolate aggregated data. Therefore, the most prominent ethical concerns concern (a) categorization, bias, and prejudice, and (b) algorithmic transparency. The following section outlines the ethical dimensions of data-driven persona development, identifying key issues that should be considered when creating personas.

6.2.1   SIX ETHICAL DIMENSIONS ANALYTICAL FRAMEWORK

Gillespie (2014) identified six ethical dimensions (ED) of "public relevance" algorithms (see Table 6.3). This framework is relevant as it covers multiple areas of ethics that are relevant to data-driven persona development. The underlying principle is one of procedural justice (Lee et al., 2019), which demands that every action in the data-driven persona development is precise, equitable, reliable, discernable, and ethical (Green and Chen, 2019; Grgić-Hlača et al., 2018).

Table 6.3: Six ethical dimensions (EDs), as identified by Gillespie (2014)

Ethical Dimension (ED)	
ED1: Patterns of Inclusion	The choices behind what makes it into the dataset in the first place, what is excluded, and how data is made algorithm ready
ED2: Cycles of Anticipation	The implications of algorithm providers' attempts to thoroughly know and predict their users, and how the conclusions they draw can matter

Ethical Dimension (ED)	
ED3: Evaluation of Relevance	The criteria by which algorithms determine what is relevant, how those criteria are obscured from users, and how they enact political choices about appropriate and legitimate knowledge
ED4: Promise of Algorithmic Objectivity	The way the technical character of the algorithm is positioned as an assurance of impartiality, and how that claim is maintained in the face of controversy
ED5: Entanglement with Practice	How users reshape their practices to suit the algorithms they depend on, and how they can turn algorithms into terrains for political contest, sometimes even to interrogate the politics of the algorithm itself
ED6: Production of Calculated Publics	How the algorithmic presentation of publics back to themselves shape a public's sense of itself, and who is best positioned to benefit from that knowledge

ED1: Patterns of inclusion: As Gillespie (2014) explains, algorithms are pointless unless paired with data points. The first aspect of Gillespie's six dimensions refers to the decisions of what data is included in a dataset and how the data is configured for algorithmic use. This relates to identifying the data sources and variables for data-driven persona development. Exclusion patterns influence the data derived from social media platforms. This includes when sensitive material is excluded and/or the data only contains user-specific content. The datasets for data-driven persona development are typically extracted from the application program interfaces (APIs) of social media sites (Jung et al., 2017).

Therefore, data are already filtered in specific ways that may encompass patterns of prejudice. Structured relationships across variables also influence user analytics in potentially misleading ways. Therefore, the ethical design problem here concerns practices of inclusion in data collection and database design. It is particularly concerned with what is included and, perhaps more significantly, what is excluded from the datasets. Furthermore, how do these selections pertain to principles of access and fairness?

ED2: Cycles of anticipation: The second dimension involves the implications of the efforts by algorithm providers to understand and define their users. In the context of data-driven persona development, a major concern is that the data that is most comprehensible to the algorithm represents actual users. Although a social media platform can document a substantial amount of data about its users, the platform is restricted to only knowing "what it is able to know" (Gillespie, 2014, p. 173). Consequently, what prevails from user analytics is merely a blunt estimation of a real user, or an "algorithmic identity," in which certain details of users are preserved, and others are neglected. These identities function as "shadow bodies" that permeate through information systems (Gillespie, 2014).

Thus, this suggests that "objectivity" of data-driven personas (An et al., 2018a, 2018b) may not be reality, particularly when the source data is biased. There may be a misalignment between actual users and their algorithmic bodies. When these faulty user analytics are reflected back into personas' development, the question arises: *How to lower the risk that a significant number of user characteristics, which play a key role in user experience and decision-making, are overlooked or biase*d?

ED3: The evaluation of relevance: Gillespie's third dimension relates to the considerations by which algorithms assess the relevance and promote certain kinds of information. The corresponding step in data-driven persona development is the process by which personas are automatically generated. The assessment of relevance is an ethical concern because algorithms may inadvertently introduce new biases or magnify existing ones (Binns, 2017). These concerns may arise when applying NLP methods in persona generation. For example, Bolukbasi et al. (2016) showed that word embeddings trained on news stories reinforce common gender stereotypes and risk maintaining patterns of discrimination.

For data-driven persona development, a major concern is the effect of racial stereotypes when creating personas (Salminen et al., 2018a). While data-driven persona development algorithms may be tasked to disregard protected attributes, this approach can be inadequate because protected attributes can be deduced from other attributes. Moreover, discarding protected attributes from personas may also lead to issues of relevance. For example, a persona by proxy has a race. Let us consider criminal personas or personas at risk (see Figure 6.1).

The selection of the persona's ethnicity can reinforce negative stereotypes (e.g., a criminal persona being African-American). As a result, data-driven persona development becomes politicized and is no longer seen as objective and unbiased. Thus, stereotypes ultimately become intertwined with algorithmic decision-making in data-driven persona development. However, equally important ethical questions are, "What if this ethnicity actually and truly represents the underlying data?" and, if so, "Is it ethical to change the ethnicity in order not to be politicized?"

Therefore, algorithmic bias concerns are related to the data-driven persona development's first steps of identifying the unique user interaction patterns from the given dataset and then matching those distinct user interaction patterns to the demographic user group. Data-driven persona development also reverses the vector of ethical inquiry when it inserts characteristics—including potentially protected attributes such as ethnicity, gender, or family status—back into the algorithm: first at the collective level (by identifying prevalent demographic groups from a dataset) and finally at the level of the individual (by creating shell personas using demographic characteristics). These are important steps that ensure the personas are credible because personas without these features are of little value.

Figure 6.1: Jason, a Criminal Persona. If ethnicity is a protected variable, how should criminal personas be portrayed? Showcasing an African-American persona would reinforce negative stereotypes while excluding this race from the datasets entirely would inaccurately reflect source data. Our recommendation is to consider the entire cast of data-driven personas instead of focus on individual personas and subsequently ensure racial parity. This means showing both white and black criminal personas, for example, if the resulting set of personas accurately reflect the source data.

Thus, the primary concern is how to fulfill the principle of fairness and non-discrimination in the latter stages of data-driven persona development, particularly when the algorithm reintroduces group demographics and characteristics (including protected attributes) into aggregated data. The issue at hand rests on an ethical understanding of algorithmic categories and estimated correlation.

ED4: The promise of algorithmic objectivity: Data-driven persona development harnesses the power of categories and algorithmic profiling by inferring demographic representations from data. Creating demographic categories around an interaction pattern requires some form of classification based on projected similarity. This raises ethical issues because the linkage of two or more variables through a seemingly objective computational logic may imply such linkages as natural and self-evident, which in turn may perpetuate existing social inequalities and prejudices. Such linkages may be applied to situations that are less than ethical (Ananny, 2016).

Additionally, categories define the different information in a fixed way that deters alternatives. The definition of demographic brackets, which includes and excludes certain demographic attributes, and how they are viewed and represented are all problems that need to be regarded in an ethical understanding of data-driven persona development.

Another key issue for fair persona creation is that only one dominant feature value can be selected for certain characteristics like age, gender, or ethnicity (Salminen, Jung, and Jansen, 2019a). In addition to the strategies discussed above, avoiding discrimination in this stage of the data-driven persona development process may require the post-processing of categories or the revision of decisions to ensure equal distribution between protected and unprotected groups (Mittelstadt et al., 2016; Salminen et al., 2019). For example, it is possible to deliberately incorporate variations in the underlying user base by creating additional information to persona profiles that highlight the diversity beyond displaying only the dominant user attributes (Salminen et al., 2019).

Therefore, the management of algorithms relates closely to algorithmic transparency. The more that is known about algorithmic decision-making, the more effectively it can be assessed for fairness. In most but not all cases, transparency of algorithmic decision-making leads to increased fairness (Lee et al., 2019; Zarsky, 2016).

Algorithmic transparency is dictated by the clarity and validity of standards, the representativeness of data, and the rationale of decision outcomes (Lee et al., 2019; see Table 6.4). In the case of data-driven persona development, these considerations lead to the following goal: Data-driven persona development should be communicated in a straightforward way that promotes decision-making in a specific scenario while outlining how the persona information is developed.

Table 6.4: Four principles for algorithmic transparency (Lee et al., 2019)

	Principle
1: Clarity of standards	Transparency about how algorithms process information from datasets, how fairness is operationally defined, and how well the algorithm achieves its objectives
2: Validity of standards	The sharing of standards to enable people to question whether they are acceptable for the decision context
3: Representativeness of information	The evaluation of overlap between algorithmic standards and the beliefs and preferences of end-users
4: Rationale of decision outcomes	The inclusion of textual, statistical, and visual evidence and examples that illustrate how the algorithm made a specific judgment

ED5–6: The entanglement with practice and the production of calculated publics: The discussion thus far has focused on the ethics of data-driven persona development from online user analytics. The way end-users engage with personas is another factor to consider, especially as persona use has been shown to contain political undertones (Marsden and Haag, 2016; Rönkkö, 2005). The concern here is with the fifth and sixth ethical dimensions of Gillespie's model: *the coupling of practice* (how users interact with algorithmic outputs) and the *development of calculated publics* (how the algorithmic portrayal of publics shapes a public's sense of itself) (Gillespie, 2014).

Political motivations and prejudices among persona users have been raised as challenges (Hill et al., 2017; Rönkkö, 2005). Personas based on statistics and data can give stakeholders more credibility and power, as data can be weaponized to facilitate political agendas within institutions, even when it is produced through procedures that are not well established (Siegel, 2010).

As such, an additional key challenge is ensuring how data-driven personas are applied ethically in stakeholders' decision-making. One approach is to ensure that the personas illustrate the cultural richness of the user base that they portray rather than only featuring users that represent the average or majority (Marsden and Haag, 2016). In a way, it is about prompting end-users to acknowledge that their user base, not just a single majority, has fringe behaviors and deviations (Turner and Turner, 2011).

6.2.2   THREE GUIDELINES FOR ETHICAL DATA-DRIVEN PERSONA DEVELOPMENT APPLICATION

Data-driven persona development offers a promising solution to the complexity of big data analytics in many important ways. By extrapolating and portraying big data as personas, data-driven persona development aims to personify algorithms and machine learning and package this information into useful personas. However, because of the unpredictability of human decision-making, both by humans and machines, the normative dimension of the interaction between the personas and end-users should be of importance in data-driven persona development.

To assess data-driven persona development's fairness, three principles of ethical decision-making serve as valuable guidelines (Green and Chen 2019; see Table 6.5).

Table 6.5: Three guidelines for ethical data-driven persona development (adapted from Green and Chen 2019)	
Guidelines	
1: Performance	Users of data-driven personas must be able to make more accurate predictions than they could without the data-driven personas.
2: Transparency	Developers of data-driven personas should accurately assess their own performance and that of the algorithmic data-driven persona development method. It should adjust their use of data-driven personas to account for the technique's accuracy.
3: Representativeness	Users must interact with data-driven personas in ways that are free of bias regarding race, gender, and other areas. This involves encouraging users to establish what information is relevant and develop the capacity to overlook some of the information presented as facts.

6.3   APG ILLUSTRATION

The Automatic Persona Generation (APG) system creates data-driven personas by leveraging behavioral and demographic user segments from social media and other analytics data and then generating data-driven personas by algorithmic means. The persona's profile is enriched with a name, nationality, and photo, which may engender stereotyping. One feature that APG uses to address this is that, via its full-stack analytics approach, it can display to the stakeholders and system users that the presented persona may represent numerous age groups, several nationalities, and multiple genders.

For example, in Figure 6.2, by explaining the dialog box that displays the algorithmic weights for the demographics, APG shows that the data-driven persona actually represents multiple age groups and nationalities.

Figure 6.2: Ashley, represented in the persona profile as a 30-something Black American female. With the display of the algorithmic weight, one can see that the persona actually represents multiple age groups and nationalities, although the Female-30-something-American is the most highly weighted.

6.4   CHAPTER TAKE-AWAYS

- Issues with data-driven persona development fall into four categories: disconnection, targeting, complexity, and outliers.

- These issues are underscored by lack of standardized measures; data availability, quality, and consistency; human and machine biases (including stereotyping); and lack of concern for outliers by the underlying algorithms.

- Each data-driven persona development method has its limitations for the final application as well as specific requirements on the data type and structure it can process. Thus, not all data works as well with all algorithms.

- Triangulation to validate data and algorithmic transparency are ways to offset some of the challenges and apply personas more effectively.

- Lack of concern for outliers in the application of data-driven personas leads to significant ethical issues. Gillespie's six ethical dimensions are (1) patterns of inclusion, (2) cycles of anticipation, (3) evaluation of relevance, (4) promise of algorithmic objectivity, (5) entanglement with practice, and (6) production of calculated publics. Each of these dimensions corresponds with a different stage of data-driven persona development.

- The four principles for algorithmic transparency are (1) clarity of standards, (2) validity of standards, (3) representativeness of information, and (4) rationale of decision outcomes.

- The three guidelines for ethical data-driven persona development application emphasize ethical issues with (1) persona performance, (2) transparency, and (3) representativeness.

6.5   DISCUSSION AND ASSESSMENT QUESTIONS

1. List the four common categories of data-driven persona development issues. Which one(s) are most harmful from an ethical point of view? Provide justifications.

2. What challenges do both data-driven personas and qualitatively developed personas share? How do these challenges manifest in different ways for persona type?

3. Among the common issues of data-driven persona development, identify two, and describe what methods can be applied to alleviate them.

4. List the six ethical dimensions for analyzing data-driven persona development. At which stage of data-driven persona development is each particular ethical dimension most relevant? Explain why.

5. List the four principles for algorithmic transparency. How can each of them be put into practice?

6. List and define the three ethical guidelines for data-driven persona development. How can each of them be put into practice?

7. How can one prevent perpetuating stereotypes in personas? Use criminal personas as an example. Select another domain andexplain why stereotypes in personas pose an issue. Describe how one prevents perpetuating stereotypes in personas in this new domain.

6.6   REFERENCES

An, J., Kwak, H., Jung, S., Salminen, J., and Jansen, B. J. (2018a). Customer segmentation using online platforms: Isolating behavioral and demographic segments for persona creation via aggregated user data. *Social Network Analysis and Mining*, 8(1), 54. DOI: 10.1007/s13278-018-0531-0. 139, 141, 143, 148

An, J., Kwak, H., Salminen, J., Jung, S., and Jansen, B. J. (2018b). Imaginary people representing real numbers: Generating personas from online social media data. *ACM Transactions on the Web (TWEB)*, 12(4), 27. DOI: 10.1145/3265986. 139, 148

Ananny, M. (2016). Toward an ethics of algorithms: Convening, observation, probability, and timeliness. *Science, Technology, and Human Values*, 41(1), 93–117. DOI: 10.1177/0162243915606523. 149

Bamman, D., O'Connor, B., and Smith, N. A. (2013). Learning latent personas of film characters. *Proceedings of the 51st Annual Meeting of the Association for Computational Linguistics*. pp. 10. 140

Binns, R. (2017). Fairness in machine learning: Lessons from political philosophy. *ArXiv Preprint ArXiv:1712.03586*. 148

Bolukbasi, T., Chang, K.-W., Zou, J. Y., Saligrama, V., and Kalai, A. T. (2016). Man is to computer programmer as woman is to homemaker? Debiasing word embeddings. *Advances in Neural Information Processing Systems*, 4349–4357. 148

Brickey, J., Walczak, S., and Burgess, T. (2012). Comparing semi-automated clustering methods for persona development. *IEEE Transactions on Software Engineering*, 38(3), 537–546. DOI: 10.1109/TSE.2011.60. 140

Dhakad, L., Das, M., Bhattacharyya, C., Datta, S., Kale, M., and Mehta, V. (2017). SOPER: Discovering the influence of fashion and the many faces of user from session logs using stick breaking process. *Proceedings of the 2017 ACM on Conference on Information and Knowledge Management - CIKM '17*. pp. 1609–1618. DOI: 10.1145/3132847.3133007. 139

Eslami, M., Krishna Kumaran, S. R., Sandvig, C., and Karahalios, K. (2018). Communicating algorithmic process in online behavioral advertising. *Proceedings of the 2018 CHI Conference on Human Factors in Computing Systems*. pp. 432. DOI: 10.1145/3173574.3174006. 146

Ford, D., Zimmermann, T., Bird, C., and Nagappan, N. (2017). Characterizing software engineering work with personas based on knowledge worker actions. *Proceedings of the 11th ACM/IEEE International Symposium on Empirical Software Engineering and Measurement*. pp. 394–403. DOI: 10.1109/ESEM.2017.54. 142

Gillespie, T. (2014). The relevance of algorithms. *Media Technologies: Essays on Communication, Materiality, and Society*, 167. DOI: 10.7551/mitpress/9780262525374.003.0009. 146, 147, 150

Goodman-Deane, J., Waller, S., Demin, D., González-de-Heredia, A., Bradley, M., and Clarkson, J. P. (2018). Evaluating inclusivity using quantitative personas. In the *Proceedings of Design Research Society Conference 2018*. *Design Research Society Conference 2018*, Limerick, Ireland. DOI: 10.21606/drs.2018.400. 139, 145

Green, B. and Chen, Y. (2019). The principles and limits of algorithm-in-the-loop decision making. *Proceedings of the ACM on Human-Computer Interaction*. Volume 3, pp. 50–74. DOI: 10.1145/3359152. 146, 151

Grgić-Hlača, N., Zafar, M. B., Gummadi, K. P., and Weller, A. (2018). Beyond distributive fairness in algorithmic decision making: Feature selection for procedurally fair learning. *Thirty-Second AAAI Conference on Artificial Intelligence*. DOI: 10.1145/3178876.3186138. 146

Hill, C. G., Haag, M., Oleson, A., Mendez, C., Marsden, N., Sarma, A., and Burnett, M. (2017). Gender-inclusiveness personas vs. stereotyping: Can we have it both ways? *Proceedings of the 2017 CHI Conference*. pp. 6658–6671. DOI: 10.1145/3025453.3025609. 145, 150

Hirskyj-Douglas, I., Read, J. C., and Horton, M. (2017). Animal personas: Representing dog stakeholders in interaction design. *Proceedings of the 31st British Computer Society Human Computer Interaction Conference*. Volume 37, pp. 1–37:13. DOI: 10.14236/ewic/HCI2017.37. 139

Holden, R. J., Kulanthaivel, A., Purkayastha, S., Goggins, K. M., and Kripalani, S. (2017). Know thy eHealth user: Development of biopsychosocial personas from a study of older adults with heart failure. *International Journal of Medical Informatics*, 108, 158–167. DOI: 10.1016/j.ijmedinf.2017.10.006. 140

Holmgard, C., Liapis, A., Togelius, J., and Yannakakis, G. N. (2014). Evolving personas for player decision modeling. *Computational Intelligence and Games (CIG), 2014 IEEE Conference On*. pp. 1–8. DOI: 10.1109/CIG.2014.6932911. 139

Jansen, B. J., An, J., Kwak, H., and Cho, H. (2016). Efforts towards automatically generating personas in real-time using actual user data. *Qatar Foundation Annual Research Conference Proceedings*, Volume 2016 Issue 1, 2016, ICTPP3230. DOI: 10.5339/qfarc.2016.ICTPP3230. 145

Jung, S., An, J., Kwak, H., Ahmad, M., Nielsen, L., and Jansen, B. J. (2017). Persona generation from aggregated social media data. *Proceedings of the 2017 CHI Conference Extended Abstracts on Human Factors in Computing Systems*. pp. 1748–1755. DOI: 10.1145/3027063.3053120. 147

Jung, S., Salminen, J., and Jansen, B. J. (2019). Personas changing over time: Analyzing variations of data-driven personas during a two-year period. *Extended Abstracts of the 2019 CHI Conference on Human Factors in Computing Systems - CHI EA '19*. pp. 1–6. DOI: 10.1145/3290607.3312955. 146

Kim, H. M. and Wiggins, J. (2016). A factor analysis approach to persona development using survey data. *Proceedings of the 2016 Library Assessment Conference*. p. 11. 143

Kirkpatrick, K. (2016). Battling algorithmic bias: How do we ensure algorithms treat us fairly? *Communications of the ACM*, 59(10), 16–17. DOI: 10.1145/2983270. 145

Kwak, H., An, J., and Jansen, B. J. (2017). Automatic generation of personas using YouTube social media data. *Proceedings of the Hawaii International Conference on System Sciences (HICSS-50)*. pp. 833–842. 142

Lee, M. K., Jain, A., CHA, H., and Ojha, S. (2019). Procedural justice in algorithmic fairness: Leveraging transparency and outcome control for fair algorithmic mediation. *Psychology*, 9, 14. DOI: 10.1145/3359284. 146, 150

Marsden, N. and Haag, M. (2016). Stereotypes and politics: Reflections on personas. *Proceedings of the 2016 CHI Conference on Human Factors in Computing Systems*. pp. 4017–4031. DOI: 10.1145/2858036.2858151. 145, 150, 151

Mijač, T., Jadrić, M., and Ćukušić, M. (2018). The potential and issues in data-driven development of web personas. *2018 41st International Convention on Information and Communication

Technology, Electronics and Microelectronics (MIPRO). pp. 1237–1242. DOI: 10.23919/MIPRO.2018.8400224. 142, 143

Mittelstadt, B. D., Allo, P., Taddeo, M., Wachter, S., and Floridi, L. (2016). The ethics of algorithms: Mapping the debate. *Big Data and Society*, 3(2). DOI: 10.1177/2053951716679679. 150

Nielsen, L. (2019). *Personas—User Focused Design*, 2nd edition, 2019 edition. Springer. DOI: 10.1007/978-1-4471-7427-1. 143

Rönkkö, K. (2005). An empirical study demonstrating how different design constraints, project organization and contexts limited the utility of personas. *Proceedings of the Proceedings of the 38th Annual Hawaii International Conference on System Sciences.* Volume 08. DOI: 10.1109/HICSS.2005.85. 150

Salminen, J., Guan, K., Jung, S., Chowdhury, S. A., and Jansen, B. J. (2020). A literature review of quantitative persona creation. *CHI '20: Proceedings of the 2020 CHI Conference on Human Factors in Computing Systems.* pp. 1–14. DOI: 10.1145/3313831.3376502. 140

Salminen, J., Jung, S., and Jansen, B. J. (2019). The future of data-driven personas: A marriage of online analytics numbers and human attributes. *21st International Conference on Enterprise Information Systems, ICEIS*, 2019. pp. 596–603. DOI: 10.5220/0007744706080615. 150

Salminen, J., Jansen, B. J., An, J., Kwak, H., and Jung, S. (2018). Are personas done? Evaluating their usefulness in the age of digital analytics. *Persona Studies*, 4(2), 47–65. DOI:10.21153/psj2018vol4no2art737. 146

Salminen, J., Jansen, B. J., An, J., Kwak, H., and Jung, S. (2019a). Automatic persona generation for online content creators: Conceptual rationale and a research agenda. In L. Nielsen (Ed.), P*ersonas—User Focused Design*, 2nd ed. Springer London. pp. 135–160 DOI: 10.1007/978-1-4471-7427-1_8. 146

Salminen, J., Jung, S., and Jansen, B. J. (2019a). The future of data-driven personas: A marriage of online analytics numbers and human attributes. *ICEIS 2019 - Proceedings of the 21st International Conference on Enterprise Information Systems.* pp. 596–603. DOI: 10.5220/0007744706080615. 148

Salminen, J., Jung, S., and Jansen, B. J. (2019b). Detecting demographic bias in automatically generated personas. *Extended Abstracts of the 2019 CHI Conference on Human Factors in Computing Systems*, LBW0122:1-LBW0122:6. DOI: 10.1145/3290607.3313034. 145

Salminen, J., Nielsen, L., Jung, S., An, J., Kwak, H., and Jansen, B. J. (2018a). "Is more better?": Impact of multiple photos on perception of persona profiles. *Proceedings of ACM CHI Conference on Human Factors in Computing Systems (CHI2018).* DOI: 10.1145/3173574.3173891. 141, 148

Salminen, J., Santos, J. M., Jung, S., Eslami, M., and Jansen, B. J. (2019b). Persona transparency: Analyzing the impact of explanations on perceptions of data-driven personas. *International Journal of Human–Computer Interaction*, 0(0), 1–13. DOI: 10.1080/10447318.2019.1688946. 145, 146

Siegel, D. A. (2010). The mystique of numbers: Belief in quantitative approaches to segmentation and persona development. *CHI '10 Extended Abstracts on Human Factors in Computing Systems*. pp. 4721–4732. DOI: 10.1145/1753846.1754221. 151

Tu, N., Dong, X., Rau, P. P., and Zhang, T. (2010). Using cluster analysis in persona development. *2010 8th International Conference on Supply Chain Management and Information*. pp. 1–5. 142

Turner, P. and Turner, S. (2011). Is stereotyping inevitable when designing with personas? *Design Studies*, 32(1), 30–44. DOI: 10.1016/j.destud.2010.06.002. 151

Tychsen, A. and Canossa, A. (2008). Defining personas in games using metrics. *Proceedings of the 2008 Conference on Future Play: Research, Play, Share*. pp. 73–80. DOI: 10.1145/1496984.1496997. 140

Vecchio, P. D., Mele, G., Ndou, V., and Secundo, G. (2018). Creating value from social big data: *Implications for Smart Tourism Destinations. Information Processing and Management*, 54(5), 847–860. DOI: 10.1016/j.ipm.2017.10.006. 139

Wöckl, B., Yildizoglu, U., Buber, I., Aparicio Diaz, B., Kruijff, E., and Tscheligi, M. (2012). Basic senior personas: A representative design tool covering the spectrum of European older adults. *Proceedings of the 14th International ACM SIGACCESS Conference on Computers and Accessibility*. pp. 25–32. DOI: 10.1145/2384916.2384922. 151, 143

Zarsky, T. (2016). The trouble with algorithmic decisions: An analytic road map to examine efficiency and fairness in automated and opaque decision making. *Science, Technology, and Human Values*, 41(1), 118–132. DOI: 10.1177/0162243915605575. 150

Zhang, X., Brown, H.-F., and Shankar, A. (2016). Data-driven personas: Constructing archetypal users with clickstreams and user telemetry. *Proceedings of the 2016 CHI Conference on Human Factors in Computing Systems*. pp. 5350–5359. DOI: 10.1145/2858036.2858523. 140

CHAPTER 7

Use Cases for Data-Driven Personas

This chapter explores use cases of data-driven personas. In particular, we discuss 12 specific use cases in 3 general types: (1) <u>analytical</u>, (2) <u>interactive</u>, and (3) <u>team-centered</u> use cases. The use cases are presented from the viewpoint of <u>end-users</u> of the personas. By "end-users", we refer to the professional stakeholders that make decisions based on the personas or communicate with other stakeholders using the personas. As such, end-users are different from the "users" that the personas represent. The chapter contains action points for both data-driven persona end-users and persona developers.

7.1 TOWARD USE CASES OF DATA-DRIVEN PERSONAS

An important concept for data-driven persona use cases is **Personas + X**, which refers to the idea that personas always require a use case to deliver value-in-use (see Figure 7.1). To realize the potential of data-driven personas as user representations, the data-driven personas need to be coupled with real use cases, tasks, decision-making scenarios, or actual problems in user-centered design.

$$\text{Personas} \quad + \quad X \left\{ \begin{array}{l} \bullet \text{ Business Goals} \\ \bullet \text{ Scenarios} \\ \bullet \text{ Assumptions} \\ \bullet \text{ Use Cases} \\ \bullet \text{ Narratives} \\ \bullet \text{ Jobs to Do} \end{array} \right.$$

Figure 7.1: To obtain value from personas, one needs to couple them with actual decision-making scenarios, use cases, or goals.

One approach for making the "X" more concrete is replacing it with a specific user-related goal. For example, in marketing, X can indicate goals such as growing sales, improving ad click-through rates, collecting less expensive sales leads, or collecting more leads. Thus, the question would become, for example, "How do we grow <u>sales</u> using data-driven personas?" In this case, <u>sales</u> is the value of the variable <u>X</u>. Such a question is a starting point in data-driven persona design.

In the following subsections, we present 12 use cases (i.e., the "X") for data-driven personas, divided into 3 general categories.

1. **Analytical use cases:** focused on finding insights from the user data using descriptive information and passive observation.

2. **Interactive use cases:** analyzing the user data based on flexible system functionality and the active participation of persona users for modifying and manipulating that data.

3. **Team-centered use cases:** practical activities for user understanding in an organizational setting.

The use cases (UCs) are based on the accumulated knowledge and insights gathered by the authors from their multi-year research on data-driven personas, developing an interactive persona system for industry use, and assisting organizations with the implementation and use of these personas. We include specific implementation examples when applicable. Table 7.1 shows an overview of the use cases, and the following subsections explain each use case.

Table 7.1: Data-driven persona use cases by type

Analytical Use Cases	Interactive Use Cases	Team Use Cases
Customer Journey Mapping	On-Demand Persona Generation	Communicating Data via Personas
Behavioral Modeling	User Sentiment Analysis	Challenging Existing Assumptions
Market Gap Analysis	Chat with a Persona	Supporting Design Activities
Longitudinal Analysis of User Interests	Persona Recommendations	Split Testing with Personas

7.2   ANALYTICAL USE CASES

7.2.1   UC1: CUSTOMER JOURNEY MAPPING

Journey mapping is plotting the stages and paths of the users' lifecycle, documenting each persona's unique state of mind, needs, and concerns at each stage. Combining customer journey mapping with data-driven personas is an exciting application area for data-driven personas. The customer journey concept relies on the notion that users or customers engage with an organization's products and messages on various channels at various times. Data-driven personas can help isolate, conceptualize, and communicate information on customer segments that are specifically salient at each step of the customer journey.

A typical manifestation of the customer journey is the conversion funnel, a popular digital marketing concept (Jansen and Schuster, 2011). Figure 7.2 offers an example of using data-driven personas in conjunction with the conversion funnel.

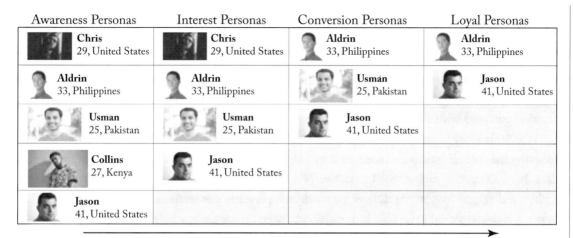

Awareness Personas	Interest Personas	Conversion Personas	Loyal Personas
Chris 29, United States	**Chris** 29, United States	**Aldrin** 33, Philippines	**Aldrin** 33, Philippines
Aldrin 33, Philippines	**Aldrin** 33, Philippines	**Usman** 25, Pakistan	**Jason** 41, United States
Usman 25, Pakistan	**Usman** 25, Pakistan	**Jason** 41, United States	
Collins 27, Kenya	**Jason** 41, United States		
Jason 41, United States			

Conversion Funnel

Figure 7.2: Conversion funnel with the appropriate and relevant data-driven personas.

The key to UC01 is to segment the user data to the corresponding stages of the conversion funnel.

For example, <u>awareness personas</u> can be derived from online advertising account user data. A web analytics metric such as **impressions** can be used for generating data-driven personas from users that were exposed to the organization's ads. Then, the same process can be repeated for users that **clicked** the ads, generating <u>interest personas</u> that showed an interest in the company's offerings. Again, from those that ended up **purchasing**, we can generate <u>conversion personas</u>. Finally, <u>loyal personas</u> represent users that converted and remained loyal over time through **repurchasing**. When altering only the interaction metric the persona generation relies upon (impression/click/purchase/repurchase) and keeping all other parameters for persona generation identical, the differences in the resulting personas reflect the differences in the customer base at each stage of the funnel.

Figure 7.2 describes funnel thinking. The company starts with a set of data-driven personas exposed to its messaging, and this set of personas decreases as users move down the conversion funnel. An alternative is keeping the number of personas <u>constant</u>, meaning that five personas are generated for each stage of the funnel, for example. By comparing the similarities and differences of those personas using quantitative metrics (Jansen et al., 2019b), one can infer insights regarding how user segments change in each step of the conversion funnel.

The choice of the representative metric based on which the data-driven personas are generated is crucial. By switching the metric, the user data changes to correspond to another aspect of user behavior, and the portrayal of the user base therefore changes. There is no right or wrong interaction metric, but the choice depends on what aspect of user behavior we are interested in for a given decision. Therefore, it is crucial to be aware of the possibilities and flexibility that this choice gives. One can create audience personas, first-time customer personas, loyal user personas, and so on. Also, the assumption with there being one metric for one specific generation of personas relies on the interaction matrix approach of APG (see Chapter 4). In this approach, the values in the matrix describe one behavioral trait, and one cannot include multiple metrics (e.g., impressions and clicks) at the same time. Using other algorithmic approaches, that could be possible, perhaps creating personas with a complex behavioral profile.

It is also easy to get lost in complexities, especially since these parallel personas can all coexist, meaning they are all real, as in "based on data." However, they all depict a certain facet of the overall data. In practice, this means that interactive persona systems need to support the flexible creation, saving, and comparison of the different data-driven personas' generations by different metrics. The persona end-users need to be able to transition between these generations, influence their creation, and be kept updated (for example, using automated email notifications) when dramatic changes take place between different persona generations.

- Action points:

    ◦ Map your customer journey or conversion funnel from the user data

    ◦ Create specific data-driven personas for each step of the journey or funnel

    ◦ Analyze commonalities and differences among the data-driven personas

    ◦ Identify opportunities and focus on serving specific personas better

7.2.2   UC2: BEHAVIORAL MODELING

In general, data-driven personas help product developers' get into character and understand their users' circumstances (Cooper, 1999). They facilitate a genuine understanding of the thoughts, feelings, and behaviors of core customers. Individuals have a natural tendency to relate to other humans, and it is important to tap into this psychological effect when making design and product development choices.

Therefore, scenarios and mental modeling have been suggested as fundamental use cases for personas (Grudin, 2006). For example, given a planned design change, we can ask, "What would Hind think of this change?" We can envision each decision's expected impact on a given persona, which can be operationalized as a payoff matrix, an idea from game theory.

For example, consider three personas: James, Hind, and Rachael. Product X is changing—the company employing personas is a start-up that has sold its product for a meager price. It now plans to increase its price and simulate how this change would affect different market segments. The start-up has identified three main segments and created a persona for each. Table 7.2 shows the expected payoffs.

Criteria	James	Hind	Rachael
Key information	Enterprise IT manager	Small-business freelancer	Mid-sized HR manager
Change scenario	Increasing monthly price by 50%	Increasing monthly price by 50%	Increasing monthly price by 50%
Payoff	Acceptable	Unacceptable	Unacceptable
Reasoning	Uses the product among other products; "somebody else" pays, so the increase in the price does not give a reason to cancel, as there is high enough perceived value.	Uses the product actively but needs to mind the overall value; a 50% increase would be too much.	Does not use the product actively, so a substantial decrease would provide an excuse to cut the whole expense.
Estimated maximum accepted change	100%	25%	15%

Table 7.2: Scenario modeling with the expected payoffs for the personas

We can also use the payoff matrix to develop more detailed analyses, for example, to define the accepted level of increase. For example, presume that the start-up runs a survey or a set of interviews with the purpose of scoping the maximum accepted price increase.

The results indicate that the enterprise segment can accept doubling the price because the absolute cost of the product is still small relative to their overall budget. The maximum tolerance would seem to situate the small freelancer segment with an increase of 25%, whereas the mid-sized HR buyer would only tolerate a 15% increase. The start-up makes the decision to create new tiers of the product: one catering to James (100% price increase) and another to Hind (25% increase) while risking losing Rachael altogether, as this segment is not seen as strategically important.

The scenarios can also be more closely related to a specific use case. Figure 7.3 illustrates how data-driven personas can predict how audience segments are likely to react to a specific headline. Using such functionalities, creative workers can simulate content responses and compare different messages before publishing the content.

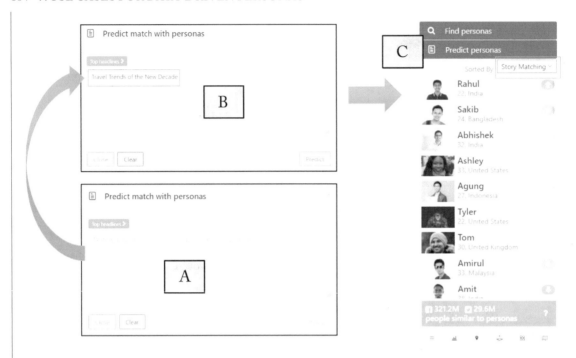

Figure 7.3: Predict personas' interest in a given content headline. A form field is given to the user [A], in which the user types the tested message [B]. By comparing the headline's topic with the personas' topics of interest, the system gives the most and least matching personas [C], indicated by arrows and the sorting function.

- Action points:

  ○ Define strategic decisions that are likely to impact users.

  ○ Identify the data-driven personas that those decisions impact.

  ○ Evaluate the positive and negative effects of the decisions on each data-driven persona (use a payoff matrix).

  ○ Based on the analysis, decide how each data-driven persona should be treated.

7.2.3   UC3: MARKET GAP ANALYSIS

In general, the concept of "intelligent analysis" refers to pre-computing insights from the data and presenting these insights in a salient way to end-users of personas. So, conceptually, this means refining information to knowledge and, more precisely, to a form of actionable knowledge. The creation of intelligent analyses in any analytics system, not only in data-driven personas, requires both creativity and understanding of the type of decisions the end-users make and the kind of information they need for those decisions.

A good litmus test for separating actionable insights from noise is by testing with real users: present them with a function and ask if they find it valuable for decision-making. Also, ask the users to elaborate on why they answered yes or no, and describe, in their own words, a situation detailing when and how they would make use of the insight.

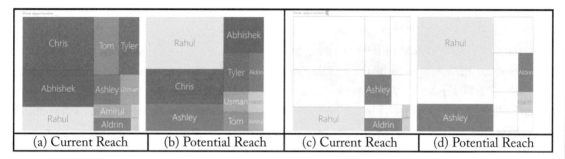

| (a) Current Reach | (b) Potential Reach | (c) Current Reach | (d) Potential Reach |

Figure 7.4: The left-side picture—(a) and (b) describe current reach and potential reach without intelligent filtering. The right-side picture—(c) and (d) has the filter enabled (toggle button on the top-left screen), which makes the potential personas visually salient for end-users. "Potential" implies that these personas (Rahul, Ashley, Aldrin, and Harith) represent larger segments than their share in the data. Screenshot from the Automatic Persona Generation system, https://persona.qcri.org.

As there are endless possibilities in creating intelligent analyses, we cannot present a comprehensive list of them. However, one example is presented in Figure 7.4 that illustrates what we mean by facilitating end-users' ability to infer insights from the personas. Users can enable the filtered view, and the system shows the opportunities to increase overall audience size, as calculated by the background algorithm. The use case scenario here is that of increasing the overall reach of the organization. The system shows the current audience sizes and the potential audience sizes of each segment, represented by a persona. Both pieces of information are derived from real user data.

Thus, by making those user segments with the highest growth potential visually salient through a heuristic calculation, the system has performed an "intelligent" analysis that serves as a starting point. The end-user can now select a data-driven persona with a large growth potential (e.g., Rahul in Figure 7.4) and learn more about this persona in order to devise persona-specific growth strategies.

- Action points:

  ○ Define the data-driven personas that together represent your overall market.

  ○ Determine how big of a representation each persona has in your current audience.

○ Determine how big of a representation each persona has in the total market.

○ Compare the two previous figures to identify gaps: situations in which the persona's share in the external market is much higher than the share in the current audience.

○ Decide what data-driven personas to pursue and how.

7.2.4   UC4: LONGITUDINAL ANALYSIS OF USER INTERESTS

An interesting and essential task where data-driven personas and automation can be beneficial is understanding the changes in or the stability of user preferences over time (Jansen et al., 2019a; Jung et al., 2019). Figure 7.5 illustrates such functionality: The persona system automatically detects periods where a certain persona is not present in the time-series. For end-users, this information can signify that activation campaigns are needed to increase the engagement of the said segment.

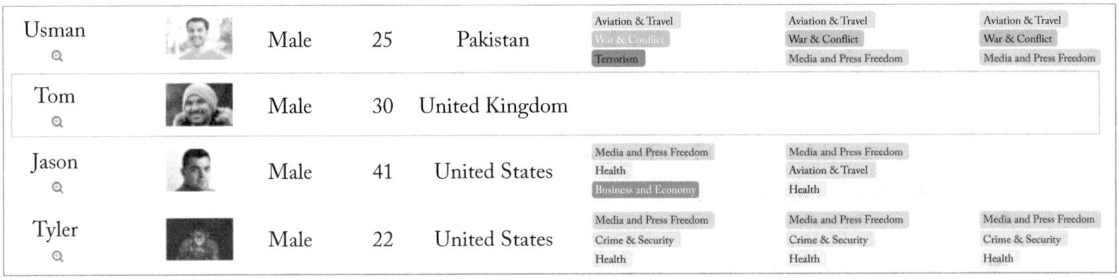

Figure 7.5: Persona chronology shows that Tom (highlighted) had dropped from the generated personas during the inspection period of the three latest months, despite his having been present previously.

• Action points:

○ Divide your user data into periods.

○ Create data-driven personas for each period, using an identical algorithmic process.

○ Analyze the results by identifying (a) loyal personas that consistently engage with your products, (b) sporadic personas whose engagement appears unpredictable, and (c) inactive personas that engaged previously but not anymore.

○ Try to explain why these patterns occur and how they could be influenced.

7.3   INTERACTIVE USE CASES

7.3.1   UC5: ON-DEMAND PERSONA GENERATION

Even though advances in HCI have led to the discovery and creation of numerous interaction techniques between end-users and computational systems, to date, data-driven personas still tend to be more descriptive. One of the most visible signs of this is that the information in data-driven personas is pre-selected, either by the algorithm or by the persona developers. In contrast, end-users cannot alter the personas' information on the fly, nor choose particular information elements before the persona is created in order to create flexible personas whose information supports the design task at hand.

In the future, persona analytics systems will most likely allow flexible segmentation based on different input metrics and/or other data (such as keywords or sentiment in the user quotes). Essentially, the more end-users are able to narrow down the datasets before the creation of data-driven personas, the more flexible, task compatible personas they can create.

An example of a flexible persona generation is presented in the following.

1. Upload data onto the persona generation system (e.g., CRM records).

2. Narrow data based on criteria of interest (e.g., gender = Female; age = 45–50 when wanting to focus on this segment).

3. Choose generation metric (e.g., number of product views).

4. Choose enrichment information (e.g., include social media quotes that correspond to product pain points).

5. Choose the number of personas (e.g., five personas).

6. Generate.

Data-driven persona users are passive consumers of information and tools and support their active involvement with the creation of personas. As the persona user is the best expert on what information is needed for a specific decision-making scenario, they are also the best experts for crafting task-specific personas from the available components afforded by interactive persona systems.

- Action points:

    ○ Ensure all team members have a say in the creation of the data-driven persona, especially regarding the personas' information design.

    ○ Investigate (e.g., by using card sorting) what kinds of personas team members would create.

○ Use these mock-up personas as a basis for a more robust, data-driven persona generation.

7.3.2 UC6: USER SENTIMENT ANALYSIS

Aspect-based sentiment analysis refers to the investigation of user sentiments in relation to a specific topic (Cambria et al., 2013). For example, what does a user think of Real Madrid? (Note: Real Madrid is a football club that is just being used as an example; it could be any football club.) Some users (i.e., fans of Real Madrid) would have a highly positive sentiment toward this brand, while others (e.g., fans of Barcelona FC) would most likely perceive it negatively.

Data-driven personas can be a gateway to investigating such sentiments. An example is given in Figure 7.6, where social media comments from the persona's most-viewed content are filtered using a specific topic ("Aviation and Travel") and sentiment (negative). Using different combinations of these sentiment and topic filters, persona users can investigate the personas' attitudes and opinions about specific issues. In the background, the system has collected a large number of social media comments, associated them with a given persona, and classified each comment for both topic and sentiment.

Figure 7.6: What issues does Chris have with the "Aviation and Travel" content? We can explore this question by filtering Chris' most-viewed content's comments using the topic and sentiment filters. For example, doing so shows that some users have issues with video translations ("Always amazes me how inaccurate the translations are on these videos").

- Action points:

    ○ Apply aspect-based approach for modeling data-driven personas' views of particular topics.

    ○ Define the topics of interest that matter for the decision-makers.

    ○ Acquire data that reflects those topics (e.g., social media comments).

    ○ Attribute the comments to each generated persona.

    ○ Classify the sentiment of each comment.

    ○ Enable stakeholders to easily filter and view sentiments by topic (deploy interactive systems).

7.3.3   UC7: CHAT WITH A PERSONA

An exciting yet highly unexplored perspective of interaction is the use of dialogue systems that enable end-users to converse with the persona (Chu et al., 2018). This can be seen as a more sophisticated version of the previous use case: instead of filtering the comments, the persona end-user can now ask the person directly using natural language. For example, we can devise ways to group user-generated social media comments by aspects by using NLP algorithms. An example of an aspect can be the comments' sentiment on a given topic. Alternatively, an aspect can represent the likely political affiliation expressed in a comment. In practice, such classes can be achieved by means of text analytics by, say, a supervised machine learning classifier.

Then, given each group has (a) enough separability, which they should have if the classifier performs well, and (b) enough samples, which they should have if the dataset is extensive enough, we would apply a text-generation algorithm. The text-generation algorithm basically learns to generate sentences that correspond with the source data and a user-given input, such as "What do you think of Israel–Palestine conflict?"

Thus, the data-driven personas can cover different opinion ranges and generate sentences that correspond with the sentiment aspect of the persona given a user question. An unknown factor is the dataset size required for accurate and representative opinions. In theory, the more generalized one wants the persona to be, the more data one needs to have. Meaning, if one wants to ask the persona about sports, politics, entertainment, and so on, many samples are needed to cover all conceivable topics. However, if one only wants to ask about politics, you need less data. In practice, this can result in the creation of narrow discussion personas, such as "political personas," "sports personas," and so on, that could be gradually combined into personas that contain more and more aspects.

Figure 7.7: Prototype implementation of chat functionality in a data-driven persona profile (middle of the picture).

In addition, one needs to define the use case: on what occasions would the end-user want to converse with a persona? What would they ask? Why? The first step would be to define these information needs and then figure out ways to collect datasets that contain the answers.

- Action points:

    ○ Explore novel ways to enable two-way interactions with data-driven personas and decision-makers.

    ○ Create a list of questions decision-makers would like to ask personas under various decision-making scenarios.

7.3.4   UC8: PERSONA RECOMMENDATIONS

An important benefit of data-driven persona systems is the creation of more personas to describe more fine-grained user segments, increasing diversity in the persona set and representing the user data more comprehensively (see Figure 7.8).

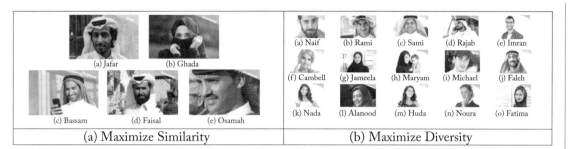

Figure 7.8: Generating data-driven personas to accommodate specific design goals. In some cases, designers may want to see the most typical personas that represent the averages in the user data (a). In other cases, they may want to see personas from a broader range of age, gender, and nationality. (b) Maximizing diversity often requires increasing the number of personas to better represent the underlying user data.

Previous research has created up to thousands of personas with more and more granular details (and smaller audience representation) (Chapman et al., 2008), but there have been no attempts to constrain the persona generations by design goals such as diversity or accuracy. As there are metrics that enable the quantification of these goals, we expect that future research and development will attempt the creation of numerous personas and then recommend a suitable number based on the end-user's goal of diversity or accuracy.

- Action points:

  ○ Capture decision-makers' choice of personas.

  ○ Analyze why decision-makers choose specific personas.

  ○ Consider these insights in persona design.

  ○ Develop ways to match specific data-driven personas with specific decision-makers.

7.4   TEAM-CENTERED USE CASES

7.4.1   UC9: COMMUNICATING DATA VIA PERSONAS

A typical use of data-driven personas is communicating across teams, departments, or organizational divisions (Nielsen, 2019). While it is challenging to discuss users using a spreadsheet, it is much easier to speak about a person or people. Thus, sharing the created persona profiles across divisions increases the chance for the realization of persona benefits for decisions that require empathetic user understanding. This is because, ideally, data-driven personas keep team members focused on customer needs.

Note that, depending on the type of decisions, other formats for presenting user data, such as charts, tables, and figures, can still be highly useful and more appropriate than data-driven personas (see Figure 7.9). The simple criterion is, "Do the decisions we are making in this meeting require an empathetic understanding of our users as people?" If not, data-driven personas are not necessarily needed or might not be the most appropriate method. If yes, data-driven personas can either replace the charts, tables, and figures or complement them as grounds for effective decision-making about users.

(a)   (b)

Figure 7.9: Information-centered analytics (a) vs. persona analytics (b). Information-centered analytics focuses on charts, numbers, and tables to present user data. Persona analytics is human-centered, meaning that all data is represented within the data-drive persona profiles. When communicating user data for strategic business decisions, an information-centered paradigm might be more appropriate. When communicating user data for design decisions that require empathetic user understanding, persona analytics is valuable.

There are various views and opinions on which decision-making situations personas fit. In their article, Salminen et al. (2018) evaluate the usefulness of personas in the age of analytics. They argue that the usefulness of personas depends on the granularity of data needed for the decision, as well as its level of automation. For strategic decisions, the level of granularity tends to be high: Decision-makers want overviews and snapshots to make important decisions based on aggregated data. For this, tables and charts are compelling. However, it has also been suggested that decision-makers can keep personas in mind while making strategic decisions. In fact, a persona can become a "silent member in the boardroom," evoked to question the customer impact of the considered decisions.

For micro-level decisions, such as those dealing with specific user segments, data-driven personas are naturally useful, as they personify the user segments. Nonetheless, Salminen et al. (2018) argue that when going to the extreme micro-level, the usefulness of personas wavers. This is because automation can take manual decision-making in situations of personalization, recommendation, dynamic pricing, and so on. While algorithms in these user cases tend to use aggregated data (e.g., in collaborative filtering), personas represent a redundant level of aggregation for the specific decision. For example, non-negative matrix factorization or similar data algorithms can be applied to discover patterns from the data for recommendation systems, but the results can be directly used for recommendations to any given individual user without the need to enrich the patterns and present them as personas. Therefore, the degree of automation matters when considering the applicability of data-driven personas.

- Action points:

  ○ Investigate the data aggregation requirements for different types of decisions taking place in the organization.

  ○ Evaluate, for each decision type, if aggregated or individual data is more usefu.

  ○ Apply data-driven analytics tools accordingly; for those decisions that require an aggregated view and empathetic understanding, deploy data-driven personas.

7.4.2 UC10: CHALLENGING EXISTING ASSUMPTIONS

Based on our practical observations in many organizations, business decision-makers often ignore systematic testing because they have a pre-defined idea of the user (i.e., the persona) and are not ready to see their ideas challenged. In psychology, this is called confirmation bias—the person seeks information that confirms their presumptions and ignores information contrary to those assumptions (Tversky and Kahneman, 1974).

It is important to note that sometimes the presumptions can be correct or in the correct direction. Heuristics and stereotypes are not always useless, as they make decision-making more efficient under incomplete information and uncertainty. Nevertheless, the question "Who is the real user?" is too important to leave to assumption alone. For this reason, a simple exercise is to make the implicit and tacit assumption of personas visible and then give a reality check by comparing them to the actual data on users.

The process for this can be carried out as follows.

1. Survey the staff, asking them to describe a small number (e.g., 3–5) of typical user types for the organization.

2. Analyze the results and build assumption-based personas constructed on the most dominant answers—these represent the construct of the assumption personas.

3. Next, investigate the actual data. Segment the user data according to the same variables that were mentioned by the staff into the same number of personas. These are your data-driven personas.

4. Compare the assumption personas with data-driven personas: what are the major differences? What about similarities?

5. Present your findings to everyone in the organization.

A practical scenario is corporate or business-to-business (B2B) sales. Salespeople tend to have entrenched views and tacit knowledge of the buyers. These tacit insights can be both a benefit and a disadvantage, depending on their accuracy and applicability. Data-driven methods can be used to corroborate the preconceived insights among the organization's professionals (Nielsen et al., 2017) and produce additional information (e.g., pain points, objections for buying). Thus, data-driven personas can help make the organization's tacit sales knowledge concrete and visible for everyone as well as test its boundaries and validity. In both cases, the level of situational awareness increases.

- Action points:

    ○ Ensure awareness of the current preconceptions that team members have about different user segments (i.e., what the segments are and their opinion of each segment).

    ○ Capture these preconceptions into assumption-based personas.

    ○ Collect real user data and create data-driven personas.

    ○ Compare the assumption-based personas with data-driven personas.

    ○ Communicate the findings in the organization to correct false preconceptions and align the team members' understanding of the users.

7.4.3 UC11: SUPPORTING DESIGN ACTIVITIES

Data-driven personas can support design activities in a variety of domains and fields of application.

For example, the online advertising industry—and the online content creation industry as well—is rapidly moving into a situation where algorithms of the "super platforms" (Salminen, 2009) decide what ads (or content) are shown to which user. This implies that the created content needs to be competitive. More emphasis will be placed on an empathetic understanding of the user, *less* on making choices regarding targeting (because the platforms take over this activity). A user study shows that persona-like "PUGs" (personified user groups) (Salminen et al., 2020b) can enhance ad performance for certain end-users, especially those experienced with personas and ad creation. The goal for research and development in this regard is to support a virtuous cycle of persona employment:

user data

➤ data-driven personas

➤ enhanced empathy among end-users

➤ more effective ads

➤ high return on investment for persona projects

Research showing tangible benefits of personas, however, is still nascent, despite extensive debate on if personas' work or not (Friess, 2012; Howard, 2015; Matthews et al., 2012; Nielsen and Storgaard Hansen, 2014; Rönkkö et al., 2004; Salminen et al., 2018). One research study shows that personas support user identification tasks better than online analytics systems (Salminen et al., 2020a). This finding supports a virtuous cycle in terms of end-users being able to locate and design for specific user segments while avoiding self-referential designs.

As a practical example, one first creates user segments, then enriches them to data-driven persona profiles. Campaigns and content (or product features/UI) are then tailored to these data-driven personas, and finally, you measure the performance-per-persona to see how well each segment works.

Each step is important. For example, deriving the test personas relies on specific logic: do we want to derive personas that represent the most loyal customers, those with the highest upsell potential or those who *perform poorly but whose performance we want to increase*? A combination of these criteria is also possible. However, the number of data-driven personas should be kept relatively low to facilitate the identification of real effects (higher power).

In practice, one can create three categories: "The Best," "The Underperformers," and "The Should-Be-Bests," with the former category containing 3–5 personas corresponding to the segments generating the most revenue; the middle category containing 3–5 personas of user segments that generate the least revenue; and the last category containing 3–5 personas of segments that should sell well but for some reason are not. Each category is then taken on by a specific design team and testing path, in which tailored campaigns for the category personas are created.

After carrying out testing with each category, it can be seen which design teams were able to achieve the highest lifts in the chosen performance metrics. Results can be reported in the form of a Persona Scorecard (see Table 7.3).

Table 7.3: Persona Scorecard. Results based on campaign testing (fictive numbers). In the scenario, campaigns were tailored for three international personas. Campaigns were run using the same budget, duration, and settings. Results were measured in terms of sales conversions. Color coding indicates campaign profitability: green = positive, yellow = borderline, red = negative.

Persona	Corresponding Ad Segment	Results (conversions)	Profitability	Next steps
James	Based on gender (Male), age (25–34), country (United States), interests (Law, Government, Politics/Legal Issues, Law, Government, Politics/Government Resources, Personal Finance/Financial News, Travel/Travel News and General Info), and language (English)	100		Increase budget (scale-up)
Pinja	Based on gender (Female), age (18–24), country (Finland), interests (Economy, Travel, Natural Environment, Health and Wellness, Religion, Anti-Discrimination, Culture, Sustainable Development, Immigration, Freedom Of Speech, Human Rights), and language (Finnish)	50		Decrease budget, revise campaign content
Niklas	Based on gender (Male), age (25–34), country (Sweden), interests (Education/Education News And General Info, Law, Government, Politics/Legal Issues, Law, Government, Politics/Politics), and language (Swedish)	33		Remove from testing

In addition to user segment creation, the *operationalization of the personas* is equally important. This refers to mapping the data-driven persona's attributes to a larger population. For a design study, this can be the focus group. For testing of marketing communications, the mapping can be done by using the attributes available in an online ad platform (e.g., Facebook Ads, Twitter Ads,

Google Ads). The more mapping criteria are applied, the more confident we can be that the obtained results correspond with the content's intended persona's reactions. For example, in the case of Facebook, we can map data-driven personas with the following information: age, gender, country/city, language, topics of interest, marital status, level of education, job. Subsequently, we can achieve a fairly accurate target group in Facebook Ads that corresponds to the persona's attributes.

- Action points:

    ◦ Integrate data-driven personas into actual optimization workflows.

    ◦ Ensure data-driven personas are part of creative work.

    ◦ Monitor and analyze the performance of the outputs created using personas.

    ◦ Operationalize personas by mapping them with external user populations.

7.4.4   UC12: SPLIT TESTING WITH PERSONAS

Say a creative agency has created two designs for Product X based on the client's brief. The brief focused on two user groups for Product X, and the design team in the creative agency created one design optimized for each of these two groups (i.e., Design A that was optimized for Persona A, and Design B that was optimized for Persona B).

To validate their designs, the team now wants to test these designs using online advertising. They conduct an A/B experiment, where the two target user groups are shown the two test designs. Both groups receive a similar number of impressions, and the design with a higher number of clicks is the winner (they assume clicks indicate interest in the product design).

The team creates an online advertising campaign in which ads are created to correspond with Design A and Design B, and those ads are targeted to Persona A and Persona B. They run the campaign for three weeks and obtain the results shown in Table 7.4.

Table 7.4: Number of clicks when A/B testing with personas (hypothetical example)

	Persona A	Persona B
Design A	500	200
Design B	150	250

Looking at the raw click counts in Table 7.4, we can see that Design A and Design B both appear to be working better for their respective personas, i.e., 500 > 150 and 250 > 200. We can also present the results in a contingency table (Table 7.5) and compute the statistical significance of the results using a 2×2 chi-square test of independence.

Table 7.5: Contingency with the following information: the observed cell totals (the expected cell totals) and [the chi-square statistic for each cell]. Compared groups are the designs.

	Persona A	Persona B	Marginal Row Totals
Design A	500 (413.64) [18.03]	200 (286.36) [26.05]	700
Design B	150 (236.36) [31.56]	250 (163.64) [45.58]	400
Marginal Column Totals	650	450	1100 (Grand Total)

These results indicate that Design A has a significantly better performance than Design B, $X^2(1, N = 1100) = 121.21$, p <.001. Therefore, if we had to choose only one product design, we would choose Design A. However, if we can choose two designs, then we would keep both as the performance of Design B among the target group corresponding to Persona B is 25% better than that of Design A.

In addition to chi-square, t-tests can also be used to measure the performance of the two groups. Such tests are easy to carry out using standard spreadsheet software or online tools.

- Action points:

    ○ Conduct statistically robust testing with personas.

    ○ Continuously develop new experimental ideas and implement them using data-driven personas and performance measurement.

    ○ Prioritize specific personas based on the results.

    ○ Use the results to enrich the person profiles further.

7.4.5   CONCLUSION

Use cases for data-driven personas can be counted in the hundreds, if not thousands. Essentially, every use case one has for user data or analytics, in general, is also a use case for data-driven personas. In this chapter, we only scratched the surface of possibilities with data-driven personas.

What tends to be lacking in the current persona use cases in the field is *interaction*—giving end-users options, features, and functionalities to flexibly alter the information in the personas. To improve upon this condition, a major transition is required from seeing the end-user as a passive recipient of persona information to seeing the user as an active agent that can interact with that information. The end result of interactive persona thinking can be seen in completely responsive and flexible systems, where the end-user *chooses* the information they want to be included in their personas, enabling truly on-demand personas.

Moreover, the transition signifies going from personas delivered in flat-file formats (e.g., PDF, paper, PowerPoint) into personas accessed via UIs that offer layered views of user information, enabling granularity and depth (Jansen et al., 2020; Salminen, Jung, and Jansen, 2019; Salminen et al., 2020c). Showing the predominant user information in the visible layer while providing one-click access to the underlying data distributions can enhance the end-users' notion of the persona being an aggregate (i.e., distribution) of people in reality, which can mitigate stereotypical thinking. Breakdowns can also help explain how the persona information was algorithmically derived (Salminen, Jung, and Jansen, 2020; Salminen et al., 2019).

Web technologies and novel interaction techniques from HCI and NLP provide interesting opportunities for enhanced persona-user interaction. In addition, there are multiple scenarios and use cases for leveraging automation techniques with personas, such as notifying users when their organization's personas change. Development and user experiments related to these scenarios and use cases will maintain the relevance of data-driven personas for the foreseeable future.

7.4.6   APG ILLUSTRATION

One of the advantages of APG system is that it can create fewer or more data-driven personas from the same data on the fly. As shown in Figure 7.10, APG has created 5 data-driven personas and 15 personas, both from the same user data. This allows for the presentation of the user data at different granularity levels, depending on the applied UC and set of stakeholders.

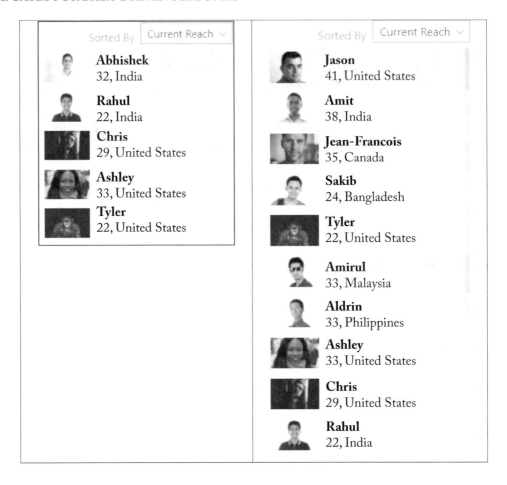

Figure 7.10: APG-generated casts of data-driven personas. These are casts of 5 data-driven personas and then 15 personas. Both casts are generated from the same foundational user data.

7.5   CHAPTER TAKE-AWAYS

- Data-driven personas need something (an "X") to be valuable in practice. This "X" can be a goal, content, use case, job to do, key performance indicator, or other points of focus that makes the application of personas concrete.

- Data-driven personas can be combined with other computational methods, such as systems, recommendation algorithms, predictive models, and so on, in order to enhance the personas' interactivity, flexibility, and applicability in a range of user tasks and scenarios.

- Data-driven personas can be deployed as thinking tools to imagine how a customer segment might react to a given change. By using predictive modeling, these changes can be quantitatively simulated.

- Data-driven personas systems can employ interaction techniques to make useful information more salient for end-users. For this, models can compute and analyze data in the background, and the outcomes can either be shown as default options or made accessible via toggles in the UI.

- The operationalization of data-driven personas can be achieved by mapping personas' attributes with those in the wider user population, such as in a designated focus group or via the use of targeting criteria in online ad platforms.

For practitioners, we offer the following advice.

- Compare customer segments (data-driven personas) in different countries, industries, and job titles. Address the question: What makes the segments different?

- Use data-driven personas to optimize your content marketing in digital channels. This can be achieved by continuously testing the performance of targeted content against the performance metrics obtained from the target group.

- Analyze advertising using data-driven personas. Create different messages for different buyer segments, test messages, and campaigns per buyer persona; also, vary the metrics (CPC/CPL). Bottom line: *How should we address different buyers? What is the advertising ROI of different personas?*

- Targeted offerings can help organizations convert more potential users to subscribers, followers, and customers. You can also use data-driven personas to tailor lead generation strategies, which can improve your lead quality and performance. By approaching your messages from a human perspective, you can create sales and marketing communication that is tailored to your core customers and, therefore, is likely to perform better.

- Carry out well-thought-out experiments with data-driven personas to produce statistically valid business insights. For example, you can run Facebook Ads campaigns targeting segments corresponding to the core personas and analyze whether the campaigns perform better than other customer segments.

7.6   DISCUSSION AND ASSESSMENT QUESTIONS

1. Explain the transition of persona users from passive consumers of information into active participants.

2. With persona users becoming active participants, discuss the requirements this sets for persona systems.

3. Explain the concept of "data-driven personas + X" and provide three examples, each from a different industry vertical.

4. Describe how data-driven personas can be used for customer journey mapping.

5. How can payoffs be used for scenario modeling with data-driven personas?

6. How can data-driven personas be used for the identification of market gaps?

7. Discuss how data-driven personas can be analyzed temporally and provide an example.

8. How can users interact with data-driven personas? List and give three examples.

9. Discuss the differences between information-centered analytics and persona analytics. What are the primary use case implications of each?

10. How can data-driven personas be used for challenging existing assumptions in the organization?

11. Explain what is meant by the "virtuous cycle of persona employment."

12. Provide an example of how to conduct A/B testing with data-driven personas.

13. Invent and present an "intelligent analysis" that a persona system could automatically conduct on user data.

7.7   REFERENCES

Cambria, E., Schuller, B., Xia, Y., and Havasi, C. (2013). New avenues in opinion mining and sentiment analysis. *IEEE Intelligent Systems*, 28(2), 15–21. DOI: 10.1109/MIS.2013.30. 168

Chapman, C. N., Love, E., Milham, R. P., ElRif, P., and Alford, J. L. (2008). Quantitative evaluation of personas as information. *Proceedings of the Human Factors and Ergonomics Society Annual Meeting*, 52(16), 1107–1111. DOI: 10.1177/154193120805201602. 171

Chu, E., Vijayaraghavan, P., and Roy, D. (2018). Learning personas from dialogue with attentive memory networks. *Proceedings of the 2018 Conference on Empirical Methods in Natural Language Processing*. pp. 2638–2646. https://www.aclweb.org/anthology/D18-1284. DOI: 10.18653/v1/D18-1284. 169

Cooper, A. (1999). *The Inmates Are Running the Asylum: Why High Tech Products Drive Us Crazy and How to Restore the Sanity*, 1st edition. Sams - Pearson Education. 162

Friess, E. (2012). Personas and decision making in the design process: An ethnographic case study. *Proceedings of the SIGCHI Conference on Human Factors in Computing Systems*. pp. 1209–1218. DOI: 10.1145/2207676.2208572. 175

Grudin, J. (2006). Why personas work: The psychological evidence. In J. Pruitt and T. Adlin (Eds.), *The Persona Lifecycle*. Elsevier. pp. 642–663 DOI: 10.1016/B978-012566251-2/50013-7. 162

Howard, T. W. (2015). Are personas really usable? *Communication Design Quarterly Review*, 3(2), 20–26. DOI: 10.1145/2752853.2752856. 175

Jansen, B. J., Jung, S., and Salminen, J. (2019a). Capturing the change in topical interests of personas over time. *Proceedings of the Association for Information Science and Technology*, 56(1), 127–136. DOI: 10.1002/pra2.11. 166

Jansen, B. J., Jung, S., and Salminen, J. (2019b). Creating manageable persona sets from large user populations. *Extended Abstracts of the 2019 CHI Conference on Human Factors in Computing Systems*. pp. 1–6. DOI: 10.1145/3290607.3313006. 161

Jansen, B. J., Salminen, J., and Jung, S. (2020). Data-driven personas for enhanced user understanding: Combining empathy with rationality for better insights to analytics. *Data and Information Management*, 4(1). https://content.sciendo.com/view/journals/dim/4/1/article-p1.xml. DOI: 10.2478/dim-2020-0005. 179

Jansen, B. J. and Schuster, S. (2011). Bidding on the buying funnel for sponsored search and keyword advertising. *Journal of Electronic Commerce Research*, 12(1), 1–18. 160

Jung, S., Salminen, J., and Jansen, B. J. (2019). Personas changing over time: Analyzing variations of data-driven personas during a two-year period. *Extended Abstracts of the 2019 CHI Conference on Human Factors in Computing Systems - CHI EA '19*. pp. 1–6. DOI: 10.1145/3290607.3312955. 166

Matthews, T., Judge, T., and Whittaker, S. (2012). How do designers and user experience professionals actually perceive and use personas? *Proceedings of the 2012 ACM Annual Conference on Human Factors in Computing Systems - CHI '12*. p. 1219. DOI: 10.1145/2207676.2208573. 175

Nielsen, L. (2019). *Personas—User Focused Design*, 2nd ed. 2019 edition. Springer. DOI: 10.1007/978-1-4471-7427-1. 171

Nielsen, L. and Storgaard Hansen, K. (2014). Personas is applicable: A study on the use of personas in Denmark. *Proceedings of the SIGCHI Conference on Human Factors in Computing Systems*. pp. 1665–1674. DOI: 10.1145/2556288.2557080. 175

Nielsen, L., Jung, S-G., An, J., Salminen, J., Kwak, H., and Jansen, B. J. 2017. Who are your users? comparing media professionals' preconception of users to data-driven personas. In *Proceedings of the 29th Australian Conference on Computer-Human Interaction (OZCHI '17)*. Association for Computing Machinery, New York, NY. pp. 602–606. DOI: 10.1145/3152771.3156178. 174

Rönkkö, K., Hellman, M., Kilander, B., and Dittrich, Y. (2004). Personas is not applicable: Local remedies interpreted in a wider context. *Proceedings of the Eighth Conference on Participatory Design: Artful Integration: Interweaving Media, Materials and Practices*. Volume 1, pp. 112–120. DOI: 10.1145/1011870.1011884. 175

Salminen, J. (2009). Power of Google: A study on online advertising exchange. Master's thesis. Turku School of Economics. 174

Salminen, J., Jansen, B. J., An, J., Kwak, H., and Jung, S. (2018). Are personas done? Evaluating their usefulness in the age of digital analytics. *Persona Studies*, 4(2), 47–65. DOI: 10.21153/psj2018vol4no2art737. 172, 173, 175

Salminen, J., Jung, S., Chowdhury, S. A., Sengün, S., and Jansen, B. J. (2020a). Personas and analytics: A comparative user study of efficiency and effectiveness for a user identification task. *Proceedings of the ACM Conference of Human Factors in Computing Systems (CHI'20)*. DOI: 10.1145/3313831.3376770. 175

Salminen, J., Jung, S., and Jansen, B. J. (2020). Explaining data-driven personas. *Proceedings of the Workshop on Explainable Smart Systems for Algorithmic Transparency in Emerging Technologies Co-Located with 25th International Conference on Intelligent User Interfaces (IUI 2020)*. p. 7. DOI: urn:nbn:de:0074-2582-4. 179

Salminen, J., Jung, S., and Jansen, B. J. (2019). The future of data-driven personas: A marriage of online analytics numbers and human attributes. *ICEIS 2019 - Proceedings of the 21st International Conference on Enterprise Information Systems*. pp. 596–603. DOI: 10.5220/0007744706080615. 179

Salminen, J., Kaate, I., Kamel, A. M. S., Jung, S., and Jansen, B. J. (2020b). How does personification impact ad performance and empathy? An experiment with online advertising. *International Journal of Human–Computer Interaction*, 0(0), 1–15. DOI: 10.1080/10447318.2020.1809246. 175

Salminen, J., Liu, Y.-H., Sengun, S., Santos, J. M., Jung, S., and Jansen, B. J. (2020c). The effect of numerical and textual information on visual engagement and perceptions of AI-driven persona interfaces. *IUI '20: Proceedings of the 25th International Conference on Intelligent User Interfaces*, 357–368. DOI: 10.1145/3377325.3377492. 179

Salminen, J., Santos, J. M., Jung, S., Eslami, M., and Jansen, B. J. (2019). Persona transparency: Analyzing the impact of explanations on perceptions of data-driven personas. *International Journal of Human–Computer Interaction*, 0(0), 1–13. DOI: 10.1080/10447318.2019.1688946. 179

Tversky, A. and Kahneman, D. (1974). Judgment under uncertainty: Heuristics and biases. *Science*, 185(4157), 1124–1131. DOI: 10.1126/science.185.4157.1124. 173

CHAPTER 8

Using Data-Driven Personas Alongside Other Human-Computer Interaction (HCI) Techniques

The persona technique came into widespread use and acceptance shortly after its inception (Cooper, 1999), although it was sometimes criticized along the way (Laubheimer, 2017; McKeen, 2019) for shortcomings relative to other user research methods. There are different approaches apart from personas that can be used during a user-centered design process. All these approaches have their advantages and shortcomings. In this chapter, we explore the employment of data-driven personas in combination with five other HCI techniques used in a user-centered design process. Personas put the focus on the user by being part of a broader user-centric design process. We also present use cases showing data-driven personas from the APG system. Data-driven personas are flexible artifacts that can be tailored to different projects and can be used at any stage of a product lifecycle. Moreover, data-driven personas can also be efficiently used in conjunction with other user research techniques to reflect (Bradley et al., 2021) a holistic understanding of the end user.

8.1 USE OF DATA-DRIVEN PERSONAS ALONGSIDE OTHER USER-EXPERIENCE RESEARCH TECHNIQUES

In this chapter, we discuss the use of data-driven personas alongside other user-experience (UX) research techniques customarily used within the field of HCI.

- **Scenarios** are stories that describe the context behind a specific user group's behavior and help designers understand their motivations, needs, and barriers.

- **Participatory design** is a collaborative design approach that actively involves different stakeholders, such as customers, partners, and employees, as full participants during a product development lifecycle.

- **Card sorting** is a technique that organizes information into logical groups frequently used to explore architecture, workflow, navigation, etc.

- **Serious games** are designed with a focus on their pedagogical value or solving business problems as opposed to pure entertainment.

- **Agile development** is a framework that advocates adaptive planning and continual updating of requirements based on iterative testing and user feedback.

We discuss each of these UX research techniques while simultaneously highlighting how each can be used alongside data-driven personas. While there are several different approaches—apart from the five mentioned above—to understand a user's needs and wants, we have chosen these techniques because they serve as examples to show the range, versatility, and benefit of data-driven personas when combined with other approaches. It is worth pointing out that this chapter is not meant to be a comprehensive treatise on these techniques. Instead, our main aim is to briefly introduce their core concepts and how they can be paired with data-driven personas. For comprehensive descriptions of each of these techniques, we refer the interested reader to the ample related literature surrounding the topic (e.g., Martin and Hanington, 2012).

8.2   USING DATA-DRIVEN PERSONAS WITH SCENARIOS

Scenarios are short stories that designers craft showing how a user might act to achieve a goal when using a system or product (Young and Barnard, 1986). Scenarios can help the designer understand users' motivations, needs, and barriers, and they can be useful tools to assist in the creation, iteration, and testing of systems and products (Carroll and Rosson, 1990). One can consider scenarios as thought-provoking storytelling exercises that are intentionally created to understand how a user would interact with a particular product or service (Gudjónsdóttir, 2010). A designer or UX practitioner might make a scenario to understand users' motivations, needs, pain points, and more in the context of using the design of a product or service. Ultimately, a scenario is a useful tool that can help in ideating, iterating, and usability testing possible optimal solutions. Scenarios and personas are often paired together where the personas can represent the target users on which the scenario was based.

During the early stages of a product design process, there is frequently a lack of shared understanding regarding the end-users and their needs. Product specifications, sketches, and diagrams can provide an agreement on what a team will attempt to achieve, but there are often also ambiguities, uncertainties, and gaps in communication between designers on the same team (Blanco et al., 2014). Because they are somewhat concrete yet flexible, scenarios on users and their goals and objectives, as well as the sequence of actions and activities, can be useful in the early stages of a project. These are also areas in which the use of personas can be complementary since a persona, by default, helps represent users, their objectives, pain points, goals, and so on. Scenarios are also good communication tools for elaborating and prioritizing requirements and can help designers focus on users and their activities, which are also some of the benefits of personas. Team members and other stakeholders can also benefit from the shared vision of what is to be developed in scenarios (Carrol, 1999), and a consistent view of users represented by personas can support this shared vision.

As scenarios were created by designers as a tool for the imagination, to better understand the motivations, needs, and barriers of a product's potential audience, they frequently focus on the task and work-oriented technology to represent people in the context of work situations. Due to this, scenarios are sometimes confused with user stories, use cases, and Jobs To Be Done (JTBD) cases. However, each is somewhat different and unique—and personas can be integrated with all of them.

User stories are short statements that describe the user's goals and are specifically focused on product features or requirements. Use cases are a stepwise set of instructions for accomplishing certain tasks. A JTBD describes the context in which a user decides to use a given product. Certainly, the boundaries among the three are blurred, but data-driven personas can assist with user stories, use cases, and JTBD in a manner similar to that of scenarios.

For example, when used on their own, scenarios can include unrealistic assumptions about technical feasibility, as scenarios are rarely empirically grounded (Grudin and Pruitt, n.d., p. 3). As such, scenarios have a potential weakness in that they may not be particularly helpful for realistic engagement with real users (Grudin and Pruitt, n.d.). This can be remedied by the use of data-driven personas alongside scenarios, as the latter help in giving a "face" to the user in the scenario. Data-driven personas, specifically, can be a great foundation for building scenarios; as noted by (Grudin and Pruitt, n.d.), they offer an *infrastructure for engagement* that story-based approaches, such as scenarios, may lack. Data-driven personas do this by providing concrete user data for the user and actions of the user presented within the scenario.

Prior work has shown that there are advantages of pairing scenarios and personas. Loke et al. (2005) applied personas and scenarios to develop an interactive, immersive environment that uses motion and presence as its main input. The resulting prototype accounted for the aesthetic and kinaesthetic qualities (i.e., awareness of the body position) of the work and the social interaction aspects of the user experience. Their movement-oriented personas and scenarios enabled the team to build robust shared understandings and *tools to think with* throughout their exhibit's design process. In a post-exercise discussion, several members of the team expressed that their exercise had provided them with surprising revelations in terms of the experience of other participants.

In an empirical study conducted by Blanco et al. (2014), two groups of industrial designers were asked to build their representation of specifications for a digital calendar product, first on their own and then collectively. One group used scenarios and personas, while the other could choose any other working method. The group of designers who had access to personas used them successfully to communicate their viewpoints, evaluate requirements, and identify conflicts. Because they had a set of standard references, the group with the personas could negotiate and take decisions more effectively than the group without them. In terms of convergence, personas and scenarios had a distinctly positive impact, mainly when it came to eliminating unnecessary user requirements that were left open by the lack of detail in the scenario.

By specifically incorporating data-driven personas with scenarios, you can create an infrastructure for engagement that has a foundation in data gathered from real people. In practice, a data-driven persona can be combined with one or more scenarios. Typically, though, a scenario will only be combined with one persona. For this pairing to be successful, however, the use of data-driven personas needs to be complemented with qualitative and quantitative data during the persona creation process. Consider the following user scenario.

> *On a Monday afternoon at work, Mae needs to submit an update to the team's project management workflow system. She is slightly concerned as this will alter the project schedule. She is unsure of the impact on the project, plus she is running late for a meeting with clients. She logs in to the system, locates the correct screen, and enters the workflow change with a note on why the change occurred. She then notifies the other team members, logs off from the system, and heads to her client meeting.*

This scenario can work together with a data-driven persona by serving as the story behind why the particular persona would interact with the system, what the persona hopes to accomplish, and what the characteristics of the persona influencing this interaction are.

For example, Figure 8.1 shows a portion of a data-driven persona from the APG system. The provided characteristics of the data-driven personas help in gaining insights into the possible user (in this case, Mae) in the scenario. Therefore, data-driven personas can be considered a starting point for scenario generation or an instantiation of the user in the already created scenario.

Mae Female, 33, Philippines

Mae is a 33-year-old female living in the Philippines, and she works in Healthcare and Medical Services field. She likes to read about Travel, Sports, Recent Movies, and Healthcare News on her Mobile Device. Her average video viewing time is about 1 minute.

Job — *Healthcare and Medical Services.*

Education Level — *College grad*

Relationship Status — *Single*

With the help of a data-driven persona, we have much more insight into Mae and her background.

Mae is in her thirties and Filipino.

She works in healthcare.

Mae is a college graduate, with a range of non-work interests.

Her primary device for consuming online content is her mobile.

Figure 8.1: Snippet of a data-driven persona from the APG system, illustrating the demographic and behavioral characteristics of the persona that can enrich the context of the user portrayed as the actor in a scenario.

8.3   USING DATA-DRIVEN PERSONAS WITH PARTICIPATORY DESIGN

Participatory design (PD) is an approach that engages stakeholders, such as designers, managers, researchers, and end-users, in the design process to help ensure that the end product meets the intended needs of the stakeholders (Hartson and Pyla, 2019). Conversely, PD can assist in prioritizing the information content in data-driven persona design if PD is used in the creation of the personas themselves.

PD welcomes all stakeholders in the design process by encompassing techniques that gather insights from observing people and working with them to create optimal solutions (Bannon and Ehn, 2012). The assumption behind the inclusion of PD in product development is that stakeholders, such as users, can approach and solve problems in similar ways to designers and developers (Hudson, 2009). Therefore, if a product's success is based on how it is experienced by its users, it is paramount to understand the users' thoughts and feelings, as well as their motivations, their preferences, their inner conflicts, and their emotional and mental models (McDonagh, 2004). In this regard, PD is tailor-made to work in conjunction with personas in order to help ensure that stakeholders have a shared view of the users.

Prior work advocates the integration of personas with PD (Reeder et al., 2014). Combining personas and PD tends to be especially beneficial in large and long-term projects (Cabrero, 2014). Personas have also been reported to be useful in various PD stages, helping bring designers closer to the actual use cases (Bødker et al., 2012).

As an example, an evidence-based self-management asthma app tailored to young people's needs was built using PD approaches and personas (Davis et al., 2018). First, participants were invited to share their lifestyle and asthma needs, as well as their concerns and goals using a paper workbook followed by a face-to-face workshop. The activities included creating artifacts like collages and worksheets that explored their identities and lifestyles, following which participants were asked to answer key research questions related to what would make an app effective, useful, practical, convenient, and emotionally engaging. The resulting data was then used to develop wireframes and create personas that were distilled based on PD sessions with users based on the information provided by the participants. Once the app was developed, participants were invited back to provide their feedback, which was overwhelmingly positive. During the design process, users expressed concern about managing their emotional health. The developers decided to include links in the app to evidence-based mental health support networks, which ended up proving to be a key area for user satisfaction.

The main benefit of using PD approaches alongside a data-driven persona is that the latter helps get an enhanced user understanding based on the results of a PD session. This enhanced understanding could be represented in an easy-to-understand way for stakeholders, enabling them to form a nuanced mental model of the persona. In a traditional data-driven personas case, the algorithm is doing all this, so the details and the "journey of persona creation" remain inaccessible for stakeholders.

However, with an approach like PD, it becomes technically possible to involve stakeholders in the process, thus regaining some of the lost immersion relative to traditional personas. These data-driven personas can serve as tools of integration of user insights to ensure a common understanding among design stakeholders. The data-driven personas can be developed at the start and refined during each step of the PD process. Additionally, the data-driven personas of the users after system development can aid in future features and product enhancements.

For example, Figure 8.2 shows a portion of a data-driven persona from the APG system. The sentiment and the online social media conversations of the data-driven persona provide insights into the sentiment and leanings of the user segment that the data-driven persona represents, helping to present a consistent understanding of the user to stakeholders participating in the design process. For example, if one is engaged in PD and wants the participants to have a shared understanding of the users' current attitude toward the product and discussions surrounding the product, a data-driven persona such as the one in Figure 8.2 would be helpful for this shared understanding.

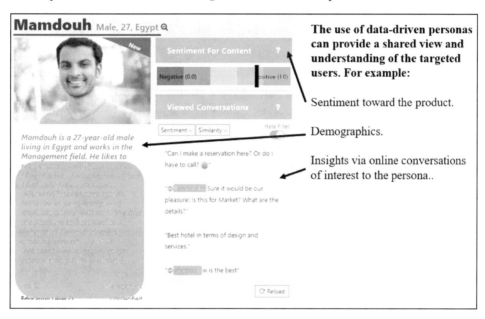

Figure 8.2: Snippet of a data-driven persona from the APG system, illustrating the sentiment and conversational characteristics that can provide insight into the cultural aspects of the users represented by the persona.

8.4 USING DATA-DRIVEN PERSONAS WITH CARD SORTING

Card sorting involves various activities that include the naming, grouping, and prioritizing of concepts (Wood and Wood, 2008). These activities usually provide terminology, relationship, and categories (Hudson, 2014) that contribute to a better understanding of users in a given problem domain. Traditionally, card sorting exercises are used to optimize information architectures (Derboven and Uyttendaele, 2008). However, these exercises can also be combined with data-driven personas to enrich the concepts with personalized user information. Conversely, card sorting can help prioritize the information content in data-driven persona design if card sorting is used in the creation of the personas themselves.

Card sorting activities are excellent tools for discovering and generating meaningful conversations among participants and researchers (Weller and Romney, 1988). Card sorting can also be used with hundreds of participants to see if a set of terminologies is understood across a large population (Fincher and Tenenberg, 2005). However, one of the risks of using card sorting is that it can result in feature fatigue (Rust et al., 2006; Thompson et al., 2005) or an over-bloating of features in a limited amount of space. Designers typically find it challenging to find a balance between making products more capable (through the functions they can perform) and making them more usable or minimalistic (Carroll, 1990). By adding personas to card sorting techniques, the issue of *featuritis* can be reduced by a clear and shared understanding of the users, their goals, and/or their pain points.

Derboven and Uyttendaele (2008) tested this integrated approach by creating personas based on existing user types of new software and reusing these profiles in a card sorting exercise. The goal of the exercise was to determine which persona should have access to which functionalities. First, several people were observed via a contextual inquiry when they used a complex digital print application. It was determined that, based on responsibilities, three general user profiles could be extracted. The profiles were reworked into personas that included a user scenario describing a typical workday. Then, expert users were given predefined cards to be sorted and grouped by functionality, always considered from the personas' points of view (participants were given color codes for easier assignment). For instance, one of the personas was Rik Cops, a print operator, who receives the laid out files and is in charge of printing them at the best possible quality. This role covers responsibilities associated with the entire end product but also includes tasks like refilling print toner and paper rolls.

The exercise helped determine which user profiles, represented by personas, should have access to which specific parts of the hardware. Additional card sorting exercises then allowed for researchers to explore which functionalities are used more often and which are not used at all, while comparisons with the personas were made again after a functionality-based structure was constructed. If the team had not had the addition of distinct types of users, the exercise might have resulted in a navigation tree with an excessive number of subcomponents.

Another successful example of using personas with card sorting is given by Lee and Price (2015). The authors explored the use of seven personas to offer a deeper understanding of the different types of commercial music information retrieval systems. First, participants were interviewed to discuss their preferred music services and narrate their actions as they used them. Then, the user data was used to create a card sorting activity based on a list of behaviors that were grouped, organized, named, and turned into personas. The card sorting activity allowed the authors to identify two relevant dimensions that expressed the differences between the groups: Companionship and Investment. In consequence, seven personas were created (Active Curator, Music Epicurean, Guided Listener, Music Recluse, Wanderer, Addict, and Non-Believer). The analysis showed a relationship between persona placements on spectrums and the type of music services preferred. Additionally, it was also determined that the user's context (mood, activities, and social context) was critical in understanding which services each user would choose.

Data-driven personas seem to be a highly beneficial addition to card sorting, an exercise that is sometimes deemed to not go deep enough into the problems it is trying to solve (Interaction

Design Foundation, 2016). By offering a better understanding of the different types of user profiles, data-driven personas can help generate meaningful conversations between card sorting participants by offering more detailed insights into the card sorting concepts.

For example, Figure 8.3 shows a portion of a data-driven persona from the APG system. The provided persona interests and content interactions offer actionable insights in gauging user topics and preferences. By interacting with the persona, stakeholders in card sorting exercises can align problems and solutions with persona interests. As participants engage in the card sorting activity, they can interact with the personas to identify how they most relate to the concepts identified in the card sorting exercises.

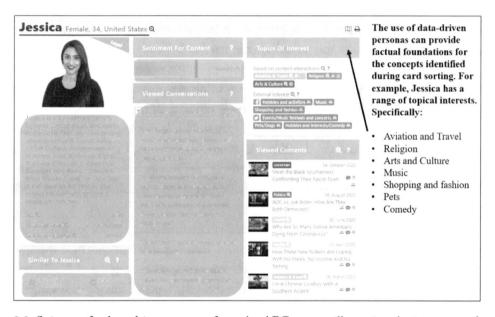

Figure 8.3: Snippet of a data-driven persona from the APG system illustrating the interests and products the persona has interacted with, which can be used to tailor serious games to specific user segments.

8.5   USING DATA-DRIVEN PERSONAS WITH SERIOUS GAMES

Serious games are systems that use gaming technologies for purposes other than entertainment (Abt, 1987; Michael and Chen, 2006). The primary objective of a serious game is learning or practicing a skill (or solving a concrete design or business problem) rather than entertainment, although it can also be designed to be "fun" for the players.

Serious games have been used in education (Zhonggen, 2019), aeronautics (Stone et al., 2011), health (Drummond et al., 2017; Lee et al., 2021), and science (Riopel et al., 2019) with purposes from teaching math to training pilots and learning a language (Raybourn, 2014). Boufera and Bendella (2014) discuss how collaborative games enhance social competencies like negotiation, communication, and decision-making. According to the two authors, the essence of serious games is to adapt according to the level of skill and desired social engagement of its users. One of the main advantages of serious games is that they transform the player from a passive receiver of information into an actively engaged agent (Li et al., 2012). These serious games have an explicit educational purpose and have been adopted in HCI, for example, as a tool to promote engaging education (Konstantakis et al., 2019).

Understanding visitors' profiles can prove essential for promoting user acceptance and identification in serious games. One way to collect the needed information and contribute toward a personalized, immersive, and engaging way is to use data-driven personas. However, there has been limited research in integrating the two approaches or using personas as player models (Yannakakis et al., 2010). User profiles have also been used for aggregating all users' input and history to create adaptation mechanisms in multiplayer serious games. While single-player games include user profiles with certain targets and saved actions, in multiplayer games, the model can also contain social parameters and behaviors. For example, Bartle (1996) has grouped role-playing game users with similar preferences into the categories of an achiever, explorer, socializer, and killer (archetypes similar to personas).

In one of the works that does explicitly investigate personas and serious games, Konstantakis et al. (2019) create personas to design a game, *The Stolen Painting*, that launches by showing the user a series of statements and asking them to rate each statement, measuring the eight dimensions of Multiple Intelligences. The game then quantifies the different types of intelligence and adapts the interface and content based on the resulting player persona. Because the personas can be dynamically updated, "*The Stolen Painting*" cannot only offer a new educational method for cultural heritage that adapts to the user, but it also can do so dynamically and over time.

Using data-driven personas techniques such as this can provide game designers with more control in shaping experiences that are immersive and tailored to a certain type of behavior and even adapt as players develop into a more active role. Such a persona can represent an agent in the game, where the persona could be presented to stakeholders as one of the roles to assume in the game (i.e., the game task is to represent "Jessica" in a given context(s), and all player acts are then based on how Jessica would react in a given situation. Although taking the role of personas has been found difficult to implement (Friess, 2012; Matthews et al., 2012), serious games could provide a framework to enhance this role-taking and the level of immersion into the circumstances of the persona.

For example, Figure 8.4 shows a cast from the APG data-driven persona system. By interacting with the various personas in the cast, designers of serious games can align problems and solutions with various user types within the population represented by the personas. They can interact with the cast of persons (by the searching and filtering afforded by the APG system) to identify which of the personas most relates to the concepts identified in the card sorting exercises. This also opens up new research areas for malleable data-driven persona systems that leverage interaction techniques (e.g., copy/paste, move, sort, organize, group) as players within a game change and evolve.

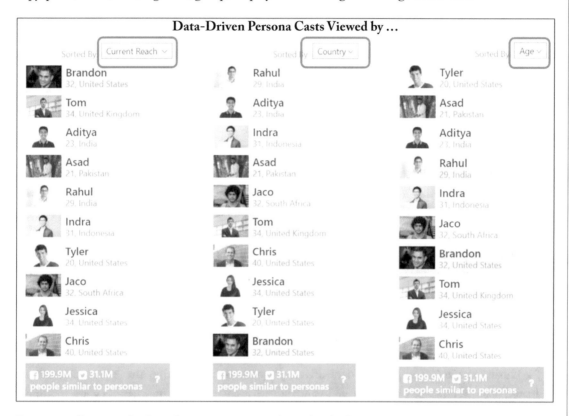

Figure 8.4: Snippet of a data-driven persona cast from the APG system illustrating the range of user types with potentially unique problems, needs, pain points, and goals to be addressed during the serious game design. The persona analytics system permits various views of the persona cast.

8.6   USING DATA-DRIVEN PERSONAS WITH AGILE DEVELOPMENT

Data-driven personas are not just useful when combined with other HCI techniques, but they can also enrich agile development, a design methodology. Agile development is an iterative framework characterized by the core principle of continuous delivery of useful software (Agile Software Development, 2001; Cockburn and Highsmith, 2001). Requirements and plans are evaluated on an ongoing basis by self-organizing cross-functional teams.

Agile development typically encompasses five phases, commonly referred to as *Envision*, *Speculate*, *Explore*, *Adapt*, and *Close* (Highsmith, 2009). Although data-driven personas can be useful across the entire cycle, they are better applied at two moments of agile development: The *Envision* phase and the *Adapt* phase (Ambler, 2008). Considering that each sprint has both exploratory and refinement phases, as the software evolves and new functionalities are built, creating a complete up-front persona design would contradict the agile philosophy. The method suggested is for an "agilized persona" (Caballero et al., 2014), one that keeps being refined as the product evolves.

During the *Envision* phase, data-driven personas are identified before any agile cycle begins or any code is released. This approach is useful for gathering the goals and speculations of users and therefore improving the results of future cycles based on research observations. Several authors have discussed the advantages of using personas before any coding is done (Chamberlain et al., 2006; Sy, 2007). Najafi and Toyoshiba (2008) support using personas during the agile development process. Singh (2008) suggests that a usability product owner should be included from the beginning of the project, working alongside the development team to define personas and helping developers to get familiar with them.

The incorporation of personas during the *Envision* phase has been analyzed by Haikara (2007), and the analysis was extended by Wolkerstorfer et al. (2008) and Hussain et al. (2008). This variation of the persona approach starts with the same user groups that will model the archetypes. However, when new knowledge suggests a persona should be changed, that persona is put through a refactoring process. This can happen as frequently as once per iteration (at the end of each data collection period).

During the *Adapt* phase, the data-driven personas defined during the exploration can be evaluated using each cycle's feedback and validated with customers. If needed, they are modified, and new ones are created, according to requirements. The use of personas has been discussed by Cleland-Huang (2013), which draws on Architecturally Significant Requirements (ASRs), the non-behavioral constraints in a system (Antoń, 1997). Examples of ASRs (Antoń, 1997) are safety, usability, portability, and reliability. ASRs are often used as selection criteria for deciding between architectural options. The personas express the quality concerns and restraints of a system for different user groups through user stories. First, the set of personas are identified and fleshed out. They are then used to drive the architectural design and analysis process, and the product architecture is broken into sprint-sized parts that populate the backlog. As the features to be developed in each sprint are chosen, the developers work on the architectural elements.

Data-driven personas can provide agile development—a way of grouping users and focusing on their needs, goals, and behaviors. By including data-driven personas in different phases, agile teams can use them to engage clients in the development life cycle and determine how a product feature should behave. Data-driven personas, with their ability to be rapidly updated, are natural "agilized" personas (Caballero et al., 2014), continually evolving throughout the product development process.

For example, Figure 8.5 shows the chronology of a cast of data-driven persona from the APG system updated overtime. These "agilized" data-driven personas are updated as new data becomes available or updated at set intervals to stay current.

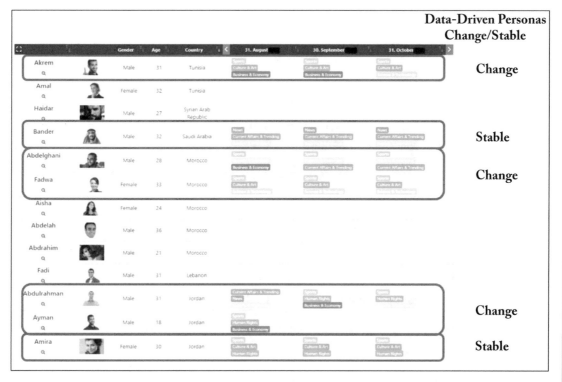

Figure 8.5: Snippet of a data-driven persona chronology from the APG system showing the changes in the casts of personas over time. These data-driven personas can be viewed as "agilized" personas, evolving throughout the development phases.

8.7   CHAPTER TAKE-AWAYS

- Data-driven personas are complementary to scenarios by providing the infrastructure and experiences that are based on real users.

- Data-driven personas can be used in a PD session by organizing user-centered and context-aware behavioral components into defined archetypes, from which appropriate stakeholders for each archetype can be engaged in the design process.

- Data-driven personas, along with card sorting, can offer a better understanding of users' behavior and context, thus providing teams with tools for more meaningful conversations and help to avoid feature fatigue.

- Data-driven personas can be used when designing serious games as they help shape different types of experiences players expect, allowing designers to improve and design the game to facilitate these experiences better.

- Data-driven personas are complementary to informing and improving usability through the agile development cycle, especially in the *Envision* and the *Adapt* phases.

8.8   DISCUSSION AND ASSESSMENT QUESTIONS

1.   Explain why data-driven personas help emphasize a "human-centered methodology" when used in combination with other UX research techniques.

2.   Describe the strengths of scenarios and how they can be reinforced by using data-driven personas.

3.   Describe how data-driven personas can help eliminate unnecessary requirements in user scenarios.

4.   Assess what makes a data-driven persona "culturally sensitive." Explain why this characteristic would be important in the context of PD.

5.   Define feature fatigue. Describe how the use of data-driven personas, combined with card sorting, can help prevent it.

6.   Discuss how data-driven personas are relevant to the employment of serious games.

7.   Describe possible differences between using data-driven personas in the *Envision* phase and the *Adapt* phase of Agile Development.

8.   You want to develop a piece of software for handling medical records (their creation, recording, transcription, and filing) using the agile framework. List and define what data variables you would need to craft data-driven personas for such a system. Explain how you would incorporate these data-driven personas during the Envision step of the agile development process.

8.9   REFERENCES

Abt, C. C. (1987). *Serious Games*. University Press of America. 195

Agile Software Development. (2001). *Manifesto for Agile Software Development*. http://agilemanifesto.org/. 198

Ambler, S. W. (2008). Tailoring usability into agile software development projects. In E. L.-C. Law, E. T. Hvannberg, and G. Cockton (Eds.), *Maturing Usability: Quality in Software, Interaction and Value*. Springer. pp. 75–95. DOI: 10.1007/978-1-84628-941-5_4. 198

Anton, A. I. (1997). Goal Identification and Refinement in the Specification of Software-Based Information Systems. Ph.D. Dissertation. Georgia Institute of Technology. Order Number: UMI Order No. GAX97-35409. 198

Bannon, L. J. and Ehn, P. (2012). Design matters in participatory design. In *Routledge Handbook of Participatory Design*. pp. 37–63. Routledge New York. 191

Bartle, R. (1996). Hearts, clubs, diamonds, spades: Players who suit MUDs. *Journal of MUD Research*, 1(1), 19. 196

Blanco, E., Pourroy, F., and Arikoglu, S. (2014). Role of personas and scenarios in creating shared understanding of functional requirements: An empirical study. In *Design Computing and Cognition'12*. Springer. pp. 61–78. DOI: 10.1007/978-94-017-9112-0_4. 188, 189

Bødker, S., Christiansen, E., Nyvang, T., and Zander, P.-O. (2012). Personas, people and participation: Challenges from the trenches of local government. *Proceedings of the 12th Participatory Design Conference on Research Papers*, Volume 1 - PDC '12. p. 91. DOI: 10.1145/2347635.2347649. 192

Boufera, H. and Bendella, F. (2014). User profiling in multiplayer serious games. *Social Simulation Conference*. https://ddd.uab.cat/record/128570. 196

Bradley, C., Oliveira, L., Birrell, S., and Cain, R. (2021). A new perspective on personas and customer journey maps: Proposing systemic UX. *International Journal of Human-Computer Studies*. DOI: 10.1016/j.ijhcs.2021.102583. 187

Caballero, L., Moreno, A. M., and Seffah, A. (2014). Persona as a tool to involving human in agile methods: Contributions from HCI and marketing. In S. Sauer, C. Bogdan, P. Forbrig, R. Bernhaupt, and M. Winckler (Eds.), *Human-Centered Software Engineering*. Springer. pp. 283–290. DOI: 10.1007/978-3-662-44811-3_20. 198, 199

Cabrero, D. G. (2014). Participatory design of persona artefacts for user eXperience in non-WEIRD cultures. *Proceedings of the 13th Participatory Design Conference: Short Papers,*

Industry Cases, Workshop Descriptions, Doctoral Consortium Papers, and Keynote Abstracts, Volume 2, 247–250. DOI: 10.1145/2662155.2662246. 192

Carrol, J. M. (1999). Five reasons for scenario-based design. *Proceedings of the 32nd Annual Hawaii International Conference on Systems Sciences. 1999. HICSS-32*. Track3, 11. DOI: 10.1109/HICSS.1999.772890. 188

Carroll, J. M. (1990). *The Nurnberg Funnel: Designing Minimalist Instruction for Practical Computer Skill*. MIT Press. 194

Carroll, J. M. and Rosson, M. B. (1990). Human-computer interaction scenarios as a design representation. *Twenty-Third Annual Hawaii International Conference on System Sciences*. Volume 2, pp. 555–561 vol.2. DOI: 10.1109/HICSS.1990.205231. 188

Chamberlain, S., Sharp, H., and Maiden, N. (2006). Towards a framework for integrating agile development and user-centred design. In P. Abrahamsson, M. Marchesi, and G. Succi (Eds.), *Extreme Programming and Agile Processes in Software Engineering*. Springer. pp. 143–153. DOI: 10.1007/11774129_15. 198

Cleland-Huang, J. (2013). Meet Elaine: A persona-driven approach to exploring architecturally significant requirements. *IEEE Software*, 30(4), 18–21. DOI: 10.1109/MS.2013.80. 198

Cockburn, A. and Highsmith, J. (2001). Agile software development, the people factor. *Computer*, 34(11), 131–133. DOI: 10.1109/2.963450. 198

Cooper, A. (1999). *The Inmates Are Running the Asylum: Why High Tech Products Drive Us Crazy and How to Restore the Sanity*. 1sy edition. Sams - Pearson Education. 187

Davis, S. R., Peters, D., Calvo, R. A., Sawyer, S. M., Foster, J. M., and Smith, L. (2018). "Kiss myAsthma": Using a participatory design approach to develop a self-management app with young people with asthma. *Journal of Asthma*, 55(9), 1018–1027. DOI: 10.1080/02770903.2017.1388391. 192

Derboven, J. and Uyttendaele, A. J. (2008). Putting personas to work: Combining card sorting and personas in requirements analysis. *New Approaches to Requirements Elicitation*. 193, 194

Drummond, D., Hadchouel, A., and Tesnière, A. (2017). Serious games for health: Three steps forwards. *Advances in Simulation*, 2(1), 3. DOI: 10.1186/s41077-017-0036-3. 196

Fincher, S. and Tenenberg, J. (2005). Making sense of card sorting data. *Expert Systems*, 22(3), 89–93. DOI: 10.1111/j.1468-0394.2005.00299.x. 193

Friess, E. (2012). Personas and decision making in the design process: An ethnographic case study. *Proceedings of the SIGCHI Conference on Human Factors in Computing Systems*. pp. 1209–1218. DOI: 10.1145/2207676.2208572. 196

Grudin, J. and Pruitt, J. (n.d.). *Personas, Participatory Design and Product Development: An Infrastructure for Engagement.* 8. 189

Gudjónsdóttir, R. (2010). *Personas and Scenarios in Use.* Skolan för datavetenskap och kommunikation, Kungliga Tekniska högskolan. http://urn.kb.se/resolve?urn=urn:nbn:se:kth:diva-12834 urn:nbn:se:kth:diva-12834. 188

Haikara, J. (2007). Usability in agile software development: Extending the interaction design process with personas approach. *International Conference on Extreme Programming and Agile Processes in Software Engineering.* pp. 153–156. DOI: 10.1007/978-3-540-73101-6_22. 198

Hartson, R. and Pyla, P. (2019). Chapter 19 - Background: Design. In R. Hartson and P. Pyla (Eds.), *The UX Book*, 2nd edition. Morgan Kaufmann. pp. 397–401. DOI: 10.1016/B978-0-12-805342-3.00019-9. 191

Highsmith, J. (2009). *Agile Project Management: Creating Innovative Products.* Pearson Education. 198

Hudson, W. (2014). Card sorting. In *The Encyclopedia of Human-Computer Interaction.* 2nd ed. https://www.interaction-design.org/literature/book/the-encyclopedia-of-human-computer-interaction-2nd-ed/card-sorting. 193

Hudson, W. (2009). Reduced empathizing skills increase challenges for user-centered design. *Proceedings of the SIGCHI Conference on Human Factors in Computing Systems.* pp. 1327–1330. DOI: 10.1145/1518701.1518901. 191

Hussain, Z., Lechner, M., Milchrahm, H., Shahzad, S., Slany, W., Umgeher, M., and Wolkerstorfer, P. (2008). Agile user-centered design applied to a mobile multimedia streaming application. In A. Holzinger (Ed.), *HCI and Usability for Education and Work.* Springer. pp. 313–330. DOI: 10.1007/978-3-540-89350-9_22. 198

Interaction Design Foundation. (2016). *The Pros and Cons of Card Sorting in UX Research.* The Interaction Design Foundation. https://www.interaction-design.org/literature/article/the-pros-and-cons-of-card-sorting-in-ux-research. 195

Konstantakis, M., Kalatha, E., and Caridakis, G. (2019). Cultural heritage, serious games and user personas based on gardner's theory of multiple intelligences: "The Stolen Painting" game. In A. Liapis, G. N. Yannakakis, M. Gentile, and M. Ninaus (Eds.), *Games and Learning Alliance.* Springer International Publishing. pp. 490–500. DOI: 10.1007/978-3-030-34350-7_47. 196

Laubheimer, P. (2017). *Personas vs. Jobs-to-Be-Done.* Nielsen Norman Group. https://www.nngroup.com/articles/personas-jobs-be-done/. 187

Lee, J. H. and Price, R. (2015). Understanding users of commercial music services through personas: Design implications. *Proceedings of the 16th International Society for Music Information Retrieval Conference (ISMIR2015)*, Malaga, Spain. DOI: 10.5281/zenodo.232222. 194

Lee, J. H., Kim, Y. M., Rhiu, I., and Yun, M. H. (2021). A persona-based approach for identifying accessibility issues in elderly and disabled users' interaction with home appliances. *Applied Sciences*, 11(1), 368. DOI: 10.3390/app11010368. 196

Li, J., Ma, S., and Ma, L. (2012). The study on the effect of educational games for the development of students' logic-mathematics of multiple intelligence. *Physics Procedia*, 33, 1749–1752. DOI: 10.1016/j.phpro.2012.05.280. 196

Loke, L., Robertson, T. J., and Mansfield, T. (2005). Moving bodies, social selves: Movement-oriented personas and scenarios. *Computer-Human Interaction Special Interest Group (CHISIG) of Australia*. https://opus.lib.uts.edu.au/handle/10453/12652. 189

Martin, B. and Hanington, B. (2012). *Universal Methods of Design: 100 Ways to Research Complex Problems, Develop Innovative Ideas, and Design Effective Solutions*, 58480th edition. Rockport Publishers. 188

Matthews, T., Judge, T., and Whittaker, S. (2012). How do designers and user experience professionals actually perceive and use personas? *Proceedings of the 2012 ACM Annual Conference on Human Factors in Computing Systems - CHI '12*. pp. 1219. DOI: 10.1145/2207676.2208573. 196

McDonagh, D. (2004). Empathic design: User experience in product design. *The Design Journal*, 7(1), 53–54. DOI: 10.2752/146069204789338406. 191

McKeen, J. H. (2019). *The Pitfalls of Personas and Advantages of Jobs to Be Done: UXmatters*. https://www.uxmatters.com/mt/archives/2019/02/the-pitfalls-of-personas-and-advantages-of-jobs-to-be-done.php. 187

Michael, D. and Chen, S. (2006). *Serious Games: Games That Educate, Train, and Inform*. 195

Najafi, M. and Toyoshiba, L. (2008). Two case studies of user experience design and agile development. *Agile 2008 Conference*. pp. 531–536. DOI: 10.1109/Agile.2008.67. 198

Raybourn, E. M. (2014). A new paradigm for serious games: Transmedia learning for more effective training and education. *Journal of Computational Science*, 5(3), 471–481. DOI: 10.1016/j.jocs.2013.08.005. 196

Reeder, B., Hills, R. A., Turner, A. M., and Demiris, G. (2014). Participatory design of an integrated information system design to support public health nurses and nurse managers. *Public Health Nursing*. 31(2), 183–192. DOI: 10.1111/phn.12081. 192

Riopel, M., Nenciovici, L., Potvin, P., Chastenay, P., Charland, P., Sarrasin, J. B., and Masson, S. (2019). Impact of serious games on science learning achievement compared with more conventional instruction: An overview and a meta-analysis. *Studies In Science Education*, 55(2), 169–214. DOI: 10.1080/03057267.2019.1722420. 196

Rust, R. T., Thompson, D. V., and Hamilton, R. W. (2006). Defeating feature fatigue. *Harvard Business Review*, 84(2), 37–47. 193

Singh, M. (2008). U-SCRUM: An agile methodology for promoting usability, *Agile 2008 Conference*, Toronto, ON, 2008, pp. 555-560, DOI: 10.1109/Agile.2008.33. 198

Stone, R. J., Panfilov, P. B., and Shukshunov, V. E. (2011). Evolution of aerospace simulation: From immersive virtual reality to serious games. *Proceedings of 5th International Conference on Recent Advances in Space Technologies - RAST2011*. pp. 655–662. DOI: 10.1109/RAST.2011.5966921. 196

Sy, D. (2007). Adapting usability investigations for agile user-centered design. *Journal of Usability Studies*, 2(3), 112–132. 198

Thompson, D. V., Hamilton, R. W., and Rust, R. T. (2005). Feature fatigue: When product capabilities become too much of a good thing. *Journal of Marketing Research*, 42(4), 431–442. DOI: 10.1509/jmkr.2005.42.4.431. 193

Weller, S. C. and Romney, A. K. (1988). *Systematic Data Collection*. Volume 10. Sage Publications. DOI: 10.4135/9781412986069. 193

Wolkerstorfer, P., Tscheligi, M., Sefelin, R., Milchrahm, H., Hussain, Z., Lechner, M., and Shahzad, S. (2008). *Probing an Agile Usability Process*. 2151–2158. DOI: 10.1145/1358628.1358648. 198

Wood, J. R. and Wood, L. E. (2008). Card sorting: Current practices and beyond. *Journal of Usability Studies*, 4(1), 1–6. 193

Yannakakis, G. N., Togelius, J., Khaled, R., Jhala, A., Karpouzis, K., Paiva, A., and Vasalou, A. (2010). Siren: Towards adaptive serious games for teaching conflict resolution. *Proceedings of ECGBL*. pp. 412–417. 196

Young, R. M. and Barnard, P. (1986). The use of scenarios in human-computer interaction research: Turbocharging the tortoise of cumulative science. *Proceedings of the SIGCHI/GI Conference on Human Factors in Computing Systems and Graphics Interface*. pp. 291–296. DOI: 10.1145/29933.275645. 188

Zhonggen, Y. (2019). A meta-analysis of use of serious games in education over a decade [Review article]. *International Journal of Computer Games Technology*; Hindawi. DOI: 10.1155/2019/4797032. 196

Part 5

Evaluating Data-Driven Personas and the Road Ahead

CHAPTER 9

Evaluating Data-Driven Personas

In this chapter, we briefly introduce the critically needed task of data-driven persona evaluation. Although we specifically focus on data-driven, nearly all of the evaluation content applies to other types of personas as well. We highlight the need for evaluation in both persona research and practice, and we introduce techniques for persona evaluation. We discuss what is a good persona and what elements combine to make a good persona. We then introduce the Persona Perception Scale (PPS) that measures user perceptions of personas, moving then to a technical definition of a good persona. We then look at a good persona in terms of use cases, introducing the concept of "personas + x". We end the chapter using APG for data-driven personas generation and evaluation, chapter takeaways, and discussion questions.

9.1   THE NEED FOR EVALUATION

Evaluation of data-driven personas in both research and practice tends to be informal and limited, so there is much room for improvement (Salminen et al., 2020a). Notable challenges include:

1. **methodological plurality,** so that different methods require different evaluation approaches,

2. **lack of standardized evaluation metrics** that apply across the methods, and

3. **lack of sharing resources**, such as data and algorithms to replicate persona generation methodologies (Salminen et al., 2020a).

Rigorous science demands replication, by definition, and the same holds for the evaluation of personas. Replication and evaluation serve to verify claimed results and to discover the strengths and limitations of different approaches, algorithms, and datasets for persona creation.

However, how does one evaluate something that is not real? This is mentioned by Grudin (2006): Personas have no odor and cannot be (physically) observed. Personas are, by definition, imaginary, so should they even be evaluated against norms of analytics metrics, such as accuracy? The rationale for the argument that personas are beyond the scope of scientific validation altogether stems from the fact that personas are, by definition, imaginary people (Cooper, 1999). There are diverse opinions on this matter. Chapman and Milham (2006) argue that personas **cannot** be scientifically validated at all. As personas have traditionally been created using subjective methods such as interviews and ethnographic work, the small sample sizes and potential creators' biases associated with these methods have raised concerns about the accuracy and reliability of personas in practice (Howard, 2015).

Our stance on this matter of debate is that, while an individual persona contains fictive elements, it also contains factual elements that correspond with a real user dataset. For example, concerning the factual elements, there is a real mean age of users in a given population, some interests among the users are more common than others, and so on.

Even the fictional aspects are open to evaluation. For example, *is the name (fictional) appropriate for this user segment in terms of metrics such as gender and nationality? Is the photo (fictional) appropriate for this user segment in terms of gender and age metrics?* Therefore, data-driven persona evaluation and validation are meaningful efforts; in fact, they are *necessary* efforts, especially on the road to implementing data-driven personas within organizations. Those stakeholders that use personas and those that doubt the usefulness of personas are going to demand validation of the personas.

Following these concerns and positions, evaluation of personas is a major issue facing researchers and creators in fields such as HCI, marketing, advertising, health care, and design. Researchers in the persona domain consistently point out that personas need justification from their end users mainly for their accuracy and usefulness in real organizations and for actual usage scenarios (Chapman and Milham, 2006; Friess, 2012; Matthews et al., 2012).

9.2   OVERVIEW OF EVALUATION APPROACHES FOR DATA-DRIVEN PERSONAS

Table 9.1 displays techniques that have been applied to the evaluation of personas in the HCI literature.

Table 9.1: Examples of persona evaluation approaches in the literature

Technique	Explanation	Reference
Case studies	Conducting qualitative case studies (interviews, ethnography) within organizations to record the use, usefulness, and impact of personas on end users' decision-making	(Friess, 2012; Jansen et al., 2017; Rönkkö, 2005; Rönkkö et al., 2004)
Information content	Investigating the information shown in persona profiles and how it serves stakeholders' needs	(Nielsen et al., 2015)
Prediction	Analyzing how well predictions made with personas hold	(An et al., 2018a)
Quantitative analysis	Employing technical metrics, such as distance, goodness-of-fit, or accuracy, to determine a persona's statistical validity	(Brickey et al., 2012; Chapman et al., 2008; Zhu et al., 2019)

Technique	Explanation	Reference
Stability analysis	Analyzing how stable personas remain over time. Rapidly changing personas would potentially indicate methodological problems	(An et al., 2017)
Survey	Measuring end users' perception of personas as latent constructs	(Salminen et al., 2018c)
Usability	Using usability standards or heuristics to evaluate persona designs	(Long, 2009)

While the list in Table 9.1 is not exhaustive, we can nonetheless contend that both qualitative (e.g., case studies) and quantitative (e.g., cluster distance; Brickey et al., 2010) methods are used. A survey-based measurement of persona perceptions adopts concepts such as likability, realism, relatability, and trustworthiness from HCI and other disciplines like psychology and marketing (Ilieva et al., 2002; Sudman et al., 1996)

Often, academic studies evaluate personas via case studies (Dharwada et al., 2007; Faily and Flechais, 2011; Jansen et al., 2017), ethnography (Friess, 2012), usability standards (Long, 2009), or statistical goodness-of-fit evaluation (An et al., 2017; An et al., 2018a; Zhang et al., 2016). For example, Friess (2012) investigated the adoption of personas among designers by counting how often personas were referred to in discussions. Long (2009) measured the effectiveness of using personas by employing usability heuristics. Nielsen et al. (2017) analyzed the match between journalists' beliefs about their audience's characteristics and the personas aggregated from the user statistics of the same organization.

Using topic modeling and quantitative persona generation, An et al. (2017) predicted how personas are likely to differ by their preferences of new online content. Miaskiewicz and Luxmoore (2017) identified specific users to represent the personas and quantitatively compared these individuals' characteristics with the generated personas. Salminen et al. (2018a) consulted qualitative data of social media users in a geographical region in the forms of Instagram profiles and semi-structured interviews. These were used to enrich further and improve the automatically generated personas. Furthermore, while some studies engaged subject-matter experts (Dupree et al., 2016; McGinn and Kotamraju, 2008), these evaluations varied and ranged from brief discussions to quantitative coding of interrater agreement levels.

A literature review (Salminen et al., 2020a) showed that there is little to no information on how persona user feedback resulted in modifications of the personas or how the personas were used for real decision-making in user-centric tasks. More efforts in external validation with real users are needed to address the applicability of personas in conjunction with their actual impact on the employing organization.

Practical evaluation is also crucial because the technical sophistication of the methods varies greatly from simple counts to complex combinations of multiple computational models and for establishing applicability, which is one of the re-emerging themes in data-driven persona research. Thoma and Williams (2009) and Holden et al. (2017) discussed the need for incorporating more qualitative methods, particularly in validation stages, to ensure representativeness in the personas. Specifically, Zhang et al. (2016), Tychsen and Canossa (2008), and Miaskiewicz et al. (2008) incorporated user evaluations in the later stages of personas creation in order to capture the most relevant yet also comprehensive traits in the final personas. This can be understood as post-hoc evaluation, resulting in adjusting or pruning the persona profiles according to user feedback.

Some researchers state plans to test their methodologies on other comparable population groups, such as different countries or universities (dos Santos et al., 2014; Kim and Wiggins, 2016; Wöckl et al., 2012). Others wish to broaden their existing data samples (dos Santos et al., 2014; Holden et al., 2017; Tu et al., 2010) or even explore current methodologies in entirely different industries (Aoyama, 2005, 2007; Chu et al., 2018). Yet, such comparative studies are currently scarce and rarely implemented in reality.

9.3   GENERAL EVALUATION APPROACHES FOR DATA-DRIVEN PERSONAS

Evaluation of personas generally adheres to either a quantitative or a qualitative approach.

9.3.1   QUANTITATIVE EVALUATION OF PERSONAS

Validation of the personas varies by the applied method. Personas created with K-means clustering are validated by calculating the Euclidean distance between the different variables (Tanenbaum et al., 2018; Wang et al., 2018) or by conducting Chi-squared tests (Tanenbaum et al., 2018). A few studies (Vosbergen et al., 2015; Zhang et al., 2016; Zhu et al., 2019) qualitatively validate clusters by engaging subject experts and users themselves in reviewing the clustering results. Based on hierarchical clustering, Miaskiewicz et al. (2008) and Mesgari et al. (2015) validated their personas by considering relations between variables within clusters. The former calculated cosine similarity of angles between pairs of non-zero vectors; the latter, on the other hand, calculated Pearson correlation (the extent of a linear relationship between two variables). Holden et al. (2017) determined the statistical significance between different variables and tested for variance with the Kruskal–Wallis test and Welch's ANOVA, respectively.

Typically, studies applying principal component analysis (PCA) for persona generation complement it with at least one other quantitative method. As a result, validation metrics also vary, including Cohen's kappa (Brickey et al., 2012; 2010), Euclidean distances of variables (Wang et al., 2018), Spearman's correlation between two ranked variables (Dang-Pham et al., 2015), and even qualitative review with survey participants (Tu et al., 2010). Similar to PCA, latent semantic analysis (LSA) is often combined with other methods, especially hierarchical clustering (Brickey et al., 2012, 2010; Miaskiewicz et al., 2008). Researchers validate their results, such as through cosine similarity tests. For NMF, An et al. (2018a) also calculated cosine similarity for pairs of personas until the closest pairs were determined. In another study employing NMF (An et al., 2018b), researchers used the Kendall rank correlation coefficient to compare the ranking of personas' demographic groups with the ranking of demographic groups in the raw data.

9.3.2 QUALITATIVE EVALUATION OF DATA-DRIVEN PERSONAS

Qualitative validation is common. Salminen et al., (2020a) found that 37% of the surveyed articles incorporated qualitative feedback into their persona validation stages. These generally involved gathering a small sample of members from the initially surveyed population to evaluate the personas in open discussion groups. An exception was Dupree et al. (2016), which recruited a mutually exclusive yet still relevant subpopulation to evaluate the personas' representativeness anecdotally. In that study, the validation stage group was tasked with self-identifying with one of the five final personas and rating how realistic they are.

Out of all the articles that used mixed quantitative-qualitative methods for persona generation, one-third incorporated qualitative methods to the validation stage only, while more than half (58.3%) incorporated qualitative methods to both the initial data collection and validation stages. The review showed that mixed quantitative-qualitative methodologies in proportion to the total number of articles published per year have consistently been incorporated, with peaks in 2010 and 2015. These peaks may be attributed to rises in popularity of incorporating qualitative aspects to validation, such as subject experts or user consultations (Salminen et al., 2020a).

9.4 WHAT OF THE PERSONA BEING EVALUATED?

Data-driven persona evaluation involves two fundamental questions.

1. What is a good data-driven persona?

2. How can the qualities of a good data-driven persona be measured?

There are *many* possible ways to evaluate data-driven personas.

On the one hand, all personas should be evaluated for their (1) accuracy—meaning how well they represent the users and are faithful to the underlying data. For example, we might say a good persona corresponds well with the baseline user data it was generated from. To measure this form of accuracy, we might compare the persona's traits to the traits that are predominant in the baseline data and obtain a numerical match. If this match is high (according to our interpretation), then the data-driven persona was of good quality because the personas are a precise reflection of the actual underlying user data.

On the other hand, personas should be evaluated for (2) <u>user perceptions</u>, such as users' willingness to use them. In other words, it is important to investigate how different individuals respond to different personas. The importance of perceptions is evident from a user study (Salminen et al., 2018d), in which the persona's ethnicity and gender affected the persona users' perceptions. Because acceptance and adoption of the personas depend on persona perceptions such as trust and credibility (Matthews et al., 2012; Rönkkö, 2005), querying user perceptions can improve a persona project's chances of being successful.

Moreover, concerning data-driven persona systems, personas should also be evaluated for (3) <u>user experience</u> or <u>usability</u> in terms of functionalities, such as navigation, search, comparison, data drill-downs, and so on of the persona analytics system. Here, one can utilize pre-existing scales and questionnaires such as the System Usability Scale (SUS) (Brooke, 1996), NASA-TLX (Cao et al., 2009), the User Experience Questionnaire (UEQ) (Schrepp et al., 2017), the Questionnaire for User Interaction Satisfaction (QUIS) (Harper and Norman, 1993), and so on.

Concerning these methodologies, persona evaluation can consist of analyzing (4) <u>user behavior</u> such as recall, task completion time, gaze movement, number and direction of transitions between the personas, and the information reviewed in each persona profile (see Figure 9.1). Behavioral user studies are somewhat novel (Salminen et al., 2020b), but they are made possible by the use of interactive data-driven persona systems, in which data concerning the use of these systems can be logged efficiently. For example, the APG system, a data-driven persona system, has a built-in mouse-tracking system that records the users' interactions with the persona profiles and different functionalities.

Experimental results from persona user studies can be combined with qualitative methods such as think-aloud (Salminen et al., 2018d) to understand both *how* and *why* individuals perceive the persona as they do (e.g., uncovering their biased thinking). Qualitative data collection can take place simultaneously with the use of personas or after asking for user feedback. In the latter case, the analysis of the feedback can shed light on what directions the qualitative inquiry should take in gathering deep insights about persona perceptions.

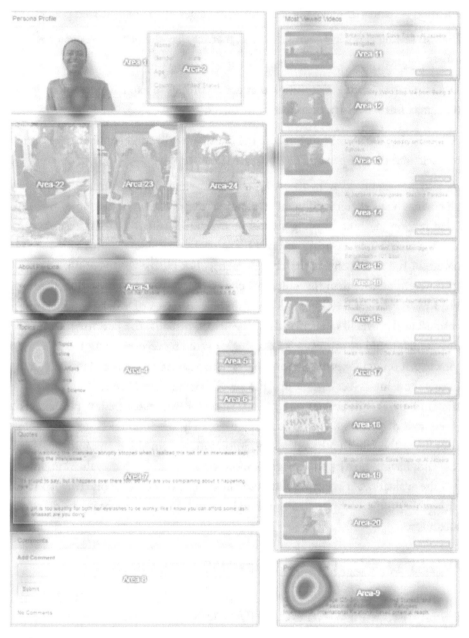

Figure 9.1: An example of evaluating personas using eye-tracking. This example shows the participants most often viewed the persona description (Area 3), topics of interest (Area 4), and audience size (Area 9). Eye-tracking is often coupled with think-aloud, i.e., asking the user to explain what part of the persona profile they are looking at and why.

Evaluation activities can take place in different stages of the data-driven persona life cycle.

- **Before:** setting explicit design goals, i.e., metrics that the generated personas need to satisfy.

- **During:** incorporating algorithms that act according to explicitly stated design goals (e.g., maximize diversity, minimize statistical distance).

- **After:** letting the algorithms process the data "naturally," then applying decision rules to select and discard personas.

It is also important to note that different subsystems and information elements of data-driven personas may require different evaluation techniques. For example, the information elements that rely on machine learning should be evaluated using metrics such as accuracy or F1 score (which is a metric for measuring accuracy). Each persona model requires a separate evaluation, and the nature of the model affects the chosen metric. For binary classification, one may want to use slightly different metrics than for multilabel classification. For text generation, the metrics (e.g., BLEU, METEOR, and ROGUE) would be different in terms of what they measure and how. When considering the overall quality of the data-driven persona, the performance scores of these various subsystems should be aggregated for a single overall score, even though studies rarely do so.

In practice, it often makes more sense to evaluate persona casts instead of individual personas (a "cast" means the same as "set" or "group;" the set of personas created simultaneously to represent a given dataset of users). This evaluation by cast is done for two reasons. First, persona stakeholders typically use a cast of personas, even when they ultimately select one persona on whom to focus. Stakeholders make the selection based on the information from the many individual personas in the cast. Second, having many personas gives more data points for the evaluation, increasing the reliability of the evaluation. It is virtually impossible in most contexts for one persona to capture all the essential qualities of a user population for a given task. Still, several personas do so with much higher probability.

9.5   WHAT IS A GOOD DATA-DRIVEN PERSONA?

9.5.1   USER PERCEPTIONS OF A PERSONA

What are good data-driven personas like? This question can be approached by reversing it, as there is plenty of literature on what constitutes a bad persona. In general, "bad" personas are misleading, confusing, untrustworthy, inconsistent, easily forgettable, not relatable, lacking important details, and not actionable (Long, 2009; Matthews et al., 2012; Nieters et al., 2007).

Therefore, it follows that "good" personas are the opposite. In other words, they are (a) truthful, (b) clear, (c) credible (trustworthy), (d) consistent, (e) memorable, (f) empathetic, and (g) complete (rounded; Nielsen, 2019) characters that (h) stakeholders find actionable. "Actionable" means that real decisions ("actions") affecting users can be made based on the information presented in the persona profile.

To measure persona quality, Salminen et al. (2020a) recommend using Credibility, Consistency, Completeness, Clarity, Empathy, and Willingness to Use (WTU) so that its user would perceive a "good" data-driven persona as credible, consistent, complete, clearly presented, and empathetic so that decision-makers would be willing to use it for their work tasks. The researchers developed a survey instrument for the measurement of these perceptions, the PPS. According to their tenet, the higher the persona perception scores are, the better the persona's overall quality. While the researchers do not provide definite cut-off points for "low" and "high" scores of persona quality, they propose different techniques for determining such values.

First, they propose using empirical distributions (e.g., interquartile range) to infer the cut-off points from the actual instrument responses. Second, they suggest heuristically dividing the Likert scale into roughly even quality ranges such that the range of 1–2 indicates *low-quality* personas, 3–5 indicates medium-quality personas, and 6–7 indicates high-quality personas. These efforts can enable practitioners and persona developers to determine an overall *persona quality score* (Salminen et al., 2020d).

We now address these key constructs in the PPS.

Credibility (trustworthiness, believability) is a key dimension of persona quality because, if decision-makers do not trust the personas, they will not adopt and use the personas (Vincent and Blandford, 2014). For example, in a study by Matthews et al. (2012), roughly a third of the participants found the created personas abstract, impersonal, misleading, and distracting. Although close to half of the participants were neutral to moderately positive about the personas, the study highlights personas' credibility challenges. Therefore, a high-quality persona needs to be credible.

Consistency arises as a problem when the personas are pieced together from several unrelated data sources. Bødker et al. (2012) refer to such patched-up personas as "Frankenstein's monsters", with information that is manually pieced together from multiple sources and either unrelated or without verifying the relations. The methodological flexibility of persona creation—i.e., the lack of strict conventions and guidelines (Nielsen et al., 2015)—has contributed to a situation in which there are many different ways to create data-driven personas. The lack of standardization and unity, therefore, promulgates inconsistency, both in terms of persona creation (a large number of different templates and designs being used) and persona perceptions (the difficulty of users "learning" and understanding different persona designs and information). Overall, a high-quality persona will have information content that is (a) internally consistent and coherent, up to a degree where the association of different information pieces can be quantitatively shown, and (b) does not leave the user under the impression that "something is not right", for example, that the name does not match the nationality, the picture does not match the age, or the interests do not match the quotes.

Consistency is a special problem for data-driven personas that often combine data from several online sources (An et al., 2018b, 2018c), especially when the data cannot be mapped with user identifications or other unique identifiers. For example, persona quotes and other information of data-driven personas can conflict if the persona is interested in sports. Still, the shown quotes talk about fashion, and the persona users may find the presented information inconsistent. These discrepancies are discussed in Salminen et al. (2019a; 2019), and observed in several user studies (Nielsen et al., 2017; Salminen et al., 2018b, 2019c).

Completeness refers to the fact that a high-quality persona has all the essential information for its successful application. Determining the information content of the persona profiles (known as "persona information design") is a crucial activity in the persona-creation process (Pruitt and Adlin, 2006). The information directly affects the perceived usefulness of the persona. Incomplete information is also associated with a lack of usefulness and willingness to use personas. For example, Bødker et al. (2012) reported that the personas developed in their study were not perceived as actionable, resulting in resistance to the adoption of personas in professional use.

Clarity of the persona profile (text, picture, visualizations, etc.) can hinder or enhance the persona user experience. For example, the persona information can be ambiguous and unclear, so the end-users are confused about what they are seeing. Madsen et al. (2014) noted that "Without clarity, it is impossible to communicate about the specific needs and goals of the users and […] meet these [needs]" (p. 1). In a user study (Salminen et al., 2019b), journalists found the provided definitions of the information in data-driven personas unclear, leading to increased confusion. For example, it was not clear if the "Quotes" section of the persona profile had comments about the persona or by the persona. For personas to be useful, they need to present the information of the user group they are describing in a clear manner (Nielsen et al., 2015).

Empathy can be defined as a feeling of understanding and compassion (Singer and Klimecki, 2014). Personas provide a shared mental model of the end-users' needs and wants, summarizing information about users in an empathetic format that is more memorable than numbers, tables, or other non-personified target group information (Goodwin, 2009). Persona-centric storytelling facilitates the absorption of persona information (Madsen and Nielsen, 2010). Persona descriptions exploit the human proneness for narratives by communicating the personas as descriptive stories, e.g., "Mary is a 35-year-old woman who likes extreme sports and dreams of having a vacation in Helsinki just by herself." A high-quality persona will convey experiences that the decision-makers would not necessarily know otherwise, facilitating immersion into the user's role and circumstances (Howard, 2015). By doing so, the persona helps mitigate the decision-makers' tendency to view the world from their own perspective (Long, 2009).

Willingness to use is a central construct for the adoption of personas in organizations (Friess, 2012; Rönkkö, 2005; Rönkkö et al., 2004). A high-quality persona is one that stakeholders want to use for decision-making. According to Rönkkö et al. (2004), decision-makers are unlikely to take low-quality personas seriously. This implies that, even when persona developers invest considerable efforts into persona creation, decision-makers may consider personas as "nice-to-have" instead of serious decision-making tools. Therefore, the true measure of persona quality is the users' willingness to deploy the personas in their work and, perhaps even more precisely, whether they *actually* deploy the personas for such purpose. Ultimately, the moment of truth for every persona system is whether it is actively used or not. Therefore, measuring both the willingness to use and the actual use is important.

Research has revealed several key perceptions relating to the creation, adoption, and use of personas. It is, therefore, worthwhile to evaluate persona perceptions. The perceptions vary individually (Hill et al., 2017; Marsden and Haag 2016; Salminen et al., 2018d), stemming from the personas' looks, demographics, behaviors, and dispositions and revealing stereotypical thinking (Ambady and Rosenthal, 1992), as well as the users' beliefs and attitudes about others (Swann, 1984). However, perceptions are not always associated with the quality of the persona. For example, making the personas "likable" or "similar to the person using them" is not a design goal, even though "likability" and "similarity" are persona perceptions. In contrast, "unlikable" and "different from me" personas can be useful in decision-making inasmuch they help avoid self-centering bias (Salminen et al., 2018a).

9.5.2 TECHNICAL DEFINITION OF A GOOD DATA-DRIVEN PERSONA

From a technical point of view, the "goodness" of data-driven personas can refer to specific properties of the persona set. Consider three cases: *diversity*, *accuracy*, and *consistency*.

Accuracy, as mentioned previously, refers to the personas corresponding to the underlying user data—to measure this, one can deploy statistical distance metrics, such as Jensen–Shannon divergence, Kullback–Leibler divergence, Hellinger distance, and so on. Essentially, these metrics compare the distribution of persona characteristics in the generated set of personas with the corresponding characteristics in the baseline data from which the personas were generated.

In the case of *diversity*, one can compute the number of unique attributes emerging in the set of personas—for example, if the persona set contains five unique demographic groups, then the demographic diversity is five. If there are three age groups, then the age group diversity is three. This measure can be turned into a metric called "coverage" by dividing the number of unique groups by the total number of unique groups in the baseline data. For example, if there are purchases from customers in 100 countries in the baseline data, and the persona set contains personas from 20 countries, then coverage would be 20/100 = 0.2, or 20%.

In turn, *consistency* refers to the personas remaining the same (or very similar) when repeating the persona generation. Note that this definition of consistency differs from the one given in the context of user perceptions—in user perceptions, consistency means that the persona information appears consistent to the end-user; for example, the picture matches the age of the persona. However, when considering consistency as a metric for algorithmic evaluation, the point is to determine how stable the results are. This is important for two reasons. First, some algorithms are stochastic in nature, meaning that the resulting personas could be different when rerunning the same algorithm, even when the same underlying data is used. Second, when increasing the number of personas, an inconsistent algorithm produces personas that are not "built upon" the smaller number of personas but, rather, selected randomly. Such behavior is extremely problematic, as it erodes the trust of stakeholders in data-driven personas.

Typically, repeated evaluations are not done in persona studies, which is why persona creators may "get away" with this randomness. A solution is to use a deterministic algorithm that generates the same (or highly similar) cast of personas every time when using the same data. An oft-used technique is setting the seed initialization of the stochastic algorithm to a constant state, through which the exact same results can be achieved on independent runs. However, this is not really a solution to the instability; while the constant initialization helps the replicability of persona generation in a specific case, it does not remove the algorithm's inherent instability. Therefore, the consistency of persona generation algorithms should be measured to see how inconsistently they behave for the specific purpose of persona generation.

Consistency can be determined by measuring personas' similarity in the persona sets generated by repeated runs of the same algorithm and data. In these evaluations, similarity is simply the overlap of the persona attribute values (e.g., the number of same age groups) between two persona sets. One can also report the mean, mode, and standard deviation in persona attributes over a set of runs. For numerical variables such as age, one can report mean and standard deviation. For categorical variables, frequencies and modes can be compared.

9.5.3   ORGANIZATIONAL PERSPECTIVE OF A DATA-DRIVEN PERSONA

"Good" can also mean that the personas serve their users (or the user organization) well. For measuring such outcomes, it is possible once again to use surveys (e.g., "How useful have the personas been for your work tasks?" "Please mention specific decisions where you made use of the personas."). It is also possible to tie the use of data-driven personas with quantitative metrics, such as views, clicks, sales, customer satisfaction, complaint rates, net promoter score (NPS), etc. If the deployment and Persona Performance Monitoring are executed correctly, then metrics are useful for this effort. Organizational aspects are further evaluated in the following section.

9.6   EVALUATING THE "REAL" IMPACT OF DATA-DRIVEN PERSONAS

The question "Do data-driven personas work?" is associated with three invalidated assumptions. By "invalidated," we mean that the empirical evidence on these matters is lacking or inconsistent. First,

a.   do data-driven personas, in fact, increase the level of empathy among persona users? Second, if data-driven personas do increase empathy,

b.   does this matter in reality—in other words, does this empathy result in persona users creating better products for end-users? Third, if so,

c.   do these better products improve the organization's key performance indicators, i.e., is there real value in persona application?

There is no existing data-driven research that shows strong empirical evidence for this chain of logic. Yet, the chain entails the crucial aspects of value creation with data-driven personas.

Consider an example from the realm of marketing. If online ad copywriters are shown data-driven personas, does this increase their empathetic understanding of customers? If so, do they create better ads that outperform ads created with an alternative technique of customer understanding? Evidence on this matter is currently inconclusive, although it tends to point to the direction that users with experience in personas and ad creation create more effective ads using data-driven personas when compared to ads created using spreadsheet information on customers (Salminen et al., 2020c).

At a more general level, the question is: *What actually drives better decision-making*? If "Factor X" positively affects decision-making and using data-driven personas positively affects "Factor X," then data-driven personas are useful. In corollary, if the returns of better decision-making exceed the costs of implementing personas, then the personas are profitable (positive ROI). Furthermore, if data-driven personas improve "Factor X" more than "Method B," then data-driven personas are better (in some specific tasks) than Method B.

Therefore, we can test the value of data-driven personas by (a) comparing the effects on a target variable before and after introducing personas (sequential testing) or (b) comparing personas with another method (controlled experiment, i.e., parallel testing). The questions of whether data-driven personas "work" and if they serve any real purpose are frequent among corporate decision-makers that tend to view the world from the perspective of measurable KPIs. While we wholeheartedly agree with the importance of showing the value of data-driven personas, at the same time, the question is somewhat trite.

Consider the analogy of web analytics—decision-makers rarely question its value.

Instead, the value of web analytics is taken for granted. In turn, data-driven personas are often not viewed as an extension of data but more as imaginary or fictive. This is perhaps the "fault" of the persona definition that traditionally highlights the fictitious part rather than the data part. For this reason, it is natural for decision-makers to focus on the word "fictional." Nonetheless, this is a fallacy since the data-driven persona is fictional, but the foundational data is not.

The solution to this thinking trap is to understand data-driven personas as extensions or presentations of the user data. We advocate "persona analytics," i.e., presenting user analytics data as personas. What comes after that is the same as any other analytics system: depending on what information is needed for a certain decision, it is reviewed, and a decision is made to act upon it.

Data-driven persona creators struggling to gain persona acceptance can pose the following questions to decision-makers in return.

> *Data-driven personas are only one way to present analytics information. Do you think analytics is valuable? What about user segmentation? What about user understanding in general?*

Typically, asking these questions makes the decision-maker realize that data-driven personas are only one instrument or tool for implementing user segmentation and achieving user understanding.

Regarding the use of technical metrics, an important question relates to the point in time of their implementation. Consider the following chain of activities.

Metrics-driven:

Define a design goal

➢ Select a metric

➢ Select an algorithm

➢ Generate metric-driven personas

Data-Driven:

Select data

➢ Select an algorithm

➢ Generate data-driven personas

Roughly speaking, we can distinguish the metric-driven persona generation from the data-driven persona generation, depending on the stage in which the metrics are incorporated. A metrics-driven approach aims to create personas that adhere to certain design goals (e.g., diversity, accuracy), whereas a data-driven approach naïvely looks at the patterns in the data to see what kind of personas emerge. Nonetheless, a data-driven approach does not mean the personas would be generated randomly or without the help of a quantitative metric. In contrast, statistical metrics (e.g., variance) drive the process of fine-tuning the hyperparameters—most importantly, the number of generated personas.

9.7   IMPLEMENTATION OF EVALUATION PRACTICES FOR DATA-DRIVEN PERSONAS

This section has implications for persona researchers, persona creators, and industry practitioners.

Practitioners can survey the end-users of personas to understand how the developed data-driven personas are perceived by the end-users, such as marketers, product managers, software developers, corporate executives, and so on. To provide further guidelines into the evaluation of personas, we describe four use cases in which one can deploy the PPS, a survey instrument included in this book's appendices.

Table 9.2: Using persona perception evaluation toward improving the data-driven personas	
Improve…	**By…**
Credibility	• ensuring personas are based on real user data (An et al., 2018c); triangulating data source such as quantitative and qualitative, behavioral, and interpretative (Pruitt and Grudin, 2003)
Consistency	• ensuring information elements in the persona match one another (Chapman and Milham, 2006)
Completeness	• investigating the information needs of persona users (Nielsen and Storgaard Hansen, 2014)
Clarity	• following conventions of persona information design for content and layout (Nielsen et al., 2015)
Empathy	• involving "depth" and personal details of the persona (Cooper, 1999)

Pre-testing data-driven personas: A potentially impactful use of the PPS is to pre-test personas for perceptions before deploying the data-driven personas into a broader use within an organization. For example, the PPS could be deployed to analyze how the perceptions of decision-makers affect the decisions taken about the customers of a company. This is an important point to address as decision-makers' perceptions of different customer groups may favor one group over another (Gabbidon and Higgins, 2007). For pre-testing, particularly important constructs are Empathy and WTU as these constructs are conceptually associated with the adoption of data-driven personas for real use.

Querying decision-makers' stereotypes about users: The PPS can reveal one's attitudes toward a persona (i.e., the underlying user segment). Thus, the deployment of the PPS can be associated with the equal and fair treatment of users, for example, by investigating the implicit biases associated with a set of data-driven personas. Additionally, conflicting views of the persona can arise despite being shown the same persona information, potentially invalidating data-driven personas as effective design tools (Rönkkö et al., 2004). To address this, the PPS can help identify situations in which different teams or individuals are interpreting the personas differently. The results can be leveraged toward the creation of data-driven personas that produce less variability in perceptions, thus helping to align decision-makers' understanding of their users.

Persona failure analysis: Moreover, with the PPS instrument, the created data-driven personas can be tested for undesirable effects, such as lack of credibility and consistency. If a data-driven persona profile or narrative is considered untrustworthy or inconsistent, this implies that the design goals for persona creation have not been achieved. Such verification is particularly important because the creation of data-driven personas tends to require major financial investments in the tens of thousands of U.S. dollars (Howard, 2015), which means that persona developers want to mitigate any barriers to persona adoption and use. As active use of data-driven personas remains a consistent challenge, systematic methodologies such as the PPS can help create solutions for adoption.

Longitudinal analysis of attitudes toward personas: The PPS instrument can be employed to measure the change in persona perceptions over time, considering, for example, the impact of seemingly minor changes to data-driven persona profiles that could result in major changes in the perception of those personas by the end-users. By quantifying the perceptions with the PPS, it is possible to measure the stability of persona perceptions over time, even when the persona undergoes radical changes. Such an analysis is highly called for, as the field of persona research is in dire need of longitudinal studies of persona use in real organizations (Friess, 2012), and the quantitative measurement of persona perceptions provides a proper toolkit for researchers to conduct longitudinal research.

Iterative improvement of personas: The PPS can be used as a part of an iterative process to improve data-driven persona designs. This works as follows. We first deploy the PPS to map potential issues with the persona design (e.g., low credibility rating). Using the PPS, practitioners can gain awareness of the perceptual problems with the persona design (as they can be quantified) and then, using qualitative inquiry, work toward solving them. To support iterative improvement, the PPS can be administered on several occasions—for example, in an iterative design loop like this: *use the PPS to find out credibility is low → use qualitative interviews to find out why → make changes to persona design → repeat the PPS and see if the credibility score has reached a satisfactory level.* From this angle, however, "How to make high-quality data-driven personas?" is an empirical question or a design journey for which the PPS provides an instrument.

Researchers can creatively develop similar questions to systematically test how (a) various manipulations in the persona profile's content/layout and (b) persona user characteristics (e.g., age, gender, similarity with the persona) affect an individual's perceptions of personas. This inquiry can take place by combining experimental persona designs (i.e., changing a variable in Version B while keeping Version A constant). For example, in ongoing research, we use a hate-detection algorithm to remove toxic comments from data-driven personas automatically created from social media data, then examine how toxic vs. non-toxic data-driven personas are perceived by individuals.

The PPS can also help uncover individual differences in attitudes toward personas. Consider this example scenario. *Persona User 1*, for whatever reason (perhaps the information does not match his stereotypical view of customers), does not like *Persona A* and is not willing to use this persona when making decisions. This is a case of non-adoption; that is, *User 1* refuses to accept the persona. On the other hand, *Persona User 2* thinks the opposite; she likes the persona and is willing to use it. Now, given that we have the PPS as an instrument, we can quantify *both* the aggregated view (composite score) of the credibility, WTU, etc., of the persona throughout the organization *and* the variation of these perceptions by individuals. The variation in itself can be crucial for enhancing the systematic adoption of personas in organizations, a longstanding issue in persona theory and practice (Chapman and Milham, 2006; Rönkkö et al., 2004).

9.8 EVALUATION APG DATA-DRIVEN PERSONAS

9.8.1 COMPARING APG TO YOUTUBE ANALYTICS

A user study (Salminen et al., 2020b) was conducted with 34 participants in an organization using both personas (APG) and YouTube Analytics (YTA) to compare how well these systems performed for a user segment identification task. The participants were asked to complete the task using both the APG and the YTA systems, and the results were recorded using a combination of eye-tracking, mouse-tracking, and think-aloud voice recordings. The results (see Table 9.3) show APG outperforming YTA for this task type.

Table 9.3: Results from a user study comparing APG's persona analytics to YouTube Analytics

Metric	APG	YTA	Comparison
Success rate	25 (73.5%)	8 (23.5%)	3.13 more successful task completions with APG compared to YTA
Completion Time (sec)	417.3	553.0	0.35 required average task completion time with APG compared to YTA
Completion Steps	10.5	17.2	0.61 required average steps for task completion with APG compared to YTA
Identified User Attributes	3.0	2.1	0.43 more correct user attributes identified with APG compared to YTA

The results showed that data-driven personas are more efficient, as measured by either time or the number of required steps for user identification, both for locating the user segment and completing the overall task. Data-driven personas required less time and effort than analytics, and they were therefore more efficient than analytics. Data-driven personas were also more effective in terms of accuracy and the ability to craft user attribute messages and generate confidence in these communications for user identification. For all measures of success, self-efficacy, and communication, personas were more effective than analytics. Figure 9.2 illustrates the data recorded in this study.

Figure 9.2: Example of using mouse- and eye-tracking for a data-driven persona user study using APG and YouTube Analytics.

Figure 9.2a shows a data-driven persona treatment example (male, 18–24, U.S.). To locate the right persona, participants had to scan the persona list and choose the persona suitable to the user segment criteria: (a) male, (b) 18–24 years of age, and (c) from the U.S. or Jordan. The extra lines relate to eye and mouse movements. Figure 9.2b shows a YouTube treatment example (male, 18–24, Jordan). To locate the right user segment, participants needed to select Analytics, and then Demographics, and then filter for (a) male, (b) 18–24 years of age, and (c) U.S. or Jordan. Note: The extra lines relate to eye and mouse movements.

9.8.2 LIST OF "STUPID" QUESTIONS TO UNDERSTAND DATA-DRIVEN PERSONAS

Finally, we provide a list of questions non-technically savvy practitioners (also useful for the technically savvy!) can ask from more technically savvy persona creators or consultants pushing data-driven personas.

We provide this list because it is advisable that the practitioners avoid the assumption that just because an algorithm was used, the data-driven persona-creation process is flawless. Since the reality does not match the ideal (i.e., none of the known data-driven persona creation algorithms are perfect), the shortcomings should be brought to light and debated transparently.

A list of "stupid" questions about data-driven personas.

1.   How did you collect the data for these personas?

2. How did you choose the algorithm for persona creation?

3. What were the algorithmic alternatives? Why were they not chosen?

4. How did you decide how many personas were created?

5. Was a statistical metric used to generate this number of personas?

6. Can you explain the statistical metric and the justification for the decisions behind any manually chosen threshold values?

7. Apart from the number of personas, were there other hyperparameters that you set manually? If so, please explain each of them and the reasoning for choosing specific values for them.

8. What are the general weaknesses of the algorithms that you used for persona creation?

9. What are the specific weaknesses in the personas created for this project (e.g., representativeness, diversity, bias)? Could these weaknesses be addressed somehow? If so, how? If so, why didn't you implement them to address the weaknesses?

9.9   SUMMARY

Evaluation of data-driven personas is critical because, in the absence of quality standards, persona creators may lack the tools for improving and justifying their personas. Fortunately, data-driven persona development relies on statistical methods, which implies that persona creators can verify their methods using quantitative metrics. As far as we can see, this potential for standardization is an enormous advantage to data-driven personas in general. However, comparing different data-driven methods requires research to develop a unified metric applicable across the different methods.

At the same time, quantitative metrics pose challenges for data-driven persona design. Using a metric as a design goal can result in the personas no longer being objective (i.e., data-driven) but value-driven. The choice of algorithms, hyperparameters, and data processing techniques are all forms of design power that can drastically alter the composition of the generated personas and, as a result, the data-driven persona users' understanding of their user population. The worst outcome is misleading the end-users of the personas. This can be very easy in practice, as most stakeholders lack the technical expertise to ask difficult questions and instead assume that "data" and "algorithms" mean the same as "objective" and "trustworthy". Therefore, it is the responsibility of the persona creators to articulate their methodologies, design choices, and any weaknesses to the stakeholders, rather than obfuscating these matters or expecting the stakeholders to ask about them.

Another issue in using metrics as goals that drive the data-driven persona generation process is that it may be counterintuitive. We mean by this that "evaluation" is a way of objectively examining the results, conducted independently from the creation of the said results. Suppose an evaluation metric is already infused in the persona-creation process, e.g., by manipulating the baseline data or applying an algorithm that is biased toward generating diverse as opposed to accurate results. In that case, the resulting personas are no longer objectively generated but are, instead, driven by values. This may be fine, depending on the case, but in all cases, such design choices should be transparently communicated to the end-users of personas so that they understand the limitations and boundaries of the personas they are using.

The relationship between the data-driven personas and their users evolve over time. Some data-driven personas are instantly forgotten; others can be remembered days, months, or years after. What governs this mechanism? So far, research has not systematically investigated the long-term effects of data-driven personas either for individuals or for organizations. The issue is that most user studies rely on first impressions—what the effects of the personas are now, but not what the effects would be tomorrow, next week, or next month. Novel evaluation techniques are needed to uncover rules or mechanisms that govern the persona user relationship.

9.10 CHAPTER TAKE-AWAYS

- The first question in data-driven persona evaluation is to determine what is being evaluated: quality, accuracy, user perceptions, user experience, usability, or something else.

- Data-driven personas should be truthful and not present inaccurate information to decision-makers about their users.

- Data-driven personas' truthfulness is difficult to verify as there are no metrics researchers commonly agree upon.

- In the persona context, accuracy is defined such that a more accurate persona better corresponds to the underlying average traits of the user segment that is being described. Conversely, a less accurate data-driven persona deviates more from these traits.

- Even though user perceptions (the way personas are perceived as human beings) should not necessarily be design goals, perceptions influence what information persona users infer from the personas and how they act upon this information.

- When applying a multidimensional survey instrument (dimension = credibility, clarity, willingness to use…), the mean of all composite scores can be seen as a measure of persona quality.

- Evaluating the consistency (stability) of data-driven persona generation algorithms is important. A deterministic algorithm always generates the same personas from the same data when using the same hyperparameters. With a stochastic algorithm, the results may vary.

9.11   DISCUSSION AND ASSESSMENT QUESTIONS

1. Address the following question: What are "good" data-driven personas? List attributes of a "good" data-driven persona.

2. Describe how data-driven personas have been evaluated in HCI research.

3. List four aspects that data-driven persona evaluation can focus on.

4. Explain why user perceptions of data-driven personas should be evaluated. Why do these perceptions matter at all?

5. Explain the "challenge of the first impression" in data-driven persona evaluation.

6. Describe why the evaluation of data-driven personas is challenging.

7. Explain why data-driven persona evaluation is needed. What are the positive outcomes?

8. Discuss qualitative and quantitative data-driven persona evaluation techniques.

9. List and define what metrics can be defined for assessing the achievement of data-driven persona design goals.

10. Explain what is meant by the division between metric-driven and data-driven persona creation.

11. Explain how evaluation can be applied toward the iterative improvement of data-driven personas.

9.12   REFERENCES

Ambady, N. and Rosenthal, R. (1992). Thin slices of expressive behavior as predictors of interpersonal consequences: A meta-analysis. *Psychological Bulletin*, 111(2), 256–274. DOI: 10.1037/0033-2909.111.2.256. 219

An, J., Kwak, H., and Jansen, B. J. (2017). Personas for content creators via decomposed aggregate audience statistics. *Proceedings of Advances in Social Network Analysis and Mining (ASONAM 2017). Advances in Social Network Analysis and Mining (ASONAM 2017)*. Sydney, Australia. DOI: 10.1145/3110025.3110072. 211

An, J., Kwak, H., Jung, S., Salminen, J., and Jansen, B. J. (2018a). Customer segmentation using online platforms: Isolating behavioral and demographic segments for persona creation via aggregated user data. *Social Network Analysis and Mining*, 8(1). DOI: 10.1007/s13278-018-0531-0. 210, 211, 213

An, J., Kwak, H., Jung, S., Salminen, J., and Jansen, B. J. (2018b). Customer segmentation using online platforms: Isolating behavioral and demographic segments for persona creation via aggregated user data. *Social Network Analysis and Mining*, 8(1), 54. DOI: 10.1007/s13278-018-0531-0. 213, 218

An, J., Kwak, H., Salminen, J., Jung, S., and Jansen, B. J. (2018c). Imaginary people representing real numbers: Generating personas from online social media data. *ACM Transactions on the Web (TWEB)*, 12(4), 27. DOI: 10.1145/3265986. 218

An, J., Kwak, H., Salminen, J., Jung, S., and Jansen, B. J. (2018d). Imaginary people representing real numbers: Generating personas from online social media data. *ACM Transactions on the Web (TWEB)*, 12(3). DOI: 10.1145/3265986. 223

Aoyama, M. (2005). Persona-and-scenario based requirements engineering for software embedded in digital consumer products. *Proceedings of the 13th IEEE International Conference on Requirements Engineering (RE'05)*. pp. 85–94. DOI: 10.1109/RE.2005.50. 212

Aoyama, M. (2007). Persona-scenario-goal methodology for user-centered requirements engineering. *Proceedings of the 15th IEEE International Requirements Engineering Conference (RE 2007)*. pp. 185–194. DOI: 10.1109/RE.2007.50. 212

Bødker, S., Christiansen, E., Nyvang, T., and Zander, P.-O. (2012). Personas, people and participation: Challenges from the trenches of local government. *Proceedings of the 12th Participatory Design Conference on Research Papers*. Volume 1 - PDC '12, p. 91. DOI: 10.1145/2347635.2347649. 217, 218

Brickey, J., Walczak, S., and Burgess, T. (2012). Comparing semi-automated clustering methods for persona development. *IEEE Transactions on Software Engineering*, 38(3), 537–546. DOI: 10.1109/TSE.2011.60. 210, 212, 213

Brickey, J., Walczak, S., and Burgess, T. (2010). A comparative analysis of persona clustering methods. *Americas Conference on Information Systems (AMCIS2010)*. p. 217. 211, 212, 213

Brooke, J. (1996). SUS: A "quick and dirty" usability. *Usability Evaluation in Industry*, 189. 214

Cao, A., Chintamani, K. K., Pandya, A. K., and Ellis, R. D. (2009). NASA TLX: Software for assessing subjective mental workload. *Behavior Research Methods*, 41(1), 113–117. DOI: 10.3758/BRM.41.1.113. 214

Chapman, C. N., Love, E., Milham, R. P., ElRif, P., and Alford, J. L. (2008). Quantitative evaluation of personas as information. *Proceedings of the Human Factors and Ergonomics Society Annual Meeting*. Volume 52, pp. 1107–1111. DOI: 10.1177/154193120805201602. 210

Chapman, C. N. and Milham, R. P. (2006). The personas' new clothes: Methodological and practical arguments against a popular method. *Proceedings of the Human Factors and Ergonomics Society Annual Meeting*, 50(5), 634–636. DOI: 10.1177/154193120605000503. 209, 210, 223, 225

Chu, E., Vijayaraghavan, P., and Roy, D. (2018). Learning personas from dialogue with aAttentive memory networks. *Proceedings of the 2018 Conference on Empirical Methods in Natural Language Processing*. pp. 2638–2646. https://www.aclweb.org/anthology/D18-1284. DOI: 10.18653/v1/D18-1284. 212

Cooper, A. (1999). *The Inmates Are Running the Asylum: Why High Tech Products Drive Us Crazy and How to Restore the Sanity*, 1st edition. Sams - Pearson Education. 209, 223

Dang-Pham, D., Pittayachawan, S., and Nkhoma, M. (2015). Demystifying online personas of Vietnamese young adults on Facebook: A Q-methodology approach. *Australasian Journal of Information Systems*, 19(1). DOI: 10.3127/ajis.v19i0.1204. 212

Dharwada, P., Greenstein, J. S., Gramopadhye, A. K., and Davis, S. J. (2007). A case study on use of personas in design and development of an audit management system. *Proceedings of the Human Factors and Ergonomics Society Annual Meeting*, 51(5), 469–473. DOI: 10.1177/154193120705100509. 211

dos Santos, T. F., de Castro, D. G., Masiero, A. A., and Junior, P. T. A. (2014). Behavioral persona for human-robot interaction: A study based on pet robot. *International Conference on Human-Computer Interaction*. pp. 687–696. DOI: 10.1007/978-3-319-07230-2_65. 212

Dupree, J. L., Devries, R., Berry, D. M., and Lank, E. (2016). Privacy personas: Clustering users via attitudes and behaviors toward security practices. *Proceedings of the 2016 CHI Conference on*

Human Factors in Computing Systems. pp. 5228–5239. DOI: 10.1145/2858036.2858214. 211, 213

Faily, S. and Flechais, I. (2011). Persona cases: A technique for grounding personas. *Proceedings of the SIGCHI Conference on Human Factors in Computing Systems.* pp. 2267–2270. DOI: 10.1145/1978942.1979274. 211

Friess, E. (2012). Personas and decision making in the design process: An ethnographic case study. *Proceedings of the SIGCHI Conference on Human Factors in Computing Systems.* pp. 1209–1218. DOI: 10.1145/2207676.2208572. 210, 211, 218, 224

Gabbidon, S. L. and Higgins, G. E. (2007). Consumer racial profiling and perceived victimization: A phone survey of Philadelphia area residents. *American Journal of Criminal Justice,* 32(1–2), 1–11. DOI: 10.1007/s12103-007-9019-6. 223

Goodwin, K. (2009). *Designing for the Digital Age: How to Create Human-Centered Products and Services.* 1st edition. Wiley. 218

Grudin, J. (2006). Why personas work: The psychological evidence. In J. Pruitt and T. Adlin (Eds.), *The Persona Lifecycle.* Elsevier. pp. 642–663. DOI: 10.1016/B978-012566251-2/50013-7. 209

Harper, B. D. and Norman, K. L. (1993). Improving user satisfaction: The questionnaire for user interaction satisfaction version 5.5. *Proceedings of the 1st Annual Mid-Atlantic Human Factors Conference.* pp. 224–228. 214

Hill, C. G., Haag, M., Oleson, A., Mendez, C., Marsden, N., Sarma, A., and Burnett, M. (2017). Gender-inclusiveness personas vs. stereotyping: Can we have it both ways? *Proceedings of the 2017 CHI Conference.* pp. 6658–6671. DOI: 10.1145/3025453.3025609. 219

Holden, R. J., Kulanthaivel, A., Purkayastha, S., Goggins, K. M., and Kripalani, S. (2017). Know thy eHealth user: Development of biopsychosocial personas from a study of older adults with heart failure. *International Journal of Medical Informatics,* 108, 158–167. DOI: 10.1016/j.ijmedinf.2017.10.006. 212

Howard, T. W. (2015). Are personas really usable? *Communication Design Quarterly Review,* 3(2), 20–26. DOI: 10.1145/2752853.2752856. 209, 218, 224

Ilieva, J., Baron, S., and Healey, N. M. (2002). Online surveys in marketing research: Pros and cons. *International Journal of Market Research,* 44(3), 361. DOI: 10.1177/147078530204400303. 211

Jansen, A., Van Mechelen, M., and Slegers, K. (2017). Personas and behavioral theories: A case study using self-determination theory to construct overweight personas. *Proceedings of the 2017 CHI Conference on Human Factors in Computing Systems.* pp. 2127–2136. DOI: 10.1145/3025453.3026003. 210, 211

Kim, H. M. and Wiggins, J. (2016). A factor analysis approach to persona development using survey data. *Proceedings of the 2016 Library Assessment Conference.* p. 11. 212

Long, F. (2009). Real or imaginary: The effectiveness of using personas in product design. *Proceedings of the Irish Ergonomics Society Annual Conference.* p. 14. 211, 216, 218

Madsen, A., McKagan, S. B., Sayre, E. C., Martinuk, M., and Bell, A. (2014). Personas as a powerful methodology to design targeted professional development resources. *ArXiv Preprint ArXiv:1408.1125.* 218

Madsen, S. and Nielsen, L. (2010). Exploring persona-scenarios—using storytelling to create design ideas. In *Human Work Interaction Design: Usability in Social, Cultural and Organizational Contexts.* Springer, Berlin, Heidelberg. pp. 57–66. DOI: 10.1007/978-3-642-11762-6_5. 218

Marsden, N. and Haag, M. (2016). Stereotypes and politics: Reflections on personas. *Proceedings of the 2016 CHI Conference on Human Factors in Computing System*s. pp. 4017–4031. DOI: 10.1145/2858036.2858151. 219

Matthews, T., Judge, T., and Whittaker, S. (2012). How do designers and user experience professionals actually perceive and use personas? *Proceedings of the SIGCHI Conference on Human Factors in Computing Systems.* pp. 1219–1228. DOI: 10.1145/2207676.2208573. 210, 214, 216, 217

McGinn, J. J. and Kotamraju, N. (2008). Data-driven persona development. *Proceedings of the SIGCHI Conference on Human Factors in Computing Systems.* pp. 1521–1524. DOI: 10.1145/1357054.1357292. 211

Mesgari, M., Okoli, C., and Guinea, A. O. de. (2015). Affordance-based user personas: A mixed-method approach to persona development. *AMCIS 2015 Proceedings.* https://aisel.aisnet.org/amcis2015/HCI/GeneralPresentations/1. 212

Miaskiewicz, T. and Luxmoore, C. (2017). The use of data-driven personas to facilitate organizational adoption: A case study. *The Design Journal*, 20(3), 357–374. DOI: 10.1080/14606925.2017.1301160. 211

Miaskiewicz, T., Sumner, T., and Kozar, K. A. (2008). A latent semantic analysis methodology for the identification and creation of personas. *Proceedings of the SIGCHI Conference on Human Factors in Computing Systems.* pp. 1501–1510. http://dl.acm.org/citation.cfm?id=1357290. DOI: 10.1145/1357054.1357290. 212, 213

Nielsen, L. (2019). *Personas—User Focused Design*, 2nd ed. 2019 edition. Springer. DOI: 10.1007/978-1-4471-7427-1. 217

Nielsen, L., Hansen, K. S., Stage, J., and Billestrup, J. (2015). A template for design personas: Analysis of 47 persona descriptions from danish industries and organizations. *International Journal Sociotechnology Knowledge Development*, 7(1), 45–61. DOI: 10.4018/ijskd.2015010104. 210, 217, 218, 223

Nielsen, L., Jung, S.-G., An, J., Salminen, J., Kwak, H., and Jansen, B. J. (2017). Who are your users?: Comparing media professionals' preconception of users to data-driven personas. *Proceedings of the 29th Australian Conference on Computer-Human Interaction*. pp. 602–606. DOI: 10.1145/3152771.3156178. 211, 218

Nielsen, L. and Storgaard Hansen, K. (2014). Personas is applicable: A study on the use of personas in Denmark. *Proceedings of the SIGCHI Conference on Human Factors in Computing Systems*. pp. 1665–1674. DOI: 10.1145/2556288.2557080. 223

Nieters, J. E., Ivaturi, S., and Ahmed, I. (2007). Making personas memorable. *CHI '07 Extended Abstracts on Human Factors in Computing Systems*. pp. 1817–1824. DOI: 10.1145/1240866.1240905. 216

Pruitt, J. and Adlin, T. (2006). *The Persona Lifecycle: Keeping People in Mind Throughout Product Design*, 1st edition. Morgan Kaufmann. DOI: 10.1145/1167867.1164070. 218

Pruitt, J. and Grudin, J. (2003). Personas: Practice and theory. *Proceedings of the 2003 Conference on Designing for User Experiences*. pp. 1–15. DOI: 10.1145/997078.997089. 223

Rönkkö, K. (2005). An empirical study demonstrating how different design constraints, project organization and contexts limited the utility of personas. *Proceedings of the Proceedings of the 38th Annual Hawaii International Conference on System Sciences*. Volume 08. DOI: 10.1109/HICSS.2005.85. 214, 218

Rönkkö, K., Hellman, M., Kilander, B., and Dittrich, Y. (2004). Personas is not applicable: Local remedies interpreted in a wider context. *Proceedings of the Eighth Conference on Participatory Design: Artful Integration: Interweaving Media, Materials and Practices*. Volume 1, pp. 112–120. DOI: 10.1145/1011870.1011884. 210, 218, 223, 225

Salminen, J., Guan, K., Jung, S., Chowdhury, S. A., and Jansen, B. J. (2020a). A literature review of quantitative persona creation. *CHI '20: Proceedings of the 2020 CHI Conference on Human Factors in Computing Systems*. pp. 1–14. DOI: 10.1145/3313831.3376502. 209, 211, 213, 217

Salminen, J., Jansen, B. J., An, J., Kwak, H., and Jung, S. (2018a). Are personas done? Evaluating their usefulness in the age of digital analytics. *Persona Studies*, 4(2), 47–65. DOI: 10.21153/psj2018vol4no2art737. 211, 219

Salminen, J., Jansen, B. J., An, J., Kwak, H., and Jung, S. (2019a). Automatic persona generation for online content creators: Conceptual rationale and a research agenda. In L. Nielsen (Ed.), *Personas—User Focused Design*, 2nd ed. Springer London. pp. 135–160. DOI: 10.1007/978-1-4471-7427-1_8. 218

Salminen, J., Jung, S., An, J., Kwak, H., and Jansen, B. J. (2018b). Findings of a user study of automatically generated personas. *Extended Abstracts of the 2018 CHI Conference on Human Factors in Computing Systems - CHI '18*. pp. 1–6. DOI: 10.1145/3170427.3188470. 218

Salminen, J., Jung, S., An, J., Kwak, H., Nielsen, L., and Jansen, B. J. (2019b). Confusion and information triggered by photos in persona profiles. *International Journal of Human-Computer Studies*, 129, 1–14. DOI: 10.1016/j.ijhcs.2019.03.005. 218

Salminen, J., Jung, S., Chowdhury, S. A., Sengün, S., and Jansen, B. J. (2020b). Personas and analytics: A comparative user study of efficiency and effectiveness for a user identification task. *Proceedings of the ACM Conference of Human Factors in Computing Systems (CHI'20)*. DOI: 10.1145/3313831.3376770. 214, 225

Salminen, J., Jung, S., and Jansen, B. J. (2019). The future of data-driven personas: A marriage of online analytics numbers and human attributes. *ICEIS 2019 - Proceedings of the 21st International Conference on Enterprise Information Systems*. pp. 596–603. DOI: 10.5220/0007744706080615. 218

Salminen, J., Kaate, I., Kamel, A. M. S., Jung, S., and Jansen, B. J. (2020c). How does personification impact ad performance and empathy? An experiment with online advertising. *International Journal of Human–Computer Interaction*, 0(0), 1–15. DOI: 10.1080/10447318.2020.1809246. 221

Salminen, J., Kwak, H., Santos, J. M., Jung, S.-G., An, J., and Jansen, B. J. (2018c). *Persona Perception Scale: Developing and Validating an Instrument for Human-Like Representations of Data*. pp. 1–6. DOI: 10.1145/3170427.3188461. 211

Salminen, J., Nielsen, L., Jung, S.-G., An, J., Kwak, H., and Jansen, B. J. (2018d). "Is more better?": Impact of multiple photos on perception of persona profiles. *Proceedings of ACM CHI Conference on Human Factors in Computing Systems (CHI2018). ACM CHI Conference on Human Factors in Computing Systems (CHI2018)*, Montréal, Canada. DOI: 10.1145/3173574.3173891. 214, 219

Salminen, J., Santos, J. M., Kwak, H., An, J., Jung, S., and Jansen, B. J. (2020d). Persona perception scale: development and exploratory validation of an instrument for evaluating individuals' perceptions of personas. *International Journal of Human-Computer Studies*, 141, 102437. DOI: 10.1016/j.ijhcs.2020.102437. 217

Salminen, J., Sengun, S., Jung, S., and Jansen, B. J. (2019c). Design issues in automatically generated persona profiles: A qualitative analysis from 38 think-aloud transcripts. *Proceedings of the ACM SIGIR Conference on Human Information Interaction and Retrieval (CHIIR)*. pp. 225–229. DOI: 10.1145/3295750.3298942. 218

Salminen, J., Şengün, S., Kwak, H., Jansen, B. J., An, J., Jung, S., Vieweg, S., and Harrell, D. F. (2018e). From 2,772 segments to five personas: Summarizing a diverse online audience by generating culturally adapted personas. *First Monday*. DOI: 10.5210/fm.v23i6.8415.

Schrepp, M., Hinderks, A., and Thomaschewski, J. (2017). Construction of a benchmark for the user experience questionnaire (UEQ). *International Journal of Interactive Multimedia and Artificial Intelligence*, 4(4), 40–44. DOI: 10.9781/ijimai.2017.445. 214

Singer, T. and Klimecki, O. M. (2014). Empathy and compassion. *Current Biology*, 24(18), R875–R878. DOI: 10.1016/j.cub.2014.06.054. 218

Sudman, S., Bradburn, N. M., and Schwarz, N. (1996). *Thinking about Answers: The Application of Cognitive Processes to Survey Methodology*. Jossey-Bass. 211

Swann, W. B. (1984). Quest for accuracy in person perception: A matter of pragmatics. *Psychological Review*, 91(4), 457. DOI: 10.1037/0033-295X.91.4.457. 219

Tanenbaum, M. L., Adams, R. N., Iturralde, E., Hanes, S. J., Barley, R. C., Naranjo, D., and Hood, K. K. (2018). From wary wearers to d-embracers: personas of readiness to use diabetes devices. *Journal of Diabetes Science and Technology*, 12(6), 1101–1107. DOI: 10.1177/1932296818793756. 212

Thoma, V. and Williams, B. (2009). Developing and validating personas in e-Commerce: A heuristic approach. In T. Gross, J. Gulliksen, P. Kotzé, L. Oestreicher, P. Palanque, R. O. Prates, and M. Winckler (Eds.), *Human-Computer Interaction – INTERACT 2009*. Springer Berlin Heidelberg. pp. 524–527. DOI: 10.1007/978-3-642-03658-3_56. 212

Tu, N., Dong, X., Rau, P. P., and Zhang, T. (2010). Using cluster analysis in Persona development. *2010 8th International Conference on Supply Chain Management and Information*. pp. 1–5. 212, 213

Tychsen, A. and Canossa, A. (2008). Defining personas in games using metrics. *Proceedings of the 2008 Conference on Future Play: Research, Play, Share*. pp. 73–80. DOI: 10.1145/1496984.1496997. 212

Vincent, C. J. and Blandford, A. (2014). The challenges of delivering validated personas for medical equipment design. *Applied Ergonomics*, 45(4), 1097–1105. DOI: 10.1016/j. apergo.2014.01.010. 217

Vosbergen, S., Mulder-Wiggers, J. M. R., Lacroix, J. P., Kemps, H. M. C., Kraaijenhagen, R. A., Jaspers, M. W. M., and Peek, N. (2015). Using personas to tailor educational messages to the preferences of coronary heart disease patients. *Journal of Biomedical Informatics*, 53, 100–112. DOI: 10.1016/j.jbi.2014.09.004. 212

Wang, L., Li, L., Cai, H., Xu, L., Xu, B., and Jiang, L. (2018). Analysis of regional group health persona based on image recognition. *2018 Sixth International Conference on Enterprise Systems (ES)*. pp. 166–171. DOI: 10.1109/ES.2018.00033. 212

Wöckl, B., Yildizoglu, U., Buber, I., Aparicio Diaz, B., Kruijff, E., and Tscheligi, M. (2012). Basic senior personas: A representative design tool covering the spectrum of European older adults. *Proceedings of the 14th International ACM SIGACCESS Conference on Computers and Accessibility*. pp. 25–32. DOI: 10.1145/2384916.2384922. 212

Zhang, X., Brown, H.-F., and Shankar, A. (2016). Data-driven personas: Constructing archetypal users with clickstreams and user telemetry. *Proceedings of the 2016 CHI Conference on Human Factors in Computing Systems*. pp. 5350–5359. DOI: 10.1145/2858036.2858523. 211, 212

Zhu, H., Wang, H., and Carroll, J. M. (2019). Creating persona skeletons from imbalanced datasets: A case study using U.S. olderadults' health data. *Proceedings of the 2019 on Designing Interactive Systems Conference - DIS '19*. pp. 61–70. DOI: 10.1145/3322276.3322285. 210, 212

CHAPTER 10

Selecting the Appropriate Persona Creation Method

In this chapter, we discuss the various methods of persona creation. Persona creation has traditionally been divided into Qualitative, Quantitative, and Mixed-Methods approaches. However, there is a lack of literature systematically contrasting the strengths and weaknesses of these three general approaches. Here, we review the literature to map the strengths and weaknesses of these approaches. We provide insights for better creation and use of data-driven personas from both researchers and practitioners, especially those who are new to personas, deploying personas in a new domain, or familiar with only one of the persona creation approaches. We end with some examples of the APG system that creates data-driven personas.

10.1 INTRODUCTION

User centricity focuses on better understanding the users toward the development of user-friendly products. A plethora of user understanding approaches have been developed within the HCI domain (Baxter et al., 2015) for this purpose. These approaches have been applied to a range of fields related to digital innovation, such as e-commerce, digital marketing, health informatics, and cybersecurity (Dupree et al., 2016; LeRouge et al., 2013; Poulain and Tarissan, 2020; Salminen et al., 2019).

The selection of a user understanding approach to support user-centric design depends on the information required for a specific task or development project. In some situations, decision-makers require highly detailed user information, while in others, an overview of very broad patterns in the user base is sufficient—personas, especially data-driven personas, can aid in both.

In the extensive body of research on persona creation, three main approaches have been established: *Qualitative*, *Quantitative*, and *Mixed-Methods* (Tu et al., 2010). These approaches (Jansen et al., 2021) contain various methods of data collection and analysis (both qualitative and quantitative), such as affinity diagrams, decision trees, factor analysis, hierarchical clustering, k-means clustering, latent semantic analysis, multidimensional scaling analysis, weighted graphs, and so on (Zhu et al., 2019).

Table 10.1 outlines a high-level stepwise process for selecting the approach persona development approach (Jansen et al., 2021).

Table 10.1: Steps for persona creation. The first and the last step are common for all methods.

	Qualitative	Quantitative	Mixed-Methods
Step 1: Decide the purpose	Decide the purpose(s) of the use of personas.		
Step 2: Gather data	Conduct manual data collection via interviews, focus groups, surveys, etc. to gather data concerning users. Data can include demographics, behaviors, goals, pain points, etc.	Gather the data via automatic means from analytics platforms or other sources such as surveys and CRM systems. Data will typically contain both demographics and behavioral attributes.	Gather the data generally via automatic means from analytics platforms or other sources such as surveys and CRM systems. Identify shortfalls and enrich via qualitative methods (or vice versa).
Step 3: Analyze the data	Analyze the collected data to identify trends, typically via mostly qualitative methods (e.g., grounded theory).	Analyze the collected data to identify trends, typically via quantitative or algorithmic methods.	Analyze the collected data to identify trends, using a mix of qualitative, quantitative, and/or algorithmic methods.
Step 4: Identify archetype users	From the results of data analysis, identify user segments.	The quantitative or algorithmic method will generally result in a specific number of user segments.	Identify the specific number of user segments of current users and/or target users.
Step 5: Create persona profiles	Enhance personas with name, picture, topics of interest, quotes, etc.		

Especially for novice persona users, this methodological plurality may feel daunting, as the persona creation methods range from qualitative interpretative approaches to complicated data science algorithms (Salminen et al., 2020). Nevertheless, a basic understanding of the available alternatives is required for selecting the appropriate persona creation approach for a given task, context, or scenario. Our synthesis of the strengths and weaknesses of the three main approaches provides help for this purpose. We predominantly target persona newcomers by summarizing the 'pros and cons' of the primary persona creation methods. Also, experienced persona users may find this synthesis useful as a refresher of persona creation approaches, and as an inspiration to explore persona creation approaches beyond their past experience and comfort zone.

This chapter addresses two questions.

1.   What are the strengths and weaknesses of the three approaches of persona creation?

2.   When should persona end-users choose each approach?

10.2   PRIMARY METHODS OF PERSONA CREATION

Qualitative persona creation (QUAL) typically involves manual data collection and analysis methods (see the comparison in Table 10.1). Examples of data collection methods are focus groups and interviews (Miaskiewicz et al., 2008; Vosbergen et al., 2015), with data that is generally unstructured and descriptive, e.g., texts and interviews (Dupree et al., 2016; Ford et al., 2017; Huh et al., 2016). Examples of qualitative analysis methods are axial and open coding (Guo and Razikin, 2015; Mesgari et al., 2015). Although personas can be created without data (Matthews et al., 2012), such as assumption-based personas (Seiden and Gothelf, 2003), they are more commonly created based solely on data or based on data with fictive elements.

When data is used, these qualitative personas are typically developed using ethnographic fieldwork and/or user interviews (Cooper, 2004; Goodwin and Cooper, 2009; Pruitt and Grudin, 2003), and they usually rely on a small volume of user data, not enough to apply quantitative analysis (Chapman and Milham, 2006). Overall, QUAL is the traditional approach among researchers and practitioners.

Quantitative persona creation (QUANT), on the other hand, typically involves automatic data collection and data science methods, at least at some level, including nearly fully automated methods for persona-analytics systems such as APG. An example would be using application programming interfaces (APIs) (Cleland-Huang et al., 2013; Wang et al., 2018), where data is generally structured by grouping performance metrics (e.g., views, likes, shares, purchases, etc.) by demographic groups. Examples of QUANT methods to analyze the collected user data are regression, clustering, and matrix factorization (An et al., 2018a, 2018b).

Historically, there were a limited number of efforts, in the literature, to create data-driven personas that are based on behavioral data in large quantities (McGinn and Kotamraju, 2008). However, the use of QUANT methods has increased since the introduction of the persona concept, driven by the increasing availability of online user data (Deng et al., 2020; Xie et al., 2020) and user-segmentation algorithms (Salminen et al., 2020).

Mixed-Methods approach (MIXED) is an integration of these two approaches. The division of approaches into QUAL and QUANT is common in many domains, as is the desire to link the two into a MIXED approach (McGinn and Kotamraju, 2008; Tu et al., 2010). The MIXED approach maintains that QUAL and QUANT methods are compatible and can be used jointly to produce complete (rounded) personas better than either approach could accomplish alone (McGinn and Kotamraju, 2008).

MIXED personas are often recommended in the literature (Pruitt and Grudin, 2003), and most QUANT approaches tend to be accompanied by some form of QUAL effort in writing and evaluation of the persona profiles (Salminen et al., 2020). Conversely, even QUAL approaches can incorporate some QUANT efforts. So, it may be best to view these three approaches, QUAL, MIXED, and QUANT, as a spectrum instead of hard and fast categories. Data-driven personas are an extreme case of the QUANT approach output.

The selection of an approach for persona creation has been discussed by a wide range of research articles in HCI (Nielsen, 2004, 2013; Pruitt and Adlin, 2006; Pruitt and Grudin, 2003). However, there is limited previous work systematically analyzing the strengths and weaknesses of each method type. We report such a systematic analysis in this chapter. The goal is to analyze the strengths and weaknesses of the three persona creation approaches, as well as to outline key opportunities for using data-driven personas to enhance digital innovations.

10.3   LITERATURE COLLECTION AND ANALYSIS

We present in this sub-section a literature analysis of persona creation approaches (Jansen et al., 2021). The analysis is conducted by reading research articles, comparing them, and systematically synthesizing the findings. The evidence base consists of 74 research articles, either conceptually discussing or empirically creating personas. These articles were identified for use, along with the authors' extensive experience of studying personas and creating them for dozens of companies and other organizations. They consist of persona articles in peer-reviewed venues that typically publish persona research.

The researchers conducted the analysis by independently reviewing a portion of the articles. A codebook was created for noting down the "codes" (Glaser and Strauss, 1967) corresponding to each approach and its strengths and weaknesses (Strengths-Qualitative, Weaknesses-Qualitative, etc.). In qualitative research tradition, a code refers to an inductive unit of observation describing a relevant theme in the data—*relevant* in terms of the research goal and *data* in terms of the articles. An example of a code is "COMPLEXITY" (see the following sub-section). To generate the codes, the researchers worked collaboratively, and each of the researchers assigned codes to each subdivision of the articles. The researchers then commented on each other's codes, and the final list of codes was obtained via mutual agreement (Jansen et al., 2021).

The following subsections present the results of this analysis. We provide supporting references (SR) for each code (see the boxes summarizing the findings).

10.4   STRENGTHS AND WEAKNESSES

10.4.1 QUALITATIVE PERSONA CREATION

In earlier HCI practice, the methods used were often quantitative, focusing on keystrokes and task completion. However, there was also a need to understand socially-based phenomena (Adams et al., 2008). From the beginning, the persona method has aimed to answer the questions "Why do people behave as they do?" and "Why do people think as they do?" along with evoking empathy for the users (Grudin, 2006). For this purpose, qualitative methods were useful, and ethnography provided tools such as observations, interviews, and contextual inquiry. The starting point for QUAL personas was software development and design. Teams used the personas method to understand user needs, pain points, work processes, etc. These areas are challenging to access via quantitative methods. One of the first articles to explore the method (Pruitt and Grudin, 2003) mentions the description of a day in the life of the persona. It also provides anecdotes and personal information that can be used to develop empathy in the persona end-users.

The QUAL approach has several strengths that explain why it is a favorite approach for many fans of the persona method. The strengths (listed in alphabetical order) are (Jansen et al., 2021) as follows.

S1.   **COMPLEXITY**: Investigating multi-layered and nuanced user behaviors (i.e., complex phenomena). SR: (Blomquist and Arvola, 2002; Mulder and Yaar, 2006).

S2.   **DEPTH:** Focusing on a limited number of cases in significant depth. SR: (Adams et al., 2008; Guo and Yan, 2011).

S3.   **DESCRIPTIVE:** Inductively producing a descriptive theory of a user type. SR: (Neate et al., 2019; Nielsen, 2004).

S4.   **EMOTIONS:** Conveying the users' interpretations, internal emotions, and beliefs. SR: (Mulder and Yaar, 2006; Pruitt and Grudin, 2003).

S5.   **EMPATHY:** Accessing the underlying context of needs, feelings, goals, behaviors, and pain points. SR: (Hisham, 2009; Nielsen, 2004; Wright and McCarthy, 2008).

S6.   **EVALUATION:** Analyzing different user types and scenarios. SR: (Aljohani and Blustein, 2015; Guo and Yan, 2011).

S7.   **EXPERIENCES:** Providing an understanding of the personal experiences of users. SR: (Adams et al., 2008; Idoughi et al., 2012).

S8.   **PERSONALIZE:** Providing individual anecdotes and insights to be used in persona profiles. SR: (Anvari et al., 2017; Nielsen, 2004).

S9.   **SPECIFICITY:** Creating rich representations of specific user circumstances. SR: (Guo and Yan, 2011; Holtzblatt et al., 2005).

The weaknesses of QUAL are (Jansen et al., 2021) as follows.

W1.   **BIAS:** Profiles can be plagued with biases and idiosyncrasies. SR: (An et al., 2018a; Chapman and Milham, 2006).

W2.   **EFFORT:** Manual creation of persona profiles is time-consuming. SR: (An et al., 2018a; Drego et al., 2010).

W3.   **INVALID:** Qualitative methods may imply low levels of credibility for users. SR: (An et al., 2018a; Mesgari et al., 2015).

W4.   **NARROW:** Might not generalize to other users or settings. SR: (Brickey et al., 2010; Chapman et al., 2015).

W5.   **REPRESENTATIVE:** Does not address the number of users; therefore, small segments might be overrepresented. SR: (An et al., 2018a; Chapman and Milham, 2006).

10.4.2 QUANTITATIVE PERSONA CREATION

The increased availability of digital user data, both for in-house sources such as CRM systems and for online analytics platforms, as well as more sophisticated algorithmic techniques (An et al., 2018a, 2018b), encourages the creation of data-driven personas from quantitative data. Data collection via online APIs has dramatically increased the feasibility of quantitative persona creation (Vecchio et al., 2018). This online user data can be collected through social media platforms (e.g., Facebook, YouTube), online analytics services (e.g., Adobe Analytics, Google Analytics), or CRMsystems.

The QUANT approach has several strengths that explain why it has gained support in many data-driven personas development cases. The strengths include (Jansen et al., 2021) the following.

S1.   **EVALUATION:** Allows for testing hypotheses that are constructed before the personas are created. SR: (Brooks and Greer, 2014; Li et al., 2016).

S2.   **PRECISION:** Data collected is more precise, concise, and quantitative. SR: (Chapman et al., 2015; Dupree et al., 2016).

S3.   **PRESENTATION:** Easier to simplify user findings when the data is founded on sufficient samples. SR: (An et al., 2018a, 2018b).

S4.   **REPEATABILITY:** Ability to simplify user findings of many different populations and segments. SR: (An et al., 2018a; Salminen et al., 2019).

S5.   **SIMPLICITY:** Ability to construct a situation that eliminates the bewildering sway of many variables, allowing one or more recognized cause-and-effect relations. SR: (Kim et al., 2019; Tempelman-Kluit and Pearce, 2014).

S6.   **SPEED:** Faster data collection and analysis than the QUAL approach. SR: (Chu et al., 2018; Ishii et al., 2018; Mijač et al., 2018).

S7.   **TESTING:** Profiles can be used for quantitative predictions. SR: (Miaskiewicz et al., 2008; Rahimi and Cleland-Huang, 2014).

S8.   **VALIDITY:** Allows validation and testing of constructed theories about users. SR: (Minichiello et al., 2018; Wöckl et al., 2012).

S9.   **VOLUME:** The approach is applicable to the study of large numbers of users. SR: (An et al., 2018b; Watanabe et al., 2017; Zhu et al., 2019).

The QUANT approach has several weaknesses, however. These include (Jansen et al., 2021) the following.

W1.   **COMPLEXITY:** User data gathered via this method may require complex algorithms for analysis. SR: (Dhakad et al., 2017; Holmgard et al., 2014).

W2.   **DISCONNECTION:** Segmentation may not reflect the goals and objectives of the end-users. SR: (Goodman-Deane et al., 2018; Hirskyj-Douglas et al., 2017).

W3.   **OUTLIERS:** The statistical weight of the majority of users may mask interesting outliers. SR: (Tychsen and Canossa, 2008; Zhang et al., 2016).

W4.   **TARGETED:** Personas created may represent existing users and not desired users. SR: (Bamman et al., 2013; Brickey et al., 2012; Holden et al., 2017).

10.4.3 MIXED-METHOD PERSONA CREATION

When the QUAL approach results are combined with those of the QUANT approach, the resulting personas may better present current user behaviors (quantitative added value) and better interpret the complexities of any given situation or targeted users (qualitative added value). As such, the MIXED approach has several strengths that may make it a worthwhile approach, which are (Jansen et al., 2021) as follows.

S1.   **COMPLETENESS:** Allows for the adding of insights that might be missed when relying on a single method. SR: (Dang-Pham et al., 2015; Tempelman-Kluit and Pearce, 2014).

S2.   **DIVERSITY:** Qualitative data (narratives) can merge with quantitative data (numbers) to add connotations. SR: (Dupree et al., 2016; Hirskyj-Douglas et al., 2017).

S3.   **FLEXIBILITY:** Can produce more complete knowledge necessary to inform actionable insights. SR: (Hirskyj-Douglas et al., 2017; Thoma and Williams, 2009).

S4.   **RANGE:** Allows for the presentation of a broader and more complete range of information due to a range of data collection and/or analysis methods. SR: (An et al., 2018a; Minichiello et al., 2018).

S5.   **RESILIENT**: Combines the strengths of quantitative and qualitative approaches. SR: (McGinn and Kotamraju, 2008; Tu et al., 2010).

S6.   **SUPPORT:** Profiles are better positioned to provide evidence of representing the users via the convergence of findings. SR: (Salminen et al., 2018; Zaugg and Ziegenfuss, 2018).

S7.   **TESTABLE:** Information in the profile can be used to generate and test hypotheses. SR: (Dupree et al., 2016; Miaskiewicz and Luxmoore, 2017).

Yet, the MIXED approach also has weaknesses, including (Jansen et al., 2021) the following.

W1.   **EFFORT:** It is more expensive and time-consuming than the other creation methods due to possible duplicate content during data collection and analysis. SR: (Holden et al., 2017; Mijač et al., 2018).

W2.   **IMPLEMENTATION:** It may prove difficult to implement by any single persona development team. SR: (Mesgari et al., 2015; Miaskiewicz and Luxmoore, 2017).

W3.   **INTEGRATION:** As a result of a mixture of different data collection techniques and methods of analysis, there may be problems interpreting conflicting results into a coherent profile. SR: (Ford et al., 2017; Salminen et al., 2018).

W4.   **PREPARATION:** It requires knowledge about many methods and techniques and how to appropriately mix them to generate coherent personas. SR: (Guo and Razikin, 2015; Salminen et al., 2018).

10.5   DISCUSSION AND IMPLICATIONS

The persona technique has inherent advantages relative to other user analytics techniques, in that personas provide human faces to "cold" numbers (Jansen et al., 2020). However, there is considerable plurality when it comes to persona creation methods, which may be confusing, especially for those who are new to personas. To help navigate this plurality, we analyzed the three primary approaches of persona creation.

Table 10.2: SWOT analysis of each of the persona creation approaches

SWOT	Qualitative	Quantitative	Mixed-Methods
Strengths	Detailed and nuanced insights	Detailed and testable observations of behaviors	More subtle explanations of observed behaviors
Weakness	Limited data and testable hypotheses	Circumscribe insights into goals, desires, pain points	Difficult to integrate disparate data
Opportunities	Enhanced methods of data collection	Availability of online analytics data	Algorithmic approaches for understanding qualitative data
Threats	Rapidly changing user population requiring further rounds of data collection	Constant change to APIs, services, and platforms	Diverge user segments resulting in conflicting insights

Our main implications for persona users—both researchers and practitioners—are three-fold. First, before choosing the approach, persona users should (1) build awareness of the strengths and weaknesses of each option. For this, we provide a standard SWOT analysis (see Table 10.2).

Second, persona users should (2) consider the context of the persona creation process and final use case. This involves understanding the context and decision process of the stakeholders using the personas. Part of this "contextual awareness" is an understanding of how well each approach is compatible with the user-centric analysis case at hand. For example, it is simply not possible to collect a large dataset for persona creation driven by quantitative analysis. Other times, specific quantitative information is requested by the decision-makers to make the personas work for them.

Third, persona users should (3) understand that there is no "one best approach" to personas. Perhaps the closest to this is, when resources and data permit, the MIXED approach. As suggested in the HCI literature (Mesgari et al., 2015; Pruitt and Grudin, 2003; Salminen et al., 2018), the MIXED approach assists in answering questions that cannot be answered under either QUAL or QUANT approaches alone. One should be aware that while integrating data, information, and results from the QUAL and QUANT approaches into a MIXED approach for persona creation, there are techniques to guide the integration. One of these is the triangulation design model (Tashakkori and Teddie, 1998), which aims to combine the qualitative and quantitative data collection into one comprehensive persona profile.

Table 10.3 presents guidelines for persona users to choose the appropriate approach for their process. These guidelines consider seven criteria: (1) *Data*, (2) *Context*, (3) *Information*, (4) *Updatability*, (5) *Interactivity*, (6) *Timeliness*, and (7) *Economics*.

Table 10.3: Guidelines for persona users to choose a suitable approach for their project. QUANT is suitable for What questions, QUAL for Why questions, and MIXED for both What and Why questions

	Choose QUAL if…	Choose QUANT if…	Choose MIXED if…
Data	You have access to users that are willing to share their experiences and expectations.	You have pre-existing quantitative data that describes user behaviors and demographics.	You have access to both quantitative and qualitative user insights.
Context	Decision-making circumstances require an in-depth understanding of the users.	Your data can be used for the decision-making purposes of the organization for which the personas are created.	The personas need to adapt to many use cases and scenarios that are difficult to anticipate.
Information	The information needs of the decision-makers are focused on qualitative insights (e.g., user pain points, motivations, goals)	Decision-makers' information needs can be satisfied with quantitative data on user segments (e.g., duration of using the product, features used).	Decision-makers required in-depth personas that have qualitative details (e.g., pain points) and numerical accuracy (e.g., audience size the persona represents).
Updatability	Personas are used for a one-time project or do not require frequent updating.	Personas need to be updated frequently (i.e., the behaviors and demographics in the user base are rapidly shifting).	If there are proper resources (time, money, expertise) to update the personas as required by the changes in the user behavior.
Interactivity	There is no need for decision-makers to interact with the personas beyond the media of paper, presentation slides, and posters.	Decision-makers need to interact and explore personas using computer-assisted media.	There is a possibility to leverage various types of data in an interactive system that provides long-term value for decision-makers.

	Choose QUAL if...	Choose QUANT if...	Choose MIXED if...
Timeliness	If persona creation is not time-sensitive but can afford the collection of data using interviews and/or ethnography.	You need to generate the personas rapidly without time to conduct manual data collection and analysis.	If there is no strict time limit for synthesizing the results of quantitative and qualitative inquiry.
Economics	Adequate budget is available for professional interviews/ethnography.	You have pre-existing resources (skills, software) that can be deployed for quantitative analysis.	If there is no strict limit on the budget, and the use of experts from qualitative and quantitative domains can be afforded.

The bottom line is that in the "perfect world," without limitations, persona creators should most likely opt for the MIXED approach (Jansen et al., 2021). Specifically, they should rely on QUANT for data-driven personas and then supplement this QUANT data with some QUAL data to "round things out." However, various realities—such as data availability, lack of specialized skills, and constraints in resources such as time and money—require persona creators in practical settings to make trade-offs.

For the final choice of persona creation methods, exploration and experimentation with different methods are highly recommended for researchers and practitioners, as venturing out from methodological comfort zones, and applying new, unfamiliar methods is crucial for learning and "becoming better" at creating personas. Even when accustomed to a certain persona creation approach, another approach might be more appropriate for specific tasks and contexts. Thus, researchers and practitioners may benefit greatly from exploring and experimenting with approaches that are new to them.

10.6   APG ILLUSTRATION

Although APG generates data-driven personas, it does incorporate some QUAL elements, including conversations that the persona has engaged in. Naturally, since the persona is not real, it did not actually engage in these conversations. The user in the segment that the persona represented engaged in these online conversations, shedding light on user perceptions and feelings represented by data-driven personas. These insights, collected automatically, provide the type of data they would expect from QUAL data collection methods. An example of social media conversations is shown in Figure 10.1.

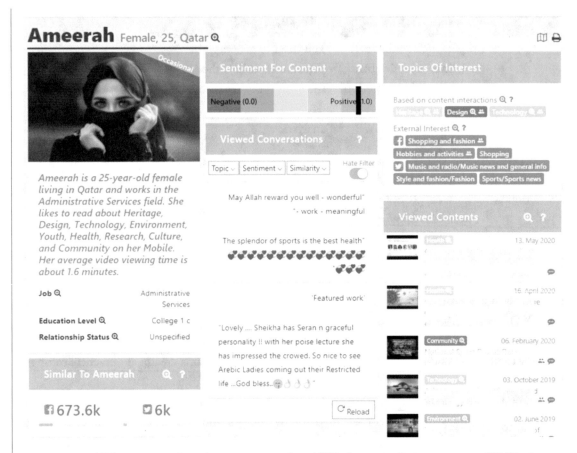

Figure 10.1: APG generates data-driven personas, but APG also typically incorporates QUAL elements, such as social media conversations. These social media comments are made by those users the persona represents engaged with online.

10.7 CONCLUSION AND THE ROAD AHEAD

To provide methodological clarity, we analyzed three approaches for persona creation: Quantitative, Qualitative, and Mixed-Methods. We arrived at the strengths and weaknesses of each approach via a systematic analysis of the literature. We presented a SWOT analysis of the three approaches to distill insights into in what situations each approach should be implored, and we summarized the implications in a framework of guidelines for persona creators. As the complexity and diversity of user populations increase, personas can serve as a valuable instrument for understanding users in digital-innovation contexts.

10.8   CHAPTER TAKE-AWAYS

- The generic benefit of personas, regardless of how they are created, arises from summarizing user information into an intuitive representation that can be communicated with little effort.

- The three main approaches for persona creation are Qualitative, Quantitative, and Mixed-Methods. Data-driven personas typically rely on quantitative methods.

- Qualitative methods are most common in persona literature and practice.

- Each of the three approaches has strengths that drive their use, but they each also come with weaknesses. Persona developers need to weigh the trade-offs of each for their specific task.

- There are seven criteria for persona stakeholders to consider when choosing the appropriate approach for their process: (1) *Data*, (2) *Context*, (3) *Information*, (4) *Updatability*, (5) *Interactivity*, (6) *Timeliness*, and (7) *Economics*.

10.9   DISCUSSION AND ASSESSMENT QUESTIONS

1. List and define the three general approaches to persona creation.

2. Describe the differences in data gathering among the three general approaches for persona creation.

3. Compare and contrast the creation of the persona profile in the Qualitative, Quantitative, and Mixed-Methods approaches.

4. List and define one strength and one weakness of Qualitative, Quantitative, and Mixed-Methods persona creation.

5. Explain why the Mixed-Methods approach to persona creation is so difficult compared to the Qualitative and Quantitative methods.

6. Identify a factor that has led to an increase in the use of the Quantitative method, and explain why this is driving the use of the Quantitative method and, therefore, the creation of data-driven personas.

10.10 REFERENCES

Adams, A., Lunt, P., and Cairns, P. (2008). A qualitative approach to HCI research. In *Research Methods for Human-Computer Interaction*. Cambridge University Press. pp. 138–157. DOI: 10.1017/CBO9780511814570.008. 243

Aljohani, M. and Blustein, J. (2015). Personas help understand users' needs, goals and desires in an online institutional repository. *World Academy of Science, Engineering and Technology International Journal of Computer and Information Engineering*, 9(2), 629–636. 243

An, J., Kwak, H., Jung, S., Salminen, J., and Jansen, B. J. (2018a). Customer segmentation using online platforms: Isolating behavioral and demographic segments for persona creation via aggregated user data. *Social Network Analysis and Mining*, 8(1), 54. DOI: 10.1007/s13278-018-0531-0. 241, 244, 245

An, J., Kwak, H., Salminen, J., Jung, S., and Jansen, B. J. (2018b). Imaginary people representing real numbers: Generating personas from online social media data. *ACM Transactions on the Web (TWEB)*, 12(4), 27. DOI: 10.1145/3265986. 241, 244, 245

Anvari, F., Richards, D., Hitchens, M., Babar, M. A., Tran, H. M. T., and Busch, P. (2017). An empirical investigation of the influence of persona with personality traits on conceptual design. *Journal of Systems and Software*, 134, 324–339. DOI: 10.1016/j.jss.2017.09.020. 243

Bamman, D., O'Connor, B., and Smith, N. A. (2013). Learning latent personas of film characters. *Proceedings of the 51st Annual Meeting of the Association for Computational Linguistics*. pp. 10. 245

Baxter, K., Courage, C., and Caine, K. (2015). *Understanding your Users: A Practical Guide to User Requirements Methods, Tools, and Techniques*, 2nd edition. Morgan Kaufmann. DOI: 10.1016/B978-0-12-800232-2.00001-8. 239

Blomquist, Aa. and Arvola, M. (2002). Personas in action: Ethnography in an interaction design team. *Proceedings of the Second Nordic Conference on Human-Computer Interaction*. pp. 197–200. DOI: 10.1145/572020.572044. 243

Brickey, J., Walczak, S., and Burgess, T. (2012). Comparing semi-automated clustering methods for persona development. *IEEE Transactions on Software Engineering*, 38(3), 537–546. DOI: 10.1109/TSE.2011.60. 245

Brickey, Jon, Walczak, S., and Burgess, T. (2010). A comparative analysis of persona clustering methods. *Americas Conference on Information Systems (AMCIS2010)*. p. 217. 244

Brooks, C. and Greer, J. (2014). Explaining predictive models to learning specialists using personas. *Proceedins of the Fourth International Conference on Learning Analytics And Knowledge – LAK '14*. pp. 26–30. DOI: 10.1145/2567574.2567612. 244

Chapman, C., Krontiris, K., and Webb, J. (2015). Profile CBC: Using conjoint analysis for consumer profiles. *Sawtooth Software Conference Proceedings*. https://research.google.com/pubs/archive/44167.pdf. 244

Chapman, C. N. and Milham, R. P. (2006). The personas' new clothes: Methodological and practical arguments against a popular method. *Proceedings of the Human Factors and Ergonomics Society Annual Meeting*, 50, 634–636. DOI: 10.1177/154193120605000503. 241, 244

Chu, E., Vijayaraghavan, P., and Roy, D. (2018). Learning personas from dialogue with attentive memory networks. *Proceedings of the 2018 Conference on Empirical Methods in Natural Language Processing*. pp. 2638–2646. https://www.aclweb.org/anthology/D18-1284. DOI: 10.18653/v1/D18-1284. 244

Cleland-Huang, J., Czauderna, A., and Keenan, E. (2013). A persona-based approach for exploring architecturally significant requirements in agile projects. In J. Doerr and A. L. Opdahl (Eds.), *Requirements Engineering: Foundation for Software Quality*. Springer. pp. 18–33. DOI: 10.1007/978-3-642-37422-7_2. 241

Cooper, A. (2004). *The Inmates Are Running the Asylum: Why High Tech Products Drive Us Crazy and How to Restore the Sanity* (2nd Edition). Pearson Higher Education. 241

Dang-Pham, D., Pittayachawan, S., and Nkhoma, M. (2015). Demystifying online personas of Vietnamese young adults on Facebook: A Q-methodology approach. *Australasian Journal of Information Systems*, 19(1). DOI: 10.3127/ajis.v19i0.1204. 245

Deng, S., Jiang, Y., Li, H., and Liu, Y. (2020). Who contributes what? Scrutinizing the activity data of 4.2 million Zhihu users via immersion scores. *Information Processing and Management*, 57(5), 102274. DOI: 10.1016/j.ipm.2020.102274. 241

Dhakad, L., Das, M., Bhattacharyya, C., Datta, S., Kale, M., and Mehta, V. (2017). SOPER: Discovering the influence of fashion and the many faces of user from session logs using stick breaking process. *Proceedings of the 2017 ACM on Conference on Information and Knowledge Management – CIKM '17* pp. 1609–1618. DOI: 10.1145/3132847.3133007. 245

Drego, V. L., Dorsey, M., Burns, M., and Catino, S. (2010). *The ROI Of Personas* [Report]. Forrester Research. https://www.forrester.com/report/The+ROI+Of+Personas/-/E-RES55359. 244

Dupree, J. L., Devries, R., Berry, D. M., and Lank, E. (2016). Privacy personas: Clustering users via attitudes and behaviors toward security practices. *Proceedings of the 2016 CHI Conference on Human Factors in Computing Systems* pp. 5228–5239. DOI: 10.1145/2858036.2858214. 239, 241, 244, 245, 246

Ford, D., Zimmermann, T., Bird, C., and Nagappan, N. (2017). Characterizing software engineering work with personas based on knowledge worker actions. *Proceedings of the 11th ACM/IEEE International Symposium on Empirical Software Engineering and Measurement* pp. 394–403. DOI: 10.1109/ESEM.2017.54. 241, 246

Glaser, B. G. and Strauss, A. L. (1967). *The Discovery of Grounded Theory: Strategies for Qualitative Research*. Transaction Publishers. DOI: 10.1097/00006199-196807000-00014. 242

Goodman-Deane, J., Waller, S., Demin, D., González-de-Heredia, A., Bradley, M., and Clarkson, J. P. (2018). Evaluating inclusivity using quantitative personas. In *Proceedings of Design Research Society Conference 2018. Design Research Society Conference 2018*, Limerick, Ireland. DOI: 10.21606/drs.2018.400. 245

Goodwin, K. and Cooper, A. (2009). *Designing for the Digital Age: How to Create Human-Centered Products and Services*. Wiley. 241

Grudin, J. (2006). Why personas work: The psychological evidence. In John Pruitt and T. Adlin (Eds.), *The Persona Lifecycle*. Elsevier. pp. 642–663. DOI: 10.1016/B978-012566251-2/50013-7. 243

Guo, H. and Razikin, K. B. (2015). Anthropological user research: A data-driven approach to personas development. *Proceedings of the Annual Meeting of the Australian Special Interest Group for Computer Human Interaction* pp. 417–421. DOI: 10.1145/2838739.2838816. 241, 246

Guo, J. and Yan, P. (2011). User-centered information architecture of University Library Website. *2011 3rd International Conference on Computer Research and Development*, 2, 370–372. 243

Hirskyj-Douglas, I., Read, J. C., and Horton, M. (2017). Animal personas: Representing dog stakeholders in interaction design. *Proceedings of the 31st British Computer Society Human Computer Interaction Conference*, 37. pp. 1-37:13. DOI: 10.14236/ewic/HCI2017.37. 245

Hisham, S. (2009). Experimenting with the use of persona in a focus group discussion with older adults in Malaysia. *Proceedings of the 21st Annual Conference of the Australian Computer-Human Interaction Special Interest Group on Design: Open 24/7 - OZCHI '09*, 333. DOI: 10.1145/1738826.1738889. 243

Holden, R. J., Kulanthaivel, A., Purkayastha, S., Goggins, K. M., and Kripalani, S. (2017). Know thy eHealth user: Development of biopsychosocial personas from a study of older adults with heart failure. *International Journal of Medical Informatics*, 108, 158–167. DOI: 10.1016/j.ijmedinf.2017.10.006. 245, 246

Holmgard, C., Liapis, A., Togelius, J., and Yannakakis, G. N. (2014). Evolving personas for player decision modeling. *Computational Intelligence and Games (CIG), 2014 IEEE Conference On.* pp. 1–8. DOI: 10.1109/CIG.2014.6932911. 245

Holtzblatt, K., Beringer, J., and Baker, L. (2005). Rapid user centered design techniques: Challenges and solutions. *CHI'05 Extended Abstracts on Human Factors in Computing Systems.* pp. 2037–2038. DOI: 10.1145/1056808.1057088. 243

Huh, J., Kwon, B. C., Kim, S.-H., Lee, S., Choo, J., Kim, J., Choi, M.-J., and Yi, J. S. (2016). Personas in online health communities. *Journal of Biomedical Informatics*, 63, 212–225. DOI: 10.1016/j.jbi.2016.08.019. 241

Idoughi, D., Seffah, A., and Kolski, C. (2012). Adding user experience into the interactive service design loop: A persona-based approach. *Behaviour and Information Technology*, 31(3), 287–303. DOI: 10.1016/j.jbi.2016.08.019. 243

Ishii, R., Ito, S., Ishihara, M., Harada, T., and Thawonmas, R. (2018). Monte-carlo tree search implementation of fighting game ais having personas. *2018 IEEE Conference on Computational Intelligence and Games (CIG).* pp. 1–8. DOI: 10.1109/CIG.2018.8490367. 244

Jansen, B. J., Jung, S., Salminen, J., Guan, K., and Nielsen, L. (2021). Strengths and weaknesses of persona creation methods: Outlining guidelines for novice and experienced users and opportunities for digital innovations. *Proceedings of the Hawaii International Conference on System Sciences (HICSS).* 239, 242, 243, 244, 245, 246, 249

Jansen, B. J., Salminen, J., and Jung, S. (2020). Data-driven personas for enhanced user understanding: Combining empathy with rationality for better insights to analytics. *Data and Information Management*, 4(1). https://content.sciendo.com/view/journals/dim/4/1/article-p1.xml. DOI: 10.2478/dim-2020-0005. 246

Kim, E., Yoon, J., Kwon, J., Liaw, T., and Agogino, A. M. (2019). From innocent irene to parental Patrick: Framing user characteristics and personas to design for cybersecurity. *Proceedings of the Design Society: International Conference on Engineering Design*, 1(1), 1773–1782. DOI: 10.1017/dsi.2019.183. 244

LeRouge, C., Ma, J., Sneha, S., and Tolle, K. (2013). User profiles and personas in the design and development of consumer health technologies. *International Journal of Medical Informatics*, 82(11), e251–e268. DOI: 10.1016/j.ijmedinf.2011.03.006. 239

Li, J., Galley, M., Brockett, C., Spithourakis, G., Gao, J., and Dolan, B. (2016). A persona-based neural conversation model. *Proceedings of the 54th Annual Meeting of the Association for Computational Linguistics (Volume 1: Long Papers).* pp. 994–1003. DOI: 10.18653/v1/P16-1094. 244

Matthews, T., Judge, T., and Whittaker, S. (2012). How do designers and user experience professionals actually perceive and use personas? *Proceedings of the SIGCHI Conference on Human Factors in Computing Systems*. pp. 1219–1228. DOI: 10.1145/2207676.2208573. 241

McGinn, J. and Kotamraju, N. (2008). Data-driven persona development. *Proceedings of the SIGCHI Conference on Human Factors in Computing Systems*. pp. 1521–1524. DOI: 10.1145/1357054.1357292. 241, 242, 246

Mesgari, M., Okoli, C., and Guinea, A. O. de. (2015). Affordance-based user personas: A mixed-method approach to persona development. *AMCIS 2015 Proceedings*. https://aisel.aisnet.org/amcis2015/HCI/GeneralPresentations/1. 241, 244, 246, 247

Miaskiewicz, T. and Luxmoore, C. (2017). The use of data-driven personas to facilitate organizational adoption–A case study. *The Design Journal*, 20(3), 357–374. DOI: 10.1080/14606925.2017.1301160. 246

Miaskiewicz, T., Sumner, T., and Kozar, K. A. (2008). A latent semantic analysis methodology for the identification and creation of personas. *Proceedings of the SIGCHI Conference on Human Factors in Computing Systems*. pp. 1501–1510. http://dl.acm.org/citation.cfm?id=1357290. DOI: 10.1145/1357054.1357290. 241, 245

Mijač, T., Jadrić, M., and Ćukušić, M. (2018). The potential and issues in data-driven development of web personas. *2018 41st International Convention on Information and Communication Technology, Electronics and Microelectronics (MIPRO)*. pp. 1237–1242. DOI: 10.23919/MIPRO.2018.8400224. 244, 246

Minichiello, A., Hood, J. R., and Harkness, D. S. (2018). Bringing user experience design to bear on STEM education: A narrative literature review. *Journal for STEM Education Research*, 1(1–2), 7–33. DOI: 10.1007/s41979-018-0005-3. 245

Mulder, S. and Yaar, Z. (2006). *The User is Always Right: A Practical Guide to Creating and Using Personas for the Web*. New Rider. 243

Neate, T., Bourazeri, A., Roper, A., Stumpf, S., and Wilson, S. (2019). Co-created personas: Engaging and empowering users with diverse needs within the design process. *Proceedings of the 2019 CHI Conference on Human Factors in Computing Systems - CHI '19*. pp. 1–12. DOI: 10.1145/3290605.3300880. 243

Nielsen, L. (2004). Engaging personas and narrative scenarios [Ph.D. Thesis, Samfundslitteratur]. http://personas.dk/wp-content/samlet-udgave-til-load.pdf. 242, 243

Nielsen, L. (2013). *Personas—User Focused Design*. Springer-Verlag. DOI: 10.1007/978-1-4471-4084-9. 242

Poulain, R. and Tarissan, F. (2020). Investigating the lack of diversity in user behavior: The case of musical content on online platforms. *Information Processing and Management*, 57(2), 102169. DOI: 10.1016/j.ipm.2019.102169. 239

Pruitt, J. and Adlin, T. (2006). *The Persona Lifecycle: Keeping People in Mind Throughout Product Design*. Morgan Kaufmann. 242

Pruitt, J. and Grudin, J. (2003). Personas: Practice and theory. *Proceedings of the 2003 Conference on Designing for User Experiences*. pp. 1–15. DOI: 10.1145/997078.997089. 241, 242, 243, 247

Rahimi, M. and Cleland-Huang, J. (2014). Personas in the middle: Automated support for creating personas as focal points in feature gathering forums. *Proceedings of the 29th ACM/IEEE International Conference on Automated Software Engineering*. pp. 479–484. DOI: 10.1145/2642937.2642958. 245

Salminen, J., Guan, K., Jung, S., Chowdhury, S. A., and Jansen, B. J. (2020). A literature review of quantitative persona creation. *CHI '20: Proceedings of the 2020 CHI Conference on Human Factors in Computing Systems*. pp. 1–14. DOI: 10.1145/3313831.3376502. 240, 241, 242

Salminen, J., Jung, S., and Jansen, B. J. (2019). The future of data-driven personas: A marriage of online analytics numbers and human attributes. *ICEIS 2019 - Proceedings of the 21st International Conference on Enterprise Information Systems*. pp. 596–603. DOI: 10.5220/0007744706080615. 239, 244

Salminen, J., Şengün, S., Kwak, H., Jansen, B. J., An, J., Jung, S., Vieweg, S., and Harrell, D. F. (2018). From 2,772 segments to five personas: Summarizing a diverse online audience by generating culturally adapted personas. *First Monday*. DOI: 10.5210/fm.v23i6.8415. 246, 247

Seiden, J. and Gothelf, J. (2003). *Lean UX: Applying Lean Principles to Improve User Experience*. O'Reilly. 241

Tashakkori, A. and Teddie, C. (1998). *Mixed methodology*. Sage. 247

Tempelman-Kluit, N. and Pearce, A. (2014). Invoking the user from data to design. *College and Research Libraries*, 75(5), 616–640. DOI: 10.5860/crl.75.5.616. 244, 245

Thoma, V. and Williams, B. (2009). Developing and validating personas in e-commerce: A heuristic approach. In T. Gross, J. Gulliksen, P. Kotzé, L. Oestreicher, P. Palanque, R. O. Prates, and M. Winckler (Eds.), *Human-Computer Interaction – INTERACT 2009*. Springer Berlin Heidelberg. pp. 524–527. DOI: 10.1007/978-3-642-03658-3_56. 245

Tu, N., He, Q., Zhang, T., Zhang, H., Li, Y., Xu, H., and Xiang, Y. (2010). Combine qualitative and quantitative methods to create persona. *2010 3rd International Conference on Informa-*

tion Management, Innovation Management and Industrial Engineering, 3, 597–603. DOI: 10.1109/ICIII.2010.463. 239, 241, 246

Tychsen, A. and Canossa, A. (2008). Defining personas in games using metrics. *Proceedings of the 2008 Conference on Future Play: Research, Play, Share*. pp. 73–80. DOI: 10.1145/1496984.1496997. 245

Vecchio, P. D., Mele, G., Ndou, V., and Secundo, G. (2018). Creating value from social big data: Implications for smart tourism destinations. *Information Processing and Management*, 54(5), 847–860. DOI: 10.1016/j.ipm.2017.10.006. 244

Vosbergen, S., Mulder-Wiggers, J. M. R., Lacroix, J. P., Kemps, H. M. C., Kraaijenhagen, R. A., Jaspers, M. W. M., and Peek, N. (2015). Using personas to tailor educational messages to the preferences of coronary heart disease patients. *Journal of Biomedical Informatics*, 53, 100–112. DOI: 10.1016/j.jbi.2014.09.004. 241

Wang, L., Li, L., Cai, H., Xu, L., Xu, B., and Jiang, L. (2018). Analysis of regional group health persona based on image recognition. *2018 Sixth International Conference on Enterprise Systems (ES)*. pp. 166–171. DOI: 10.1109/ES.2018.00033. 241

Watanabe, Y., Washizaki, H., Honda, K., Noyori, Y., Fukazawa, Y., Morizuki, A., Shibata, H., Ogawa, K., Ishigaki, M., Shiizaki, S., Yamaguchi, T., and Yagi, T. (2017). ID3P: Iterative data-driven development of persona based on quantitative evaluation and revision. *Proceedings of the 10th International Workshop on Cooperative and Human Aspects of Software Engineering*. pp. 49–55. DOI: 10.1109/CHASE.2017.9. 245

Wöckl, B., Yildizoglu, U., Buber, I., Aparicio Diaz, B., Kruijff, E., and Tscheligi, M. (2012). Basic senior personas: A representative design tool covering the spectrum of european older adults. *Proceedings of the 14th International ACM SIGACCESS Conference on Computers and Accessibility*. pp. 25–32. DOI: 10.1145/2384916.2384922. 245

Wright, P. and McCarthy, J. (2008). Empathy and experience in HCI. *Proceedings of the SIGCHI Conference on Human Factors in Computing Systems*. pp. 637–646. DOI: 10.1145/1357054.1357156. 243

Xie, I., Babu, R., Lee, T. H., Castillo, M. D., You, S., and Hanlon, A. M. (2020). Enhancing usability of digital libraries: Designing help features to support blind and visually impaired users. *Information Processing and Management*, 57(3), 102110. DOI: 10.1016/j.ipm.2019.102110. 241

Zaugg, H. and Ziegenfuss, D. H. (2018). Comparison of personas between two academic libraries. *Performance Measurement and Metrics*, 19(3), 142–152. DOI: 10.1108/PMM-04-2018-0013. 246

Zhang, X., Brown, H.-F., and Shankar, A. (2016). Data-driven personas: Constructing archetypal users with clickstreams and user telemetry. *Proceedings of the 2016 CHI Conference on Human Factors in Computing Systems*. pp. 5350–5359. DOI: 10.1145/2858036.2858523. 245

Zhu, H., Wang, H., and Carroll, J. M. (2019). Creating persona skeletons from imbalanced datasets—A case study using u.s. older adults' health data. *Proceedings of the 2019 on Designing Interactive Systems Conference - DIS '19*. pp. 61–70. DOI: 10.1145/3322276.3322285. 239, 245

Part 6

Data-Driven Personas and the Future

CHAPTER 11

Conclusion: Dispelling Myths and Laying Out the Grand Challenges of Data-Driven Personas

In this concluding chapter, we address three myths concerning data-driven personas. In some respects, these myths are the foundational drivers for the grand challenges in the data-driven persona domain. We then present and discuss the grand challenges that must be addressed, in a multidisciplinary manner, to take data-driven personas to the next level of fully functional persona analytics in order to achieve enhanced user understanding across the many domains that employ personas.

11.1 DATA-DRIVEN PERSONA MYTHS

Our experience has shown there are many myths concerning data-driven personas. Three common ones are as follows.

MYTH 1: Data-driven personas are only for big companies. There is a misconception that data-driven personas are only for big companies. This is not true because data-driven personas' suitability depends on the data volume (i.e., size), not company size. In the era of social media, there can be small companies that have large customer bases or even individuals ("influencers") that have large audiences. So, it needs to be clear that data size (i.e., number of contents, number of viewers, the variation of viewers, number of products, number of services) matters more than company size.

In reverse, it is also true that a very big company may not have enough data for data-driven personas, or the company user population has too little variety (i.e., too homogenous) to make data-driven personas appropriate.

MYTH 2: Data-driven personas are cheap. While data-driven techniques democratize personas for organizations that can access data, many organizations do not have the data. So, the democratization of personas does not necessarily always take place. In this case, data collection can be costly. Moreover, expertise for data-driven persona creation (i.e., data science skills) and the associated steps that require human labor (e.g., data annotation for interest classification) can similarly increase the price tag. Third, the creation of a complete persona analytics system with the capability to generate data-driven personas from big data can be quite expensive in terms of time and cost, along with requiring significant technical expertise, which would seem to put it out of the reach of small companies (see MYTH 1).

However, Software as a Service (SaaS) of persona analytics systems, such as the APG system, can create personas for a single company relative inexpensively, as the overall development cost is not borne by a single entity.

MYTH 3: The narrow quantitative persona. This myth refers to the assumption that <u>quantitatively derived</u>, data-driven personas contain shallow information limited to numerical analysis, and not insightful qualitative information, such as pain points, needs, and wants. To some extent, this is a predominant case for some personas; nonetheless, it is not necessarily true, and it is becoming increasingly rare as personas analytics systems emerge on the scene. New studies are proposing advanced techniques to generate more personas insights, such as personality traits (Salminen et al., 2020d) using deep learning.

Moreover, social media (Spiliotopoulos et al., 2020) comments, user reviews, and customer relationship management survey responses are rich sources of information about users' thinking and address this issue at least partially. Dispelling the myth of narrow quantitative personas is important because it is an assumption that may prevent researchers from pursuing the difficult tasks of including more in-depth information in the quantitative personas and encourage departmentalization in which persona creators assume certain trade-offs, depending on their choice of method.

Overall, it is important to dispel these (and other) myths to advance data-driven persona research and progress of the domain, from flat personas to data-driven personas to fully functional persona analytics systems and address the grand challenges of data-driven personas.

11.2   THE GRAND CHALLENGES FOR DATA-DRIVEN PERSONAS

11.2.1   DEFINING GRAND CHALLENGES

A grand challenge is a fundamental problem in a domain with broad internal and external applications and whose solution would enable applying an approach that could become available in the near term. A driver of a grand challenge is the clear articulation of the desired objective to focus attention and resources on the problem in order to promote innovative solutions to the problem. The grand challenge approach does not define an immediately obvious answer but steers efforts in a given direction.

One benefit of articulating grand challenges is the galvanization of action from various researchers, agencies, research labs, universities, and companies. Grand challenges can catalyze substantial research advances for a set of priorities within the domain. Grand challenges typically have some or all of the following attributes.

- **A broad vision:** grand, ambitious but explicitly targeted;

- **A collaboration need:** because of their scope, there is often a need for multidisciplinary research;

- **An achievable task set:** the targets are ambitious and audacious but have a defined and unambiguous outcome even though the exact solution has not yet been articulated; and

- **A flexible agenda:** the journey to achieve the explicit target is not yet known or defined.

A second benefit of articulating grand challenges is the changing of the perception in the field. The articulation and outlining of a grand challenge serve to shift thinking in a domain from "Why would we work on that?" to "Why aren't we working on that?"

This is the primary motivator for the inclusion of this chapter on grand challenges. We provide these grand challenges to serve as a call to action for data-driven personas and analytics, design, marketing, advertising, health, engineering, and other researchers to push the field forward.

For each grand challenge described in this chapter, the authors believe that the scientific and practical payments are likely to result from research efforts in the near term. We begin by identifying the grand challenge then discuss the underlying problem and articulate the benefits of addressing the specific grand challenge. We list more focused research areas that are especially deserving of intensive study for some grand challenges although these lists are not intended to be comprehensive.

The authors also do not claim that these grand challenges are the only challenges for research and development in the data-driven personas domain. Rather, we have identified these as among the most important and, in our experience, the most achievable with the most impact in the near term.

11.2.2 THE GRAND CHALLENGES OF DATA-DRIVEN PERSONAS

The grand challenges of data-driven personas are shown in Figure 11.1, and each grand challenge is discussed below.

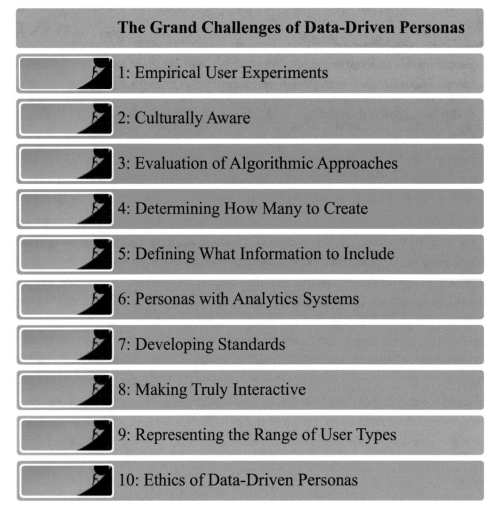

Figure 11.1: The 10 grand challenges of the data-driven persona domain.

Grand Challenge 1: Empirical User Experiments—Shift from Assumptions to Evidence for Data-Driven Personas. To rigorously evaluate data-driven personas against other methods of enhancing user understanding for a range of user standing tasks, see the discussion in Chapter 7 on "personas + X." This will require a series of carefully controlled, empirical, and mainly quantitative system studies with carefully articulated tasks, domains, and criteria for evaluation by a wide range of researchers. For scientific progress, data-driven persona research should empirically demonstrate that *personas engender empathy for the users*, and *empathy for the users improves design* across a range of domains, use cases, and tasks.

To our knowledge, as of this writing, there is no peer-reviewed research demonstrating, in an empirically valid manner, that (non-data-driven) personas are better than any other method for a given user understanding task. Data-driven personas have been validated as of this writing (Salminen et al., 2020b) for at least one user understanding task. Currently, most persona studies fail to address this aspect of persona evaluation, instead of relying on assumptions, which is why conducting empirical experiments across a wide range of user understanding tasks is one of the grand challenges.

Grand Challenge 2: Creating Data-Driven Personas That Are Culturally Aware. To create data-driven personas that are culturally aware of the stakeholders who will employ and use these personas. Cultural meanings and differences are extremely difficult to encode and detect using automated systems, and it is not so easy using qualitative methods, either. These meanings are difficult even for untrained humans to distinguish. An automatic persona system is entirely oblivious to them unless specifically trained to classify information based on its cultural meanings. Such efforts are lacking from the literature, despite there being an extensive body of literature concerning culture-specific use of personas (Cabrero, 2014; Cabrero et al., 2016a, 2016b; Jensen et al., 2017; Nielsen, 2010, 2013; Nielsen and Storgaard Hansen, 2014).

One possible solution has humans in the loop: Have end-users flag culturally inappropriate content in the personas, which would help the underlying algorithm to learn what is culturally appropriate and what is not. However, scaling this approach is difficult, which is why this is a grand challenge for the data-driven persona domain.

Grand Challenge 3: Evaluation of Algorithmic Approaches for Data-Driven Personas' Creation. To evaluate the implications of creating data-driven personas algorithms and determine appropriate algorithms for generating data-driven personas in line with organizational goals and key performance indicators (KPIs). There are several open questions in this area, including (a) identifying algorithmic bias in design goals that impact diverse, fair, and consistent data-driven personas; (b) creating ethically robust data-driven personas that fairly represent the underlying user data; (c) identifying suitable algorithms to be used for data-driven persona segmentation; (d) maintaining consistency and fairly representing the underlying user data as different algorithms generate different personas from the same data; (e) detecting how to deal with imbalanced user data and how to generate data-driven personas of marginalized user groups; and (f) developing computational techniques to infer user attributes such as pain points, needs, wants, and culture-specific meanings and incorporate these into the persona profiles. Given the multivariable issues at play, this is a grand challenge for data-driven personas.

Grand Challenge 4: Determining How Many Data-Driven Personas to Create. To determine the "best" number of data-driven personas to create that both represent the underlying user population and are also optimal for stakeholders to employ and use for their tasks. Persona stakeholders may generalize traits presented in the personas due to the limited number of final personas that they see fit to create. While stakeholders can create more data-driven personas to capture subtler and esoteric characteristics, this might result in personas that may be too numerous to apply in familiar contexts. "Is it reasonable to expect the end-users to employ hundreds of personas?" We do not know, as this aspect has not been investigated in prior work to our knowledge. However, we do know that it may take hundreds of data-driven personas to adequately represent some user populations (Jansen et al., 2019).

Thus, the stakeholders must consider the opportunity cost of including and excluding fringe personas, depending on their goals. Such trade-off questions also exist for the information design of data-driven personas. Brickey et al. (2010), Bamman et al. (2013), and Holden et al. (2017, 2018, 2020) highlighted their limitations in contextualizing personas when it came to unexpected outliers in the clusters, such as deciding which traits are applicable. These decisions are currently made by technically oriented persona creators who are not necessarily the same people as persona stakeholders and end-users. Therefore, simple user interfaces for persona analytics design are needed, with "simple" referring to point-and-click interfaces that require little technical sophistication.

Grand Challenge 5: Defining What Information Data-Driven Personas Should Contain. To create flexible personas and persona profiles that are adaptable and confirm to stakeholder needs. *Persona users' goals vary. Persona users' information needs vary*. Persona users' tasks vary. The variation in these three aspects underlines the need for flexibility in persona analytics systems and data-driven personas. Through flexibility, persona analytics systems can accommodate many-fold more use cases than static flat personas that cannot be modified after their creation. These interactive personas from such persona analytics systems should be malleable. The stakeholders can manipulate both the information included in the persona and its presentation; the stakeholders can quickly switch between personas; the stakeholders can choose to view majority personas, minority personas, or a mix thereof; and the stakeholders can input scenarios into the system and observe simulated or predicted behaviors of the personas. Incorporating flexibility is, therefore, needed in persona analytics systems and is challenging to do. Therefore, this is one of the grand challenges of data-driven personas.

Grand Challenge 6: Integration of Personas with Analytics Systems. To conceptually and practically define the boundaries among personalization—segmentation—data-driven personas via theoretical construct development, rigorous user research, and applied design of personas analytics systems. As data-driven personas are presented as interactive services, these data-driven personas become components of full-stack personas analytics systems (Jansen et al., 2020). In such personas analytics systems, data-driven persona profiles serve as interfaces to analytics systems and enable efficient use of API interfaces for exporting persona profiles to other systems to enable the users to conceptualize their user data in an ad-hoc manner as personas.

However, this situation raises conceptual questions about defining the boundaries of what a persona is in the concept of a system allowing for personalization, segmentation, and personas. Where does one begin and the next end? Can *every* person be a persona? If so, how is this different than personalization? If not, what value does the persona bring relative to personalization? How different does one person have to be from another to be distinct and require a different persona? Are personas within an analytics system really personas in the traditional sense? Or are they representative segments? Is the traditional conceptualization of personas outdated in the age of analytics? These conceptualization, research, and implementation issues are complex, so this is a grand challenge.

Grand Challenge 7: Developing Data-Driven Persona Standards. Data-driven personas suffer from a lack of standards. This is paradoxical because data-driven personas are, in theory, in a perfect position for standards to emerge. Yet, no known universal metrics to evaluate persona quality even exist as of this writing! There are no standards, for example, as to how many personas should be created, how to choose the algorithm(s), what metrics should be used to evaluate the personas, or what ethical considerations there should be when collecting and processing data. The lack of standards hinders the progress of data-driven personas on multiple fronts: creation, use, and understanding user behavior.

The choice of methods is unclear, as is the mutual comparison of methods. *What are the standard use cases for data-driven personas? How many personas do users view? On average, how long do they spend on persona profiles? What information is the most crucial for decision-making?* Apart from limited exploratory work (Salminen et al., 2018, 2020b, 2020c), no convincing standards for data-driven persona user behavior have been developed to date.

Also, data-driven personas can be generated from many alternative metrics to describe different behaviors, but often, one core metric is used at a time (An et al., 2018a). *Which metric(s) should be chosen, then?* This issue is akin to that in the field of analytics, where stakeholders need to define their questions well to avoid getting lost in the dozens of reports afforded by most analytics systems. For data-driven personas, there is virtually no guidance for this metrics selection; researchers and practitioners carry out the selection in an ad-hoc manner.

Grand Challenge 8: Making Personas Truly Interactive. Current data-driven personas are still immature in the sense that end-users cannot truly "interrogate" them. Stakeholders cannot ask the persona what it thinks of a given design, how it would behave in a certain situation, or explain why the personas have a certain, for example, pain point. Interaction techniques for data-driven personas are still at early stages, and quantitative methods are not efficiently deployed to predict the persona's behavior in unforeseen scenarios. Technologies in text-generation and dialogue systems can, in theory, enable real conversations with personas, but even the state-of-the-art NLP techniques are not yet ripe for this use case.

To truly engage with a persona as if it were a human being, a considerable leap in artificial intelligence is required. Until that leap, the approach that can be taken relies on adding gradual interactivity, such as filters for persona sentiments (Jansen et al., 2020) and text-based prediction of interests (An et al., 2018b). In the addition of such features, the crucial question is that of user needs—do the new features serve specific needs, and do they work enough to provide value for persona users in their daily jobs?

Grand Challenge 9: Representing the Whole Range of User Types. The typical definition of personas is that they describe typical users (Cooper, 2004). Therefore, creating an average persona is the conceptual and practical default of many persona creation projects. Its challenges relate, firstly, to stereotyping when focusing on the mean/average user (Haag and Marsden, 2019; Turner and Turner, 2011) and secondly, to the focus of data-driven algorithms on the central tendency in the data. What we mean by this can be illustrated with a simple example. Assume two data points about users, with numerical values of "1" and "5." Their average is "3," which is equally far from both observations and thus does not well represent either data point.

This "flaw of averages" is documented in a classic study conducted by the U.S. Air Force in 1950 that found that, among 4,000 measured pilots, no pilots matched all the average attributes of height, weight, etc. (Hertzberg et al., 1954). Similarly, by picking "representative" behaviors and characteristics for the data-driven personas, we overlook the extremes. These extremes, anomalies, deviations, minorities, and fringe groups are, therefore, not considered by the stakeholders using the data-driven personas; as far as the stakeholders are concerned, they do not exist (Salminen et al., 2020a). To correct the issue, experimental work will be needed to discover and isolate extreme personas (to determine the range of personas in a dataset), as well as to separate the creation of average personas from that of outlier personas.

Grand Challenge 10: The Ethics of Data-Driven Personas. The final challenge deals with ethics. According to the escalating demands for normative analyses of algorithms, an ethical review of data-driven persona development is necessary. While data-driven persona development may increase objectivity (Jansen et al., 2019), current methods may present new sources of prejudice and lack of transparency (Salminen et al., 2019), as well as other ethical challenges. Overall, data-driven persona development may be thought of as an attempt to disaggregate aggregated data, which is how analytics platforms typically present such individual user data. Therefore, the most prominent ethical concerns involve categorization bias and algorithmic transparency.

Thus far, research on ethics in data-driven personas is extremely scarce (Goodman-Deane et al., 2018). It is, therefore, uncertain whether the HCI researchers and practitioners even recognize these ethical issues. For example, replacing the persona generation algorithm can have a drastic effect on the generated personas, even when the underlying data is the same. Apart from the research presented in Brickey et al. (2012) that only focuses on clustering algorithms, we are unaware of any work actually comparing what kinds of personas are generated by different algorithms based on the same baseline data. Thus, it is uncertain whether data-driven personas are biased and, if so, how?

11.3   VISION OF THE PERFECT DATA-DRIVEN PERSONA

So, what are the implications if these grand challenges are addressed in the near future? In an ideal world, what would it look like? What persona information would we have? What features? In what ways would users be able to interact with data-driven personas?

Answering these questions, addressing the grand challenges, and speculating on the direction of the research are thought-provoking, but one possible outcome in an idealized persona analytics system would be one that possesses the following attributes:

- validated benefits for enhanced user understanding as measured by both effectiveness and efficiency relative to other methods;

- data-driven personas profiles that are sensitive to the cultural aspects in which they are employed and of those who employ them;

- ensemble of algorithmic approaches that adapt to organizational goals and key performance indicators;

- problem aware (i.e., you sense you have a problem but do not know there is a solution) where the "best" number of data-driven personas is dependent on the problem to be addressed;

- problem aware where the "best" information to present to the end user is dependent on the problem to be addressed;

- fully integrated data from individual users to conceptual data-driven personas;

- standardized data-driven personas allowing for sharing across projects and systems;

- interactive data-driven personas capability of communicating with stakeholders via multiple mediums and channels;

- representation of each user segments in the population; and

- explainability of the possible data and/or algorithmic biases self-contained.

11.4   FUTURE CONSIDERATIONS

Grand challenges have been employed in various domains to innovate and advance the field toward high-payoff research, practice, and development. In the domain of data-driven personas, the grand challenges presented here are, to our knowledge, the first grand challenges articulated for the field. The successful achievement of these grand challenges will require the rapid sharing of information, insights, and resources among many researchers and practitioners to make informed research decisions. However, if the domain is successful in these efforts, the results are a substantial leap forward in the development of personas analytics systems, enhanced user understanding, and better-designed systems, content, and products.

11.5 REFERENCES

An, J., Kwak, H., Jung, S., Salminen, J., and Jansen, B. J. (2018a). Customer segmentation using online platforms: Isolating behavioral and demographic segments for persona creation via aggregated user data. *Social Network Analysis and Mining*, 8(1), 54. DOI: 10.1007/s13278-018-0531-0. 269

An, J., Kwak, H., Salminen, J., Jung, S., and Jansen, B. J. (2018b). Imaginary people representing real numbers: Generating personas from online social media data. *ACM Transactions on the Web (TWEB)*, 12(4), 27. DOI: 10.1145/3265986. 269

Bamman, D., O'Connor, B., and Smith, N. A. (2013). Learning latent personas of film characters. *Proceedings of the 51st Annual Meeting of the Association for Computational Linguistics*. p. 10. 268

Brickey, J., Walczak, S., and Burgess, T. (2012). Comparing semi-automated clustering methods for persona development. *IEEE Transactions on Software Engineering*, 38(3), 537–546. DOI: 10.1109/TSE.2011.60. 270

Brickey, J., Walczak, S., and Burgess, T. (2010). A comparative analysis of persona clustering methods. *AMCIS 2010 Proceedings*. https://aisel.aisnet.org/amcis2010/217. 268

Brickey, Jonalan. (2010). *System For Persona Ensemble Clustering: A Cluster Ensemble Approach To Persona Development*. University of Colorado at Denver. 268

Cabrero, D. G. (2014). Participatory design of persona artefacts for user eXperience in non-WEIRD cultures. *Proceedings of the 13th Participatory Design Conference: Short Papers, Industry Cases, Workshop Descriptions, Doctoral Consortium Papers, and Keynote Abstracts*. Volume 2, pp. 247–250. DOI: 10.1145/2662155.2662246. 267

Cabrero, D. G., Winschiers-Theophilus, H., and Abdelnour-Nocera, J. (2016a). A critique of personas as representations of "the other" in cross-cultural technology design. *Proceedings of the First African Conference on Human Computer Interaction*. pp. 149–154. DOI: 10.1145/2998581.2998595. 267

Cabrero, D. G., Winschiers-Theophilus, H., Abdelnour-Nocera, J., and Kapuire, G. K. (2016b). A hermeneutic inquiry into user-created personas in different Namibian locales. *Proceed-

ings of the 14th Participatory Design Conference: Full Papers. Volume 1, pp. 101–110. DOI: 10.1145/2940299.2940310. 267

Cooper, A. (2004). *The Inmates Are Running the Asylum: Why High Tech Products Drive Us Crazy and How to Restore the Sanity*. 2nd edition. Pearson Higher Education. 270

Goodman-Deane, J., Waller, S., Demin, D., González-de-Heredia, A., Bradley, M., and Clarkson, J. P. (2018). Evaluating inclusivity using quantitative personas. *Proceedings of Design Research Society Conference 2018. Design Research Society Conference 2018*, Limerick, Ireland. DOI: 10.21606/drs.2018.400. 270

Haag, M. and Marsden, N. (2019). Exploring personas as a method to foster empathy in student IT design teams. *International Journal of Technology and Design Education*, 29(3), 565–582. DOI: 10.1007/s10798-018-9452-5. 270

Hertzberg, H. T., Daniels, G. S., and Churchill, E. (1954). *Anthropometry Of Flying Personnel-1950*. Antioch Coll Yellow Springs OH. 270

Holden, R. J., Daley, C. N., Mickelson, R. S., Bolchini, D., Toscos, T., Cornet, V. P., Miller, A., and Mirro, M. J. (2020). Patient decision-making personas: An application of a patient-centered cognitive task analysis (P-CTA). *Applied Ergonomics*, 87, 103107. DOI: /10.1016/j.apergo.2020.103107. 268

Holden, R. J., Joshi, P., Rao, K., Varrier, A., Daley, C. N., Bolchini, D., Blackburn, J., Toscos, T., Wagner, S., Martin, E., Miller, A., and Mirro, M. J. (2018). Modeling personas for older adults with heart failure. *Proceedings of the Human Factors and Ergonomics Society Annual Meeting*, 62(1), 1072–1076. DOI: 10.1177/1541931218621246. 268

Holden, R. J., Kulanthaivel, A., Purkayastha, S., Goggins, K. M., and Kripalani, S. (2017). Know thy eHealth user: Development of biopsychosocial personas from a study of older adults with heart failure. *International Journal of Medical Informatics*, 108, 158–167. DOI: 10.1016/j.ijmedinf.2017.10.006. 268

Jansen, B. J., Jung, S., and Salminen, J. (2020). From flat file to interface: Synthesis of personas and analytics for enhanced user understanding. *Proceedings of the Association for Information Science and Technology*, 57(1). DOI: 10.1002/pra2.215. 268, 269

Jansen, B. J., Jung, S., and Salminen, J. (2019). Creating manageable persona sets from large user populations. *Extended Abstracts of the 2019 CHI Conference on Human Factors in Computing Systems*. pp. 1–6. DOI: 10.1145/3290607.3313006. 268, 270

Jensen, I., Hautopp, H., Nielsen, L., and Madsen, S. (2017). Developing international personas: A new intercultural communication practice in globalized societies. *Journal of Intercultural Communication*. p. 43. 267

Nielsen, L. (2010). Personas in Cross-Cultural Projects. In D. Katre, R. Orngreen, P. Yammiyavar, and T. Clemmensen (Eds.), *Human Work Interaction Design: Usability in Social, Cultural and Organizational Contexts*. Volume 316, pp. 76–82). Springer Berlin Heidelberg. DOI: 10.1007/978-3-642-11762-6_7. 267

Nielsen, L. (2013). *Personas—User Focused Design*, 1st edition. Springer-Verlag. DOI: 10.1007/978-1-4471-4084-9. 267

Nielsen, L. and Storgaard Hansen, K. (2014). Personas is applicable: A study on the use of personas in Denmark. *Proceedings of the SIGCHI Conference on Human Factors in Computing Systems*. pp. 1665–1674. DOI: 10.1145/2556288.2557080. 267

Salminen, J., Froneman, W., Jung, S., Chowdhury, S., and Jansen, B. J. (2020a). The ethics of data-driven personas. *Extended Abstracts of the 2020 CHI Conference on Human Factors in Computing Systems Extended Abstracts*. pp. 1–9. DOI: 10.1145/3334480.3382790. 270

Salminen, J., Jung, S., Chowdhury, S. A., Sengün, S., and Jansen, B. J. (2020b). Personas and analytics: A comparative user study of efficiency and effectiveness for a user identification task. *Proceedings of the ACM Conference of Human Factors in Computing Systems (CHI'20)*. DOI: 10.1145/3313831.3376770. 267, 269

Salminen, J., Liu, Y.-H., Sengun, S., Santos, J. M., Jung, S., and Jansen, B. J. (2020c). The effect of numerical and textual information on visual engagement and perceptions of AI-driven persona interfaces. *IUI '20: Proceedings of the 25th International Conference on Intelligent User Interfaces*. pp. 357–368. DOI: 10.1145/3377325.3377492. 269

Salminen, J., Nielsen, L., Jung, S., An, J., Kwak, H., and Jansen, B. J. (2018). "Is more better?": Impact of multiple photos on perception of persona profiles. *Proceedings of ACM CHI Conference on Human Factors in Computing Systems (CHI2018)*. DOI: 10.1145/3173574.3173891. 269

Salminen, J., Rao, R. G., Jung, S., Chowdhury, S. A., and Jansen, B. J. (2020d). Enriching social media personas with personality traits: A deep learning approach using the big five classes. *International Conference on Human-Computer Interaction*, 101–120. DOI: 10.1007/978-3-030-50334-5_7. 264

Salminen, J., Santos, J. M., Jung, S., Eslami, M., and Jansen, B. J. (2019). Persona transparency: Analyzing the impact of explanations on perceptions of data-driven personas. *International Journal of Human–Computer Interaction*, 0(0), 1–13. DOI: 10.1080/10447318.2019.1688946. 270

Spiliotopoulos, D., Margaris, D., and Vassilakis, C. (2020). Data-assisted persona construction using social media data. *Big Data and Cognitive Computing*, 4(3), 21. DOI: 10.3390/bdcc4030021. 264

Turner, P. and Turner, S. (2011). Is stereotyping inevitable when designing with personas? *Design Studies*, 32(1), 30–44. DOI: 10.1016/j.destud.2010.06.002. 270

APPENDIX A

Persona Perception Scale Items

Salminen, Joni, Joao M. Santos, Haewoon Kwak, Jisun An, Soon-gyo Jung, and Bernard J. Jansen. 2020. Persona perception scale: Development and exploratory validation of an instrument for evaluating individuals' perceptions of personas. *International Journal of Human-Computer Studies*, 141.

Construct	Item	Item content
Consistency	CN01	The quotes of the persona match other information shown in the persona profile.
	CN02	The picture of the persona matches other information shown in the persona profile.
	CN03	The persona information seems consistent.
	CN04	The persona's demographic information (age, gender, country) corresponds with other information shown in the persona profile.
Completeness	CM01	The persona profile is detailed enough to make decisions about the customers it describes.
	CM02	The persona profile seems complete.
	CM03	The persona profile provides enough information to understand the people it describes.
	CM04	The persona profile is not missing vital information.
Willingness to use	WTU01	I would make use of this persona in my task of [insert task].
	WTU02	I can imagine ways to make use of the persona information in my task of [insert task].
	WTU03	This persona would improve my ability to make decisions about the customers it describes.
Credibility	CR01	The persona seems like a real person.
	CR02	I have met people like this persona.
	CR03	The picture of the persona looks authentic.
Clarity	CL01	The information about the persona is well presented.
	CL02	The text in the persona profile is clear enough to read.
	CL03	The information in the persona profile is easy to understand.

Construct	Item	Item content
Similarity	SM01	This persona feels similar to me.
	SM02	The persona and I think alike.
	SM03	The persona and I share similar interests.
	SM04	I believe I would agree with this persona on most matters.
Likability	LK01	I find this persona likable.
	LK02	I could be friends with this persona.
	LK03	This persona feels like someone I could spend time with.
	LK04	This persona is interesting.
Empathy	EM01	I feel like I understand this persona.
	EM02	I feel strong ties to this persona.
	EM03	I can imagine a day in the life of this persona.

APPENDIX B

User Interview Questions for Persona Data Collection

Here are an integrate set of user interview questions that have been used to create personas.

Question	Source Author Name	Source URL	Theme
How do you prefer to communicate (e.g., by phone, email, in person)?	Carol Ann Tan	https://www.sprk-d.com/blog/21-essential-questions-to-ask-during-a-buyer-persona-interview	Consumer Habits
Which social networks do you prefer to use (personally and professionally)?	Carol Ann Tan	https://www.sprk-d.com/blog/21-essential-questions-to-ask-during-a-buyer-persona-interview	Consumer Habits
How do you stay current on developments in your industry?	Carol Ann Tan	https://www.sprk-d.com/blog/21-essential-questions-to-ask-during-a-buyer-persona-interview	Consumer Habits
If you were to search for a product/service you needed, what search terms would you use?	Carol Ann Tan	https://www.sprk-d.com/blog/21-essential-questions-to-ask-during-a-buyer-persona-interview	Consumer Habits
Think back on a recent purchase. How did you research the purchase?	Carol Ann Tan	https://www.sprk-d.com/blog/21-essential-questions-to-ask-during-a-buyer-persona-interview	Consumer Habits
Think back on a recent purchase. How did you research the purchase? What factors were most important to you in evaluating your options? What doubts did you have? Did anyone help you make the final decision?	Carol Ann Tan	https://www.sprk-d.com/blog/21-essential-questions-to-ask-during-a-buyer-persona-interview	Consumer Habits
What do you watch on TV?	Carly Ries	https://www.smartbug-media.com/blog/55-questions-to-ask-when-developing-buyer-personas	Consumer Habits

Question	Source Author Name	Source URL	Theme
What offline resources do you use?	Carly Ries	https://www.smartbug-media.com/blog/55-questions-to-ask-when-developing-buyer-personas	Consumer Habits
What online resources do you use?	Carly Ries	https://www.smartbug-media.com/blog/55-questions-to-ask-when-developing-buyer-personas	Consumer Habits
Where do you prefer to do your shopping?	Carly Ries	https://www.smartbug-media.com/blog/55-questions-to-ask-when-developing-buyer-personas	Consumer Habits
How important is it to get a good deal?	Carly Ries	https://www.smartbug-media.com/blog/55-questions-to-ask-when-developing-buyer-personas	Consumer Habits
What types of mobile devices do you own?	Carly Ries	https://www.smartbug-media.com/blog/55-questions-to-ask-when-developing-buyer-personas	Consumer Habits
What could make us even better? Whether it be in the buying process you went through or afterward?	Kaitlyn Petro	https://www.impactbnd.com/blog/buyer-persona-questions-to-ask-in-your-persona-interviews	Consumer Habits
What could we do to reach more people just like you?	Kaitlyn Petro	https://www.impactbnd.com/blog/buyer-persona-questions-to-ask-in-your-persona-interviews	Consumer Habits
How often do you check emails on your phone, at home, at work?	Kaitlyn Petro	https://www.impactbnd.com/blog/buyer-persona-questions-to-ask-in-your-persona-interviews	Consumer Habits
Do you use the internet to research vendors or products? If yes, how do you search for information?	Lindsay Kolowich	https://blog.hubspot.com/marketing/buyer-persona-questions	Consumer Habits

Question	Source Author Name	Source URL	Theme
Describe a recent purchase.	Lindsay Kolowich	https://blog.hubspot.com/marketing/buyer-persona-questions	Consumer Habits
What do you like to do in your free time?	Mark Loehrke	https://www.clariantcreative.com/blog/creating-personas-interview-questions-to-get-you-started	Consumer Habits
If yes, which ones?	Sujan Patel	https://sujanpatel.com/marketing/150-buyer-persona-questions/	Consumer Habits
If no, why not? Are they unsure how to use them? Perhaps they don't trust them?	Sujan Patel	https://sujanpatel.com/marketing/150-buyer-persona-questions/	Consumer Habits
What's their preferred method of communication? Emailing, texting, using an app (such as WhatsApp), or do they prefer to pick up the phone?	Sujan Patel	https://sujanpatel.com/marketing/150-buyer-persona-questions/	Consumer Habits
Do they shop online?	Sujan Patel	https://sujanpatel.com/marketing/150-buyer-persona-questions/	Consumer Habits
If yes, which websites do they usually buy from?	Sujan Patel	https://sujanpatel.com/marketing/150-buyer-persona-questions/	Consumer Habits
If no, why not? As with Question #336, this may come down to trust (not feeling confident supplying their bank details online) or ability (not understanding how to make purchases online). However, they may simply prefer to make purchases in person.	Sujan Patel	https://sujanpatel.com/marketing/150-buyer-persona-questions/	Consumer Habits
Again if no, could they be persuaded to start shopping online?	Sujan Patel	https://sujanpatel.com/marketing/150-buyer-persona-questions/	Consumer Habits
What cell phone do they use?	Sujan Patel	https://sujanpatel.com/marketing/150-buyer-persona-questions/	Consumer Habits

Question	Source Author Name	Source URL	Theme
Why do they need your product (or service)? Think about the benefits it will offer your specific buyer (not the general public at large).	Sujan Patel	https://sujanpatel.com/marketing/150-buyer-persona-questions/	Consumer Habits
When will they need your product? Is it something they'll need for a specific occasion, something that lends itself to repeat purchases, or something that, while useful, will not be required at any specific point?	Sujan Patel	https://sujanpatel.com/marketing/150-buyer-persona-questions/	Consumer Habits
What other products (if any) on the market offer the same (or similar) benefits?	Sujan Patel	https://sujanpatel.com/marketing/150-buyer-persona-questions/	Consumer Habits
If you're up against competing products, why would your persona choose to buy from you, rather than one of your competitors? Think about your USPs; specifically, how your USPs will benefit your buyer.	Sujan Patel	https://sujanpatel.com/marketing/150-buyer-persona-questions/	Consumer Habits
What questions will they ask before deciding to buy your product?	Sujan Patel	https://sujanpatel.com/marketing/150-buyer-persona-questions/	Consumer Habits
What's their number one concern when deciding whether or not to make a purchase? (Price, quality, brand, etc.)	Sujan Patel	https://sujanpatel.com/marketing/150-buyer-persona-questions/	Consumer Habits
How would they prefer to purchase your product? Online, over the phone, or in person?	Sujan Patel	https://sujanpatel.com/marketing/150-buyer-persona-questions/	Consumer Habits

Question	Source Author Name	Source URL	Theme
Are they willing to make the purchase by alternative means, or is there only one means by which they are happy or able to buy?	Sujan Patel	https://sujanpatel.com/marketing/150-buyer-persona-questions/	Consumer Habits
When making a purchase online, which payment method do they prefer to use? Think PayPal, debit card, or credit card, but consider the card provider too.	Sujan Patel	https://sujanpatel.com/marketing/150-buyer-persona-questions/	Consumer Habits
When making a purchase in person, do they prefer to pay by card or with cash?	Sujan Patel	https://sujanpatel.com/marketing/150-buyer-persona-questions/	Consumer Habits
What accomplishments are you most proud of?	Carly Ries	https://www.smartbug-media.com/blog/55-questions-to-ask-when-developing-buyer-personas	Decision Making
What are the top three things on your bucket list?	Carly Ries	https://www.smartbug-media.com/blog/55-questions-to-ask-when-developing-buyer-personas	Decision Making
What value is typically associated with your industry?	Carly Ries	https://www.smartbug-media.com/blog/55-questions-to-ask-when-developing-buyer-personas	Decision Making
What is the preferred type of sales experience in your industry?	Carly Ries	https://www.smartbug-media.com/blog/55-questions-to-ask-when-developing-buyer-personas	Decision Making
(If a customer) Why did you choose [your company] over another company?	Kaitlyn Petro	https://www.impactbnd.com/blog/buyer-persona-questions-to-ask-in-your-persona-interviews	Decision Making

Question	Source Author Name	Source URL	Theme
(If not a customer) Why did you choose X Company over us?	Kaitlyn Petro	https://www.impactbnd.com/blog/buyer-persona-questions-to-ask-in-your-persona-interviews	Decision Making
What is your decision-making process when planning on buying [your product/service]?	Kaitlyn Petro	https://www.impactbnd.com/blog/buyer-persona-questions-to-ask-in-your-persona-interviews	Decision Making
Was anyone else involved in this process? If so, who? And why or why not?	Kaitlyn Petro	https://www.impactbnd.com/blog/buyer-persona-questions-to-ask-in-your-persona-interviews	Decision Making
What would you say influences your purchasing decision the most?	Kaitlyn Petro	https://www.impactbnd.com/blog/buyer-persona-questions-to-ask-in-your-persona-interviews	Decision Making
What is most important to you when selecting a vendor?	Kaitlyn Petro	https://www.impactbnd.com/blog/buyer-persona-questions-to-ask-in-your-persona-interviews	Decision Making
What are some key factors that would deter you from making a purchase?	Kaitlyn Petro	https://www.impactbnd.com/blog/buyer-persona-questions-to-ask-in-your-persona-interviews	Decision Making
What kind of customer- or user-related decisions you make?	Persona Writer	https://persona.qcri.org/blog/how-to-create-personas-a-list-of-common-interview-questions/	Decision Making
What are the goals you're trying to achieve?	Mark Loehrke	https://www.clariantcreative.com/blog/creating-personas-interview-questions-to-get-you-started	Decision Making
Why are these goals important?	Mark Loehrke	https://www.clariantcreative.com/blog/creating-personas-interview-questions-to-get-you-started	Decision Making
What steps are you taking to achieve these goals?	Mark Loehrke	https://www.clariantcreative.com/blog/creating-personas-interview-questions-to-get-you-started	Decision Making

Question	Source Author Name	Source URL	Theme
If it didn't, what would you do differently next time?	Mark Loehrke	https://www.clariantcreative.com/blog/creating-personas-interview-questions-to-get-you-started	Decision Making
Who is involved in the buying process for products or services like ours?	Mark Loehrke	https://www.clariantcreative.com/blog/creating-personas-interview-questions-to-get-you-started	Decision Making
Who do you consult with and trust for advice and information?	Mark Loehrke	https://www.clariantcreative.com/blog/creating-personas-interview-questions-to-get-you-started	Decision Making
What are your biggest complaints about our product or service?	Mark Loehrke	https://www.clariantcreative.com/blog/creating-personas-interview-questions-to-get-you-started	Decision Making
What must happen for you to overcome these complaints?	Mark Loehrke	https://www.clariantcreative.com/blog/creating-personas-interview-questions-to-get-you-started	Decision Making
What is your income?	Kaitlyn Petro	https://www.impactbnd.com/blog/buyer-persona-questions-to-ask-in-your-persona-interviews	Demographics
What is your current occupation?	Kaitlyn Petro	https://www.impactbnd.com/blog/buyer-persona-questions-to-ask-in-your-persona-interviews	Demographics
What city do you live in? Work in?	Mark Loehrke	https://www.clariantcreative.com/blog/creating-personas-interview-questions-to-get-you-started	Demographics
What is their name?	Sujan Patel	https://sujanpatel.com/marketing/150-buyer-persona-questions/	Demographics
Are they male or female?	Sujan Patel	https://sujanpatel.com/marketing/150-buyer-persona-questions/	Demographics
Which country were they born in?	Sujan Patel	https://sujanpatel.com/marketing/150-buyer-persona-questions/	Demographics
Which city were they born in?	Sujan Patel	https://sujanpatel.com/marketing/150-buyer-persona-questions/	Demographics
What's their racial background?	Sujan Patel	https://sujanpatel.com/marketing/150-buyer-persona-questions/	Demographics
In which country and city do they live now?	Sujan Patel	https://sujanpatel.com/marketing/150-buyer-persona-questions/	Demographics

Question	Source Author Name	Source URL	Theme
What websites or publications do you read regularly?	Carol Ann Tan	https://www.sprk-d.com/blog/21-essential-questions-to-ask-during-a-buyer-persona-interview	Information Sources
Where do you go to learn about a product or service?	Carly Ries	https://www.smartbug-media.com/blog/55-questions-to-ask-when-developing-buyer-personas	Information Sources
Who do you ask for product/service recommendations?	Carly Ries	https://www.smartbug-media.com/blog/55-questions-to-ask-when-developing-buyer-personas	Information Sources
What type of online or print information articles do you read?	Kaitlyn Petro	https://www.impactbnd.com/blog/buyer-persona-questions-to-ask-in-your-persona-interviews	Information Sources
Which social media networks do you use personally? How often?	Kaitlyn Petro	https://www.impactbnd.com/blog/buyer-persona-questions-to-ask-in-your-persona-interviews	Information Sources
Which search engine do you use the most? What's your process for finding something online?	Kaitlyn Petro	https://www.impactbnd.com/blog/buyer-persona-questions-to-ask-in-your-persona-interviews	Information Sources
Do you belong to any social, professional, or networking groups?	Mark Loehrke	https://www.clariantcreative.com/blog/creating-personas-interview-questions-to-get-you-started	Information Sources
Do you attend any industry events, conferences, or trade shows?	Mark Loehrke	https://www.clariantcreative.com/blog/creating-personas-interview-questions-to-get-you-started	Information Sources
What information formats do you engage with the most?	Mark Loehrke	https://www.clariantcreative.com/blog/creating-personas-interview-questions-to-get-you-started	Information Sources
How do you do your research on new products and/or services for your business?	Mark Loehrke	https://www.clariantcreative.com/blog/creating-personas-interview-questions-to-get-you-started	Information Sources
How did you find out about our company?	Mark Loehrke	https://www.clariantcreative.com/blog/creating-personas-interview-questions-to-get-you-started	Information Sources

Question	Source Author Name	Source URL	Theme
How adept are they at using technology?	Sujan Patel	https://sujanpatel.com/marketing/150-buyer-persona-questions/	Information Sources
Do they tend to embrace new technologies or do they prefer to stick with systems they know?	Sujan Patel	https://sujanpatel.com/marketing/150-buyer-persona-questions/	Information Sources
Are they a fluent internet user?	Sujan Patel	https://sujanpatel.com/marketing/150-buyer-persona-questions/	Information Sources
What operating system do they use?	Sujan Patel	https://sujanpatel.com/marketing/150-buyer-persona-questions/	Information Sources
What internet browser do they use?	Sujan Patel	https://sujanpatel.com/marketing/150-buyer-persona-questions/	Information Sources
Which is their preferred search engine?	Sujan Patel	https://sujanpatel.com/marketing/150-buyer-persona-questions/	Information Sources
Do they use any social media websites?	Sujan Patel	https://sujanpatel.com/marketing/150-buyer-persona-questions/	Information Sources
Do they use their cell phone for browsing the internet?	Sujan Patel	https://sujanpatel.com/marketing/150-buyer-persona-questions/	Information Sources
Do they use their cell phone to make purchases?	Sujan Patel	https://sujanpatel.com/marketing/150-buyer-persona-questions/	Information Sources
What is your HHI?	Carly Ries	https://www.smartbug-media.com/blog/55-questions-to-ask-when-developing-buyer-personas	Life Situation
Are you a homeowner or renter?	Carly Ries	https://www.smartbug-media.com/blog/55-questions-to-ask-when-developing-buyer-personas	Life Situation
What do you do for fun?	Carly Ries	https://www.smartbug-media.com/blog/55-questions-to-ask-when-developing-buyer-personas	Life Situation
Who are the people in your life that are most important?	Carly Ries	https://www.smartbug-media.com/blog/55-questions-to-ask-when-developing-buyer-personas	Life Situation

Question	Source Author Name	Source URL	Theme
What type of vehicles do you own and why?	Carly Ries	https://www.smartbug-media.com/blog/55-questions-to-ask-when-developing-buyer-personas	Life Situation
What type of indulgent or luxurious purchases do you make?	Carly Ries	https://www.smartbug-media.com/blog/55-questions-to-ask-when-developing-buyer-personas	Life Situation
Do you have any hobbies? Are you involved in any activities or organizations?	Kaitlyn Petro	https://www.impactbnd.com/blog/buyer-persona-questions-to-ask-in-your-persona-interviews	Life Situation
Tell us about your family life.	Mark Loehrke	https://www.clariantcreative.com/blog/creating-personas-interview-questions-to-get-you-started	Life Situation
Who were they raised by (mother and father/single parent/grandparents/etc.)?	Sujan Patel	https://sujanpatel.com/marketing/150-buyer-persona-questions/	Life Situation
If applicable, what did their mother do for a living?	Sujan Patel	https://sujanpatel.com/marketing/150-buyer-persona-questions/	Life Situation
Again, if applicable, what did their father do for a living?	Sujan Patel	https://sujanpatel.com/marketing/150-buyer-persona-questions/	Life Situation
Alternatively, if they weren't raised by their mother or father, what did their primary caregiver do for a living?	Sujan Patel	https://sujanpatel.com/marketing/150-buyer-persona-questions/	Life Situation
What was the parenting style they were raised with? Strict, laid back, or somewhere in between?	Sujan Patel	https://sujanpatel.com/marketing/150-buyer-persona-questions/	Life Situation
Were they raised in a religious household? If yes, which religion were they raised under?	Sujan Patel	https://sujanpatel.com/marketing/150-buyer-persona-questions/	Life Situation

Question	Source Author Name	Source URL	Theme
Do they have any brothers or sisters? If yes, how many brothers and how many sisters?	Sujan Patel	https://sujanpatel.com/marketing/150-buyer-persona-questions/	Life Situation
Where in the birth order did they arrive? (This is said to have a significant impact on the kind of person we grow up to be.)	Sujan Patel	https://sujanpatel.com/marketing/150-buyer-persona-questions/	Life Situation
What was the social status of their family growing up?	Sujan Patel	https://sujanpatel.com/marketing/150-buyer-persona-questions/	Life Situation
Did they grow up in the city, the suburbs, or in a rural area?	Sujan Patel	https://sujanpatel.com/marketing/150-buyer-persona-questions/	Life Situation
What type of home did they grow up in? (An apartment, small house, large house, etc.)	Sujan Patel	https://sujanpatel.com/marketing/150-buyer-persona-questions/	Life Situation
Do they have any debt? How much?	Sujan Patel	https://sujanpatel.com/marketing/150-buyer-persona-questions/	Life Situation
Is this debt (if there is any) a result of the cost of necessary landmarks in their life (i.e., a college loan or a mortgage) or irresponsible spending (such as credit card debt)?	Sujan Patel	https://sujanpatel.com/marketing/150-buyer-persona-questions/	Life Situation
How much are they worth (total cash and assets, minus liabilities)?	Sujan Patel	https://sujanpatel.com/marketing/150-buyer-persona-questions/	Life Situation
Are they very conscientious about the purchases they make or are they liable to make impulse buys?	Sujan Patel	https://sujanpatel.com/marketing/150-buyer-persona-questions/	Life Situation
Are they the main breadwinner in their household?	Sujan Patel	https://sujanpatel.com/marketing/150-buyer-persona-questions/	Life Situation
Are they responsible for most of the purchasing decisions in their household?	Sujan Patel	https://sujanpatel.com/marketing/150-buyer-persona-questions/	Life Situation

Question	Source Author Name	Source URL	Theme
How do they feel about their current marital status? Happily single or happily married? Or, are they single but looking for a partner?	Sujan Patel	https://sujanpatel.com/marketing/150-buyer-persona-questions/	Life Situation
What's their sexual orientation?	Sujan Patel	https://sujanpatel.com/marketing/150-buyer-persona-questions/	Life Situation
Which political party (if any) do they support?	Sujan Patel	https://sujanpatel.com/marketing/150-buyer-persona-questions/	Life Situation
Are they actively involved in politics?	Sujan Patel	https://sujanpatel.com/marketing/150-buyer-persona-questions/	Life Situation
Are they environmentally conscious?	Sujan Patel	https://sujanpatel.com/marketing/150-buyer-persona-questions/	Life Situation
Which news sources do they read?	Sujan Patel	https://sujanpatel.com/marketing/150-buyer-persona-questions/	Life Situation
Also if yes, are they girls, boys, or a mix of both?	Sujan Patel	https://sujanpatel.com/marketing/150-buyer-persona-questions/	Life Situation
If they don't have children, is this a conscious decision or do they want children but have been unable to have them? Are they likely to have children in the future?	Sujan Patel	https://sujanpatel.com/marketing/150-buyer-persona-questions/	Life Situation
Do they have any pets?	Sujan Patel	https://sujanpatel.com/marketing/150-buyer-persona-questions/	Life Situation
If yes, how many and what are they? Interestingly, people's preferences toward particular animals can tell us a lot about their character.	Sujan Patel	https://sujanpatel.com/marketing/150-buyer-persona-questions/	Life Situation
What type of home do they currently live in?	Sujan Patel	https://sujanpatel.com/marketing/150-buyer-persona-questions/	Life Situation
Who (if anyone) shares their home with them?	Sujan Patel	https://sujanpatel.com/marketing/150-buyer-persona-questions/	Life Situation

Question	Source Author Name	Source URL	Theme
How many friends do they have? Explore this further by asking how many close friends they have vs. more casual acquaintances.	Sujan Patel	https://sujanpatel.com/marketing/150-buyer-persona-questions/	Life Situation
Do they see their friends often? Are they a social butterfly or do they prefer spending their free time at home?	Sujan Patel	https://sujanpatel.com/marketing/150-buyer-persona-questions/	Life Situation
Are they religious?	Sujan Patel	https://sujanpatel.com/marketing/150-buyer-persona-questions/	Life Situation
If yes, which religion are they part of?	Sujan Patel	https://sujanpatel.com/marketing/150-buyer-persona-questions/	Life Situation
Also if yes, have they always been part of this religion or is something they chose to embrace as an adult?	Sujan Patel	https://sujanpatel.com/marketing/150-buyer-persona-questions/	Life Situation
What hobbies (if any) do they have?	Sujan Patel	https://sujanpatel.com/marketing/150-buyer-persona-questions/	Life Situation
Do they exercise regularly?	Sujan Patel	https://sujanpatel.com/marketing/150-buyer-persona-questions/	Life Situation
If yes, what type/s of exercise do they do?	Sujan Patel	https://sujanpatel.com/marketing/150-buyer-persona-questions/	Life Situation
If no, why don't they exercise? Time? Laziness? Health problems?	Sujan Patel	https://sujanpatel.com/marketing/150-buyer-persona-questions/	Life Situation
Do they play any competitive sports?	Sujan Patel	https://sujanpatel.com/marketing/150-buyer-persona-questions/	Life Situation
Do they prefer baths or showers? Seriously—the answer says more about us than you might think.	Sujan Patel	https://sujanpatel.com/marketing/150-buyer-persona-questions/	Life Situation
What TV shows do they enjoy watching?	Sujan Patel	https://sujanpatel.com/marketing/150-buyer-persona-questions/	Life Situation
What genre of movies do they like best?	Sujan Patel	https://sujanpatel.com/marketing/150-buyer-persona-questions/	Life Situation

Question	Source Author Name	Source URL	Theme
What genre of movies do they like least?	Sujan Patel	https://sujanpatel.com/marketing/150-buyer-persona-questions/	Life Situation
What type of music do they enjoy listening to?	Sujan Patel	https://sujanpatel.com/marketing/150-buyer-persona-questions/	Life Situation
Who do they most look up to/admire? This could be somebody they know or a celebrity.	Sujan Patel	https://sujanpatel.com/marketing/150-buyer-persona-questions//	Life Situation
Do they enjoy reading?	Sujan Patel	https://sujanpatel.com/marketing/150-buyer-persona-questions/	Life Situation
If yes, what do they tend to read?	Sujan Patel	https://sujanpatel.com/marketing/150-buyer-persona-questions/	Life Situation
Do they regularly go on vacations?	Sujan Patel	https://sujanpatel.com/marketing/150-buyer-persona-questions//	Life Situation
If yes, where do they go? Do they usually go to the same place? Do they go abroad?	Sujan Patel	https://sujanpatel.com/marketing/150-buyer-persona-questions/	Life Situation
Also if yes, what do sort of vacations do they usually go on? Beach? City? Skiing? Cruise?	Sujan Patel	https://sujanpatel.com/marketing/150-buyer-persona-questions/	Life Situation
If they don't go on many vacations, why not? Does money hold them back or do they simply prefer staying at home?	Sujan Patel	https://sujanpatel.com/marketing/150-buyer-persona-questions/	Life Situation
Have they ever been backpacking?	Sujan Patel	https://sujanpatel.com/marketing/150-buyer-persona-questions/	Life Situation
If yes, where did they go?	Sujan Patel	https://sujanpatel.com/marketing/150-buyer-persona-questions/	Life Situation
Also if yes, who did they go with?	Sujan Patel	https://sujanpatel.com/marketing/150-buyer-persona-questions//	Life Situation
If no, do they ever want to go traveling?	Sujan Patel	https://sujanpatel.com/marketing/150-buyer-persona-questions/	Life Situation
How often do they treat themselves?	Sujan Patel	https://sujanpatel.com/marketing/150-buyer-persona-questions/	Life Situation
Do they drink alcohol?	Sujan Patel	https://sujanpatel.com/marketing/150-buyer-persona-questions/	Life Situation

Question	Source Author Name	Source URL	Theme
Do they smoke?	Sujan Patel	https://sujanpatel.com/market-ing/150-buyer-persona-questions/	Life Situation
If no to either of the above, are they an ex-drinker or smoker?	Sujan Patel	https://sujanpatel.com/market-ing/150-buyer-persona-questions//	Life Situation
Are they introverted or ex-troverted? Or somewhere inbetween?	Sujan Patel	https://sujanpatel.com/market-ing/150-buyer-persona-questions/	Life Situation
How spontaneous are they?	Sujan Patel	https://sujanpatel.com/market-ing/150-buyer-persona-questions/	Life Situation
Are they a risk taker?	Sujan Patel	https://sujanpatel.com/market-ing/150-buyer-persona-questions/	Life Situation
Do they tend to break or fol-low rules?	Sujan Patel	https://sujanpatel.com/market-ing/150-buyer-persona-questions/	Life Situation
Are they mostly optimistic or pessimistic? Or are they a realist?	Sujan Patel	https://sujanpatel.com/market-ing/150-buyer-persona-questions/	Life Situation
Are they driven more by their right brain or their left brain? Are they more creative or more logically minded?	Sujan Patel	https://sujanpatel.com/market-ing/150-buyer-persona-questions/	Life Situation
Do they adapt easily to change?	Sujan Patel	https://sujanpatel.com/market-ing/150-buyer-persona-questions/	Life Situation
Are they independent or do they tend to follow the crowd?	Sujan Patel	https://sujanpatel.com/market-ing/150-buyer-persona-questions/	Life Situation
Do they get jealous easily or are they easily pleased for others?	Sujan Patel	https://sujanpatel.com/market-ing/150-buyer-persona-questions/	Life Situation
Do they worry about what others think of them?	Sujan Patel	https://sujanpatel.com/market-ing/150-buyer-persona-questions/	Life Situation
How would their friends de-scribe them?	Sujan Patel	https://sujanpatel.com/market-ing/150-buyer-persona-questions/	Life Situation
How would they describe themselves?	Sujan Patel	https://sujanpatel.com/market-ing/150-buyer-persona-questions/	Life Situation

Question	Source Author Name	Source URL	Theme
What technical and demographic information do you have about your website visitors?	Carly Ries	https://www.smartbug-media.com/blog/55-questions-to-ask-when-developing-buyer-personas	Marketing Team
How do you currently market?	Carly Ries	https://www.smartbug-media.com/blog/55-questions-to-ask-when-developing-buyer-personas	Marketing Team
Describe marketing campaigns that have been the most successful.	Carly Ries	https://www.smartbug-media.com/blog/55-questions-to-ask-when-developing-buyer-personas	Marketing Team
Describe marketing campaigns that have failed.	Carly Ries	https://www.smartbug-media.com/blog/55-questions-to-ask-when-developing-buyer-personas	Marketing Team
Which blog posts have received the most traffic?	Carly Ries	https://www.smartbug-media.com/blog/55-questions-to-ask-when-developing-buyer-personas	Marketing Team
What are the most frequently asked questions from customers?	Carly Ries	https://www.smartbug-media.com/blog/55-questions-to-ask-when-developing-buyer-personas	Marketing Team
Which page on the website receives the most impressions?	Carly Ries	https://www.smartbug-media.com/blog/55-questions-to-ask-when-developing-buyer-personas	Marketing Team
What is the most frustrating part of your day?	Carly Ries	https://www.smartbug-media.com/blog/55-questions-to-ask-when-developing-buyer-personas	Paint Points
What is the worst customer service experience you've ever had?	Carly Ries	https://www.smartbug-media.com/blog/55-questions-to-ask-when-developing-buyer-personas	Paint Points

Question	Source Author Name	Source URL	Theme
What regular activity do you find stressful?	Carly Ries	https://www.smartbug-media.com/blog/55-questions-to-ask-when-developing-buyer-personas	Paint Points
What makes you nervous?	Carly Ries	https://www.smartbug-media.com/blog/55-questions-to-ask-when-developing-buyer-personas	Paint Points
What is the fastest way for somebody to make you angry?	Carly Ries	https://www.smartbug-media.com/blog/55-questions-to-ask-when-developing-buyer-personas	Paint Points
What is your least favorite part of your job?	Carly Ries	https://www.smartbug-media.com/blog/55-questions-to-ask-when-developing-buyer-personas	Paint Points
What is the worst job you can imagine?	Carly Ries	https://www.smartbug-media.com/blog/55-questions-to-ask-when-developing-buyer-personas	Paint Points
What purchase under XX dollars did you most regret?	Carly Ries	https://www.smartbug-media.com/blog/55-questions-to-ask-when-developing-buyer-personas	Paint Points
What do you worry about?	Carly Ries	https://www.smartbug-media.com/blog/55-questions-to-ask-when-developing-buyer-personas	Paint Points
What frustrates you the most about your job?	Mark Loehrke	https://www.clariantcreative.com/blog/creating-personas-interview-questions-to-get-you-started	Paint Points
What do you enjoy most?	Mark Loehrke	https://www.clariantcreative.com/blog/creating-personas-interview-questions-to-get-you-started	Paint Points

Question	Source Author Name	Source URL	Theme
What types of customers do you typically meet?	Carly Ries	https://www.smartbug-media.com/blog/55-ques-tions-to-ask-when-develop-ing-buyer-personass	Sales Team
Why do different types of customers typically make a purchase?	Carly Ries	https://www.smartbug-media.com/blog/55-ques-tions-to-ask-when-develop-ing-buyer-personas	Sales Team
What reasons do customers cite for selecting your busi-ness over a competitor?	Carly Ries	https://www.smartbug-media.com/blog/55-ques-tions-to-ask-when-develop-ing-buyer-personas	Sales Team
What are the most common objections you hear?	Carly Ries	https://www.smartbug-media.com/blog/55-ques-tions-to-ask-when-develop-ing-buyer-personas	Sales Team
Were they popular at school?	Jesse Ness	https://www.ecwid.com/blog/how-to-create-buyer-personas-for-an-ecommerce-store.html	School Life
What type of school did they attend? Public or private? Small or large? Was it a well-rated and respected school or a struggling school?	Sujan Patel	https://sujanpatel.com/market-ing/150-buyer-persona-questions/	School Life
What were they like at school? Were they popular? A loner? Somewhere in be-tween?	Sujan Patel	https://sujanpatel.com/market-ing/150-buyer-persona-questions/	School Life
What "social group" (if any) did they fit into?	Sujan Patel	https://sujanpatel.com/market-ing/150-buyer-persona-questions/	School Life
How well did they do at school? Did they tend to fail, excel, or were they an average student?	Sujan Patel	https://sujanpatel.com/market-ing/150-buyer-persona-questions/	School Life
Did they get into much trou-ble at school?	Sujan Patel	https://sujanpatel.com/market-ing/150-buyer-persona-questions/	School Life
What was their favorite sub-ject?	Sujan Patel	https://sujanpatel.com/market-ing/150-buyer-persona-questions/	School Life

Question	Source Author Name	Source URL	Theme
What was their least-favorite subject?	Sujan Patel	https://sujanpatel.com/marketing/150-buyer-persona-questions/	School Life
What did they want to be when they were growing up?	Sujan Patel	https://sujanpatel.com/marketing/150-buyer-persona-questions/	School Life
Did they go to college?	Sujan Patel	https://sujanpatel.com/marketing/150-buyer-persona-questions/	School Life
If so, which one?	Sujan Patel	https://sujanpatel.com/marketing/150-buyer-persona-questions/	School Life
Without wanting to repeat myself, which extra-curricular activities (if any) did they take part in at college?	Sujan Patel	https://sujanpatel.com/marketing/150-buyer-persona-questions/	School Life
Did they join a sorority or fraternity?	Sujan Patel	https://sujanpatel.com/marketing/150-buyer-persona-questions/	School Life
What was their social life like at college?	Sujan Patel	https://sujanpatel.com/marketing/150-buyer-persona-questions/	School Life
What kinds of grades did they get?	Sujan Patel	https://sujanpatel.com/marketing/150-buyer-persona-questions/	School Life
If they didn't go to college, what stopped them? Cost? Grades? Or did college simply not fit with their goals?	Sujan Patel	https://sujanpatel.com/marketing/150-buyer-persona-questions/	School Life
If they didn't go to college, what did they do after high school? Get their first job? Go traveling? Nothing?	Sujan Patel	https://sujanpatel.com/marketing/150-buyer-persona-questions/	School Life
What is their current literacy level?	Sujan Patel	https://sujanpatel.com/marketing/150-buyer-persona-questions/	School Life
What are your career goals?	Carol Ann Tan	https://www.sprk-d.com/blog/21-essential-questions-to-ask-during-a-buyer-persona-interview	Work Life
What are your responsibilities in that role?	Carol Ann Tan	https://www.sprk-d.com/blog/21-essential-questions-to-ask-during-a-buyer-persona-interview	Work Life
What industry (or industries) is the company a part of?	Carol Ann Tan	https://www.sprk-d.com/blog/21-essential-questions-to-ask-during-a-buyer-persona-interview	Work Life

Question	Source Author Name	Source URL	Theme
What does success in your job look like to you?	Carol Ann Tan	https://www.sprk-d.com/blog/21-essential-questions-to-ask-during-a-buyer-persona-interview	Work Life
What are some of your biggest priorities when making decisions for the company?	Carol Ann Tan	https://www.sprk-d.com/blog/21-essential-questions-to-ask-during-a-buyer-persona-interview	Work Life
What are the company's short- and long-term objectives?	Carol Ann Tan	https://www.sprk-d.com/blog/21-essential-questions-to-ask-during-a-buyer-persona-interview	Work Life
How long have you been in your current position?	Carly Ries	https://www.smartbug-media.com/blog/55-questions-to-ask-when-developing-buyer-personas	Work Life
What does a typical day look like for you?	Carly Ries	https://www.smartbug-media.com/blog/55-questions-to-ask-when-developing-buyer-personas	Work Life
How much time do you spend at work and at home?	Carly Ries	https://www.smartbug-media.com/blog/55-questions-to-ask-when-developing-buyer-personas	Work Life
What are the top questions asked by customers?	Carly Ries	https://www.smartbug-media.com/blog/55-questions-to-ask-when-developing-buyer-personas	Work Life
What are the top questions asked by prospects?	Carly Ries	https://www.smartbug-media.com/blog/55-questions-to-ask-when-developing-buyer-personas	Work Life
Take me back to the day when you first decided to explore your [product/service] options. What was going on in your life that made you think about making this purchase?	Kaitlyn Petro	https://www.impactbnd.com/blog/buyer-persona-questions-to-ask-in-your-persona-interviews	Work Life

Question	Source Author Name	Source URL	Theme
How did you hear about [your company]?	Kaitlyn Petro	https://www.impactbnd.com/blog/buyer-persona-questions-to-ask-in-your-persona-interviews	Work Life
What initially attracted you to us?	Kaitlyn Petro	https://www.impactbnd.com/blog/buyer-persona-questions-to-ask-in-your-persona-interviews	Work Life
What was your first impression of us?	Kaitlyn Petro	https://www.impactbnd.com/blog/buyer-persona-questions-to-ask-in-your-persona-interviews	Work Life
Were you the main person doing research when you found us? If not, who was?	Kaitlyn Petro	https://www.impactbnd.com/blog/buyer-persona-questions-to-ask-in-your-persona-interviews	Work Life
What three words would you have used to describe [your company] while you were comparing other companies? (If you don't mind me asking, what words would you have used to describe the other companies you were evaluating?)	Kaitlyn Petro	https://www.impactbnd.com/blog/buyer-persona-questions-to-ask-in-your-persona-interviews	Work Life
What was your biggest concern or reservation (if any) about buying from us?	Kaitlyn Petro	https://www.impactbnd.com/blog/buyer-persona-questions-to-ask-in-your-persona-interviews	Work Life
Describe your career path.	Lindsay Kolowich	https://blog.hubspot.com/marketing/buyer-persona-questions	Work Life
What is your job role? Your title?	Lindsay Kolowich	https://blog.hubspot.com/marketing/buyer-persona-questions	Work Life
How is your job measured?	Lindsay Kolowich	https://blog.hubspot.com/marketing/buyer-persona-questions	Work Life
What does a typical day look like?	Lindsay Kolowich	https://blog.hubspot.com/marketing/buyer-persona-questions	Work Life

Question	Source Author Name	Source URL	Theme
What knowledge and which tools do you use in your job?	Lindsay Kolowich	https://blog.hubspot.com/marketing/buyer-persona-questions	Work Life
What are you responsible for?	Lindsay Kolowich	https://blog.hubspot.com/marketing/buyer-persona-questions	Work Life
What does it mean to be successful in your role?	Lindsay Kolowich	https://blog.hubspot.com/marketing/buyer-persona-questions	Work Life
How do you learn about new information for your job?	Lindsay Kolowich	https://blog.hubspot.com/marketing/buyer-persona-questions	Work Life
Which publications or blogs do you read?	Lindsay Kolowich	https://blog.hubspot.com/marketing/buyer-persona-questions	Work Life
Which associations and social networks do you participate in?	Lindsay Kolowich	https://blog.hubspot.com/marketing/buyer-persona-questions	Work Life
What are your general job objectives?	Persona Writer	https://persona.qcri.org/blog/how-to-create-personas-a-list-of-common-interview-questions/	Work Life
What kind of customer or user information do you need?	Persona Writer	https://persona.qcri.org/blog/how-to-create-personas-a-list-of-common-interview-questions/	Work Life
What analytics information are you currently using?	Persona Writer	https://persona.qcri.org/blog/how-to-create-personas-a-list-of-common-interview-questions/	Work Life
What kind of customer- or user-related questions are currently not answered using the available data?	Persona Writer	https://persona.qcri.org/blog/how-to-create-personas-a-list-of-common-interview-questions/	Work Life
How would you use personas in your own work?	Persona Writer	https://persona.qcri.org/blog/how-to-create-personas-a-list-of-common-interview-questions/	Work Life
What information you find useful in a persona profile?	Persona Writer	https://persona.qcri.org/blog/how-to-create-personas-a-list-of-common-interview-questions/	Work Life
(OPTIONAL: What information is missing from the shown persona profile?)	Persona Writer	https://persona.qcri.org/blog/how-to-create-personas-a-list-of-common-interview-questions/	Work Life
What was their first full-time job?	Jesse Ness	https://www.ecwid.com/blog/how-to-create-buyer-personas-for-an-ecommerce-store.html	Work Life

Question	Source Author Name	Source URL	Theme
How did they end up where they are today?	Jesse Ness	https://www.ecwid.com/blog/how-to-create-buyer-personas-for-an-ecommerce-store.html	Work Life
Has their career track been traditional or did they switch from another industry?	Jesse Ness	https://www.ecwid.com/blog/how-to-create-buyer-personas-for-an-ecommerce-store.html	Work Life
How often you buy high ticket items?	Jesse Ness	https://www.ecwid.com/blog/how-to-create-buyer-personas-for-an-ecommerce-store.html	Work Life
How much are they worth?	Jesse Ness	https://www.ecwid.com/blog/how-to-create-buyer-personas-for-an-ecommerce-store.html	Work Life
Are they responsible for making purchasing decision in the household?	Jesse Ness	https://www.ecwid.com/blog/how-to-create-buyer-personas-for-an-ecommerce-store.html	Work Life
What's important to them and what's driving the change?	Ardath Ablee	https://marketinginteractions.typepad.com/marketing_interactions/2013/02/personas-in-the-closet.html	Work Life
What's impeding or speeding their need to change?	Ardath Ablee	https://marketinginteractions.typepad.com/marketing_interactions/2013/02/personas-in-the-closet.html	Work Life
How do they go about change?	Ardath Ablee	https://marketinginteractions.typepad.com/marketing_interactions/2013/02/personas-in-the-closet.html	Work Life
What do they need to know to embrace change?	Ardath Ablee	https://marketinginteractions.typepad.com/marketing_interactions/2013/02/personas-in-the-closet.html	Work Life
Who do they turn to for advice or information?	Ardath Ablee	https://marketinginteractions.typepad.com/marketing_interactions/2013/02/personas-in-the-closet.html	Work Life

Question	Source Author Name	Source URL	Theme
What's the value they visualize once they make a decision?	Ardath Ablee	https://marketinginteractions.typepad.com/marketing_interactions/2013/02/personas-in-the-closet.html	Work Life
Who do they have to sell change to in order to get it?	Ardath Ablee	https://marketinginteractions.typepad.com/marketing_interactions/2013/02/personas-in-the-closet.html	Work Life
What could cause the need for this change to lose priority?	Ardath Ablee	https://marketinginteractions.typepad.com/marketing_interactions/2013/02/personas-in-the-closet.html	Work Life
What is your job title?	Mark Loehrke	https://www.clariantcreative.com/blog/creating-personas-interview-questions-to-get-you-started	Work Life
What are your responsibilities?	Mark Loehrke	https://www.clariantcreative.com/blog/creating-personas-interview-questions-to-get-you-started	Work Life
What is a typical workday like for you?	Mark Loehrke	https://www.clariantcreative.com/blog/creating-personas-interview-questions-to-get-you-started	Work Life
How many years of experience do you have?	Mark Loehrke	https://www.clariantcreative.com/blog/creating-personas-interview-questions-to-get-you-started	Work Life
What is your professional background?	Mark Loehrke	https://www.clariantcreative.com/blog/creating-personas-interview-questions-to-get-you-started	Work Life
How do you measure success in your position?	Mark Loehrke	https://www.clariantcreative.com/blog/creating-personas-interview-questions-to-get-you-started	Work Life
To whom do you report? Who reports to you?	Mark Loehrke	https://www.clariantcreative.com/blog/creating-personas-interview-questions-to-get-you-started	Work Life
What was their first ever job (remember that this may overlap with school or college)?	Sujan Patel	https://sujanpatel.com/marketing/150-buyer-persona-questions/	Work Life

Question	Source Author Name	Source URL	Theme
What was their first ever full-time job?	Sujan Patel	https://sujanpatel.com/marketing/150-buyer-persona-questions/	Work Life
What job are they currently doing?	Sujan Patel	https://sujanpatel.com/marketing/150-buyer-persona-questions/	Work Life
How long have they been in their current role?	Sujan Patel	https://sujanpatel.com/marketing/150-buyer-persona-questions/	Work Life
Why did they choose this job? Were they head-hunted? Or perhaps the role is a stop-gap until they find something more suited to their skill set?	Sujan Patel	https://sujanpatel.com/marketing/150-buyer-persona-questions/	Work Life
What are their key responsibilities?	Sujan Patel	https://sujanpatel.com/marketing/150-buyer-persona-questions/	Work Life
How much do they earn?	Sujan Patel	https://sujanpatel.com/marketing/150-buyer-persona-questions/	Work Life
Do they feel their current salary offers fair compensation for the work they do?	Sujan Patel	https://sujanpatel.com/marketing/150-buyer-persona-questions/	Work Life
Do they enjoy their job?	Sujan Patel	https://sujanpatel.com/marketing/150-buyer-persona-questions/	Work Life
Do they like the people they work with?	Sujan Patel	https://sujanpatel.com/marketing/150-buyer-persona-questions/	Work Life
Do they like their boss?	Sujan Patel	https://sujanpatel.com/marketing/150-buyer-persona-questions/	Work Life
What, if anything, would they change about their current role?	Sujan Patel	https://sujanpatel.com/marketing/150-buyer-persona-questions/	Work Life
How do they see their role progressing? Will they be looking to move to another company or progress within their current firm?	Sujan Patel	https://sujanpatel.com/marketing/150-buyer-persona-questions/	Work Life
Are they considering a career change?	Sujan Patel	https://sujanpatel.com/marketing/150-buyer-persona-questions/	Work Life
What is their dream job?	Sujan Patel	https://sujanpatel.com/marketing/150-buyer-persona-questions/	Work Life
Do they have any plans to pursue their dream job?	Sujan Patel	https://sujanpatel.com/marketing/150-buyer-persona-questions/	Work Life

APPENDIX C

Persona Profile Attribute Comparison

We compared the attributes utilied in 12 online persona creation systems. We categorized the attributes and then show the specific attributes common in each personas profile from each system. Table C-1 presented these results.

Table C-1: Comparison of 12 persona profile templates

Source .No.			1	2	3	4	5	6	7	8	9	10	11	12	#	%
Elements		Source	Dribble 1	Behance	Applied By Design	Dribble 2	Xtension	Personapp	User Forge	Just In Mind	Content Harmony	Buyer Persona	Compose.ly	Hubspot	#	%
Picture			x	x	x	x	x	x	-	x	x	-	x	x	10	83%
Demographics	Name		x	x	x	x	x	x	x	x	x	x	x	x	12	100%
	Age		x	x	x	x	x	-	x	x	x	-	x	x	10	83%
	Location		x	-	-	-	x	-	x	x	x	-	x	x	7	58%
	Salary		-	-	-	x	-	-	x	-	-	-	x	-	3	25%
	Relationship Status		-	-	-	-	x	-	-	x	x	-	x	x	5	42%
Other Basic Information	Quotes		-	-	x	-	-	-	x	-	x	-	-	-	3	25%
	Bio		x	x	x	x	x	-	-	x	x	x	x	x	10	83%
	Job Title		x	x	x	x	x	x	-	x	x	x	x	x	11	92%
	Education		-	x	x	-	-	-	x	-	x	x	x	x	7	58%
	Years Of Experience		-	-	x	-	-	-	-	-	-	-	-	-	1	8%
User Story			x	x	-	-	-	-	x	x	x	-	-	-	5	42%
Psychographics	Goals		x	x	-	x	x	x	x	x	x	-	x	-	9	75%
	Motivation		-	x	-	x	x	x	-	x	x	-	-	-	6	50%
	Influencers		-	x	-	x	-	-	-	x	-	-	-	-	3	25%
	Pain Points		-	x	-	x	x	-	-	x	x	-	x	-	6	50%
	Personal Values		-	-	x	-	-	-	-	-	-	-	x	-	2	17%
	Personality		-	x	-	-	x	x	-	x	x	-	x	-	6	50%
	Defining Traits		-	-	-	-	-	-	-	-	-	-	x	-	1	8%
	Archetype		-	-	-	-	x	-	-	x	x	-	-	-	3	25%

Source .No.			1 Dribble 1	2 Behance	3 Applied By Design	4 Dribble 2	5 Xtension	6 Personapp	7 User Forge	8 Just In Mind	9 Content Harmony	10 Buyer Persona	11 Compose.ly	12 Hubspot	#	%
Elements	Source														#	%
Skills		Skills	x	-	-	-	-	-	-	-	x	x	-	-	3	25%
		Areas of Expertise	-	-	x	-	-	-	-	-	x	-	-	-	2	17%
		Technology	-	x	x	-	-	-	-	-	x	-	-	-	3	25%
Personal		Fav App/Preferred Channels	x	-	x	-	x	-	-	x	-	-	x	x	6	50%
		Preferred Brands	-	-	-	-	x	-	-	-	-	-	x	-	2	17%
		Trusted Resources	-	-	-	-	-	-	-	-	-	x	-	-	1	8%
Other Attributes		Work Experience	-	-	-	-	-	-	-	-	-	-	x	-	1	8%
		Relationship with Company	-	x	-	-	-	-	-	-	-	-	-	-	1	8%
		Collaboraters	-	-	x	-	-	-	-	-	-	-	-	-	1	8%
		Time Management	-	-	x	-	-	-	-	-	-	-	-	-	1	8%
		Current Tools	-	-	x	-	-	-	-	-	-	-	-	-	1	8%
		Event Attendance Attributes	-	-	-	x	-	-	-	-	-	-	-	-	1	8%
Add Additional Section			-	-	-	-	x	-	x	-	-	-	-	x	3	25%

Online Sources

- Dribble 1 — https://dribbble.com/
- Behance — https://www.behance.net/
- Applied By Design — http://appliedbydesign.com/#/home
- Dribble 2 — https://dribbble.com/
- Xtension — https://xtensio.com/user-persona/
- Personapp — http://personapp.io/
- User Forge — https://userforge.com/
- Just In Mind — https://www.justinmind.com/

- Content Harmony   https://www.contentharmony.com/blog/customer-persona-tools/

- Buyer Persona Institute (BPI)   https://www.buyerpersona.com/

- Compose.ly   https://compose.ly/strategy/user-persona-guide/

- Hubspot   https://www.hubspot.com/make-my-persona

Glossary

A/B testing: using personas as a part of a split testing process, e.g., to increase team members' empathy toward users before creating test versions that target said users

Ad hoc type personas: personas created based on one's current understanding of the users (without performing additional data collection). (See also "assumption-based personas.")

Adoption: the real use of personas in an organization for tasks and/or decision making

Agile development: a framework that advocates adaptive planning and continual development to define requirements and develop a (software) product

Agile personas: personas used in agile development. When new knowledge suggests agile personas should be changed, the personas are modified. This modifying can happen several times during the agile development process.

Algorithmic bias: the influence of an algorithm or algorithms on the deviation of the created persona set from a persona set that is regarded as ideal

Analytics: generation of user information and insights from computational processing of data

Assumption-based personas: created based on one's rough guess about target user type rather than actual user data. Assumption-based personas can be seen as a starting point for more thorough persona research. (See also "ad-hoc personas.")

Automated persona generation: the creation of personas from analytics data using statistical algorithms

Card Sorting: a technique that organizes information into logical groups, frequently used to explore architecture, workflow, and navigation of systems

Consistency: the degree to which the personas have the same or similar attributes when applying an identical algorithm and dataset to their creation over a number of iterations

Curse of dimensionality: as more attributes (dimensions) are added to a persona, the number of users represented by the persona decreases

Data: numerical or qualitative information about users. Qualitative data may need to be converted to numbers before used in data-driven persona creation.

Data-driven persona development: creating personas based on trends and patterns identified via quantitative analysis on actual user data

Data-driven persona readiness: the degree to which an organization is ready for the creation and employment of data-driven personas

Data-driven personas: humanized user segments of a given user population generated as the output of a data-driven persona development process

Decision making: using personas to make decisions concerning users of products (e.g., choosing or prioritizing features to develop)

Design: using personas for creating tangible or intangible offerings (e.g., products, systems, services, campaigns, messages, tools)

Desk-drawer personas: personas that, for some reason, are not used by stakeholders in a meaningful way (i.e., they are created and placed into a mental or actual desk drawer and remain there)

Diversity: the variability of personas by an attribute of interest (e.g., a persona set with more personas from different ages would be more diverse than a persona set with personas centered around a narrow age range)

Empathy: the ability to understand others (a central benefit of using personas)

Fairness: the degree to which the personas correspond with the distribution of persona attributes in the user data from which they were created

Flat-file personas: static personas, represented in the form of paper-like medium, and pose limited interactivity to persona users

Full-stack personas: personas that serve as interactive interfaces making the persona, related analytical information, and the underlying data easily accessible

Gap analysis: the process of comparing the current performance of some objective with a future or projected performance for that objective. From this comparison, one ascertains the gaps and identifies the corrective measures to close the gap.

Goal-directed personas: personas created to target a common goal of a specific set of users

Goodness of data-driven personas: an idea implying that persona creation should be driven by certain desiderata

Interaction: how persona users engage with data-driven personas and/or persona systems (e.g., clicking, typing, voice direction)

Interactive persona system: a tool that comprises user interface, functionalities, and data. Users can interact with the personas via different interaction techniques in the system (see "Interaction").

Layered information: the presentation of persona information at multiple levels (e.g., using data breakdowns to provide additional details on the persona or tooltip definitions to provide explanations on how the information was generated)

Metric-driven personas: personas that are based on specific design goals (e.g., diversity, accuracy, impact, revenue) rather than particular patterns in user data

Mixed methods approach: collecting and analyzing qualitative and quantitative data to create personas

Negative personas: personas that represent the less-than-ideal users. They are composed of a collection of behaviors, demographics, and real-life scenarios that separate them from the ideal users.

Participatory design: a cooperative approach that actively involves different stakeholders such as customers, partners, and employees in the design of a system

Persona analytics system: creating personas using analytics data and algorithmic methods and presenting them via an interactive interface

Persona analytics: the process of analyzing data to create data-driven personas based upon interpretation and communication of meaningful patterns in the user data

Persona attribute: one of the information pieces in a persona profile (e.g., the persona's age)

Persona cast: an organized collection of personas created from the same underlying user data. (See also "persona set.")

Persona choice: the factors that influence which persona a persona user selects for a given task

Persona end-user (aka "persona stakeholder," "user"): an individual that uses data-driven personas for decision-making

Persona information design: the selection of information elements (attributes, characteristics) that the finalized persona profiles will communicate to persona users

Persona narrative: a textual description of the persona

Persona number preference: the number of data-driven personas an end-user wants to see

Persona Perception Scale (PPS): a survey instrument for evaluating how individuals perceive data-driven personas

Persona Performance Monitoring (PPM): a formal document explaining how the personas will be used after their creation and how the results will be measured

Persona profile: typically, a one- or two- "page" description of the persona, usually containing a name, photo, demographic, behaviors, and other information about the persona

Persona subset: a collection of data-driven personas to which end-users refer. (See also "persona cast.")

Persona template: a layout used to create a persona profile, including, for example, name, picture, and demographics of the persona in a certain position and size

Persona viewing behavior: the style and manner in which a user perceives the persona profile and processes its information (e.g., the order and duration of viewing different information elements)

Persona-as-an-interface: the idea that data-driven personas are an alternative interface to user data, similar to graphs, figures, and tables that also act as interfaces to user data

Personas: fictional characters created to represent the target users/customers/audience to help stakeholders enhance their user understanding

Qualitative approach: a method for persona data collection focused primarily on words. Such an approach can be useful to understand concepts, thoughts and/or experiences of people. This approach enables the collection of in-depth insights on topics that are not well understood.

Quantitative approach: a method for persona data collection using primarily numbers and statistics. This data can be presented using charts and graphs, and mathematical or statistical knowledge is needed to carry out the analysis.

Role-based personas: personas that describe the demands, challenges, and context of the (social) role of a user segment

Rounded persona: a persona that contains all the necessary information for persona users to complete a task or a range of tasks

Scenarios: stories that describe the context behind a specific user group behavior and help designers understand their motivations, needs, and challenges

Segmentation: the approach of dividing a target market population into smaller, homogeneous categories based on shared characteristics

Serious games: games designed with a focus on pedagogical value or decision-making scenarios (e.g., strategy formulation) as opposed to pure entertainment

Skeleton persona (AKA, "skeletal personas"): prototypes of personas containing the bare basic information but not all the characteristics typical of personas, such as names and images

Stakeholder: an individual either using personas or being affected by the use of personas

Target groups: potential users to which a system or product is directed

Transparency: the degree to which the persona user is made aware of how the data-driven personas were created (e.g., by providing explanations of the algorithms)

User interface: a visual presentation of the persona that enables user actions such as filtering, selecting, refreshing, comparing, and so on

User stories: short statements that describe user goals. (See also "scenarios.")

User studies: user research conducted to understand persona users' reactions, behaviors, and perceptions concerning personas. User studies are conducted toward creating more useful personas.

User-centricity: a focus on understanding the users better so that user-friendly systems can be designed for them

Users: either the people who will interact with personas ("use personas"), or the people the created personas are based on

Willingness to use: a persona user's implicit or explicit desire to use personas for a task

Afterword

Much of this book's content is the result of efforts by the core team members of the Automatic Persona Generation (APG) Project, pictured here the year the book was written.

Pictured: Soon-gyo Jung, Jim Jansen, and Joni Salminen, the APG Team's core members.

The APG Project encompasses a range of efforts, working with many collaborators, to push and define the boundaries of efforts in the human computer interaction field to enhance user understanding via more accurate, more recent, and more updateable data-driven personas. The research findings impact other domains, including healthcare, marketing, advertising, and education.

This book is not the end but rather the beginning of the next stage of this research—to integrate data-driven personas and analytics into fully functional persona analytics systems for the range of goals from user understanding, user segmentation, and user personalization.

Follow the APG Team at https://persona.qcri.org and https://quecst.qcri.org.

Authors' Biographies

Bernard J. Jansen is a Principal Scientist in the social computing group of the Qatar Computing Research Institute. He is a graduate of West Point and has a Ph.D. in computer science from Texas A&M University. Professor Jansen is Editor-in-Chief of the journal, *Information Processing and Management* (Elsevier).

Joni Salminen is a research scientist at Qatar Computing Research Institute, Hamad Bin Khalifa University, and at Turku School of Economics. His current research interests include automatic persona generation from social media and online analytics data, the societal impact of machine decision making (#algoritmitutkimus), and related social computing topics.

Soon-gyo Jung is a software engineer focused on news/data analytics and implementing related systems at Qatar Computing Research Institute. He received a B.E. degree in computer software from the Kwangwoon University, Seoul, Korea, in 2014, and an M.S. degree in electrical and computer engineering from the Sungkyunkwan University, Suwon, Korea, in 2016.

Kathleen Guan is a graduate student with the University College London. She has a Bachelor of Science in Foreign Service in International Law from Georgetown University, and research training in Public Health from Johns Hopkins University. In addition to research consulting for industry, Kathleen is currently a research student in Neuroscience and Psychopathology through a joint graduate program between University College London and Yale School of Medicine.